MW00448524

GIVING GROUND

The Politics of Propinquity

Each volume of this series will contain original essays from leading theorists focusing on one topic of immediate cultural and political concern. While experts from a variety of fields will contribute to each volume, the avowed aim of the series is to demonstrate the fundamental psychoanalytic character of the issues raised and the solutions required. Against the narrowing and reduction of psychoanalysis to a specialized vocabulary, which so often takes place in cultural studies, the project of these volumes is to enlarge the scope of psychoanalysis by equating it, more properly, with its concepts, no matter what term designates them. From the perspective of this enlargement, our modernity – including its 'postmodern' inversion – will be shown to be more thoroughly defined by psychoanalysis than was previously thought, and the strategies for thinking our current conditions will be rigorously overhauled.

GIVING GROUND

The Politics of Propinquity

◆

edited by
JOAN COPJEC
and
MICHAEL SORKIN

VERSO
London • New York

First published by Verso 1999
This collection © Verso 1999
Individual contributions © Individual contributors 1999
All rights reserved

The moral rights of the individual contributors have been asserted

Verso
UK: 6 Meard Street, London W1V 3HR
US: 180 Varick Street, New York, NY 10014–4606

Verso is the imprint of New Left Books

ISBN 1–85984–892–3
ISBN 1–85984–134–1 (pbk)

British Library Cataloguing in Publication Data
A catalogue record for this book is available from the British Library

Library of Congress Cataloging-in-Publication Data
A catalog record for this book is available from the Library of Congress

Giving ground : the politics of propinquity / edited by Joan Copjec
    and Michael Sorkin.
        p.   cm.
    ISBN 1–85984–892–3 (cloth).—ISBN 1–85984–134–1 (pbk.)
    1. City planning.   2. Sociology, Urban.   3. Political culture.
I. Copjec, Joan.   II. Sorkin, Michael, 1948–   .
HT166.G575   1999
307.76—dc21   99–17417
                                                                      CIP

Typeset by SetSystems Ltd, Saffron Walden, Essex
Printed by Biddles Ltd, Guildford and King's Lynn

CONTENTS

For Ann Armento Copjec, with love

INTRODUCTION
Traffic In Democracy

MICHAEL SORKIN

A few months ago, Mayor Giuliani closed the 50th Street crosswalks at
Fifth and Madison Avenues. The reason was to combat 'congestion'
in midtown Manhattan (of course, what he meant was automotive
congestion). Forcing walkers to cross the street in order to cross
the street enabled cars to turn right or left onto the opposing one-
way avenues without having to worry about negotiating with
pedestrians.

In the mayor's scheme, pedestrians are inconvenienced to
convenience cars. As a result, 50th Street has become a contested zone
in the fight over the right to move: crossing the street is now an act of
civil disobedience. Reflecting this proscription, a policeman has been
installed on each corner to assure compliance. Although this breaches
the historic understanding between New York pedestrians and police
that jaywalking laws are ridiculous and will therefore be ignored, it is
consonant with the mayor's (the ex-prosecutor's, the urban
disciplinarian's) penal comprehension of time and space. A prison, after
all, is built on the abstraction of every dimension of time but length and
on the devolution of spatial choice to a clockwise or counter route
around the exercise yard.

The mayor's strictures against crossing derive from a desire to
enhance the 'flow' of traffic. Flow seeks to increase speed (and save
time) by prioritizing the faster means of movement. Safety is often
foregrounded as the reason for this system of preferences; the potential
for danger, confusion and slow-down resulting from the undisciplined
mix gives rise to elaborate structures for vetting what traffic engineers
call 'conflict' between modes. Typically, this means slower vehicles yield

to faster ones and pedestrians to all, walkers deferring to cars, cars to trains, trains to planes, and so on.

Modern city planning is structured around an armature of such conflict avoidance. Elevated highways, pedestrian skyways, subway systems and other movement technologies clarify relations between classes of vehicles for the sake of efficient flow. This traffic strategy is mirrored in (and derived from) the idea of zoning by use, another gambit based on the idea of separating 'incompatible' activities and persons. For both, the segregating clarity of the movement hierarchy is presented as evidence of the 'rationality' of the system.

Chandigarh, the north Indian city designed by Le Corbusier – modernity's leading enthusiast for the city of efficient flow – is perhaps the most elaborate and self-conscious example of this type of traffic 'zoning'. Here, seven categories of road traffic are distinguished – based on speed – and the city is designed efficiently to separate them. Likewise, in a kind of nightmarish Taylorization of caste, the city distributes residents of various income levels among more than a dozen different income-based housing types.

The result is a city altogether different from the older Indian cities with their indigenous styles of motion that so appalled the fastidious Corbusier. Typically, Indian traffic is completely mixed up, a slow-moving mass of cows and pedicabs, motor-rickshaws, trucks and buses, camels and people on foot, the antithesis of 'efficient' separation. Motion through this sluggish maelstrom does not proceed so much by absolute right as through a continuing process of local negotiation for the right of passage.

There's something deeply satisfying about the movement through these old cities, not only because everyone is obliged to slow down but because this slow-down is the material basis for the tractability of the system. A student of mine who recently studied traffic patterns in Istanbul observed that its glacial pace guaranteed the safe and convenient crossing of pedestrians. In this decelerated system, slow may not become fast, but it does become fast for pedestrians.

Traffic codes and historic laws of rights of way codify urban styles of deference in motion. These rules of accessibility form criteria for determining who may go where and when. As such, these rights of way – which grant temporary permission to use private or public property for passage – structure a primal rite of *giving ground* and can thus serve us here as a concrete, that is, physical, exemplum of the deference to one's neighbor that urban existence daily demands. The homey concreteness of this instance should not, however, trivialize it or turn it into some plodding metaphor for more 'abstract' instances of giving way. For, though speed – and indeed almost instantaneous 'movement' – is now conceived as the determining factor of our new global economic and political order, the slower, physical flow of vehicular and human traffic remains a neglected issue. Not only is it true that it is primarily information and capital that travels at lightning speed and crosses all territorial barriers while the diaspora of despised peoples moves at a much slower pace and while strictures against movement – set up by inhospitable nations and opportunistic corporations – increase, it is also the case that urban density and movement through it has to be thought through politically, in these terms, rather than approached as merely a set of technical problems.

Growth complicates matters by introducing a vector of continuous transformation into the general pattern of urban distances. Under the contemporary regime of growth, this relationship has escaped rational management. The typical American – and increasingly global – result has been sprawl without end, the rapid outward movement of the urban periphery. As stable adjacencies and proximities are disrupted by the growth of the edge and the resultant transformation of the center, the system has produced its characteristic form: the 'edge city' in which uses are continuously relocated to re-establish proximity both by introducing new lateral relations oblivious to the center and by creating a physical texture in which hierarchies are highly repetitive and places increasingly indistinguishable.

There is a potentially ethical relation between speed and purpose, a system of rights that awards access to speed (and space) differentially. This demands a nuanced – and contested – ethics of privilege in a complex system that must weigh the rights of ambulances and strollers against more general rights of way and place. Such an ethics can derive from a very large number of criteria which – taken altogether – describe the politics of urban circulation. Indeed, the negotiated character of any urban spatial encounter begs an ethical reading of all of its components.

Energy, for example, is needed to produce motion. The ethics of energy expenditure – which is today articulated largely on the side of conservation – could arguably be invoked in defense of either side of the pedestrian/automotive question. On behalf of cars, the argument would come from their greater momentum (derived from both greater mass and greater speed), from the idea that their efficiency derives from smooth and speedy operation. The economy of stop and start opposes – in its inefficiency – the conservation of automotive energy.

The counter-argument is that cars are *intrinsically* wasteful of energy. This is a large claim, based on a global paradigm of conservation, not just a local one. Here, pedestrians become the alpha-means of low-energy travel, the ideal movers. This hierarchy puts walkers at the top, followed by human-powered transport – such as bikes, and so on down the line – the criterion being that the more energetic always yields to the least, reversing orthodox priorities. Of course, at the moment the rising curve of teleological privilege crosses the sinking curve of energy output, the whole becomes impossible.

This mathematical system defines walkers as energyless movers, as '0'. Once their actual expenditure is introduced into the equation, a difficulty arises. On the one hand, it's clear that the expenditure of aerobic energy by the organism increases (or at least conserves) the potential for further expenditure. This is called exercise. On the other hand, this calculation is based on individual potential and therefore on the difference between old and young, disabled and fit, and so on. The collision is between life conceived as pure physiology and life conceived in human terms (in which pleasure and convenience play important roles).

By identifying this priority of individual benefit (versus the class benefits of traffic), the way is open to a system that offers preferences based on the ability to derive benefit from locomotion. This would be based on a blending of physiological issues (whose ambulatory efficiency would be most increased by a given expenditure of energy) and human purpose (whose functioning arrogates the highest degree of necessity). While the road to the absurd is opened up by this calculation, it remains true that systems of traffic must be based on precepts beyond pure speed, on ideas about the distribution of rights.

The politics of traffic derives from the degree of access to the malleability of – the right to – time, the ability to speed up and slow down at will as well as the general enjoyment of the right of way. *This* right is ultimately to entropy since the individuation of desires tends (in a condition of freedom) to an increase in variation, a chaos of happinesses. Under such a system, older people, disabled people and the encumbered would – in order to enjoy temporal parity with other citizens – be the first candidates for the allotment of the energy that would become the means for a fair distribution of time.

Propinquity – neighborliness – is the ground and problem of democracy. Agnes Heller has described politics as the concretization of the universal value of freedom. The city – because of its intensity – is the privileged place of this politics of freedom, if not of freedom itself. The old Hanseatic maxim, 'city air makes people free' was based on the liquidity of association that characterizes urban life. City politics is deeply inscribed in questions of propinquity and access, in the legibility and tractability of routines of circulation and contact: the *currency* of propinquity is exchange, the most vital measure of the city's intensity.

The public spaces of the city are pre-eminently the spaces of circulation and exchange, overwhelmingly streets and sidewalks. We judge the good city by the quality of its public life and hence of its public space, yet the very idea of public space is now under siege. Formerly, attempts to *limit* it hid behind expressions of fear of its decline, but this disguise is now unnecessary. The notion of public space is attacked outright as itself a mask. The forces arrayed against public space come from a number of different and even opposed directions: from economic and social drives toward privatization; identity politics; communitarianism; from sprawl and the resulting growth of cyburbia, that pale blue zone of connectivity without place. As the idea of a universal public is supplanted by a desire for and embrace of multiple publics, traditional formulations of physical consent are becoming strained.

While the notion of public space was never meant to refer exclusively to a geographically delimited space that was open to all, it seems indisputable that the broader notion cannot dispense with such spaces. It is most likely because public space is so often and so readily conceived as dependent on a decorporealization of its citizenry – a demotion and even denigration of the particular and the physical – that the notion of public space has become so *abstract*, so divorced from any theorization of physical locations. This is also why notions such as the 'electronic town hall' have been so easy to sell, as though its very incorporeality guaranteed its publicity. Public space never comes down to a social abstraction from the individual body (in a famous quip, Marx mocked the naivety of such formulations: 'I have never encountered an abstract man, only concrete men'), it is, rather, a matter of reconfiguring the individual citizen's relation to his or her body and to those of other citizens.

What must be acknowledged and understood is the enormous anxiety that marks the decline of space as the primary medium of urban exchange. This need not take place on the terrain of nostalgia, as a simple mourning of the loss of once-familiar, now disappearing forms of human contact. It is a matter of grasping the consequences of – and often altering – the ways in which contemporary strategies of the virtual compete with historic ideas of location as the basis of propinquity. We've got to watch out: the fundamental epistemology of the city – the way it constructs its meanings – is being transformed as physical presence ceases to be the privileged means of participation and enjoyment of urban life.

The human character of cities begins with face to face interactions. From the city's styles of intensifying such intercourse descends any description of the urban economy and its politics. Traffic is one medium of this commerce, the sum of those instrumentalities of motion by which propinquity is engineered, the means by which we are enabled physically to encounter different circumstances within the city. While no mode of movement will make a difference if the character and variety of places between which we travel fail to reflect a sufficient range of differences, the dialogue of intersection between public and private is mediated and – in part – invented by the available means of circulating between them.

The relationship between propinquity and publicity begins with this statistical necessity: democratic deliberation is only possible in an environment that conduces both consensus and accident. This continual potential for conflict is vital to deliberation and marks the vigor of difference within culture. The design of urban systems demands a beautifully negotiated balance between the predictable and the unexpected, in order to produce the largest number of accidental discursive events.

Accidental encounter is produced by the character of urban access. One of the by-products of density and adjacency in cities is a continual testing of access. Propinquity – the ongoing legibility of adjacencies – always harbors a *testing* function and the power to reveal the limits of urban boundaries. This is analogous to the 'testing' of public accommodation that was part of the civil rights movement's strategy in the early 1960s, when groups of blacks would seek to be served at restaurants, hotels and other 'public' sites in order to establish the facts of discrimination as antecedent to legal intervention. An older form of such testing is the continuing and systematic use by walkers in England of historic 'rights of way' across private property, a form of close reading and measurement of the health and dimensions of the public environment and a means for setting the algorithms of territorial convenience.

While metropolitan citizens may choose to ignore what they happen to see in the city, their physical presence at the scenes of urbanity assures the likelihood of direct observation of the sites of stricture, conflict, conversion, appropriation and other negotiations. The approaching US census is now raising a procedural question which is in fact more than that: should we continue to take the national census by a door-to-door head count or should we rely on statistical information to arrive at a determination of our numbers? We have been repeatedly told that statistics make visible the individuals who once composed an invisible feudal mass, but it is more than clear that statistical calculations bring into being new classes of the uncounted whose invisibility is perhaps more profound for being now disavowed. Urban ghettos are fast becoming not only the blind spots in the modern game of statistics, but also areas we would just as soon see burned to the ground as see.

Founded on the rule of law, democracy demands the continual application of legality as well as the continual review of the nature and quality of the justice that inheres in the system of legal sanction. The functioning of that system is, in turn, contingent on presence, on the drawing in of citizens to the rites and routines of adjudication so that the plurality and variety of citizen-observers produce another guarantee of fairness via the statistical likelihood that urban encounters will often include – if only at their periphery – substantial numbers of disinterested parties.

Of course, this idea of constant encounter inevitably produces friction, the simple result of rubbing subjects together. (It's no accident that *frottage* is the 'classic' urban perversion.) Urban friction is the signal of boundary and a symptomatic constituent of urban social gradients. Such friction – by signaling difference – locates the internal edges of the city as well as potential sources of conflict. Yet, the very idea of accommodation is produced by such conflict, heightened by the physical character of urban life. It is no tautology to suggest that the only training for living together is living together. Racial tolerance is never concretized in the absence of the other, which is why anti-Semitism, and racism of all forms, thrives where there are no Jews, no racial others, in sight.

The city thus produces citizenship through the repetitive confrontation of citizens with an environment that organizes its prejudices and privileges physically, which is to say measurably. Unfortunately, traffic today is never thought about against the background of these concerns; it is approached as merely a technological problem and thus is saddled with the myths of technology, pinioned between visions of tractability and autonomy. Traffic engineers seek utopian solutions and fear 'Frankensteinian' rebellions, see-sawing on the only two possibilities offered by technology and its discontents.

Modernist urbanism collapsed as the result of its blind thrall to such scientism, whether in the form of its devotion to technology and the social 'sciences', or in its dreary mimesis of tech-forms. When – in reaction to this – cities ceased to be planned in the old physical sense, the prerogatives of planning activity were taken over by 'infrastructure', by something supposed to be underneath, invisible, common, neutral. This, of course, is simply modernism stripped of its iconic veneer. Traffic planning was quickly subsumed under this logic, becoming the favored visibility of planning, the thing that could tolerably be seen.

The foregrounding of the means of motion in city planning has proved disastrous. Cities have historically been obliged to play catch-up with existing transportation technologies, successively refitting themselves with systems that do not love them; urban space has been rent and scarred by railways and freeways, clogged and scored by pollution and metal. Yet the appeal of motion-based urbanism is rendered 'obvious' by discourses that effectively substitute the freedom to move unobstructed and in isolation for freedom of association. To the list of freedoms we have added the freedom of speedy dissociation.

Modern movement culture is increasingly serviced by capsules of intermediacy, by trains, planes, automobiles and elevators. These instrumentalities now make time for sitting in front of the video and computer screens with which they are being fitted. Just as the view from the railway car window forever altered not simply the landscape but our fundamental perceptions of time and space, so the window of the monitor represents a shift in our perceptual and psychical relationship to exteriority. Virtual travel embodies a remarkable economy of energy as the experience of motion is efficiently stripped from actual mobility.

Walter Hudson is this virtual dream turned flesh. At the time of his death on Christmas Eve 1991 he weighed 1,125 pounds, down from the 1,400 pounds that had established his Guinness-certified record as the world's fattest human. Hudson was so large that when he died a wall of his house had to be demolished to permit the removal of his body by a fork-lift. This body was towed *behind* a hearse to the cemetery where his piano-case coffin was buried in a double plot.

What made Hudson truly exemplary, though, was not his bulk but his immobility: except for a tragically brief period of slimming, Hudson never left his house, unable for years to rise from his specially-constructed bed. Sustained by a high-tech personal *Existenzminimum* of computer and television, toilet and refrigerator – a Big Mac in one hand, the remote control in the other – he led his contracted life.

Hudson's heft was both the medium of his immobility and the reason for his celebrity. Although his baroque corpulence bespoke spatiality (his achievement, after all, was to have occupied more space than anyone in history), his presence on the world stage was pure mediation. Hudson managed – without ever being present – to be incredibly *visible,* lavishly attended to by the media, who made him a poster child for America's prurient obsession with the consumption of space. Hudson represented the flip side of anorexia – the spatial neurosis of the age – and evoked the nation's prurient censure of overweight, a moral failure that infringes on the rights of the rest of us to space and aesthetic conformity.

On the other hand, Hudson's 'luxurious' occupation of physical space bore a striking resemblance to the delimiting privileges of the global élite, who circle the globe with effortless efficiency immobilized in their business-class seats, strapped and wired in, stuffed like Strasbourg geese. As they cruise through the ether on the way to a distant place that they are increasingly at pains to distinguish from the one left twelve hours ago and half a world away, questions of status and comfort are reduced to a consideration of the extra inches they occupy for the duration.

This global movement system trades access for privacy: constant surveillance is the price of 'freedom' of movement. Ironically, this surveillance is at its most Draconian for those with the greatest 'rights'. World travelers, for example, are subject to microscopic attention, their activities recorded, correlated, and made available to an enormous invisible government of customs authorities, shadowy credit agencies, back-office computer banks, market research firms, private security companies, advertisers, database gatherers and an endlessness of media connections. Pull out your Amex card and we know exactly where you are. Turn on your home security system and we know you've left. Order a special meal and we know there's a non-smoking Muslim in seat 3K.

The most dramatically efficient solution to the traffic problem is elimination of the reasons to move, whether through Walter Hudson-style immobility or the suppression of evocative qualities of difference in the environment. Location today is under intense competition from position, that is from location emptied of locality, proximity defined through virtual relations with other entities around the globe and with others living life on the Net. Location more and more rules at the expense of place. A tremendous rescaling is under way and with it a fattening culture of post-adjacent propinquity, configured at global scale.

Traffic – at whatever scale – is defined by the relationship between speed and flow, a quality that has by now obtained a quasi-metaphysical status. Like the circulation of capital, the circulation of traffic is most perfectly efficient when it attains the status of a constant – perpetual motion. But, while stasis is the enemy of a flowing system of perfect efficiency, it is also indispensable to its functioning: flow needs nodes.

The node is the corollary of flow, implying not simply centrality (and therefore directionality) but cease, the place where motion stops, enabling transfer (to foot, to another means, to another purpose). Flow imposes its own idea of efficiency, always calibrated to keeping going, not stopping, overcoming impedance and resisting inertia. The consequences are dramatic: nodal architecture subsumed by strategies of flow is predominant in the American landscape: the strip, the shopping mall, the suburbs, the edge city. Walter Hudson was a living node.

In America, the car is the main means for activating this landscape, for a variety of reasons, few of which are functional. It is well-observed that cars, in America, are idealized objects of identification and desire ('I love my Buick'). We hold the right to bear arms and own a car most dear. This auto-eroticism is responsible for the exponential enlargement of America's pavement – over one third of the total area of Los Angeles, for example, is devoted to the car. Indeed, no longer content to ply the confines of the pavement, the largest growth sector in the American automobile market is for off-the-road vehicles and for space-aggrandizing, home-surrogate, minivans.

Because the car seeks to optimize both speed and flow it looks for a conflict-free environment. In a mixed system, this means that either traffic must be separated strictly or a hierarchy must arise. Stop signs and traffic lights (as well as pedestrian barricades and cops on the corner) are means for sorting out this conflict. Traffic lights, which are meant to increase the efficient utility of the street, are, however, designed from the position of the car, directed primarily at resolving potential conflicts among vehicles. By any measure, pedestrians are disadvantaged: the space of the car, which predominates, is always a danger to them. Although the ideal for traffic is an easy mingling, we only produce technologies predicated on separation. The automobile system seeks invariably to exclude other modes that might come into conflict with it.

Los Angeles is the omega of the spatial city and the prototype of the city of the edge. Los Angeles – and cities like it – seek to create a consistent culture of the particle, in which an ostensibly egalitarian set of property relations is matched to a similarly conceived strategy of circulation. The experiment conducted with the use of cars in Los Angeles succinctly recapitulates Thomas Jefferson's Cartesian fantasy of the organization of American space. The grid – the instrument of an equality achieved by the surrender of difference in space or rather by the reduction of the arena of difference to a rigidly circumscribed territory – functions only if there is an even distribution of use, or if it runs like 'clockwork,' no caesura, no surcease, *and* if there are no intersections. This was Jefferson's fundamental error: he saw the grid as constituted purely of the aggregated surfaces of infinite squares, their boundaries immaterial, pure edge.

The Jeffersonian grid, however, generates both territories *and* interstices. Each square contains not simply its own surface but also four extra-territorial intersections which must be shared through negotiation. The conundrum is that an intersection is both a deterrent to flow and a necessity for contact. As a practical matter, the grid system only works at very low loadings, where the possibilities of conflict are greatly reduced. As anyone who has driven the LA grid late at night knows, this kind of geometrical freedom – in which one encounters public space as almost purely private – can be exhilarating. At higher rates of utilization, though, contact becomes impediment.

In cities like Los Angeles, the loadings on the grid are thrown into disequilibrium by the inequalities of use that culture imposes on the system. Zoning by class and by function, as well as the extremely uneven distribution of energy and motion over the diurnal cycle, distort the stable, static relationships that are at the core of the Cartesian fantasy: Thomas Jefferson never imagined the rush hour. Planning in Los Angeles is a history of successively failed panaceas for this problem. Co-ordinated traffic signals (traffic timing being the bedrock of the fantasy of flow) is one strategy for introducing hierarchy, great blocks of traffic shifted around the gridded zones, like trains of space in a synchronicity of flow. Urban expansion is another, but such growth – that old frontiersperson's hankering after infinity – reaches its limits in LA, the edge of the continent. Thus, the classic LA solution was to introduce the next order of physical gridding: the freeway.

Freeways are a symptom of both the spatial and temporal disequilibrium of real life, a mismatch of a technological fix with a conceptual difficulty. Freeways understand the city from the position of the car. Like other concentrating styles of motion, they try to reconcile the actual nodality of the system (the exits, if not the communities, are discreet) with the fantasy of a continuous fabric of equalized relationships. Los Angeles traffic effectively models the condition of American democracy with its inherent conflicts between an egalitarian model of social relations and a rapidly expanding system of privileges increasingly at odds with it.

America's national book of virtues celebrates the frontier and locates our autonomy in property, the literal possession of space. On the frontier, the quality of space lies in its boundlessness and our share must thus also share in this infinitude. In a system of generous dimensions – the mile-square grid, for example – privacy can be both elective and absolute. After all, if our neighbor is always invisible, our domain will appear unbounded: American polity is not founded on the fantasy of collectivity but on the right to be left alone. The contemporary fight over immigration reflects this anxiety over the loss of space and the excess visibility of the other. Where Alberti famously conceived the city as a magnified house, the American house summarizes the nation, the family isolated in its dominion of space. Such a vision is re-read back onto the body of the city itself, whether in conversions of territory directly to value or, more darkly, in the strategies of enclaving and exclusion that dominate so much contemporary place-making.

Disneyland – the objective correlative for everything – is a time-space bordello. With its carefully marked 'photo opportunities' and its scrupulous control of the marketing of its images, it is the high-capitalist field of seeing. At Disneyland, the stroll – slowed to a tortoise creep in the form of lines – is the means of circulation between attractions that are themselves based on a kind of pure interior speed, roller-coasting in the dark. All other means of motion offer no benefit in convenience or time. The wait in line precedes a brief burst of speed on a journey to nowhere, a potlatch of haste aestheticized. High speed is totally decoupled from convenience and transferred to the territory of pure – if highly marketable – enjoyment.

It's no coincidence that Disneyland first appeared in – or rather *near* – Los Angeles and represents a world's fair model 'solution' to the problem of the city. Viewed as a critique of modern urbanism, it is remarkable for its re-establishment of a version of pedestrian morality. Disneyland, located at a site that exists *only* because of the conjunction of freeways, forsakes the grid for the node. The huge, warped, point-grid of freeway nodes raises the grid a notch, finding its curves at topographic scale. But again, like the city itself, the system feels intermediate. There is a dialectic of distortion produced by the relationship of the efficient placement of freeway exits and the prior claims of the existing condition – farms, forests, houses, towns, and so on. Unlike the Jeffersonian grid which seeks to organize nothingness into a map of potential, the freeway grid is predicated on the prior existence of places of value and therefore lacks the geometric rigor of its Jeffersonian counterpart, reversing its priority of dispersal by searching out the already existing intersection, seeking concentrations or their potential. And, a further notch, Disneyland constructs a cultural grid. In its juxtapositions of simulated versions of different historical and cultural moments, Disneyland adds the fourth dimension to the grid – another substitution of location for place – and thus harbingers in the physical the possibilities now everywhere actualized by strategies of the virtual.

Disneyland is a playground of mobility, it entertains with pleasure-motion. For all its depredations, regimentation, surveillance and control, part of what is experienced as enjoyable at Disneyland really is the passage through an environment of urban density in which both the physical texture and the means of circulation are not simply entertaining but stand in invigorating contrast to the dysfunctional versions back home. One thus extracts from Disneyland a shred of hope, the persuasive example that pedestrianism coupled with short distance collective transport systems can be both efficient and fun, can thrive in the midst of an environment completely otherwise constituted, and that the space of flow sufficiently decelerated can become the space of exchange. But only if we're not just passing through. The paranoiacly privatized space of Disneyland could never make itself home to any but the most abstract – that is, monetary – exchange.

Democratic traffic deprivileges unimpeded flow and favors concrete exchange. To promote the enabling deceleration, cities need to adopt supply-side transport management strategies. This will not necessarily be easy. Our culture – nursed on advertising around the clock – makes a fetish of demand: the whole system thrives on spurious need. But this is no signal of the autonomy of our desires, these, rather, are the sounds of their silencing and reveal how thoroughly entrapped we have become in someone else's entrepreneurial dream.

To begin again will mean reconsidering the place of the body in democracy. For the most part, democracy does not traffic in bodies; it is instead theorized in terms of disincorporation, the beheading of the monarch, the emptying out of the central place of power, the establishment of body-blind tribunals of public justice, and so on. Yet, as I argued earlier, it is a mistake to take this disincorporation literally, as the mere excision of the physical body from space, for what democratic theory actually represents is a radical clearing of old notions of the body and an invitation to invent it anew.

The grid prefers a movement monoculture, and monoculture is tyranny. Uniform transit helps produce uniform neighborhoods. Conversely, it seems clear that the ability of neighborhoods to act autonomously is enhanced by their accessibility. Indeed, the solution to the traffic problem is not continuously to model its operations at larger and larger scales, but radically to disconnect locality from larger systems which, on balance, ill serve it. For many places, the only way to come to terms with the hegemony of the automotive system is to secede from it. In inner city areas, starved for useful public space and clotted with traffic, the most logical and effective step is to reduce the physical area actually available to the car. Roadways constitute the major portion of the commonly maintained public realm in cities. Cars have been given an enormous franchise on the use of this space – public property – for both circulation and storage.

Recently, working on a plan for East New York, a poor neighborhood in Brooklyn, I wondered what a minimum intervention might be that would begin to recapture the order of the neighborhood from motor traffic, promote greening and reinforce new patterns of relative self-sufficiency and local autonomy. The answer, I decided, was to plant a tree in an intersection. Several consequences were anticipated. First, the space devoted to the automobile would be reduced by the instant creation of four dead-end streets: the tree would oblige traffic either to find collateral means of circulation or keep out. Second, the quieted zone would permit dramatic alteration of the ratios of green and built space with accompanying possibilities for new agricultural activities and architectural types. Finally, I hoped that street-life – its sparse commerce having been attenuated into useless, center-crushing linearity – would be densified in a series of locally-scaled commercial and social centers that would restore legibility, convenience and conviviality to a place ragged, over-large and devoid of all character.

Accident demands the retention of urban difference, not its reduction to a series of empty, abstracted, visual distinctions. But if not by abstraction, how should the city be divided? In the age of identity politics, what is the meaning and purchase of the ghetto? While we think of it as primarily carceral, we know it can breed great dynamism. Common experiences and common cause sometimes produce a variety of solutions and goals. The ghetto begs the question of the boundary, of the morphology of difference. In a city dedicated to free circulation, how is it possible to construct the boundaries that will make variety both legible and accessible?

The antidote to the ghetto would be the neighborhood, a place of social and physical semi-permeability, if it were not for the fact that the notion of neighborhood is now often appropriated by those who conceive it as a fortress against 'neighborliness' in all its properly vexatious and thus productive aspects. For these people, the neighborhood is little more than an inverse ghetto – that is, elective and privileged. It is time to reinstate a notion of neighborhood that is simultaneously bounded and open. To achieve appropriate legibility, and to engender productive rates of and settings for accidental encounter, neighborhoods must be secured to the body, to both its scale and constraints. Thus, a neighborhood must be meaningfully physical, configuring the blend of the social and the dimensional.

It is necessary to bear in mind, however, that the constraints, and even the scale, of the body are not what they were in the classical age when Aristotle famously called for a limitation of the agora to the space of a shout. We can hear and see much farther now than then, the result of a myriad of prosthetic devices of our own invention. It is easy to say – and so it often *is* said – that these prostheses have annulled, or alienated us from, our bodies. The truth, I believe, is more complex: the body itself is not what it once was. With the rise of capitalism it acquired the potential of a tool, something that could be used. What has never been adequately dealt with by urban theorists or planners is the effect this redefinition of the body has on the notion of neighborhood. If public space, the agora, was defined by Aristotle through the imprinting of the capability of the body on it, this is because *incorporation* was the metaphor by which the alien – the foreign – difference could be accommodated without threatening their integrity and autonomy. Once the notion of the body changed, once it became conceivable as a tool, the notion of incorporation was replaced by that of *assimilation* and the foreign came under increasing pressure to surrender its difference in favor of some unqualified substrate.

No modern neighborhood – inasmuch as it is home to computers, televisions, phones, faxes, and so on – will ever be as small as the agora of antiquity; it is thus impossible to return to this scale in some real sense. Nor is it possible voluntaristically to return to the older metaphor of incorporation, since our bodies and our conditions are *materially* different. But it is possible – and indeed necessary – to think about and construct our cities in a way that binds them to the body and what it can do. For the modern body has, it turns out, redoubled and contradictory functions: it serves not only as tool but as that which incarnates the accident as such. That is, whereas in antiquity accidents had a place and thus a body could expect to *meet* with them, in modernity accidents are not given a place and thus a body could only *be* one. The body now bears the burden of being the only place where the accident resides. In other terms, only the body – through work – can introduce difference into an otherwise uniform system.

Consumer research and focus groups, the media of planning not only for Disney's town of Celebration but for many of our global cities, are busy designing urban environments suited to the programmable body-as-tool. The task this volume sets itself is to begin thinking about what place the other modern body – the body-as-accident – does and might occupy in the global city. Against all the arguments about the dematerialization attendant on our 'information age', it seemed important to us to recognize that the modern body has the impossible role of giving a place to place. Neither nostalgic nor humanist, this recognition stresses the historical novelty of this role and the radical impossibility that conditions it. That is to say, what is at issue here is *not* an argument for an urbanism that would allow the body to develop its full potential. Cities must make room, not for what is possible, but for what is still *impossible*. This latter never wears a human face, which is the source of a great deal of difficulty, the major urban difficulty we now confront.

I

THE GLOBAL,
THE INTIMATE,
AND THE EMPTY

1 . . . THREE, TWO, ONE, CONTACT:
Times Square Red, 1998[1]

SAMUEL R. DELANY

> . . . in this great preoccupation about the way to govern and the search for the
> ways to govern, we identify a perpetual question which would be: 'how not to be
> governed *like that*, by that, in the name of those principles, with such and such an
> objective in mind and by means of such procedures, not like that, not for that,
> not by them.' And if we accord this movement of govermentalization of both
> society and individuals the historic dimension and breadth which I believe it has
> had, it seems that one could approximately locate therein what we could call the
> critical attitude.
>
> Michel Foucault, What is Critique?

0 The primary thesis is simply that, given the mode of capitalism under which
we live, life is at its most rewarding, productive and pleasant when the greatest
number of people understand, appreciate, and seek out interclass contact and
communication conducted in a mode of good will.

My secondary thesis is, however, that the class war rages constantly and often
silently in the comparatively stabilized societies of the developed world, though
it is at times as hard to detect as Freud's unconscious or the structure of
discourse, perpetually works for the erosion of the social practices through
which interclass communication
takes place, and the institutions
holding those practices stable, so that
new institutions must always be
conceived and set in place to take
over the jobs of those that are
battered again and again till they are
destroyed.

A. Among other things, this essay is an
attempt to explain what is going on in
the following anecdote:

A group of friends entered a Soho gallery opening – some young painters and
their acquaintances. At the group's center was a woman painter – we'll call her
Jane Pharnim – who had a show up
currently at a nearby gallery we'll call
Quincunx.

My tertiary thesis, to which now
and again I shall return, is that, while
the establishment and utilization

As Jane and the group stood around
talking and sipping from plastic glasses
of white wine, a man joined them, saying

to Jane: 'You're Jane Pharnim, aren't you? I saw your show just yesterday over at the Quincunx. I was very impressed. Probably, I shouldn't tell you this, but I'm going to be reviewing it for *Color and Form*. I don't think it'll be a problem though, since I was planning to give it a pretty good review anyway. But it's nice to get a chance to meet you and say hello. The only picture that somewhat puzzled me was that big gray and yellow one in the back. It seemed so different from all the others.'

'It is, in many ways,' replied Pharnim. 'But in others – do you remember the little red one right beside the door . . .?'

'One of my favorites – yes.'

'Well, the big gray and yellow one has the identical structure, turned upside down and rotated left/right, as the little red one. I wanted to see if I could make it work like that, larger and with a cooler palette. That's why it's there with the others – even though, yeah, I know it doesn't *really* look like it belongs.'

'Now, that's interesting. No, I didn't see that. I'll have to rethink that one before I hand in the review.'

The conversation drifted on. Soon – and separately – both the reviewer and Pharnim left.

But the next morning one of the painters who had been part of the group (and who, unlike Pharnim, hadn't yet had a gallery show but would very much have liked one) explained to a friend: 'You know, today in the art world it's all who you know, who you meet, who you network with. Last night, I was at an opening with Jane, when this art reviewer came over to talk to her. She practically dictated her review to him, word for word . . .'

Now, despite the young man's somewhat over-glib analysis, certain things *did*

tion of those institutions always involves specific social practices, the effects of my primary and secondary theses are regularly perceived at the level of discourse. Therefore, it is only by a constant renovation of the concept of discourse that society can maintain the most conscientious and informed field for both the establishment of such institutions and practices and, by extension, the necessary critique of those institutions and practices – a critique necessary if new institutions of any efficacy are to develop. At this level, in its largely stabilizing/destabilizing role, superstructure (and superstructure at its most oppositional) *can* impinge on infrastructure.

1.1 We are all aware that landlords and tenants exist in a fundamentally antagonistic relationship with one another. Generally speaking, throughout most of what we might call the middle classes of our society, landlords tend to be somewhat better off financially than their tenants. Certainly the class war is as strong there as between any groups save, perhaps, workers and employers.

With that in mind, here is a tale:

A black woman born in Nottaway, Virginia, my maternal grandmother came from Petersburg to New York City at age eighteen, in 1898, and moved to Harlem in 1902 when it was still a German neighborhood. With my grandfather, an elevator operator in a downtown office building and go on in the encounter at the art opening and certain things *did not.*

We can clarify some points right away. The encounter did not bring about the writing of the review. (The reviewer had been assigned the review before he met Pharnim.) The encounter did not change a bad review into a good one. (If the reviewer had already decided to write a bad one, it's unlikely he would have introduced himself – or he would have avoided letting Pharnim know who he was.) Most obviously, the encounter did not acquire for Pharnim her show at the Quincunx. Taken out of context, however, what the young male artist, who lusts after just such a show himself ['. . . today in the art world it's all who you know, who you meet, who you network with . . .'], said could easily be taken to mean that such contacts might well lead to shows.

Gallery openings and such art gatherings are typical fields for networking. The exchange was typical of those that easily and often occur in networking venues. What *did* happen at the gallery opening was an exchange of specialized information about one somewhat problematic canvas in Pharnim's show – information that may or may not find its way into an already favorable review; and, yes, it is information that might not have been available to the reviewer had there been no networking venue to bring him, even so briefly, together with the artist.

By the end of this essay, I hope we shall have an even clearer idea not only of what went on and what did not go on in this networking situation, but we will also have some understanding of what the young man who witnessed the encounter *thought* he was seeing and what he felt his stake was in drawing the

later a Grand Central Terminal redcap, she took rooms in the first house in Harlem opened to blacks, on 132nd Street, between Seventh and Lenox. Owned by a black man married to a white woman, the house rented to men and women working as servants in the neighborhood. My grandmother told of returning to her rooms after work, while the Germans, sitting in front of their houses along Seventh Avenue played zithers through the evening.

A number of times in the sixties and seventies, Grandma spoke of the social practice in the twenties, thirties, and, in a few places, into the forties, of the landlord's annual or sometimes semiannual visit to her apartment: my sense is that these visits were notably different from the monthly visits *to* the landlord to pay the rent – in the days before universal banking.

Expected by both tenants and landlords, the practice allowed tenants to point out directly to the building's owner any breakages, or repairs that were needed. The owner got a chance to see how the tenant was treating his or her property. By opening the door for less formal ones, these visits established an arena for social interchange. From them, landlords gained a sense of the tenants as individuals and tenants took a sense of the landlord as a person.

Yes, there might be a spate of cleaning in the apartment in the days before the landlord came. Certainly, there might be a rush of painters and conclusion from it *about* the necessity of plumbers in that same month – both, networking that he did. so that, during the visit itself, everyone might come off at his or her best. But the visits meant that in those situations in which there were problems on either side that could be resolved only by the greater forces of the class war itself (an eviction, a suit against a landlord for a major dereliction of necessary repairs), there was nevertheless a social field in which either side could ask for leniency or at least understanding from the other; and often it could be granted. Similarly, either side could personally entreat the other to straighten up and fly right, and many times this was enough to avert major confrontations.

In no way did the social practice obviate the socio-economic antagonism between the *classes*. But it tended to stabilize relationships at the personal level and restrict conflict to the economic level itself – keeping it from spilling over into other, personal situations.

What eroded this practice of landlord visits were, first, the economic forces of the Depression. Pressures on tenants (from the exhaustion of having two or three jobs to the anomie of having no job at all) became such that they began housing extra materials or extra people in their apartments to the point that a good day's cleaning could not cover over the evidence. Models for bourgeois living standards became less available as did time and energy to implement them. And landlords found themselves unable to afford keeping the facilities in the first-class shape tenants expected.

Tenants began to see the visits as prying.

Landlords began to see the visits as a formal responsibility empty of content and – finally – an unnecessary nuisance, in which they had to listen to demands they could not afford to meet.

Repair work was now delegated to a superintendent whose job was to carry out those repairs as inexpensively as possible. While more stringent rules were instituted to restrict property-damaging wear and tear, in practice tenants were now allowed greater leeway in what they might do to the house. Older tenants saw the failure of the landlord to visit as a dereliction of responsibility. But younger tenants cited the 'privilege' of better-off tenants in more lavish properties, often paying far higher rents, to forego such visits. Why shouldn't the privilege of the better off be a right – the right of privacy – for all?

1.2 For the last twenty-one years, I have lived in a fifth-floor walk-up, rent-stabilized apartment at the corner of Amsterdam and 82nd Street. In that time, the owner of the building has *never* been through my apartment door. Once, five years ago, he shouted threats of legal action against me from the landing below – threats which came to nothing when, in retaliation, I hired a lawyer.

B. During tight times the landlord's visit facilitated a comparatively humane prioritizing of repairs – allowing tenant complaints to be looked at somewhat more holistically in terms of how much discomfort each involved. A loose window sash in the bathroom of a twenty-year-old student, spending weekends with his family, and who is willing to wait till March to have it fixed is not necessarily the same complaint as a loose window sash of the bathroom of a seventy-year-old couple, more sensitive to cold and temperature change. A family with two working adults' incomes may be amenable to the suggestion: 'Have the window repaired at your own expense, give me the receipt, and I'll subtract half the cost of the repairs from this coming December's rent and the other half from January's, giving you a monetary break for the holidays.'

By exploiting such prioritizing strategies the landlord could sometimes stabilize and smooth out his or her cash flow problems and the seasonal crunches that invariably fell to such a business.

Of course, such prioritizing could be abused – repairs might be put off indefinitely. It is as frustrating for tenants to have to ask for the same repair month after month, as it is for landlords, month after month, to have to nag their tenants for the rent. In cases of landlord abuse, however, tenants sought refuge in a system in which a loose sash was a loose sash, no matter who had it, and wanted, as well, a time limit for when it would be fixed. Nevertheless, when a landlord used prioritizing intelligently and responsibly, it could work as a social gift to everyone.

In the situation where a loose sash is a loose sash, to be fixed within a given

This past February, when what became a four-alarm fire broke out in the building at five in the morning, he visited his property for a brief half hour at 7:30 a.m., and, standing out on the street among the fire engines, declared how grateful he was that no one had been hurt, then – in his shako and (the only man I've ever seen wear one) fur-collared overcoat – left. But those are the only two times I have ever seen him in person – or he has ever, I assume, seen me.

On the one hand, when repairs have been needed, and even more so after that brief shouting match in the hall, occasionally I've thought that the more personal relations my grandmother maintained with her landlord during the early decades of this century might well have made things go more easily. Were my landlord someone with whom, twice a year, I sat over a cup of coffee in my kitchen, I might have been able to negotiate speedier, and better quality, repairs – repairs for which, often, I would have been willing to share the financial weight; repairs which would have benefited the property itself. And certainly we both might have bypassed the emotional strain of the aforementioned shouting match.

On the other hand, I try to imagine my landlord's response if he had visited during the first ten months after I had to collapse my Amherst apartment with my New York digs (when I was under precisely the same sort of socio-economic pressures that had time, general repair quality tends to be lower, with poorer grade materials. Though the tenants benefit as a group, often as individuals they suffer more inconvenience. ('The repairman is coming at 10:00 am on Tuesday. You'll just have to take a day off from work.')

The visit from the landlord recalls another sort of visit – the charity visit – that goes back at least (in England) to the 1840s, and continues to this day with the social worker's visit.

The particular aspect of the visits I am interested in, however, is when the visitor him- or herself has the money and the authority to instigate repairs and effect material changes. When a visitor functions *precisely as a mediator between* the tenant and whoever authorizes (and pays for) the changes, we have a situation that I will designate as the linear chain model. Such chains function largely to filter out the specific, social, idiosyncratic information that made prioritizing possible. Such chains – even of two or three people – become a major mechanism to ensure not only that a loose sash is a loose sash, but that a broken pane, a loose sash, and a window frame pried out and shattered by an organized gang of apartment robbers are, all of them, just a 'window repair'.

eroded away the practice of visits in the first place), and my apartment's back three rooms looked more like an over-full Jersey warehouse space than a home with people living in it. What if he had come during the previous five years when, regularly, I let friends use the place, two and three times a month, as an Upper West Side party space? (More than half a dozen years after the fact, I still meet people who tell me they have been to 'great parties' at 'my' house, when *I* wasn't in attendance.) During the same period, I let a succession of friends and acquaintances stay there during the 130-odd days a year I was in Amherst, teaching at the University of Massachusetts. Such visits would have curtailed such practices severely – though, in neither case, on my side or on his, was the *letter* of the law violated.

1.3 At the rhetorical level, the trace of the social practice my decade-and-a-half dead grandmother spoke about still lingers in the language, as tenants in the Upper West side still speak of our landlord's 'seeing to' certain repairs – even though the landlord will not and does not intend to set eyes on anything within the front door of the building – just as the term 'landlord' is, itself, a rhetorical holdover from a time and set of social practices when the *important* things the owner was 'lord' over were, indeed, 'land,' and the 'tenants to the land', rather than the buildings erected on it.

1.4 The betraying signs that one discourse has displaced or transformed into another is often the smallest rhetorical shift: a temporal moment (and a sociological location) in the transformation between a homosexual discourse and a gay discourse may be signaled by the appearance in the 1969 Fall issues of *The Village Voice* of the locution 'coming out to' one's (straight) friends, co-workers and family (a verbal act directed toward straights) and its subsequent displacement of the demotic locution 'coming out into' (gay) society – a metaphor for one's first major gay sexual act. Between the two locutions lies Stonewall and the post-Stonewall activities of the Gay Liberation Movement. Equally, such a sign might be seen to lie at another moment, at another location, in the changeover from 'that's such a camp' to 'that's camp.' The intervening event there is Susan Sontag's 1964 *Partisan Review* essay, 'Notes on Camp'. I have written of how a shift in postal discourse may be signed by the rhetorical shift between 'she would not receive his letters' and 'she would not open his letter'. What intervened here was the 1848 introduction of the postage stamp, which changed letter writing from an art and entertainment paid for by the receiver, to a form of vanity publishing paid for by the sender. (There *is* no junk mail before 1848.) One might detect a shift in the discourse of literature by the changeover between 'George is in literature', and 'George's library contains mostly history and literature'. The explosion of print in the 1880s, occasioned by the typewriter and the linotype, intervene. The shift between a practice of landlord visits and superintendents in charge of repairs is signaled by the rhetorical shift between 'the landlord saw to the repairs' as a literal statement and the 'landlord saw to the repairs' as a metaphor. I say shifts – but these rhetorical pairings are much better looked at, on the level of discourse, as rhetorical collisions. The sign that a discursive collision has occurred is that the former meaning has been forgotten, and the careless reader, not alerted to details, reads the older rhetorical figure as if it were the newer.

As are the space of the unconscious and the space of discourse, the space where the class war occurs as such is, as are all three spaces in their pure form, imaginary – imaginary *not* in the Lacanian sense but rather in the mathematical sense. (In the Lacanian sense, those spaces are specifically symbolic.) Imaginary numbers – those involved with i, the square root of minus-one – do not exist. But they have measurable and demonstrable effects on the real (that is, political) materiality of science and technology. Similarly, the structures, conflicts and, displacements that occur in – yes – the unconscious, the class war, and the space of discourse are simply too useful to ignore in explaining what goes on in the world we live in, unto two men yelling in the hall, one a landlord and one a tenant, if not mayhem out on the streets themselves, or the visible changes in a neighborhood like Times Square, or, indeed, the Upper West Side, over a decade or so, to the specificities of rhetorical shift.

(Repeatedly Foucault described discourse, or at least a part of it, as 'an' unconscious, in a 1968 interview: 'In a positive manner we can say that

structuralism investigates an unconscious. It is the unconscious structure of
language, of the literary work, and of knowledge that one is trying at this
moment to illuminate', and, in his 1971 Foreword to the English edition of *The
Order of Things*, he wrote that his work intended to 'bring to light a *positive
unconscious* of knowledge: a level that eludes the consciousness of the scientist
and yet is part of scientific discourse', italics in original.)[2]

1.5 Starting in 1985, in the name of 'safe sex', New York City began to
criminalize every individual sex act by name, from masturbation to vaginal
intercourse, whether performed with a condom or not – a legal situation that
has catastrophic ramifications we may not crawl out from under for a long,
long time. This is a legal move that arguably puts gay liberation, for example,
back to a point notably before Stonewall – and doesn't do much for heterosexual freedom either.

This is a rhetorical change that may well adhere to an extremely important
discursive intervention in the legal contouring of social practices whose ramifications, depending on the development and the establishment of new social
practices that promote communication between the classes (specifically sexual
and sex related), are hard to foresee in any detail.

1.6 An important point: I do not think it is in any way, shape, or form, nostalgic
to say that, under such a social practice as my grandmother knew, both landlord and tenant were better off than I am today. The practice was a social arena
of communication which, when utilized fully, meant that both landlord and
tenant had to expend more time, energy and money in order to maintain a
generally higher standard of living for the tenant and a generally higher level
of property upkeep, restricting the abuse of that property, for the landlord.
On both tenant and landlord, greater restrictions obtained as to what was
expected and what was not. The practice eroded when the money was no
longer there, when the time and energy had to be turned, by both, to other
things, and when practices formerly unacceptable to both had, now, to be
accepted, so that the practice of the visits became a futile annoyance to both
sides and was dropped.

But the establishment of, say, tenant associations – at which landlords are
occasionally invited to speak and meet with their tenants – *begins* to fulfill the
vacuum in the array of social practices that erosion leaves.

At the same time, they do not fill it in the same way.

The fact that such relations may have been more pleasant does not, however,
mean that those relations were somehow more authentic than mine to Mr.
Buchbinder. All that relative pleasantness suggests is a confirmation of my

primary thesis – which *is* about pleasure, after all – pleasure in its lowest form, though pleasure no less important or social for that: the pleasant.

1.7 So stated, these points appear harmless enough. Over the last two decades, however, a notion of safety has arisen, a notion that runs from safe sex (once it becomes anything more than using condoms during anal sex with men of unknown HIV status) and safe neighborhoods, to safe cities, and committed (that is, safe) relationships, a notion which currently functions very much the way the notion of 'security' and 'conformity' did during the 1950s. As, in the name of 'safety', society dismantles the various institutions that promote inter-class communication, attempts to critique the way such institutions functioned in the past to promote their happier sides are often seen as – at best – nostalgia for an outmoded past and, at worst, a pernicious glorification of everything dangerous: unsafe sex, neighborhoods filled with undesirables (read 'unsafe characters'), promiscuity, an attack on the family, the stable social structure, and dangerous, non-committed, 'unsafe' relationships – that is, psychologically 'dangerous' relations, though the danger is rarely specified in any way other than to suggest its failure to conform to the ideal bourgeois marriage.

Such critiques are imperative, however, if we are ever to establish new institutions that will promote similar ends.

2 The linear chain into which the practice of landlord visits to tenants in the twenties, thirties, and forties might be said to have degenerated reminds us that the linear chain is as an information conduit, a relatively artificial social form. Most social interchanges of information and material occur in various forms of social nets.

Generally speaking, in a net situation, because information comes from several directions and crosses various power boundaries, separate processes – modulating, revisionary, additive, recursive and corrective – can compensate for the inevitable reductions that occur in the constitutive chains. Considered as information dispersal processes, nets are far more efficient than chains. But not all nets are the same.

Social nets can be more or less complex, of greater or lesser density. When the net density is comparatively low, we often focus on the contacts between individual net members and ignore the net-like structure in which these contacts occur. When the density is high, we are more likely to focus on the overall network.

Starting from the above as the most arbitrary and provisional of observations, the two modes of social-net practice I shall discuss for the rest of this paper – and the discourses around them that allow them to be visible as such – I

designate as 'contact' and 'networking'. Like all social practices they create/
sediment discourses, even as discourses create, individuate and inform with
value the material and social objects that facilitate and form the institutions
that both support and contour these practices.

2.1 Contact is the conversation that starts in the line at the grocery counter
with the person behind you while the clerk is changing the paper roll in the
cash register. It is the pleasantries exchanged with a neighbor who has brought
her chair out to take some air on the stoop. It is the discussion that begins with
the person next to you at a bar. It can be the conversation that starts with any
number of semi-officials or service persons – mailman, policeman, librarian,
store clerk or counter person. It can also be two men watching each other
masturbating together in adjacent urinals of a public john – an encounter
which – later – may or may not become a conversation. For contact – very
importantly – is also the intercourse, physical and conversational, that blooms
in and as 'casual sex', in public rest rooms, sex movies, public parks, singles
bars, sex clubs and on street corners with heavy hustling traffic, and the
adjoining motels or the apartments of one or another participant, from which
non-sexual friendships and/or acquaintances lasting for decades or a lifetime
may spring, not to mention the conversation of a john with a prostitute or
hustler encountered on one or another street corner or in a bar – a relation
that, a decade later, has devolved into a smile or a nod, even when (to quote
Swinburne) 'You have forgotten my kisses, / And I have forgotten your name.'
Mostly, these contact encounters are merely pleasant chats, adding a voice to a
face now and again encountered in the neighborhood. But I recall one such
supermarket-line conversation that turned out to be with a woman who'd done
graduate work on the Russian poet Zinaida Hippius, just when I happened to
be teaching Dmetri Merejkowski's Christ and anti-Christ trilogy in a graduate
seminar at the University of Massachusetts: Merejkowski was Hippius's husband,
and I was able to get some interesting and pertinent information about the
couple's wanderings in the early years of the century.

I have at least one straight male friend who, on half-a-dozen occasions, has
gotten editorial jobs for women he first met and befriended as they were
working as topless dancers in various strip clubs that put them on the fringe of
the sex workers' service profession.

A young street hustler in the 42nd Street area whom I knew (but was not a
client of) introduced me to a new client of his once – a twenty-six-year-old
lapsed Jesuit priest – for whom I shortly secured a job at a paperback publishing
house, in much the same manner.

Another supermarket-line conversation was with a young man who was an aspiring director, looking for some science fiction stories to turn into brief teleplays; I was able to jot down for him a quick bibliography of young SF writers and short stories that he might pursue. Whether or not it came to anything, I have no way of knowing. But it was easy and fun.

Still another time, it was a young woman casting director who needed someone to play the small part of a fisherman in a film she was working on – and decided I would be perfect for it. I found myself with a weekend acting job.

One Saturday morning in January 1998, my vacuum cleaner shorted out and an hour later I set it on the street by the gate before the garbage cans for my building, after making a mental note to shop for a replacement that weekend. Forty minutes on, at my local copy center, I was getting a set of xeroxes for a draft of this very paper, when a broad-faced, grey-eyed Italian-American in his late thirties, wearing a shiny red and blue jacket, wandered in: 'Anyone wanna buy a wet-dry vacuum cleaner? Ten bucks.' My first suspicion was that he was reselling the one I'd just abandoned. My second was that the one he was selling didn't work. A look disproved the first. Plugging his machine into an outlet at the sidewall of the shop for a minute disproved the second. So I went home once more with a vacuum cleaner: contact.

Contact encounters so dramatic are rare – but real. The more ordinary sorts of contact yield *their* payoff in moments of crisis: when there is a fire in your building (of the sort I mentioned above), it may be the people who have been exchanging pleasantries with you for years who take you into their home for an hour or a day – or even overnight. Contact includes the good Samaritans at traffic accidents (the two women who picked me up when my cane gave way and I fell on the street, dislocating a finger, and got me a cab), or even the neighbor who, when you've forgotten your keys at the office and are locked out of your apartment, invites you in for coffee and lets you use her phone to call a locksmith: or, as once happened to me in the mid-1960s when my then-neighborhood, the Lower East Side, was at its most neighborly and under the influence of the counter-culture, and a London guest arrived on Wednesday when I was out of town and expecting him on Thursday. Someone living across the street, who didn't know me at all, saw a stranger with two suitcases on my apartment stoop looking bemused, invited him in to wait for me, then eventually put him up for a night until I returned.

And finally: my lover of eight years, Dennis, and I first met when he was homeless and selling books from a blanket spread out on 72nd Street. Our two best friends for many years now are a gay male couple, one of whom I first met in a sexual encounter, perhaps a decade ago, at the back of the now closed-down Variety Photoplays Movie Theater on Second Avenue just below 13th

Street. Outside my family, these are among the two most rewarding relationships I have: both began as cross-class contacts in a public space.

Visitors to New York might be surprised that such occurrences are central to my vision of the City at its healthiest. Lifetime residents won't be. Watching the metamorphosis of such vigil and concern into considered and helpful action is what gives one a faithful and loving attitude toward one's neighborhood, one's city, one's nation, the world.

An undertaking such as this must acknowledge Jürgen Habermas's analysis of the public sphere – and, more important, the critique of that work leveled in the late 1970s by Oskar Negkt. But, finding them even more suited to my purposes here, I have taken 'contact', both term and concept, from Jane Jacobs's instructive 1961 study, *The Death and Life of Great American Cities*. Jacobs describes contact as a fundamentally urban phenomenon and finds it necessary for everything from neighborhood safety to a general sense of social well-being. She sees it supported by a strong sense of private and public in a field of socio-economic diversity that mixes living spaces with a variety of commercial spaces, which, in turn must provide a variety of human services if contact is to function in a pleasant and rewarding manner. Jacobs mentions neither casual sex nor public sexual relations as part of contact – presumably because she was writing at a time when such things were not talked of or analysed as elements contributing to an overall pleasurable social fabric. Today we can.

When social forces menace the distinction between private and public, people are most likely to start distrusting contact relations. In *The Death and Life of Great American Cities*, Jacobs analyses how limited socio-economic resources in the area around a public park (lack of restaurants, bathrooms, drugstores and small shops) can make the mothers who use the playground feel that the privacy within their home is threatened – thus markedly changing their public attitude to interclass contact[3]. Briefly, a park with no public eating spaces, restaurants or small-item shopping on its borders forces mothers who live adjacent to it and thus use it the most to 'share everything or nothing' in terms of offering the use of their bathroom and an occasional cup of coffee to other mothers and their children who use the park but do not live so near. Because the local mothers feel they must offer these favors to whomever they are even civil to (since such services are not publically available), they soon become extremely choosy and cliquish about whom they will speak to; the feel of the park becomes exclusive and snobbish – and uncomfortable (and inconvenient) for mothers who, in carriage, dress, race, or class, do not fit a rigid social pattern.

Similarly, if *every* sexual encounter involves bringing someone back to your house, the general sexual activity in a city becomes anxiety filled, class-bound and choosy. This is precisely *why* public restrooms, peepshows, sex movies, bars with grope rooms and parks with enough greenery are necessary for a relaxed and friendly sexual atmosphere in a democratic metropolis.

Jacobs's analysis stops short of contact as a specifically stabilizing practice in interclass relations – signaled by her (largely understandable in the pre-Stonewall 1950s when she was collecting material for her book, but nevertheless unfortunate) dismissal of 'pervert parks' as necessarily social blights – though she *was* ready to acknowledge the positive roles winos and destitute alcoholics played in stabilizing the quality of neighborhood life at a *higher* level than the neighborhood would maintain without them.[4] I would recommend her analysis, though I would add that, like so much American thinking on the left, it lacks not so much a class analysis as an *interclass* analysis.

2.2 Here is one of my favorite contact stories, told to me by a friend:

'I run annually in the Boston Marathon. I'm not a first class runner, and my goal is to finish in the top hundred – last year I was in a hundred and seventh place – but I train regularly. Every morning for the first half of the year I take a ten-mile run. Then, as the Marathon gets closer, I up it to twelve, fifteen, then twenty miles. One morning in March I was just starting my run across the Brooklyn Bridge, when I heard some woman scream – I looked around, and this fifteen- or sixteen-year-old kid had just snatched her pocket book and was taking off. I called: 'Stay here, ma'am, I'll get that back for you', turned around, and took off after him.

'It was a really interesting feeling, knowing as I ran after that kid that there was no way, unless he'd been in training for a marathon three years himself, he was going to outrun me. I stayed about five yards behind him – we were running around street corners there in Williamsburg. I didn't think he was going to make a full ten minutes. But he lasted for almost thirteen or fourteen. Finally when he was leaning against a wall, falling down on one knee, I went up to him, took the pocket book out of his hand, gave him a slap on the back of his head, and said, "Okay, now don't *do* that again!" Then I took off back to the Bridge. It was almost twenty minutes later, and the woman was gone by then. But there was some identification in the pocket book. I called her up and took it over to her that evening. She's a very interesting woman . . .'

Rare, heroic, and certainly not to be counted on, such contact nevertheless represents one of the gifts the human variety of the city can bestow.

3.0 There is, of course, another way to meet people. It's called 'networking.' Networking is what people have to do when those with like interests live too far apart to be thrown together in public spaces through chance and propinquity.

Networking is what people in small towns have to do to establish any complex cultural life today.

But contemporary 'networking' is notably different from 'contact.'

At first one is tempted to set contact and networking in opposition: networking tends to be professional and motive driven; contact tends to be more broadly social and appears random. Networking crosses class lines only in the most vigilant manner. Contact regularly crosses class lines in those public spaces in which interclass encounters are at their most frequent. Networking is heavily dependent on institutions to promote the necessary propinquity (gyms, parties, twelve-step programs, conferences, reading groups, signing groups, gatherings, workshops, tourist groups, classes) where those with the requisite social skills can maneuver. Contact is associated with public space and the architecture and commerce that depend on and promote it. Thus contact is often an outdoor sport; networking tends to take place indoors.

The opposition between contact and networking may provisionally be useful for locating those elements between the two that do, indeed, contrast. But we must not let that opposition sediment onto some absolute, transcendent, or ontological level that it cannot command. If we do, we will simply be constructing another opposition that we cannot work with at any analytical level of sophistication until it has been deconstructed – a project to which we shall return.

3.1 The benefits of networking are real and can look – especially from the outside – quite glamorous. But I believe that, today, such benefits are fundamentally misunderstood. More and more people are depending on networking to provide benefits that are far more likely to occur in contact situations – and that networking is specifically prevented from providing for a variety of reasons. Put up with me while I speak a bit about the networking institution with which I am most familiar, the writers' conference.

3.2 To most young writers, the writers' conference represents a social field where, each hopes, one of three things will occur. Either s/he will (1) be discovered (by some nebulously defined power group) because of his or her extraordinary talent; (2) bring her- or himself, by some 'heroic' extraliterary act, to the attention of someone perceived as powerful; or (3) because of social proximity someone in a position of power will take a liking to him or her and do him or her some favor to improve the young writer's lot. Certainly other desires are present as well – the desire for sociality among one's equals, in that field of desire which we mark with the terms 'ambition' and 'opportunity'. But, I submit, those others are, if only because they cannot be officially articulated, the shared form of inner, expectant concern.

Indeed, the prizes to be won at such an affair look extraordinary – at least at first: A well-known writer befriended there might eventually write a blurb for your novel or introduce you to his friends, moving you onto a new social level. The editor encountered over drinks might say, 'Sure, *send* me your manuscript', and thus launch an entire writing career; the writer on your own level, befriended there, may favorably review your first novel, if and when it is eventually completed, accepted, and published . . . Looking at the reality of the situation, however, we have to ask: how many times do any of these things actually happen? The answer is: precisely enough times to stabilize the notion of such conferences in the minds of a general aspiring writer population – and not a lot more.

The stated and articulated reason to attend the conference is, of course, to learn what will be taught about the practice of writing itself, its aesthetics and its business. But it is the rare writer who attends a writing conference without, at least from time to time, some fantasy about one or all of the primary three occurring. For just that reason, the conference will appear to be that much *more* exciting at precisely the points where something of that order appears to occur, so that the folklore about such occurrences, answering the secret desires we bring with us, when they do happen, often provides our major picture of the event.

I want to discuss all three of these possibilities in terms of anecdotes from my experience of writers' conferences, which I began attending thirty-seven years ago.

3.21 In July 1960 when I was eighteen, I received a work scholarship (I had to wait tables for the summer) to the Breadloaf Writers' Conference at Middlebury College in Vermont. The scholarship was arranged for me by an editor at Harcourt Brace who had been impressed by one of my early novels.

Although I did not know it at the time, writers' conferences often develop 'stars' among the attendant writers – one or a few aspiring writers who, for one reason or another, are singled out ('discovered') and, for the duration of the conference, are the envy of the other participants. They are the person or people on whom all the good things and tangible benefits of the conference appear to heap themselves.

On the second day at Breadloaf, to my surprise, I became such a 'star' – it was a discovery of precisely the sort I and, indeed, thousands of fledgling writers, have dreamed about at thousands of writers' conferences, before and since.

Among the 300-odd attendees at Breadloaf that year, I had submitted a novel for the novel-writing workshop. (There were some thirty people in the workshop, who met in a country-style meeting house.) Conducting the opening session, William Sloan, of William Sloan Associates, began by saying that, after looking over all thirty-odd submissions in the novel category, the only one that 'seemed to have any novelistic life whatsoever' was one from which he was going to read a passage: I was surprised when, from my seat in the third row, I heard him read a section from the third 'chapter' of my 'novel' (actually, as has been practically every MFA thesis I've encountered in the past decade, my 'novel' was, rather, a series of loosely connected stories with some common characters – and equally uninteresting): visiting a community center where a black band has just finished rehearsing, a young white man sits at an unused set of drums and begins to play an impassioned jazz percussion improvization.

When Mr. Sloan finished reading (he read it *very* well), he made the point from the podium that such writing could only come from someone who loved this sort of music. Then he asked if the author were in the room and could confirm this.

Sheepishly I stood up and confessed that, actually, I truly disliked jazz as a musical form. My father had an extensive collection of jazz records, however, and for a brief while (two or three weeks) had played cornet with Cab Callaway's band back in the early days of the Cotton Club. Yes, I had heard jazz all my life: for better or worse, I knew a fair amount about it. With one or two exceptions, however, I found it really distasteful – and the character who played it so well in my novel was a psychotically manipulative young white fellow, the villain of the piece, who subsequently maneuvered one after the other of the main black characters to their doom.

Immediately, Mr. Sloan revised his statement: such writing, then, could only come from *strong feeling*, one way or the other. And things proceeded.

But after having been singled out on the first day, I was then invited to the professional parties at the conference with the faculty. I remember several of the young writers saying, 'You've got it made.'

A woman editor at Random House attending the conference, who had once worked with Sloan and had great respect for him, invited me to lunch, once Breadloaf was over. She also read my novel – and told me, at that lunch, pretty much what half-a-dozen editors had told me before the conference, when I had been submitting the book here and there. 'You write well, but the basic subject matter is just not what makes a commercial novel.' Today, I would add the following to her articulate advice: to deal with the type of material I was dealing with (young people, mostly juvenile delinquents) would require a much more linear structure than I was using: had I been able to organize that material into a more linear 'adventure' form, rather than a mosaic of anecdotes, character sketches, and impressions (imagine as much of the plot as I've already discussed presented in the manner of *The Notebooks of Malte Laurids Brigge*), I would have had a substantially better chance of placing my book. In short, while the conference responded to the talent I showed, once the conference was over, the realities of publishing, in the form of the Random House editor who had kindly befriended me there, fell into place. And to the extent that the book represented a literary experiment (and, in my own mind, it did) the fact is, it was not a strong enough experiment to win over any of the dozen-odd commercial editors who, over the two years before and in the year afterward, read it.

My Breadloaf and Breadloaf-connected experiences doubtless made it easier for me to talk to the editors at Ace Books, who, a year and a half later, oversaw the publication of my first novel – an entirely new book that I had not even thought about writing back in Vermont. But when, in June 1962, Ace Books accepted that new novel for publication, *none* of the social contacts, either with editors or with the half-dozen other 'big-name writers', Robert Frost, John Ciardi, John Frederic Nyms (then editor of *Poetry*), or that year's Pulitzer Prize winner Allen Drury, whom I had met at Breadloaf – at which I had 'starred' and been, indeed, 'discovered' – were even tangentially involved, directly or indirectly, with my actual breaking into print.

3.22 A second anecdote addresses that second desire, the 'heroic' extra-literary act: a dozen years after Breadloaf, at a writing workshop in Michigan, *I* was now the (relatively) well-known writer, called upon to lead a group of some twenty younger writers. One particularly determined young man in his late twenties (happily married and a father of two) had his leg in a cast for the duration of the conference. He had written a story that I felt was fairly good – certainly putting him in the top fifth of the talent quotient, as I judged it. His view of what was to be gained by networking was, however, sadly inflated. One night, cast and all, he climbed through my window – and into my bed! (Later, I learned this had begun as a somewhat inebriated dare by the other students, when he had declared to them that he would 'fuck anything' and they had immediately picked me out as the . . . *Ahem*, impossible object of desire.) Our post-coital conversation lasted till dawn. Its result was that, since I thought he had talent as well as moxie, once the conference was over I told him he could use my name and send his story to a couple of editors whom I knew. Neither editor bought it. Moreover, though I have remained a desultory and distant friend of the young man's, he wrote no new work. After those two submissions, he became discouraged with his story and stopped sending it out.

(He is – still happily – married to the same woman and only this year became a new grandfather. We are still friends. And he is still unpublished.)

The fact is, the kind of energy and imagination it takes to crawl through a window and, however 'heroically' (read the import of the quotations marks as you wish), bed your instructor, is very different from the kind of imaginative energy it takes to write and craft a succession of stories and novels.

And, for those who are interested, despite this single case of a bold and vigorous young man, having taught at that particular writers' conference for almost thirty years, I have recommended many more women writers to editors than I have young male writers – for no other reason than that I found more talented women writers in attendance at such conferences than men: two from *that* particular conference – which recommendations *also* did nothing.

3.23 My third anecdote addresses the third hope of those who attend writers' conferences though, in this case, it is not a tale from my own experience, but from the folklore of science fiction. It is the story of how, back in the mid-1950s, Ray Bradbury first came to the attention of readers beyond the boundaries of the science fiction 'ghetto' (as it has been called).

Having been published the year before, Bradbury's second hardcover collection of stories, *The October Country,* was on a remainder table in Brentano's Bookstore, then on Eighth Street in Greenwich Village. In the bookstore to buy up a few of the volumes, the young Bradbury struck up a conversation with a man standing next to him. Bradbury pointed out that, at the time, newspapers and literary magazines ignored *all* SF books that came in, leaving them unread, giving them, at best, a 'Books Received' mention. His volume had gotten almost no reviews in the course of its shelf life.

Bradbury was articulate enough about the situation that the man – who turned out to be the writer Christopher Isherwood – was struck by his argument. A few issues on, in *The Saturday Review of Literature,* Isherwood (a regular reviewer for the magazine, who happened to have some say in what books he covered – a rare situation) took it upon himself to review Bradbury's book of poetic SF stories, so unlike the usual pulp fare of the day, and to do so more or less favorably. In the same review Isherwood also mentioned the situation that Bradbury had outlined. The review and the position it adopted became somewhat notorious, and, as the first SF writer to be reviewed in *The Saturday Review of Literature* (and the last for *quite* a while!), Bradbury's career moved to a new level, from which it has never really retreated.

Though many attendees at writers' conferences arrive at them with such models of writerly generosity in mind, for a complex of material reasons this is precisely the sort of thing that is, however, *not* likely to happen in such a networking situation.

The first thing to realize in the rehearsal of such a mythic tale, is that, in *all* its elements – the chance meeting in a bookstore, the happenstance conversation with a stranger over the remainder table – quintessentially it's a tale of 'contact,' *not* 'networking'. Also, the contact brought about the *reviewing* of a book already in print, not the *publication* of one still in manuscript – as most of the attendees at writing conferences are hoping for.

At writers' conferences, what *is* likely to happen?

There might be a panel presentation on the difficulties or impossibilities of science fiction securing good review venues. Such a panel might mean that, instead of flickering as a vague and passing notion, now and again, in the minds of one or three writers specifically faced with it, the problem would, for the next few months be the subject of awareness for an entire population of writers and readers who would also be aware of the forces keeping the problem in place. Thus, if a chance to break through it arose (either through contact or some institutional impetus), that chance would occur in a field that has been primed to a greater awareness of, if not sympathy for, the problem. (*That* is the benefit of networking.) Unfortunately today, unclear on the difference between the results each mode fosters, many people go into networking situations expecting or hoping for the extreme benefits of contact.

3.3 With these three anecdotes in mind, it is time to look at the reason why so few stars are discovered at writing conferences (and why, when they are, it usually does them little direct good); why the 'heroic' (i.e, extra-literary) attempt to bring oneself to the attention of the 'powerful' at a writers' conference results in so little; and finally why simple acts of friendship are unlikely to produce major changes in career or reputation when they occur at a writers' conference – and, by extension, when they occur in any general networking situation.

The reason the networking situation is not likely to produce the sometimes considerable rewards that can come from contact situations is because the *amount* of need present in the networking situation is too high for the comparatively few individuals in a position to supply the boons and favors *to distribute them in any equitable manner.* The pleasant and chatty cash bar reception at the end of the first day of panels and workshops at the writers' conference, may *look* like a friendly and sociable gathering, but at the socio-economic level, where the class war occurs, the situation is analogous to a crowd of seventy-five or a hundred beggars pressed around a train station in some underdeveloped colonial protectorate, while a handful of bourgeois tourists make their way through, hoping to find a taxi to take them off to the hotel before they are set upon and torn to pieces. Because of the way the networking situation is initially structured (at the class-war level), the competition for favors, and even rewards of merit, is too great for them to be dispensed in anything like a fair and efficient manner – efficient to the people in need, fair as those in power judge it – the desire that holds the conference stable (quite a separate thing from the epistemological rewards it promises), cannot be fulfilled by the conference without eroding the conferences themselves. The professed structure of the writers' conference is that of an epistemological dispensary. But the structure of desire that actually holds it stable and facilitates whatever dispersion of knowledge that takes place is that of a lottery one has a very small chance of winning.

Just as with the old-style social relations between tenant and landlord, the social practices and friendly interchanges that not only appear to, but *do*, fill the writers' conference reception halls, work to stabilize, retard and mitigate the forces of the class war. In no way, however, can they halt or resolve that war. They can allow it to proceed in a more humane manner, maintaining 'war' merely as a metaphor. In such situations, stabilization mitigates for *less* change in the power relations at the infrastructural level than might happen in a less concentrated and less competitive situation, even while existing social relations, happenstance, and sometimes even merit might appear to be producing the odd 'star' or lucky social 'winner'.

3.4 Having said all that, let me say that I attend writers' conferences regularly – and science fiction conventions even more so. The clear and explicable reasons for my attendance *are* networking's epistemological benefits. Those networking benefits result from the particularly dense field produced by the networking situation in which knowledge – not social favors – moves with particular speed. (The desire for social favor *is* the fuel – or the form – which propels that information through the social field.) At both formal sessions and informal gatherings, I find out about new writers and interesting books, as well as new publishing programs and changes in the business, much more quickly than I would without its benefits. By the same token, people find out about what I'm doing and get a clearer picture of my work. Because I'm comparatively comfortable appearing in public and discussing a range of topics from a podium or behind a panel table, people can get a taste of the sort of analysis I do and can decide whether they want to pursue these thoughts in my non-fiction critical work. Since I am a formal academic critic as well as a fiction writer – and a fiction writer who works in several genres – this is particularly important and promotes, in a small group of concerned readers at least, a more informed sense of my enterprise.

I feel my career benefits regularly from the results of my networking. My ultimate take on networking is, however, this: no single event in the course of my career has been directly *caused by* networking. Nevertheless, the results of networking have regularly smoothed, stabilized, and supported my career and made it more pleasant (there is that term again) than it would have been without it.

In general I would say (and I would say this to young writers particularly): rarely if ever can networking *make* a writing career when no career is to be made. It can make being a beginning writer more pleasant; it can make being a relatively established writer more pleasant. But little or nothing will happen there that will impel you from one state to the other. If anything, in the manner of stabilizing institutions, the social mechanics of conferences are more likely to retard career transitions, especially if you lean on them too heavily.

Basically the thing to remember is this:

One does not get publication by appearing in public.
One gets further invitations to appear in public.
Networking produces more opportunities to network – and that's about all.

Foucault gave us an analysis of power/knowledge. Desire/knowledge is just as important to understand – and, possibly and provisionally, in the current climate, even more so. Networking situations are self-replicating structures of knowledge and desire. Desire is what holds them stable and replicates them: and the absence on which the desire is based is the paucity of socio-material benefits everyone who attends hopes to receive. The writer will get the most from the available networking situations if he or she attends them with a clear sense of this.

4.1 Briefly, what makes 'networking' a different process from 'contact' is that the networking situation, unlike the contact situation, is one in which the fundamentally competitive relationship between all the people gathered together in the group within which networking is supposed to occur is far higher than it is in the population among which contact occurs.

The competition may be only barely perceptible at any given moment (or, under the camaraderie and good will of the occasion, all but invisible – it *is* the class war). Like the overriding economic forces of the class war and its effects on the individuals whose lives are caught up in and radically changed by it, they are seldom experienced *as* a force. It is pervasive nevertheless. Because of this the social price tag on the exchange of favors and friendly gestures is much higher here than it is in contact situations.

The people in line with you at the grocery counter are rarely *competing* with you for the items on the shelves in the way that young writers are competing for the comparatively rare number of publishing slots for first novels that can, under the best of conditions, appear each year. (Department store sales, however . . .) Even fewer in the grocery line will be competing for your specialized knowledge of the life of Zinaida Hippius. And they are not – at the moment – in competitive relations at all for the favors (whether of data or material help) that the established writer might be able to offer.

4.2 Two orders of social force are always at work. One set is centripetal and works to hold a given class stable. Another set is centrifugal and works to break a given class apart.

The first set runs from identity, through familiarity, to lethargy, to fear of difference – all of which work to hold a class together. These are the forces that the networking situation must appeal to, requisition, and exploit.

The second set has to do with the needs and desires that define the class in the first place: hunger, sex, ambition in any one of a dozen directions – spatial to economic to aesthetic or intellectual. These forces militate toward breaking up a class, driving it apart, and sending individuals off into other class arenas. This is the level where, in a democracy, contact functions as an anti-entropic method of changing various individuals' material class groundings. The reason these forces work the way they do is simply because when such desires and needs concentrate at too great a density in too small a social space over too brief a time, they become that much harder to fulfill – even when you pay generous honoraria to people who might help fill them, to move briefly into that crowded social space and dispense

C. The same principle which makes contact more likely to cede major material, social, or psychological prizes than networking makes interclass/intercommunity contact more likely to cede such prizes than intra-class or intra-community contact: At the inter-class and inter-community level, competition for those prizes is likely to be less than it would be within a class, within a community.

data about the process, without dispensing the actual rewards and benefits that those involved in the process seek. Love/desire/awe/fear/terror/abjection (horror) *is* the human response range to greater or lesser power differentials.

The centripetal forces work to tame the components of that response.

Those components underlie and *are* all the centrifugal forces.

4.3 Recently when I outlined the differences between contact and networking to a friend, he came back with the following examples: 'Contact is Jimmy Stewart; networking is Tom Cruise. Contact is complex carbohydrates. Networking is simple sugar. Contact is Zen. Networking is Scientology. Contact can effect changes at the infrastructural level; networking effects changes at the superstructural level.'

Amusing as these examples are, it's important to speak about the very solid benefits of both forms of sociality. Otherwise we risk falling into some dualistic schema, with wonderful, free-form, authentic, Dionysian contact on the one side, and terrible, calculating, inauthentic, Apollonian networking on the other. Such would be sad and absurd. The way to do this is not to install the two concepts in our minds as some sort of equal, objective and unquestioned pair of opposites. Rather we must analyze both, so that we can see that elements in each have clear and definite hierarchical relations with elements in the other, as well as other elements that are shared. But this sort of vigilant approach alone will produce a clear idea of what to expect (and not expect) from one and the other – as well as produce some clear knowledge of why we should not try to displace one *with* the other and ask one to fulfill the other's job.

> D. Contact is random only in the sense that diversity represents a web of random needs *vis-à-vis* the constraints on the needs of all the members of a single profession, a single class.

In terms of the Bradbury tale, Greenwich Village in the 'fifties was, for example, a neighborhood in which the chance of two writers running into one another at a bookstore remainder table were far higher than they would have been, say, three miles away across the river in a supermarket in Queens.

The same could be said of the Upper West Side, where I managed to snag the information about Zenaida Hippius or, indeed, the Variety Photoplays Theater, where I met my long-term social friend (and, a decade before, another long-term lover), lying as it did between the East and West Village.

Were we so naive as to assert that in networking situations *there were* selection procedures while in contact situations *there were none*, we would only be rushing to set up false and invalid oppositions.

But while contact may be, by comparison, 'random' (but doesn't one move to – or from – a particular neighborhood as part of a desire to be among, or to avoid – certain types of people, whether that neighborhood be Greenwich Village, Bensonhurst, or Beverly Hills?), and while networking may be, by comparison, 'planned' (yet how many times do we return from the professional conference unable, a month later, to remember having met anyone of particular interest or, next Monday morning in the office, having retained no useful idea?), it is clear that contact is contoured, if not organized, by earlier decisions, desires, commercial interests, zoning laws and immigration patterns. The differences seem to be rather matters of scale (the looser streets of the neighborhood versus the more condensed hotel or conference center spaces) and the granularity that allows others to dilute the social density with a range of contrasting needs and desires, as well as differences in social skills and, yes, institutional access.

4.4 Contact is likely to be its most useful when it is cross-class contact. Bradbury and Isherwood were, arguably, in the same profession, that is, both were writers. But they were also clearly at different class levels: beginning genre writer and established literary writer.

4.5 Two modes of social practice: I call them contact and networking. They designate two discourses that, over the range of society, conflict with and displace each other, re-establish themselves in new or old landscapes, where, at the level of verbal interaction, they deposit their rhetorical traces . . .

4.6 In one nineteenth-century novel that I've recently been teaching, Flaubert's *L'Education Sentimentale*, the two most important relationships to the protagonist, Frédéric Moreau, are definitely contact relationships. First and foremost is his relation with Monsieur and Madame Arnoux: he is attracted to Madame Arnoux as she sits on the deck of a ferry leaving Paris for the countryside along the Seine. The meeting is impelled wholly by desire, and Frédéric must put out a good deal of energy to make the contact occur, and stabilize it as a social friendship across the class boundaries (provincial bourgeois youth/urban sophisticate adults) that exist. His second cross-class contact friendship is with the young, good-hearted worker, Dussardier, whom he meets in a street demonstration when he and a Bohemian friend, Hussonet – also just met – decide, all-but-arbitrarily, to rescue the young worker from the clutches of the police. Both these relationships have elements of the tragic about them: Frédéric's inability to possess Madame Arnoux causes him a pain that pervades and contaminates every subsequent love relationship of his life. And Frédéric uses and abuses Dussardier in a positively shameful manner: Frédéric tells his bourgeois friends that Dussardier has committed a 12,000 franc theft (which Frédéric uses as an excuse to borrow a like amount to spend on his mistress, Rosannette) and, because the young man is working class, none of Frédéric's friends thinks to question this. But when one compares *these* relationships to two that Frédéric has acquired through networking, they come off pretty well. Compare them with his relationship to Madame Dambreuse, the fantastically avaricious and vicious widow whom Frédéric barely escapes marrying: Frédéric knows her because he is given a letter of introduction by M. Rocque to her husband, the business tycoon M. Dambreuse – pure networking. The other distinctly networking relation is Frédéric's deeply vexing friendship with Sénécal, the mathematician who believes in a purely scientific politics – to whom Frédéric is first sent by his school friend Charles Deslauriers. In short, his networking ends up aligning him with extremely – even lethally –

vicious men and women. Frédéric's fiancée-through-networking, Madame Dambreuse, delights in the destruction of the social standing of his love-object through contact, Madame Arnoux, when the Arnoux's personal belongings are sold at auction.

At the book's end, Frédéric's networking friend Sénécal shoots and kills his contact friend Dussardier during a military encounter; confronted with Madame Dambreuse's viciousness, Frédéric escapes her (she also, it turns out, has been done out of her fortune by the dead hand of her husband; Flaubert cannot pass up the irony). But Frédéric's own ability to love has been sadly, permanently injured. Nevertheless, because it plays out identically with both a man *and* a woman, it's hard to avoid the suggestion that the antipathy between friends or lovers acquired by networking and those acquired by contract may well have been a conscientious part of Flaubert's complex allegory. Indeed, when one surveys the range of the great nineteenth-century social novels, from *Illusions Perdues* and *Les Misérables* to *Great Expectations*, many, though they do not name the contrasting modes, nevertheless present dramatic evaluations of the benefits and costs of the two modes of sociality. They even have sharp comments to make on what happens when one or another character relies too heavily on relationships that begin in one or the other mode.

5.1 The current transformation of Times Square is a Baron Haussmann-like event. But like Haussmann's rebuilding of Paris, this event comprises many smaller ones, among them the destruction of acres of achitecture, numerous commercial and living spaces, and, so far, the permanent obliteration of over two-dozen theater venues, with (as of May 1997) more than a half-dozen other theater demolitions planned within the next three months. With this dies a complex of social practices, many of which turned on contact, affecting hundreds of thousands of men and women a year, some native to the city, some visitors. Further material developments alone will determine whether or not the changes in the legal status of specific sex acts that legally precedes them (but, in the class war, only accompanies them) will generate the rhetorical collisions that finally litter what already shows signs of being a major shift in the discourse of sexuality, straight and gay, as well as architecture, commerce and quality of life for New York City.

5.2 At a conference at Columbia University sponsored by the Buell Architecture Center (*Times Square: Global, Local*, March 1997), organized by Marshal Blonsky on the renovation of Times Square, the keynote speaker was Marshall Berman. The general sense I received (though it would be stunningly incorrect to call it a consensus) extended from, on the one hand, the view that, outside the general difficulties involved in going ahead with the project, there was no problem at all because the developers and architects were supremely sensitive to the needs of the city and its populace (a position put forward by spokesperson-architect Robert Stern) to, on the other hand, an only slightly less sanguine view (put forward by Berman) that, if there *was* a problem, we might as well go along with it, since there was nothing we could do about it anyway.

5.21 In a revised version of his Buell Center talk, 'Signs of the Times: The Lure of Times Square', Berman claims that I (along with Rem Koolhaas and photographer Langdon Clay) am nostalgic for what he terms 'the pre-AIDS golden age of hustling'.[5]

If there was any such 'golden age', I never had any experience of it, nor was I aware of any such thing at the time. (I assume he must mean pre-1982, possibly pre-1984.) The only thing I can imagine might lie behind Berman's misunderstanding is the erroneous assumption that all or most of the homosexual contact around Times Square was commercial, that is, involved hustlers or other sex workers, when the whole point is that, while the lure of hustlers most certainly helped attract the sexually available and curious to the area, a good 80 or 85 percent of the sexual contacts that occurred there (to make what is admittedly a totally informal guesstimate) were *not* commercial.

I do not want to demonize the profession of sex worker *per se*, but, as a material social practice that can be carried on in many ways and at many levels, the sex work that occurred there can in many respects be criticized – or, indeed, praised. And the relation of commercial sex to non-commercial sex was intricate and intimate.

What I regret personally is, however, the dissolution of that 80 percent where my own sexual activity and that of many other gay men was largely focused – though I am quite sure others, both gay and straight, do equally miss the commercial side. The two orders of sexual relationship sat by one another in the sex movie theaters, drank shoulder to shoulder in the same bars, and walked down the same streets, lingering by the same shop windows to make themselves available for conversation in the afternoons and evenings. Though the relation between commercial and non-commercial sex was not without its hostilities (occasionally intense), in such a situation there is a far greater interpenetration of the two modes than in other areas – due to contact.

E. If, as I say, 80 to 85 percent of the (gay) sexual encounters in the Times Square neighborhood were non-commercial, why does hustling so dominate the fictional accounts of the area's sexual machinery? (John Rechy's *City of Night*, Paul Roger's *Saul's Book*, and Bruce Benderson's *User*, to name three excellent examples.) I can offer three reasons.

First, fictive rhetoric tends to reproduce its own form. The assumption –

Because of the Forty-Second Street

certainly stemming from fiction – that all sex, gay or straight, generating in the Times Square area was commercial is rather like the assumption of readers who, from a brush with novels by Anne and Charlotte Brönte, assume that thousands and thousands of poor but honest young women worked as live-in governesses. Steven Marcus in *The Other Victorians* suggests that there were never more than a relatively small number of live-in governesses working in London at any one time during the early nineteenth century – while, in the same years, the number of *prostitutes* in the city was in the hundreds of thousand. But we generalize from our fictions.

Second, if only because of its economic motivation, hustling work is relatively more stable (the same men, *working* in the sex professions, are likely to show up on their beats day in and day out over a given period) and thus is more visible than even the frequent visitor, availing himself of the hustlers' services, or the movies and/or peepshows, three or four times a week. A man may show up two, three, or even five times a week for anything from a spontaneous jack-off session in a public restroom, taking a few minutes, or drop in for anywhere between a few minutes and a few hours or more at one of the sex movies. These would be among the committed habitués of the non-commercial – already far less visible than the hustler. And many more non-commercial utilizers of the neighborhood are there only once a week, once a month, or once every six months – and thus even more difficult to chronicle. The hustlers will linger, however, around a given street corner or in a particular bar five or six hours a day, four to six days a week. What will appear more consistent is not

area, my personal life as a New Yorker was a lot more pleasant from, say, 1980 to 1992 than it has been, after a five year transition period, from 1995 to now. What made it more pleasant was the cheap films and the variety of street contact available – the vast majority of *that*, let me make it clear (so that I do not appear more of a roué than I am) was *not* sexual at all; though, of course, much of it was. And of those sexual contacts, in my case less than 10 percent were with hustlers: it's *not* my favorite form of sexual content. With no intention of sounding holier than any particular thou, one resorted to hustlers (and, in my case, not with much enthusiasm), when the non-commercial population seeking sex had been largely driven from the neighborhood. As I tell my classes regularly when I come out to them, my sexual ideal today tends to be substantially over forty. But many of the most pleasant non-sexual encounters would not have occurred if so many of the people there had not been open to sexual contacts. But it is not nostalgic to ask questions such as the ones that inform the larger purpose of this meditation.

How did what was there inform the quality of life for the rest of the city?
How will what is there now inform that quality of life?
Can anything of use be learned from answering such questions?

6.1 Four great office towers are currently in various stages of construction the far more numerous – but fleeting – non-commercial encounters, but the more consistent presence of the hustlers. Thus, because it is more easily observed and researched, hustling is more frequently written about.

Third, the line between the commercial and the non-commercial is itself highly permeable and often not easily fixed. By general consensus, a hustler is someone who sets a price beforehand and, if the payment is not agreed to, no encounter takes place.

But what of the poor or homeless man in the back orchestra of the sex movie who, after the sexual act is satisfactorily completed, asks: 'Say – you wouldn't happen to have a couple of bucks on you – so I can go out, get something to eat, and get back in here to catch some sleep?' – who may, indeed, be as easily told, 'Sorry, I don't have any money with me,' as, 'Oh, sure. Here.' Is that commercial?

What of the encounter that starts off particularly well, so that one person pauses, and says: 'Hey, I'm going to go out, get some sandwiches, and a couple of cans of beer. I'll be back in ten minutes. What kind of sandwich you want? This way we can make an afternoon of it,' and is told: 'Great, man. Bring me a ham and cheese on rye with mustard.' Is *that* commercial?

Finally, what about the man who, before the incident, presents himself as hustling, asking (however) for only five dollars, but who, when you shrug and say, 'Sorry. I'm not paying,' waits ten, silent seconds, then responds, 'Ah, *fuck* . . . we'll do it anyway. Besides, I did it with you before. I know you're good.' Is *this* commercial?

These, and numerous other scenarios the long-time visitor to the area might recount (the laborer from Queens who,

at the cardinal points of the new Times Square. As I write this (January 30, 1998), one, still lacking its curtain walls, is rising over the square above the blue board fences as a complex of girders. The demolition clearing room for a second has been completed. Two are still in the planning stages. Major construction is going on and has been going on for years now up and down Eighth Avenue from 42nd Street to 52nd Street.

The Times Square problem I perceive entails the economic 'redevelopment' of a highly diversified neighborhood, with working class residences and small human services (groceries, drugstores, liquor stores, dry cleaners, diners, and speciality shops ranging from electronic stores and tourist shops to theatrical memorabilia and comic book stores, interlarding a series of theaters, film and stage rehearsal spaces, retailers of theatrical equipment, from lights to make-up, inexpensive hotels, furnished rooms, and restaurants at every level, as well as bars and the sexually-orientated businesses that, in one form or another, have thrived in the neighborhood since the 1880s) to an upper middle class ring of luxury apartments around a ring of tourist hotels clustering around a series of theaters and restaurants in the center of which a large mall, and a cluster of office towers is slowly but inexorably coming into being.

6.2 The generally erroneous assumption about how new buildings make after sex, insisted on giving *me* fifteen dollars, because he 'only went with hustlers' and would have felt uncomfortable if I didn't take *some* money from him; so, after five minutes of polite protest, I obliged), trouble the line between the commercial and the non-commercial encounter.

Because the reality of the situation is intricate and often difficult to articulate – and because an overall fictional model pre-exists that is simpler and generally accepted; and because the whole situation lies outside the boundaries of the 'socially accepted' anyway – often it's easier to let the extant rhetoric hold unchallenged sway. The result is an image of who is and who isn't a hustler that is as hard to pin down overall as who is and who isn't a whore – a concept which runs, as we all know, from the agented call girl to the woman who simply enjoys sex with several partners over a period of time.

money is something like this: a big company acquires the land, clears it for construction, and commences to build. After three to five years, when it is complete, the company rents the building out. If the building is a success and all the offices (or apartments, as the case may be) are leased and the site is a popular one, then and only then does the corporation that owns the building begin to see profits on its earlier outlays and investments. Thus the ultimate success of the building as a habitation is pivotal to the building's future economic success.

If this were the way new office buildings were actually built, however, few would even be considered, much less actually begun.

Here is an only somewhat simplified picture of how the process *actually* works. Simplified though it is, it gives a much better idea of what goes on and how money is made, nevertheless:

A large corporation decides to build a building. It acquires some land. Now it sets up an extremely small ownership corporation, which is tied to the parent corporation by a lot of very complicated contracts – but is a different and autonomous corporation, nevertheless. That ownership corporation, tiny as it might be, is now ready to build the building. The parent corporation also sets up a much larger construction corporation, which hires diggers, subcontracts construction companies, and generally oversees the building proper.

The little ownership corporation now borrows a lot of money from a bank – enough to pay the construction corporation for constructing the building proper. The small ownership corporation also sells stock to investors – enough to pay back the bank loan. The tiny ownership corporation (an office, a secretary and a few officers who oversee things) proceeds to pay the parent construction corporation with the bank funds to build the building. It uses the stock funds to pay back the bank. Figured in the cost of the building is a

healthy margin of profit for the construction corporation – the large corporation which got the whole project started – while the investors pay off the bank,
so that *it* doesn't get twisted out of shape.

Yes, if the building turns out to be a stunningly popular address, then
(remember all those contracts?) profits will be substantially greater than
otherwise. But millions and millions of dollars of profits will be made by the
parent corporation just from the construction of the building alone, even if no
single space in it is ever rented out. (Movies are made in the same manner,
which is why so many awful ones hit the screen. By the time they are released,
the producers have long since taken the money and, as it were, run.) Believing
in the myth of profit only in return for investments, public investors will swallow
the actual cost of the building's eventual failure – if it fails – while the ownership
corporation is reduced in size to nothing or next to nothing: an office in the
building on which no rent is paid, a secretary and/or an answering machine,
and a nominal head (with another major job somewhere else) on minimal
salary who comes in one a month to check in . . . if that.

6.3 Two facts should now be apparent:

First Fact: the Times Square Development Corporation *wants* to build those
buildings.

Renting them out is secondary, even if the failure to rent them is a major
catastrophe for the city, turning the area into a glass and aluminum graveyard.
A truth of high-finance capitalism tends to get away from even the moderately
well-off investor (the successful doctor or lawyer, say, bringing in two- to four-
hundred thousand a year), though this truth is, indeed, what makes capitalism:
in short-term speculative business ventures of (to choose an arbitrary cut-off
point) more than three million dollars, such as a building or civic center,
(Second Fact:) the profits to be made from dividing the money up and moving
it around over the one to six years, during which that money must be spent,
easily offset any losses from the possible failure of the enterprise itself as a
speculative endeavor, once it's completed.

The interest on a million dollars at 6.5 percent is about 250 dollars a *day*; on
a good conservative portfolio it will be 400 dollars a day; and the interest on
ten million dollars is ten times that. Thus the interest on ten millon dollars is
almost a million and a half a year. The Times Square Corporation is determined
to build those buildings. The question is: how long will it take to persuade
investors to swallow the uselessness of the project for them?

Far more important than whether the buildings can be rented out or not is
whether *investors think the buildings can be rented out*. In the late 1970s, three of
those towers were tabled for ten years. The ostensible purpose of that ten-year

delay was to give economic forces a chance to shift and business a chance to rally to the area. The real reason, however, was simply the hope that people would forget the arguments against the project, so clear in so many people's minds at the time. Indeed, the crushing arguments against the whole project from the middle 1970s were, by the middle 1980s, largely forgotten, the forgetting of which has allowed the project to take its opening steps over the last ten years. The current ten-year delay means that public relations corporations have been given another decade to make the American investing public forget the facts of the matter and convince that same public that the Times Square project is a sound one. It gambles on the possibility that, ten years from now, the economic situation might be better – at which point the developers will go ahead with those towers, towers which, Mr. Stern has told us, *will* be built.

Berman's article in *Dissent*, which I referred to above, concludes with a PS: it begins, 'I have just read in the *Times* of August 1 [1997], about a deal in the works to bring Reuters to Times Square. It wants to build an 800,000-square foot office tower on Seventh Avenue and 42nd Street.' He goes on to say that Reuters is an interesting company (as if it would have anything more to do with the building than, perhaps, rent 10 percent, or less, of its space) and he seems appalled that the awful Philip Johnson plan, designed over a decade ago will be utilized for the construction – as if, for a moment, *anyone* in a position of power involved in the deal cared. (Millions were paid for it; it must be used.) He concludes by suggesting that people who care about the square raise the roof before the deal gets done.

Consider my roof raised.

7.1 At the Buell Conference a young sociologist countered my suggestion that there were some serious losses involved in the renovation process with the counter suggestion that the new Times Square would at least be safer for women.

7.11 Which brings me to a survey of three topics – topics I will look at as systems of social practice related by contact: crime and violence on the street: the public sex practices that have been attacked and so summarily wiped out of the Times Square area; the general safety of the neighborhood – and the problem of safety for women.

First, the street-level public sex that the area was famous for, the sex movies, the peep-show activities, the street corner hustlers and hustling bar activity were overwhelmingly a matter of contact.

Call-boy and call-girl networks, not to mention the various forms of phone sex, follow much more closely the 'networking' model. But what *I* see lurking behind the positive foregrounding of 'family values' (along with, and in the

name of such values, the violent suppression of urban social structures, economic, social, and sexual) is a wholly provincial and absolutely small-town terror
of cross-class contact.

7.12 A salient, stabilizing factor that has helped create the psychological
smoke screen behind which developers of Times Square and every other
underpopulated urban center in the country have been able to pursue their
machinations in spite of public good and private desire is the small-town fear
of urban violence. Since the tourist to the big city is seen as someone *from* a
small town, the promotion of tourism is a matter of promoting the image of
the world – and of the city – that the small town holds.

Jane Jacobs has analyzed how street crimes proliferate in the city: briefly, lack
of street level business and habitation diversity produces lack of human traffic,
lack of contact, and a lack of those eyes on the street joined in the particularly
intricate self-policing web Jacobs claims is our greatest protection against urban
barbarism on the street. Many people have seen Jacobs as saying merely that the
number of eyes on the street do the actual policing. But a careful reading of her
arguments shows that these 'eyes' must be connected to individuals with very
specific and intricate social relations of both stability and investment in what we
might call the quality of street life. Too high a proportion of stranger to
indigenes, too high a turnover of regular population, and the process breaks
down. Such lacks produce the dangerous neighborhoods: the housing project,
the park with not enough stores and eating spaces bordering on it, the blocks
and blocks of apartment residences without any ameliorating human services.

7.13 Many non-city residents still do not realize that their beloved small
towns are, per capita, far more violent places than any big city. New York has
an annual rate of one murder per 108,000 inhabitants. Some large cities have
as few as one per 300,000.

In 1967, however, I spent the winter months in a Pennsylvania town, which
had a cold-weather population of under 600. That winter the town saw five
violent deaths, homicides or manslaughters.

If New York City had five murders per 600 inhabitants per winter, it would
be rampant chaos! The point, of course, is that the *structure* of violence is
different in cities from the structure of violence in small towns. Three of those
small-town violent deaths, with their perpetrators and victims, occurred within
two families who had a history of violence in the town going back three
generations – along with a truly epic rate of alcoholism. A social profile of those
families would yield one not much different from the stereotyped pictures of
the Hatfields and the McCoys of early sociological studies. The other two violent
deaths that winter came when three adolescent boys from comparatively 'good'

families, bored out of their gourds during two solid weeks of snow, on a February evening's adventure pushed a car over a cliff. In the car a young couple was necking. The two young people died – but they were from out of town. Strangers. Not residents – from another small town twenty-five or thirty miles away. That particular incident produced an ugly and finally very sad court trial; one of the boys was sent to reform school. The other two got off with strong reprimands. But the town's general sense was that the victims shouldn't have been there in the first place. You stay in your own locality. Shut them in too long by the snow like that with nothing to do, and boys will be boys . . .

In a small town the majority of the violence that occurs (say, three out of five cases) does not really surprise anyone. People know where it's going to occur and in which social units (that is, which two families) 60 percent of it will happen. They know how to stay out of its way. Your biggest protection from the rest of it is that you're *not* a stranger to the place; and you should probably stay out of places where you are. Comparatively speaking, the violence in cities is random. No one knows where it's going to fall, who the next mugging victim, house breaking victim, rape victim, not to mention victim of an apartment fire or traffic accident, will be.

Small towns control their violence by rigorously controlling – and often all but forbidding – interclass contact, unless in carefully controlled work situations. The boys of good families who killed the young couple (people in the town would be appalled that today I described the incident in such terms, though few of them would argue with me that that's what happened) did not associate with the sons and daughters of the local Hatfield/McCoys. When small towns are beautified and developed, their development generally proceeds in ways that make easier the location, unofficial segregation, and separation of the classes.

7.14 Because our new city developments, such as Times Square, are conceived largely as attractions for incoming tourists, they are being designed to look safe *to* the tourist, even if the social and architectural organization laid down to appeal to them is demonstrably inappropriate for large cities and promotes precisely the sort of isolation, inhumanity and violence that everyone abhors.

The traditional way that cities keep their violence rate monumentally lower than in small towns is by the self-policing practices that come from 'eyes on the street' *supported by a rich system of relatively random benefits and rewards that encourage pleasant sociality based entirely on contact.* That system of random rewards results in everything from the base ground of intra-neighborhood 'pleasantness' to the heroic prizes of neighborly assistance in times of catastrophe. But even more important, in a society that prides itself on the widespread existence of opportunity, interclass contacts are the site and origin of a good many of what can later be seen as life opportunities, or at least the site of many elements that make the seizing of such opportunities easier and more profitable.

7.15 The small-town way to enjoy a big city is to arrive there with your family, your friends, your school group, your church group, or – if you are really brave – your tour group, with whom you associate (these are all pre-selected network groups) and have fun, as you sample the food and culture and see the monuments and architecture. But the one thing you do not do is go out in the street alone and meet people. The fear of such an activity in New York City is, for most out-of-towners, one with the fear of bodily contagion from AIDS coupled with the equally bodily fear of hurt and loss of property.

Around 1990, I was returning on a plane to New York from a reading in Boston, with the Russian poet André Vosnesensky. Vosnesensky was staying at the Harvard Club, just a block or two north of Grand Central Station, and was unaware that one could take a bus directly there from the airport and save considerably on the taxi fare.

When we got off at Grand Central, I suggested that he might want to use the facilities at the station. Very worriedly, he told me: 'Oh, no. I don't think we better do that.'

Naively, I asked: 'Why not?'

'Because,' he told me, leaning close, 'I don't want to catch AIDS.'

Used to dealing with people who were afraid of touching people with AIDS or eating after them, I was nevertheless so surprised to discover someone who thought he would be at risk of contagion from using a public urinal, that I was non-plussed. We were to part less than five minutes later – and I have not seen him since.

But rather than take this as a spectacular example of misinformation and/or information, I think it is more interesting to see it as a cross section of the process by which AIDS functions, on an international level, as a discursive tool to keep visitors to the city away from all public facilities and places where, yes, one might, if so inclined, engage in or be subject to any sort of interclass contact.

7.16 Paradoxically, the specifically gay sexual outlets – the sex movies that encouraged masturbation and fellatio in the audience, the rougher hustler bars, the particular street corners that had parades of active hustlers – are or were locales where the violence that occurs is closer to the high small-town level than it is to the overall lower big-city level: but, there, to complete the paradox, that violence tends to be structured, rather, *like* small-town violence. If you frequent the place, quickly you learn from where and/or from whom it is going to come. A stranger or first-time visitor is probably far more vulnerable than a long-time, frequent habitué of the facility: the hustler bar, the sex theater, or the low-life street corner. Someone who visits such places two or three times a week, or monthly, is likely to be pretty clear which person – or, prejudicial as it sounds, which kind of person – will likely be the source of violence. That is why prostitutes can work the streets and neighborhoods they do. That is why, gay and straight, so many middle-class and working-class men feel perfectly safe visiting such urban spaces on a regular basis, often several times a week over years, even when, from statistics or just their own observation, they know perfectly well that every couple of weeks or months – in extreme cases two or three times a day – some sort of robbery or fight happens, or bodily injury is done to a customer. In such places, however, the violence is *not* random. It follows more or less clear patterns that are fairly easily learned. Thus habitués feel – and, indeed, usually are – as safe as most people in any other small-town-*structured* violent environment. And of course – the one thing Jacobs's analysis leaves out – during the times of non-violence, which *still* make up the majority of the time, in such locations the same principles of traffic, social diversity and self-policing hold sway, yes, even here.

Another point that people forget is: public sex situations are not Dionysian and uncontrolled but are rather some of the most highly socialized and conventionalized behavior human beings can take part in.

7.2 The sexual activity of the Times Square area (and by that I mean both commercial and non-commercial) has been hugely decried, called awful and appalling by many – including architect Robert Stern. We do *not* want a red-light district there, is the general cry of planners and organizers. People who utilized, or worked in it, however, are sometimes a bit more analytical than those issuing blanket dismissals. A good deal of what made the situation awful, when it was awful, was not the sex work *per se* but the illegal drug traffic that accompanied it, that worked its way all through it, and that, from time to time, controlled much of it. The middle 1980s saw an explosion of drug activity, focusing particularly around crack, that produced some of the most astonishing and appalling human behavior I personally have ever seen. Its extent, form and general human face have yet to be chronicled.

In 1987 I had a conversation with an eighteen-year-old Dominican, who was indeed hustling on the strip. He was worried because he was living with a seventeen-year-old friend – another young crackhead – in a project further uptown.

The younger boy had been regularly selling all the furniture in the apart-ment, and, when his mother had objected, he had killed her.

Her body, the other boy told me, was still in the closet. The older boy did not know what to do.

I suggested that he tell his younger friend – whom I did not know and had not met – to go to the police.

Some days later, when I ran into the older boy, he told me that is indeed what his young friend did. The older boy was now homeless.

One would have to be a moral imbecile to be in any way nostalgic for this situation.

Indeed, the major change in the area over the period between 1984 and 1987 was that professional prostitutes and hustlers – women generally between, say, twenty-three and forty-five, and men somewhat younger, asking (the women among them) thirty-five to seventy-five dollars per encounter (and the men ten or fifteen dollars less) – were driven out of the area by a new breed of 'five-dollar whores' or 'hustlers,' often fifteen-, sixteen-, and seventeen-year-old girls and boys who would go into a doorway and do *anything* with anyone for the four-to-eight dollars needed for the next bottle of crack. Some of that situation is reflected in the scream that ends Spike Lee's film *Jungle Fever.*

It was that appalling.

It was that scary.

I hope we can look on even that period of human atrocity, however, with a clear enough vision to see (as was certainly evident to anyone who walked through the neighborhood who, during those years, lingered and spoke to and developed any concern for any of these youngsters) that this activity clotted in the area, that it grew and spread from there to other neighborhoods, that it reached such appalling dimensions as *a direct result* of the economic attack *on* the neighborhood *by* the developers, Mr. Stern's employers, in their attempt to destroy the place as a vital and self-policing site, as a necessary prelude to their Brave New Manhattan.

The old Times Square and 42nd Street was an entertainment area catering largely to the working classes who lived in the city. The middle class and/or tourists were invited to come along and watch or participate if that, indeed, was their thing.

The New Times Square is envisioned as predominantly a middle-class area of entertainment, to which the working classes are welcome to come along, observe and take part in, if they can pay and are willing to blend in.

What controls the success (or failure) of this change are the changes in the city population itself – and changes in the working- (and middle-) class self-image. Sociologists will have to look at this aspect and analyse what is actually going on.

7.31 Here I return to the question of Times Square as a space safe for women – which some, looking at the new development, have somehow managed to see it as. The first thing one must note is that there have always been women in Times Square, on 42nd Street, and on its appendage running up and down Eighth Avenue. They were bar-maids. They were waitresses. They were store clerks. They were ticket takers. I do not know much about the female work population of the twenty-story Candler office building on the south side of 42nd Street at number 220, between the former site of the Harris and the Liberty theaters, but for many years I regularly visited a friend who worked at a translation bureau run by a Mrs. Cavanaugh on the nineteenth floor: and I will hazard that at least 40 percent of the workers there were women. Also, women *lived* in the neighborhood. Until the end of the 1970s it was a place where young theater hopefuls – more men, yes, than women; but women, nevertheless – lived in a range of inexpensive apartments and furnished rooms around Hell's Kitchen (renamed, somewhat more antiseptically, 'Clinton' a few years back). The vast majority of these women are not there now. And the developers see themselves as driving out (the minuscule proportion of) those women who were actual sex workers.

To see such a development, which makes a city space safe for one class of women by actively driving out another class, as having any concern for women *as* a class is at best naive. The Times Square developers' concern for women and women's safety extends no further than seeing women as replaceable nodes with a certain amount of money to spend in a male-dominated economic system.

Some of what was in the old Times Square worked. Some didn't work. Often what worked – about, say, the sexual activity (and, despite the horror of the planners, much of it did: we have too many testimonies to that effect by both customers *and* the sex workers themselves), worked by accident. It was not planned. But this does not mean it was not caused, analyzable, and (thus) instructive.

The new Times Square is simply not about making the area safe for women. It is not about supporting theater and the arts. It is not about promoting economic growth in the city. It is not about reducing the level of AIDS or even about driving out perversion (that is, non-commercial sexual encounters between those of the same sex who can find each other more easily in a neighborhood with sex movies, peep show activities and commercial sex) nor is it about reducing commercial sex, hustling and prostitution.

The new Times Square is about developers doing as much demolition and renovation as possible in the neighborhood, and as much construction work as they possibly can. Some old-fashioned Marxism might be useful here: infrastructure determines superstructure – not the other way around. And for all their stabilizing or destabilizing potential, discourse and rhetoric are superstructural phenomena.

There is, of course, that particularly important corollary for late-consumer media-dominated capitalism – that is largely absent from classical Marxism: 'Superstructure stabilizes infrastructure.'

Briefly and more dramatically, superstructural forces (personal relations, the quality of life in the neighborhood) may make small business decide to shut down and vacate to Queens (as my local drycleaners, Habanna San Juan, is currently doing after twenty-five years in three different locations in the Upper West Side – each location smaller than the space before, and the last further from the main thoroughfare than the previous two: there are fewer Hispanics here than before, the Spanish owner is older, he lives in Queens and has been commuting into this neighborhood at seven in the morning for more than two decades and is tired of it). But infrastructural forces will determine whether *his* landlord has three bids from white-owned businesses for the same space two months before his long-term Puerto Rican drycleaner tenant leaves – or whether the same space will sit vacant for the next eighteen months with a crack across the glass behind the window gate.

F. One of the problems with getting people to accept the first tenet of Marxism (infrastructure determines superstructure) is that we can look around us and *see* superstructural forces feeding back into the infrastructure and making changes in it. Because we are the 'political size' we are (and thus have the political horizons we do), it's hard for individuals to see the extent (or lack of it) of those changes – we have no way to determine by direct observation whether those changes are stabilizing/destabilizing or causative. And when we are unsure of (or wholly ignorant of) the infrastructural forces involved, often we assume that the superstructural forces that we have seen at work are responsible *for* major (i.e., infrastructural) changes. Infrastructural forces, however, often must be ferreted out and knowledge of their existence and effects disseminated by the superstructure.

That is to say, infrastructural forces will determine whether most of the neighborhood perceives Habanna San Juan's closing as another Puerto Rican business going as the neighborhood improves – or as another business-in-general folding as the neighborhood declines.

Infrastructure makes society go. Superstructure makes society go smoothly (or bumpily).

To confuse a stabilizing mechanism with a producing one is to create all the problems a mechanic might have were he to confuse a gyroscope with an internal combustion engine, or a farmer were he to confuse his sack of fertilizer with his bag of seeds. (In the field of human endeavor language is a stabilizing mechanism, not a producing mechanism – regardless of what both artists and critics would prefer. This in no way contradicts the notion that the world that we have access to is constituted entirely of language, i.e., that it is constituted entirely by the structure of its stabilizing forces. All else is metaphysics.)

Again and again, however, such confusion causes people who should know better to decide that, because they have located some pervasive superstructural pattern (a prevalence of petty street crime in neighborhood X, say), superstructure here is actually *producing* all the visible infrastructural changes:

'There was an influx of Puerto Ricans in neighborhood X, and a subsequent rise in drugs and petty street crimes, and because of this, eventually the neighborhood deteriorated till it became an all-but-abandoned slum where nobody, not even the Puerto Ricans, would live anymore . . .' when, at the infrastructural level, what has actually happened is that landlords-as-a-class have realized that the older buildings in neighborhood X require more maintenance and thus a greater expenditure to maintain, so they are now concentrating all their economic interest on newer properties with larger living units in neighborhood Y to the east, which is popular with young white upwardly mobile executives. The result is the decline of neighborhood X, of which street crime, drugs, and so on are only symptoms – though, as superstructural elements, those symptoms stabilize (that is, help to assure) that decline and combat any small local attempts to reverse it by less than a major infrastructural change.

Finally, there is an important rider to the corollary: in much the same way as contact and networking, infrastructure and superstructure are ultimately relative terms. They are vectors rather than fixed positions, so that there *are* some locations where, depending on the vectors around them, for brief periods it may be indeterminant whether something will operate with superstructural or infrastructural force. But while these are important intervention locations, they are not particularly germane to the analysis at hand – though an awareness of this is what makes me a marxian, rather than a Marxist.

My argument may at points appear incomplete because I am not writing about superstructural elements most people write about *not* as stabilizing (or destabilizing) but as formative on the infrastructural level – whereas I have chosen to ignore them because they are *only* stabilizing or destabilizing.

(One example may be how much of the 'lure' of Times Square was *because* that lure was illicit . . .)

In an army jet, it is sometimes hard for a civilian passenger to tell whether she is hearing the engine or the gyroscope. The gyroscope is in the body of the

plane – and both of them, running, make a fair amount of noise. Moreover, if
you turn off the gyroscope, the plane will start to bounce around and buck
through the air. In rough weather, this can be really disconcerting – leaving
the civilian to think something awful has been done to the 'motor'.

Nevertheless, what makes the plane fly is *still* the jet engine.

7.33 There is a conservative, stabilizing discourse already in place that sees
interclass contact as the source of pretty much everything dangerous, unsafe or
undesirable in the life of the country right now – from AIDS, and 'perversion' in
all its forms, to the failures of education and neighborhood decay, to homeless-
ness and urban violence. It is this discourse, which stabilizes the rhetoric in its
particular anti-AIDS, anti-sex and anti-crime (and even pro-theater) form, that is
generated by infrastructural changes – even though anyone who has spent any
time in the Times Square area can see that what is actually going on has nothing
to do with what this rhetoric purports and often contradicts it so flagrantly as to
produce some Kafkaesque, if not Orwellian, nightmares.

Because of this discourse, any social form (or, indeed, architectural form)
that steers us away from contact and contact-like situations and favors networking, or relatively more network-like situations is likely to be approved. (The
shift in popularity from professional sports to university sports is a shift from a
comparatively contact-orientated audience to a comparatively network-orien-
tated one; the growing audience for professional wrestling, however, represents
an audience more amenable to contact. The split is – but certainly not entirely
– a middle-class/working-class split, as well.) And more and more people flock
to networking situations, looking for the break, the chance, the pleasure, the
lucky encounter, the hand up that will allow them to move through social, class,
and/or economic strata – breaks, chances, pleasures and lucky encounters that
networking is not set up to provide, and often specifically retards.

7.41 I hope – and hope very much – that the new Times Square works.
Because cities function the way they do, however, *if* it works, parts of it will work
by accident. Mr. Stern says that his employers want to promote more economic
diversity. Well, I have to ask: more diversity relative to what? Certainly not to
the old Times Square. Take the now-completed section of the north face of the
block between Seventh and Eighth Avenues: in the old Times Square there was
a cigar store on the corner, followed by a tie store, followed by a working
entrance to a theater whose main body was around on Seventh Avenue,
followed by the Brandt Theater, followed by the Victory Theater: that is to say,
there were seven commercial spaces, three of which were theaters and four of
which were small sales outlets.

Along that same stretch of The New Times Square, there is Ferrara's on the corner (selling pastry and coffee). Last October, the next commercial space was occupied by a shop called Shade (which sold sun hats and sun glasses), but already it is out of business. Its papered-over store window currently announces: *Coming Soon! The Brooklyn Pastrami Company.* But the fact that one business has already folded in the new Times Square on what is supposed to be one of the world's busiest corners is *not* a good sign. This site is followed by Dapy (which sells a variety of tourist junk), followed by Magic Max, a magic store (and there has traditionally been a magic store in the area; for years, it was at the Eighth Avenue end of the block, down in the subway entrance); after that is the New Victory Theater, on the site of the old Victory: that's five commercial spaces – one theater and four stores. The drop from seven to five is a drop of almost 30 percent. Certainly prices, goods and other factors will contribute to economic diversity. But the architectural separation of the space represents a fairly firm 'bottom line' beyond which diversity cannot go, unless those spaces are further broken up.

G. The neighborhoods that have best exploited the principals of variety, self-policing, and contact are (at least in Jacobs's view in '61) those which have come about without particular planning. But if I have left any readers with the impression that, therefore, the 'opposition' between contact and networking is somehow allied to an 'opposition' between the planned and the architecturally unplanned (and that I am somehow on the side of 'the unplanned'), then they will have doubly misread me.

The problem is (and the argument is presented in Jacobs as well) that our tradition of city planning goes back through some of the great architectural heros of modernity (such as Le Corbusier) to the Victorian 'garden city'. That tradition operates by and continues to enforce two general assumptions, all but unquestioned.

The first assumption is: since cities are fundamentally ugly places, the best way to combat this ugliness is to make them look as little like cities as possible. That means we hide the small, the poor, the dirty, the grubby – shrugging them off to the edges, putting them behind a veil of parkland or public greenery. The assumption is that the best city neighborhoods are those that look as little like cities as possible. The *best* the city can produce is the boring, boring suburb.

The second assumption is: the only thing of intrinsic interest in the city is the gigantic, the colossal, the monumental. This alone is what makes a city interesting, great, unique.

Nostalgia for the seven spaces over the former four is no more in question here than some fancied nostalgia for the half-dozen years of rampant under-age crack prostitution in the mid-1980s. Rather, what we are speaking of is the public presentation of the Square by its developers, who say the builders are trying to promote economic diversity (when they are designing for relative economic homogeneity), or that they are opposed to drugs or violence against women, in

The approach to planning I propose flies in the face of both these asumptions as principles – with the result that, to most people, it may look at first like no planning at all.

Today our zoning practices are overwhelmingly exclusionary: they function entirely to keep different kinds of people, different kinds of business, different kinds of income levels and social practices from intermingling.

I suggest that we start putting together policies that mandate, rather, a sane and wholesome level of diversity in as many urban venues as possible.

New York Mayor Giuliani's current plan to move all sex business to the Westside waterfront area with a zoning mandate that each of the businesses must be at least 500 feet from any other is a perfect example of the exclusionary policies about which I am protesting. The 'five-hundred foot' rule not only makes such businesses relatively difficult to access by the people who use them; it also makes them harder to police in any effective way. The dispersal, coupled with the general desertedness at night of the neighborhood to which these businesses are being confined, makes those in the area far more vulnerable to street crimes. This seems either to be planned punishment for those who will use the services of these businesses on foot in the after-work hours when most people will get to them, or to privilege car visits (because being in a car will be safer) in a city that is desperately trying to discourage extra vehicular traffic.

It would be far more sensible to encourage the sex businesses to clump. At the same time, eating places, other entertainment venues, drug stores, groceries and living spaces should be encouraged to mix in with them. With order to make us feel that the project has some benefits for us. I am only pointing out that they have already – ruthlessly and vigorously – promoted all three (drugs, violence and underage prostitution) in the pursuit of what they are after. The idea that they will suddenly turn around and actually oppose them for any reason other than that it is clearly profitable is, once more, naive.

7.42 An example of (non-sexual) contact in Times Square:

While I was walking around the area this past summer, a young man taking pictures engaged me in conversation. A graduate student at the Columbia School of Journalism, he was there taking pictures and researching a thesis on the current reconstruction of the Times Square area. We chatted for about ten minutes. Then I left. The next day, passing through the square again, again I saw the young man with his camera. Again we said hello. Again we chatted. This time we exchanged addresses. When I got home I mailed him an earlier version of this essay, as I had told him I would, as well as an extra copy I had of *Policing Public Sex*, which I'd mentioned to him as a useful volume but which he had not yet read.

Since the publishers had sent me two copies, as well as a set of galleys, I was perfectly happy to send one to him.

I do not know if his thesis benefitted either from our talk, this essay, or the book. We have not run into one such a policy set in place as part of a long-term plan, it might well encourage a new, lively bohemian living and entertainment neighborhood for the city.

Certainly, I would say, build for large commercial spaces along the street level. But intersperse them with smaller commercial spaces that will hold the human services that make utilizing the larger services pleasant.

My approach is not to forbid the towering office building, but rather to make sure that there is a variety of housing not only nearby *but intermixed with* such undertakings. And that means housing on several social levels.

Cities are attractive to businesses because of transportation, availability of materials and skilled workers. Cities are attractive to *people* because of the pleasures the city holds. Much of that pleasure is cultural, certainly. Jobs are necessary to afford those pleasures. But it is absurd to think that, when the average male thinks about sex once every thirty seconds and the average female thinks about sex once every three minutes, pretty much throughout their lives, that sexual pleasure and sexual opportunity are somehow exempt from the equations that make city life attractive – even liveable.

another since. But I can certainly hope.

A conservative commentator might ask: 'Well, why are these beneficial non-sexual (that is, 'safe') encounters threatened by the severe restriction of sexual (that is, 'unsafe') encounters, especially if, as you say, the sexual ones are in the minority?'

My answer is:

Desire is just as inseparable from the public contact situation as we have already seen it to be in the fundamental structure of the networking situation. Desire and knowledge (like body and mind) are *not* a fundamental opposition; rather they are intricately imbricated and mutually constitutive aspects of political and social life. It is situations of desire (as Freud noted in *Leonardo da Vinci and a Memory of His Childhood* [1910]) that are the first objects and impellers of intellectual inquiry. Our society has responded to this in everything from putting the novel and poetry at the center of our study of the humanities, to developing the old Times Square area at the center of the city that has been called the Capitol of the twentieth Century in much the way Paris was called the Capitol of the nineteenth.

But we might give more thought to the necessary and productive aspect of this imbrication between knowledge and desire as it expresses itself so positively in so many forms of contact, before – with a wrecking ball and even more sweeping legislation – we render that central structure asexual and 'safe' in the name of family values and corporate giantism.

7.43 The nature of the social practices I am interrogating is such that specific benefits and losses cannot be systematized, operationalized, standardized or predicted. I can no more promise you a vacuum cleaner than I can an in-training marathon runner to return your pocket book or a relevant volume for your research in the mail out of the blue. Even *less* can I say that no one will ever do anything nice for you at a professional gathering! What I *am* saying, however, is that most people – especially those who live in cities – if they look over the important occurrences in their lives, are likely to notice that a substantial number of the important or dramatic ones, in the material or psychological sense, were brought about by encounters with strangers in a public space. This tendency is not an accident. It is a factor of the relative concentration of specific needs and suppliers in various social venues.

Networking situations start by gathering a population with the same or relatively similar needs. While this concentration creates a social field that promotes the rapid spread of information among the members *about* those needs, the relatively high concentration of need itself militates *against* those needs being materially met *within* the networking situation – indeed, militates against their being met until the members physically abandon the network group and disperse into other venues.

Without in any way disparaging the excellences, pleasures and rewards of small-town life, one must still acknowledge that the greater population and subsequently greater variety of needs and beneficial excesses to be found in cities make public contact venues, from the social to the sexual, a particularly important factor for social movement, change and a generally pleasant life in a positive and pleasant democratic urban atmosphere.

7.44 When I say I hope Times Square will work, my major fear is that the developers themselves do not know that they are lying. It is only the very young (who have seen too many mob movies) who believe criminals make better businessmen than fools. The fact is, there is just as large a percent of foolish criminals as there are foolish businessmen. Those who have *seen* criminals in business usually don't like it any more than they like to see fools running things. Theoreticians like Jacobs have given us some conceptual tools to understand the workings of certain city functions that, before her books, were largely invisible. It would be warming to think that developers might use those principles to produce profitable and vigorous urban spaces. What I'm afraid may happen is, however, that after the immediate profits of the sweetheart deals that have allowed them to build their Brave New Mall, they will take the money and run, having bamboozled the rest of us into letting them build another artificial over-extended downtown graveyard. The reason the famous four office towers were temporarily condensed to one (a fact which seems to warm Marshal Berman's heart) – with an 'interim ten-year plan to promote theater and entertainment' that is pure Orwellian Newspeak – is because the

H. Architect Robert Stern has pointed out that the aura of theatricality that inheres in Times Square because of the theater district is a marvellous and vivid attraction not only to the area but to the whole city.

I don't know if this analysis has been done by the developers, but that aura is made to glow by three forces: the glamour and excitement of the image of entertainment; the underlying image of the theater as art, as site of social critique and topicality, of dissemination of important social images; and the money that we all know accrues to successful stars, producers and works. The theater requires all three of these to maintain its aura. Remove any one, and theater becomes that much less attractive, appealing to a more limited group.

During the Buell Center conference where architect Robert Stern spoke of his employers' 'Ten Year Plan to Promote Theater and the Arts', theater critic Frank Rich, during his own presentation, pointed out that the organization of the legitimate theaters is moribund, with the two corporations that divide New York's legitimate theaters between them, the Schubert Organization and the Neiderlander Company, both on their last legs. Because of current Broadway costs, only a handful of Broadway theaters can even afford to run a full-scale musical. Even if most of the theaters are sold out nightly weeks on end, the houses are too small to support the running costs of an elaborate production today. Thus most of the theaters on Broadway are already considered by the companies that lease them 'throw away' theaters.

Should you want to experience that moribundity of the theater first hand, sit on the steps of the permanently closed fact that they would be impossible to rent has been given enough media play to discourage investors. The Times Square renovations have already demolished thirty theater and film spaces in thirty separate buildings in the area – and refurbished two: plans are to replace the destroyed spaces with *two* multiplex theater buildings. And at the end of the ten years? The four towers *will* be built.

8.0 In 1992 we emerged from twelve years of a national Republican administration that favored big business – with the result that we now have some very strong big businesses indeed. The argument which the Reagan/Bush leaders used to convince the public that this was a good thing was the promise of tax cuts and the 'trickle-down' economic theory. The 'trickle-down' economic theory, you may recall, was the notion that somehow big business would be helpful and supportive to small businesses.

It has taken a half dozen years for New Yorkers to learn, at least, what anyone over thirty-five could have told them in 1980 when Reagan was elected: big businesses drive out small businesses. Left unsupervised, big businesses stamp out small businesses, break them into pieces, devour the remains, and dance frenziedly on their graves. Now that we have watched Barnes & Noble destroy Books & Company on the East Side and Shakespeare & Company on the West and, in my own neighborhood, seen the Duane

Biltmore Theater on 47th Street, beside the metal gate, the bottom of which has been eaten away with uric acid, and chat with one of the homeless men who regularly sleep on a piece of cardboard under the dark marquee during the summer. Go along 39th Street along the theater back, where a dozen homeless men and women huddle or sleep in a welter of cardboard and garbage.

The best thing that could happen to the theater district is that, on the eventual break-up of the organizations, the theaters are sold off to a number of smaller and competing organizations. A number of the city's many theatrical experimental groups – La Mama and/or the Manhattan Theater Club, the Theater for the New City, Westbeth, CBA in Brooklyn, the LAB – should be given Broadway outlets, among precisely those theaters that Rich noted as too small to produce megaprofits.

I do not think there is anything nostalgic or any yearning for authenticity in my suggestion that what is far more likely to happen, however, is that the remnants of the organizations will be bought up by a single megacorporation, the 'throw away' theaters will go the way of the Helen Hays and the Morosco, torn down to make way for more office buildings and hotels. (For all this love of the theater, under pressure from the Times Square Development Corporation, since 1980, at least five theater buildings in the area have already been pulled down [the old Helen Hayes, the Morosco, the Adonis, the Circus], and one on the south side of 42nd between Sixth and Seventh, whose name I cannot find out] and five more [including the Capri, the Eros, the Cameo, the Venus, and one on the north side of 42nd Street between Sixth and Seventh], have

Reade Pharmacy chain put Lasky's and Ben's and several other small drugstores out of business, people have some models for the quality of service and the general atmosphere of pleasant interchange to be lost when big businesses destroy small ones.

Small businesses thrive on contact – the word-of-mouth reputations that contact engenders: 'You're looking for X? Try Q's. It's really good for what you want.'

Big businesses promote networking as much as they possibly can: 'Shop at R's – and be part of today!' vibrating over the airwaves in a three-million dollar ad campaign.

In one sense, the Times Square takeover is one of the larger and more visible manifestations of the small having been obliterated by the large. We are in a period of economic growth, we all know. But most of us are asking: why, then, isn't *my* life more pleasant? The answer is because 'pleasantness' is controlled by small business diversity and social contact – with, in a democratic society which values social movement, social opportunity, class flexibility, and interclass contact as the most re-warding, productive and thus privileged element.

Big business is anti-contact in the same way that it is anti-small business. But there are many jobs – like bookstores and, often, drugstores – that small businesses can fulfill more efficiently for the customers and more pleasantly (that word again) than can big businesses.

been totally remodeled into something that can never again be used as a theatrical space. Nor does this count any of the nine theaters on 42nd Street that stand closed and awaiting demolition. Since that time, one theater has been built – The New Victory children's theater – and one, the New Amsterdam, has been renovated. This should give the lie to any protestations of serious concern with theater in New York made by any spokesperson of Times Square Development Corporation. What the Corporation wants to do is exactly what it wanted to do in the 1970s when this plan got under way: build its office towers and its mall – and preserve a handful of theaters as museum pieces . . . only because they don't think they can get away with destroying them all. If, for a minute, they thought they could, they would.) The remaining theaters will be, at best, theatrical museums for more glitzy productions of *Guys and Dolls*, *Grease*, and *The King and I*, and, at their worst, new and bigger and more gorgeous productions referring to less and less of the social and material world around us. The amount and variety of Broadway theater will be drastically reduced – and with it will go the aura of theatricality that Mr. Stern has cited as one of our city's most valuable assets.

And, again, certain benefits from contact, networking simply *cannot* provide.

8.1 An academic who heard an earlier version of this argument told me that it explained a family phenomenon which, in his younger years, had puzzled – and sometimes embarrassed – him.

'Whenever we would go with my grandfather to a restaurant – my grampa who had been born and grew up in Italy – within ten minutes, he had everybody in the restaurant talking not only to him but to everybody else.'

The question in his grandson's mind: 'Why do you always have to *do* that, Gramps?'

The answer he realized, from my talk: how else could an unlettered laborer such as his grandfather, in the 1930s and 40s, go into a new neighborhood, a new area, and get work?

A reasonable argument might be made that a notable percentage of the homeless population in our cities today is comprised of men and women who grew up in social enclaves that counted on contact relations to provide those prized necessities, jobs, shelter, and friendship – a social practice at which we can still see that they were often very good – but who were unsuited, both by temperament and education, for the more formal stringencies of networking relations, which include securing work and social necessities through want ads, resumés, job applications, real estate listings and social interest groups; a mode of social practice which, in urban venue after urban venue, has displaced contact relations ('You want a job? Show up tomorrow morning at six-thirty: I'll put you to work') till there are hardly any left. Indeed, it is my deep suspicion that the only consistent and ultimately necessary learning that occurs across the field of 'universal higher education' toward which our

I. Because isolated, low-level, optionless poverty that shifts between poor homes and the very bottom of the job system (where the 'system' itself is seen as a fundamentally bureaucratic network phenomenon) has been called 'feminized', one is tempted to call 'masculinized' that homeless poverty where one has dropped through the system's very bottom into a world where ever-shrinking contact opportunities are the only social relations available. One of Gordon's points was that more and more men find themselves caught up in 'feminized' poverty structures. Well, many, many women and children are on the streets barely surviving, suffering, and dying in 'masculinized' poverty. I think that the gendering of such states merely overwrites and erases contextual power divisions and questions of wealth deployment with vague suggestions of a wholly inappropriate, bogus, and mystifying psychologization (men *choose* one kind of poverty; women *choose* another; when poverty is precisely about *lack* of choices) – and so should be discouraged, however well-intentioned it all first seems.

country leans more and more is the two-to-four years of acclimation to the bureaucratic management of our lives that awaits more and more of the country's working classes – and that goes along directly with (if it is not the institutional backbone of) Richard Gordon's analysis of the 'homework economy' and the 'feminization of poverty', that Donna Haraway brought to our attention more than a decade ago in her widely read, *A Cyborg Manifesto.*

8.2 What has happened to Times Square has already made my life, personally, somewhat more lonely and isolated. I have talked with a dozen men whose sexual outlets, like many of mine, were centered on that neighborhood. It is the same for them.

We need contact.

In these notes I have tried to go over some of the material and economic forces that work – on 42nd Street and in general – to suppress contact in the name of 'giving people what they want'. For I hope I've made it clear: the erosion of contact on 42nd Street is only an instance of a larger trend, in which in some places sex is involved and in others not – though desire and/or the fear of desire works through them all.

How can we promote more contact – and possibly even reverse this current trend?

Education is certainly one answer – particularly education about the way complex social units, such as cities and city neighborhoods, function. People about to come to the city need a more realistic view of what they will find when they get there. Most important, they must be disabused of the notion of the city as a unified and pervasive place of homogenized evil – and of the equally false image folks such as the Times Square Development Corporation would replace it with: the image of a space of pervasive and homogenized safety.

Those images are, of course, simpler to hold onto than the politically more

useful one that tells us: in general the city is a pretty safe place, though the
violence that occurs there is largely random. While there are certainly specific
types of big-city smarts (walking next to the curb on dark streets; listening, on
sparsely populated streets, to make sure the group of people coming up behind
you are engaged in conversation; a sense of what streets to avoid at which
hours), those areas where violence may be reasonably expected with some
frequency – often the first places the tourist sees: the bus station, the train
station, the streets around Times Square – tend to operate on a largely small-
town model and thus can usually be negotiated with ordinary (dare I say it)
small-town common sense. But the comparative paucity of urban violence is
among the most powerful factors constituting the freedom of action and
thought – so often called opportunity – that small towns simply cannot proffer.

8.3 City dwellers need to be educated as well. Investors need to know more
about the economics of large-scale real estate construction – and that they, the
investors, alone depend on the final success of the building for their returns,
while the corporation overseeing the actual construction need only be concerned with getting the object built in order to make substantial profits. City
dwellers need to be educated to the necessity of contact and contact venues;
they also need to have a clear notion of why contact *cannot* be replaced with
networking institutions in some ill-conceived attempt to sidestep urban
violence.

Because of that fear, developers are – in the name of family values, safety,
and profits – designing the New Mall-of-America to suppress as much street
contact as they possibly can, however vital it is to city life. In no way is this *just*
Times Square's problem. It is the multi-urban problem of the country – and
arises anywhere in the West where designers have stepped in to model various
civic centers. The reason we allowed, and even encouraged it, is because
people, not understanding the workings of the urban mechanisms, and believing that networking institutions can supply the same or even better benefits
than contact can, have been convinced they *should* fear contact.

People educated in the realities of city functioning must make *their* demands
– and their fears – articulate. Because we have a system where the public's
perception is, indeed, as powerful as it is (it can put off a greedy, money-
grabbing set of construction deals by a decade), it can also promote the
planning and construction of civic spaces designed to encourage rather than
discourage contact, and make it appear a profit-making process. (A park
surrounded only by residences, especially towering apartments, soon becomes
a locked fortress like Gramercy Park, and/or a criminal inferno like the central
parks in so many low-cost housing projects. A park sided by a variety of human

services, including coffee shops, inexpensive restaurants liberally intermixed with residences and other commercial establishments soon becomes a self-policing venue that promotes relaxed, anxiety-free use – and urban contact.) We have to educate people to look not so much at social objects and social monuments but to observe, analyze, and value a whole range of social relationships.

8.4 Because of its topological site in the city, the Times Square area – that is, the major entrance and exit to and from the city, thanks to the Port Authority and the Lincoln Tunnel – is the perfect place to encourage all forms of entertainment *and* desire.

8.5 City planners, architects and the people who commission them must be alerted to the long-term benefits – the social necessity – of designing for diversity:

Large and small must be built side by side.
Living spaces, commercial spaces, eating establishments, repair spaces, and entertainment spaces must all be interspersed.
Large businesses and offices must alternate with small businesses and human services, even while places to live at all levels, working-class, middle-class, and luxurious, large and small, must embraid with them into a community.

This flies in the face of more than a hundred years of architectural practice: Our society wants to condense, distill, centralize, and gigantize. But when this becomes a form – *the* form – of social engineering, whether in the form of upper-class residential neighborhoods with no stores and no working class residents, business neighborhoods with no residences at all, or industrial neighborhoods with no white collar businesses and no stores, the result is a social space that can do well only as long as money is constantly poured into it. Such locations have no way of producing the economic cushioning that holds things stable at the infrastructure level. While such neighborhoods may be, at their outset, provisionally convenient, or uncrowded, or even beautiful, they can never remain pleasant to move around in over any extended period. Without a web of social pleasantry, uncrowded soon becomes lonely; beautiful becomes artificial; and even the convenience of propinquity transforms into the oppressing necessity to be where one would rather not be. Under such valuative shifts, those material transformations wrought by time alone follow all too quickly, where neat and well-cared-for become abandoned, dirty, filled with trash, and rundown – while another neighborhood, three, five or ten times as old, which has nevertheless been able to maintain that stabilizing web of lived social pleasantry and diversity, is perceived – however shabby it may be – as quaint and full of historical interest.

What I and many other small voices are proposing is that we utilize consciously the same principals of socio-economic diversity through which those pleasant, various and stable neighborhoods that were never planned grew up naturally. We must purposely reproduce those multiform and variegated social levels to achieve similar neighborhoods as ends.

If our ideal is to promote movement among the classes – and the opportunity for such movement – we can do it only if we create greater propinquity *among* the different elements that make up the different classes.

That *is* diversity.

Today, however, diversity has to claw its way into our neighborhoods as an afterthought – often as much as a decade after the places have been built and thought out. (It is not just that there were once trees and public ashtrays on 42nd Street between Seventh and Eighth Avenues. There was also an apartment house and grocery stores, an automat, a sporting goods store, clothing stores, bookstores, electronics stores, a cigar store and several newstands, and half a dozen restaurants at various levels, all within a handful of meters of the Candler office tower – as *well* as the dozen movie theaters and amusement halls (Fascination, Herbert's Flea Circus), massage parlors and sex shows for which the area was famous for almost fifty years – years that encompassed the heyday and height of the strip as the film and entertainment capitol of the city, of the world.) Why not begin by designing *for* such variety?

At the human level, such planned diversity promotes – as it stabilizes the quality of life and the long-term viability of the social space – human contact.

9 Here's a composite entry from my last Spring's journal (1997).

After a trip to the 34th Street Central Post Office to mail a book to a friend, I walked up Eighth Avenue to the Port Authority, where I stopped to speak to Todd – of the spectacularly missing front tooth. His clothes were clean and his shirt was new, but he is still homeless, he explains. (In his middle thirties, he *has* been for over a decade.) Just come from a stint sleeping on the subway, he asked me for some change to get something to eat. I gave him a handful that probably totaled about a $1.75. 'Oh, thanks, man,' he said, 'now I can go get me some chicken wings.'

I was in the city to participate in a three-day conference at the Center for Lesbian and Gay Studies (CLAGS) at the SUNY Graduate Center: *Forms of Desire*. It's April, and after the snowstorm on the first, warmer weather seemed to have doubled the daytime Times Square traffic. Ben, gone to vacation with his wife in Germany for the winter, was back setting up his shoeshine stand behind the subway kiosk on the northwest corner. To the southeast, under the Port's marquee, Mr. Campbell was taking the afternoon shift. And Christos was there, among the pretzel and hotdog vendors, with his shiskabob wagon. (More and more these days he leaves the actual running of the stand to a Pakistani assistant.) Darrell and David have not been in evidence awhile now. Back in January and February, I'd run into Darrell a few times, either on the corner or coming out of the peep-shows further up Eighth Avenue. Street life wasn't so good for him, he admitted. But the long-awaited publication of the picture in *OUT Magazine*, he told me, had opened up some model work for him with *The Latin Connection*. Months ago, someone introduced him to some film makers (pure networking), but the OUT photo (pure contact) apparently pushed them to act on his application a lot more quickly.

I hope things go well for him.

Back in January I saw David over on Ninth Avenue, running after drugs. ('Hey, there – man! Hey, there! So long!') But not since.

There on the crowded corner, however, Jeff and Lenny and Frank were still hanging out – even while a scuffle between two young men created a widening circle under the Port's marquee, till a sudden surge of police tightened it into a knot of attention. A policeman sped past me through the crowd, while the woman beside him shrieked. Then, for a solid minute, the knot pulled tight enough to become impenetrable to sight. Moment's later, however, the same policeman led away a white kid in a blue checked shirt with a backwards baseball cap and a bleeding face (as he stumbled in the policeman's grip, he bumped against Christo's stand), while a Hispanic kid in a red jacket, shaking his head, talked to another policeman. Beside me, tall Frank tells me, 'Wow! They *got* him. They actually caught him. Man, that was cool. I didn't think they were going to get him. But they caught him!' Like Jeff, Frank, a long-time hustler on that corner, has no brief for violence that might keep his customers away.

The third evening after the conference, at the back of the 104 Broadway bus, half a dozen riders (four middle-aged women, two middle-aged men), each with his or her copy of *Playbill*, spontaneously began to discuss the matinées they'd seen that afternoon. In the full bus, the conversations wound on, and I found myself talking to a woman next to me from Connecticut, who had just come from the theater. It is spring, and New York is full of contact – though I note the conversation in the back of the bus is not cross-class contact, but pretty well limited to folks who can afford the sixty or seventy dollars for a Broadway ticket, and so partakes a bit more of the economic context of networking – the *Playbills* acting as signs of the shared interest (and shared economic level) characteristic of a networking group. Also, characteristic of networking groups, what circulated among them was knowledge about which actors were good, which plays were strong or enjoyable, which musicals had good voices but weak songs, and which just did not seem worth the time to attend.

Let me be specific. In the ten years I've known Todd, I'm sure the handouts I've given him, a dollar here, two dollars there (say, once a month), easily total 180 dollars or more – that is, over twice the price of a Broadway show ticket. If, on the bus, however, one of the *Playbill* wavers were to ask me or one of the others with whom she had been chatting amiably, 'Say, here's my name and address. The next time you're going to the theater, just pick up an extra ticket and drop it in the mail to me', it would bring the conversation to a stunned halt; and however the theater-going passengers might have dealt with it in the public space of a twenty minute bus ride, certainly no one would have seriously acceded to the request.

That is to say, once again, the material rewards from street contact (the quintessential method of the panhandler) are simply greater, even if spread out over a decade, than the rewards from a session of networking – which rewards take place (I say again) largely in the realm of shared knowledge.

That evening, around 7:20, I got home to comet Hale-Bopp, bright and fuzzy-bearded above the west extremity of 82nd Street, against an indigo evening only a single shade away from full black. At the corner, I phoned up to Dennis in the apartment (one payphone was broken; I had to cross over to use the one on the far corner), who hadn't seen it yet, to come out and take a look. Two minutes later he was down on the stoop; to prepare him, I pointed out a couple of diamond-chip stars overhead. 'Now that's a star. And *that's* a star. But if you look over there – '.

Without my even pointing, he declared: 'Wow, *there* it is!' – the fuzzy star-like object with its gauzy beard of light fanning to the east (I'd first seen it on my birthday, two nights before, in Massachusetts).

Dennis dashed back up to get his binoculars and to check it out from our roof; I turned up the street to make a quick trip to the supermarket. On my way back down 82nd Street, Hale-Bopp created a veritable wave of contact.

First an overheard father and two kids, son and daughter: 'Hey, do you see the comet up there . . .?'

'Yeah, I saw it last week.'

Moments later, I pointed it out to a heavy, white-haired plain-clothes police-man lounging in jeans and a blue sweat shirt by the gate at the precinct, who responded: 'Do I see it? Sure. It's right up there, isn't it?'

Which turned two women around in their tracks, one in a brown rain coat, both in hats. 'Is *that* it? Oh, yes.'

'Yes, right there. *My* . . .!'

'You can really see it, tonight! Maybe we should go down to the river and look.'

I left the policeman explaining to them why they *didn't* want to do that.

Thirty yards further down the block, I pointed it out to a stocky young Hispanic couple who passed me hand in hand: 'Yeah, sure. We already seen it!'

And a minute later I pointed it out again to a homeless man in his twenties with blackened hands and short black hair, who'd set his plastic garbage bag down to dig in a garbage container for soda and beer cans. 'Oh, wow! Yeah – ' slowly he stood up to rub his forehead – 'that's neat!' While I walked on, a moment later I glanced back to see he'd stopped an older Hispanic gentleman in an overcoat with a pencil-thin moustache, who now stood with him, gazing up: 'There – you see the comet . . .?'

With my cane, I walked up my stoop steps, carrying my groceries and my notebook into the vestibule, where I unlocked the door and pushed into the lobby.

10.1 How does this set of urban interactions beneath a passing celestial portent differ from similar encounters, on the same evening 100 or 500 miles away, on some small-town street? First, these encounters are in a big city. Second, over the next eight months, I have seen none of the people involved in them again – neither the homeless man nor the Hispanic gentleman, the young couple nor the pair of women, nor the policeman (one among the seventy-five-odd officers who work out of the precinct at the far end of my block, perhaps fifteen of whom I know by sight). Their only fallout is that they were pleasant – and that pleasantness hangs in the street under the trees and by the brownstones' stoops near which they occurred, months after Hale-Bopp has ellipsed the sun and soared again into solar night. That fallout will remain as long as I remain comfortable living here.

10.2 Not a full year after the CLAGS *Forms of Desire* conference that took place under the auspices of Hale-Bopp and provoked the journal entry above, at the February '88 Out/Right Conference of Lesbian and Gay Writers in Boston, Massachusetts, one of the Sunday morning programs began with two questions:

'Why is there homophobia?' and 'What makes us gay?'

As I listened to the discussion over the next hour and a half, I found myself troubled: rather than attack both questions head on, both discussants tended to veer away from them, as if the questions were somehow logically congruent to the two great philosophical conundrums, ontological and epistemological, that ground Western philosophy – 'Why is there something rather than nothing?' and, 'How can we know it?' – and, as such, could only be approached by elaborate indirection.

It seems to me (and this will bring the multiple arguments of this lengthy discussion to a close under the rubric of my third thesis: the mechanics of discourse) there are pointed answers to be given to both questions, answers that are imperative if gays and lesbians are to make any progress in passing from what Urvashti Vaid has called, so tellingly, 'virtual equality' (the appearance of equality with few or none of the material benefits) to a material and legally-based equality.

During the 1940s and 1950s my uncle (my mother's brother-in-law) Myles Paige, a black man who had graduated from Tuskegee, was a Republican and a Catholic, and a respected judge in the Brooklyn Domestic Relations Court. By the time I was ten or eleven, I knew why 'prostitutes and perverts' (my uncle was the first to join them for me in seductive alliteration; it is not without significance that, in the 1850s in London, 'gays', the plural term for male homosexuals today, meant female prostitutes) were to be hated, if not feared. I was told the reason repeatedly during half a dozen family dinners, where, over the roast lamb, the macaroni and cheese, the creamed onions and the kale, at the head of the family dinner table my uncle, the judge, held forth.

'Prostitutes and perverts,' he explained, again and again, 'destroy, undermine and rot the foundations of society.' I remember his saying, again and again, if he had his way, he 'would take all those people out and shoot 'em!' while his more liberal wife – my mother's sister – protested futilely. 'Well,' my uncle grumbled, 'I *would . . .*' The implication was that he had some arcane and secret information about 'prostitutes and perverts' that, while it justified the ferocity of his position, could not to be shared at the dinner table with women and children. But I entered adolescence knowing that the law alone, and my uncle's judicial position in it, kept his anger, and by extension the anger of all right-thinking men like him, in check – kept it from breaking out in a concerted attack on 'those people', who were destroying, undermining and rotting the foundations of society – which meant, as far as I understood it, they were menacing my right to sit there in the dining room in the Brooklyn row-house on Macdonnah Street and eat the generous, even lavish Sunday dinner that my aunt and grandmother had fixed over the afternoon . . .

These were the years between, say, 1949 and 1953, that I – and I'm sure, many others – heard this repeatedly as the general social judgement on sex workers and/or homosexuals. That is to say, it was about half a dozen years after the end of World War II. Besides being a judge, my Uncle Myles had also been a Captain in the US Army.

What homosexuality and prostitution represented for my uncle was the untrammeled pursuit of pleasure; and the untrammeled pursuit of pleasure was the opposite of social responsibility. Nor was this simply some abstract principle to the generation so recently home from European military combat. Many had begun to wake, however uncomfortably, to a fact that problematizes much of the discourse around sado-masochism today. In the words of Bruce Benderson, writing in the *Lambda Book Report 12*: 'The true Eden where all desires are satisfied is red, not green. It is a blood-bath of instincts, a gaping maw of orality, and a basin of gushing bodily fluids.' Too many had seen 'nice ordinary American boys' let loose in some tiny French or German or Italian town where, with the failure of social contract, there was no longer any law – and they had seen all too much of that red 'Eden'. Nor – in World War II – were these situations officially interrogated, with attempts to tame them for the public with images such as 'Lt. Calley' and 'My Lai', as they would be a decade-and-a-half later in Vietnam. Rather, they circulated as an unstated and inarticulate horror whose lessons were supposed to be brought back to the States while their specificity was, in any collective narrativity, unspeakable, left in the foreign outside, safely beyond the pale.

The clear and obvious answer (*especially* to a Catholic Republican army officer and judge) was that pleasure must be socially doled out in minuscule amounts, tied by rigorous contracts to responsibility. Good people were people who accepted this contractual system. Anyone who rebelled *was* a prostitute or a pervert – or both. Anyone who actively pursued prostitution or perversion was working, whether knowingly or not, to unleash precisely those red Edenic forces of desire that could only topple society, destroy responsibility, and produce a nation without families, soldiers or workers – indeed, a chaos that was itself no state, for clearly no such space of social turbulence could maintain any but the most feudal state apparatus.

That was and will remain the answer to the question, 'Why is there hatred and fear of homosexuals (homophobia)?' as long as this is the systematic relation between pleasure and responsibility in which 'prostitution and perversion' are seen to be caught up. The herd of teenage boys who stalk the street with their clubs, looking for a faggot to beat bloody and senseless, or the employer who fires the worker who is revealed to be gay or the landlord who turns the gay tenant out of his or her apartment, or the social circle who refuses to associate with someone who is found out to be gay, are simply the Valkyries – the *Wunschmadchen* – to my uncle's legally constrained Wotan.

What I saw in the conversation at Out / Right was that the argument exists today largely at the level of discourse, and that younger gay activists find it hard to articulate the greater discursive structure they are fighting to dismantle, as do those conservatives today who uphold one part of it or the other without being aware of its overall form. But discourses in such conditions tend to remain at their most stable.

The overall principle that must be appealed to in order to dismantle such a discourse is the principle that claims desire is *never* 'outside all social constraint'. Desire may be outside one set of constraints or another; but social constraints are what engender desire; and, one way or another, even at its most apparently catastrophic, they contour desire's expression.

On the particular level where the argument must proceed case by case, incident by incident, before it reaches discursive (or counter-discursive) mass, we must look at how that principle operates in the answer to our second question: 'What makes us gay?'

There are at least three different levels where an answer can be posed.

First, the question, might be interpreted to mean, 'What do we do, what qualities do we possess, that signal the fact that we partake of the pre-existing essence of "gayness" that gives us our gay "identity" and that, in most folks' minds, means that we belong to the category of "those who are gay".' This is, finally, the semiotic or epistemological level: how do we – or other people – know we are gay?

There is a second level, however, on which the question might be interpreted: what forces or conditions in the world take the potentially 'normal' and 'ordinary' person – a child, a fetus, the egg and sperm before they conjoin as a zygote – and 'pervert' them (that is, turn them away) from that 'normal' condition so that now we have someone who does some or many or all of the things we call gay – or at least wants to, or feels compelled to, even if she or he would rather not. This is, finally, the ontological level: what makes these odd, statistically unusual, but ever-present, gay people exist in the first place?

The confusion between questions one and two – the epistemological and the ontological – is already enough to muddle many arguments. People who think they are asking question two are often given (very frustrating) answers to question one – and vice versa.

But there is a third level where the question can be interpreted, which is often associated with queer theory and academics of a poststructuralist bent. Many such academics have claimed that their answer to (and thus their interpretation of) the question is the most important one, and that this answer absorbs and explains what is really going on at the first two levels.

This last is not, incidentally, a claim that I make. But I do think that this third level of interpretation (which, yes, is an aspect of the epistemological, but might be more intelligibly designated today as the theoretical) is imperative if we are to explain to a significant number of people what is wrong with a discourse that places pleasure and the body in fundamental opposition to some notion of a legally constrained social responsibility, rather than a discourse that sees that pleasure and the body are constitutive elements of the social as much as the law and responsibility themselves.

One problem with this third level of interpretation of 'What makes us gay?' that many of us academic folk have come up with is that it puts considerable strain on the ordinary meaning of 'makes'.

The opposition to our interpretation might begin like this (I start here because, by the polemic against it, the reader may have an easier time recognizing it when it arrives in its positive form): ' "To make" is an active verb. You seem to be describing a much more passive process. It sounds like you're describing some answer to the question "What allows us to be gay?" or "What facilitates our being gay?" or even "What allows people to speak about people as gay?" Indeed, the answer you propose doesn't seem to have anything to do with "making" at all. It seems to be all about language and social habit.'

To which, if we're lucky enough for the opposition to take its objection to this point, we can answer back: 'You're right! That's *exactly* our point. We now believe that language and social habit are much more important than until now, historically, they have been assumed to be. Both language and social habit perform many more jobs, intricately, efficiently and powerfully, into shaping not just what we call social reality, but even what we call reality itself (against which we used to set social reality in order to look at it as a separate situation *from* material reality). Language and social habit don't simply produce the appearance of social categories: rich, poor, educated, uneducated, well-mannered, ill-bred – those signs that, according to Henry Higgins in *My Fair Lady*, can be learned and therefore faked. They produce as well what until now were considered ontological categories: male, female, black, white, Asian, straight, gay, normal and abnormal . . . as well as trees, books, dogs, wars, rainstorms and mosquitoes: and they empower us to put all those ironizing quotation marks around words like 'normal', 'ordinary', and 'pervert' in our paragraph describing the ontological level.

'Because we realize just how powerful the socio/linguistic process is, we *insist* on coupling it with those active verbs, "to make, to produce, to create" – although, early in the dialogue, there was another common verb for this particular meaning of "make" that paid its due to the slow, sedentary and passive (as well as to the inexorable and adamantine) quality of the process: "to sediment" – a verb that fell away because it did not suit the polemical nature of the argument, but which at this point it might be well to retrieve: "What makes us gay?" in the sense of, "What produces us as gay? What creates us as gay? What sediments us as gay?" '

The level where these last four questions overlap is where our interpretation of the question – and our answer to it – emerges.

Consider a large ballroom full of people.

At various places around the walls there are doors. If one of the doors is open, and the ballroom is crowded enough, after a certain amount of time there will be a certain number of people in the other room on the far side of the open door (assuming the lights are on and nothing is going on in there to keep them out). The third-level theoretical answer to the question, 'What makes us gay?' troubles the ordinary man or woman-on-the-street for much the same reason it would trouble them if you said, of the ballroom and the room beside it, 'The open door is what makes people go into the other room.'

Most folks are likely to respond, 'Sure, I *kind* of see what you mean. But aren't you just playing with words? Isn't it really the density of the ballroom's crowd, the heat, the noise, the bustle in the ballroom that drives (that is, that *makes*) people go into the adjoining room? I'm sure you could come up with experiments where, if, on successive nights, you raised or lowered the temperature and/or the noise level, you could even correlate that to how much faster or slower people were driven out of the ballroom and into the adjoining room – thus proving crowd, heat and noise were the causative factors, rather than the door, which is finally just a facilitater.'

The answer to this objection is: 'You're answering the question as though it were being asked at level two. And for level two, your answer is fine. The question *I* am asking, however, on level three, is: 'What makes the people go into *that* room rather than any number of other possible rooms that they might have entered, behind any of the other *closed* doors around the ballroom?' And the actual answer to *that* question really *is*, 'That particular *open* door.'

Now, it's time to turn to the actual and troubling answer to the newly interpreted question, 'What makes us gay?' The answer is usually some version of the concept: 'We are made gay because that is how we have been interpellated.'

'Interpellate' is a term that was revived by Louis Althusser in his 1969 essay, 'Ideology and Ideological State Apparatuses'. The word once meant 'to interrupt with a petition'. Prior to the modern era, the aristocrats who comprised many of the royal courts could be presented with petitions by members of the *haute bourgeoisie*. These aristocrats fulfilled their tasks as subjects of the King by reading over the petitions presented to them, judging them and acting on them in accord with the petitions' perceived merit. Althusser's point is that 'we become subjects when we are interpellated'. In the same paragraph, he offers the word 'hailed' as a synonym, and goes on to give what has become a rather notorious example of a policeman calling out or hailing, 'Hey, you!' on the street. Says Althusser, in the process of thinking, 'he must mean me', we cohere into a self – rather than being, presumably, simply a point of view drifting down the street.

That awareness that 'he must mean me', is the constitutive *sine qua non* of the subject. It is the mental door through which we pass into subjectivity and selfhood. And (maintains Althusser) this cannot be a spontaneous process, but is always a response to some hailing, some interpellation, by some aspect of the social.

In that sense, it doesn't really matter whether someone catches you in the bathroom, looking at a same-sex nude, who then blurts out, 'Hey, you're gay!' and you look up and realize 'you' ('He means me!') have been caught, or if you're reading a description of homosexuality in a text book and 'you' think, 'Hey, they're describing me!' The point is, rather, that anyone who identifies him- or herself as gay must have been interpellated, at some point, as gay by some individual or social speech or text to which he or she responded, 'He/she/it/they must mean me.' That is the door opening. Without it, nobody can say, proudly, 'I *am gay*!' Without it, nobody can think guiltily and in horror, 'Oh, my God, I'm *gay* . . .!' Without it, one cannot remember idly or in passing, 'Well, I'm gay.'

Because interpellation only talks about one aspect of the meaning of making/producing/creating/sedimenting, it does not tell the whole story. It is simply one of the more important things that happens to subjects at the level of discourse. And in general, discourse constitutes and is constituted by what Walter Pater once called, in the 'Conclusion' to *The Renaissance,* 'a roughness of the eye'. Thus, without a great deal more elaboration, the notion of interpellation is as reductive as any other theoretical move. But it locates a powerful and pivotal point in the process. And it makes it clear that the process is, as are all the creative powers of discourse, irrevocably anchored within the social, rather than somehow involved with some fancied breaking out of the social into an uncharted and unmapped beyond, that only awaits the release of police surveillance to erupt into that red Eden of total unconstraint.

What the priority of the social says about those times in war where that vision of hell was first encountered by people like my uncle, possibly among our own soldiers: look, if you spend six months socializing young men to 'kill, kill, kill', it's naive to be surprised when some of them, in the course of their pursuit of pleasure, do. It is not because of some essentialist factor in 'perversion' or 'prostitition' (or sexuality in general) that always struggles to break loose.

It is language (and/as social habit) that cuts the world up into the elements, objects and categories we so glibly call reality – a reality that includes the varieties of desire; a reality where what is real *is* what must be dealt with, that is one with the political: the world *is* what it is cut up into – all else is metaphysics. That is all that is meant by that troubling post-structuralist assertion that the world is constituted of and by language and not something more to which we have any direct access.

The problem with this assertion is that one of the easiest things to understand about it is that if language/social habit makes/produces/sediments anything, it makes/produces/sediments the meanings of words. Thus, the meaning of 'makes' on the semiological/epistemological level is a socio/linguistic sedimentation. The meaning of 'makes' on the ontological level is a socio/linguistic sedimentation. And, finally, the meaning of 'makes' on the theoretical (that is, socio/lingustic) level is also a socio/linguistic sedimentation. This is all those who claim the third meaning encompasses and explains what the other two are saying. When I said above that I do not make that claim, what *I* was saying in effect was: I am not convinced this is an important observation that tells us something truly interesting about ontology or epistemology. It may just be an empty tautology that can be set aside and paid no more attention to. Personally, I think the decision as to whether it is or is not interesting is to be found *in* ontology and epistemology themselves, rather than in theory – that is to say, if the observation emboldens us to explore the world, cut it up into new and different ways, and learn what new and useful relationships can result, then the observation is of use and interest – but it is not interesting to the extent that it leads only to materially unattended theoretical restatements of itself.

Following directly from my primary thesis, my primary conclusion is that, while still respecting the private/public demarcations (I do *not* believe that property is theft), we'd best try cutting the world up in different ways socially and rearranging it so that we may benefit from the resultant social relationships. For decades the governing cry of our cities has been: 'Never speak to strangers.' I propose that in a democratic city it is *imperative* to speak to strangers, live next to them, and learn how to relate to them on many other levels as well as speech, unto the sexual – and that city venues must be designed to allow these multiple interactions to occur easily, safely, comfortably and conveniently. This is what politics – the way of living in the polis, in the city – is about.

While one thrust of this essay is that catastrophic civic interventions such as the Times Square Redevelopment Program are incorrectly justified by the assumption that interclass contact is somehow unsafe (it threatens to unleash the sexual, crime, mayhem, murder . . .) and its benefits can be replaced by networking (safe, monitored, controlled, under surveillance . . .), a second thrust has been and is that social contact is of paramount importance in the

J. The Times Square renovation is not just about real estate and economics, however unpleasant its ramifications have been on that front. Because it has involved the major restructuring of the legal code relating to sex, and because it has been a first step not just toward the moving, but toward the obliteration, of certain businesses and social practices, it has functioned as a massive and destructive intervention in the social fabric of a non-criminal group in the city – an intervention I for one deeply resent.

If the range of heterosexist homophobic society as a system wants to ally itself to an architecture, a life-style and a range of social practices that eschew contact out of an ever inflating fear of the alliance between pleasure and chaos, then I think it is in for a sad, unhappy time, far more restrictive, unpleasant and impoverishing than the strictures of monogamy could ever be.

The thousands on thousands of gay men, contingently 'responsible' or 'irresponsible', who utilized the old Times Square and like facilities for sex already know that contact is necessary. I would hope this essay makes clear that it is necessary for the whole of a flexible, democratic society – and I feel it is only socially responsible to say so.

specific pursuit of gay sexuality: The fact is, I am not interested in the 'freedom' to 'be' 'gay' without any of the existing gay institutions or without other institutions that can take up and fulfill like functions.

Such 'freedom' means nothing. Many gay institutions – clubs, bars of several persuasions, baths, tea-room sex, gay porn-movie houses (both types), brunches, entertainment, cruising areas, truck stop sex, circuit parties, and many more – have grown up outside the knowledge of much of the straight world. But these institutions have nevertheless grown up very much *within* our society, not outside it. They have been restrained on every side. That is how they have attained their current form. They do not propagate insanely in some extra-social and unconstrained 'outside'/ 'beyond', apart from any concept of social responsibility – and that includes what goes on in the orgy rooms at the baths. The freedom to 'be' 'gay' without the freedom to choose to partake of these institutions is just as meaningless as the freedom to 'be' 'Jewish' when, say, any given Jewish ritual, or Jewish text, or Jewish cultural practice is outlawed; it is as meaningless as the 'freedom' to 'be' 'black' in a world where black music, black literature, black culture, black language, and all the black social practices that have been generated through the process of black historical exclusion were suddenly suppressed. I say this not because a sexual preference is in any necessary way identical to race, or for that matter to religion. (Nor am I proposing the equally absurd notion that race and religion are equivalent.) I say it rather because none of the three – race, religion or sexual preference – represents some absolute essentialist state; I say it because all three are complex social constructs, and thus do not come into being without their attendant constructed institutions.

Tolerance – not assimilation – is the democratic litmus test for social equality.

10.3 It is impossible to hear such urban proposals as these and not think immediately of gender differences, divisions, barriers . . .

Our marginal consideration of 'feminized' and 'masculinized' poverty in section F has already suggested what I must articulate here. That so many women suffer 'feminized poverty', that so many men suffer 'masculinized poverty', as well as the fact that more and more of the 'wrong' sex show up in each, are not demonstrations of psychological difference but are, rather, an all-but-crushing demonstration that, in the symbolic space of the class-war, men and women are primarily different socio-economic classes, formed by different political and socio-economic forces. Indeed, they demonstrate just how powerful class markers are, since, in a society where men and women relate as they do and regularly cohabit and marry, such markers cut through that all important public/private boundaries, even when it is comfortably in place.

'Traditional psychological differences' between genders, when they occur, are replicating superstructural elements that work to stabilize a basic infrastructural situation; and the basic structure that grounds patriarchal (that is, heterosexist) society is one of artificial sexual scarcity – that is to say, institutions that fulfill the unstated mandate of the state to produce a certain number of children who will grow up into a certain range of various socially responsible adults, performing one or more of a range of functions: parents, workers, administrators, soldiers . . .

Because of the current world population problem and the changes in technology, that mandate has changed radically since the Revolution of 1848 (that is, the last 150 years). At this point, in an age of easy birth control, it is fairly clear that the nations most likely to prevail are those most successful in dissociating sex from procreation, though this all but reverses the earliest patriarchal form of the mandate: 'Go forth and multiply.'

From this point, let us turn to one of the more unpleasant urban phenomena: the wolf whistle, the cat-call, the lewd jeers and comments constantly passed from men in groups and singly to women on the street: the behavior that, at his shoe-shine stand at 42nd Street and Eighth Avenue, for twenty-five years, Ben has taunted, exploited, destabilized, and aestheticised. Away from the center of desire at which Ben holds sway, in the surrounding city streets, such comments pass as more or less ritualized expressions of hostility and aggression toward women by men who, to the extent they are thinking at all, glibly blame women for the situation of heterosexual scarcity. The message that underlies such jeers and comments, no matter how much they seem to highlight her attractiveness, is not, as every woman knows, 'I want to fuck *you*,' but rather, 'I *know* you won't fuck me, no matter *how* available I make myself – so the hell with you!' The fact that at 12:30 in the afternoon the average construction worker on his lunch hour is no more available for a quick fuck than the average secretary on hers, is not really the point: that's what keeps it ritualized – what allows it to leap back and forth across some fibrillating boundary between the just bearable and the wholly intolerable.

Gay urban society learned early on how to overcome the sexual scarcity problem, in a population field where, if anything, scarcity *should* be even greater. Suppose heterosexual society took a lesson from gay society and addressed the problem, not through anti-sex superstructural modifications, but through pro-sex infrastructural change:

Consider a public sex institution, not like the Show World Center that Ben so decries, thirty yards across the avenue, set up and organized for men, but, rather, a large number of hotels throughout the urban areas, scattered about the city, located in many neighborhoods, privately owned and competing to provide the best services, all of which catered to women, renting not by the day but by the hour, so that women can bring their sexual partners for a brief one, two, three, four hour tryst. Such hotels would be equipped with a good security system, surveillance, alarms and bouncers (as well as birthcontrol material) available for emergency problems. Moreover, the management would make clear that, within its precincts, all decisions were women's call, with everything designed for women's comfort and convenience.

Some people will recognize that in many cities prostitutes (and gay men) have had access to institutions now closer to, now further from, just this model for hundreds of years. In a sense, the only change I am suggesting is to move such institutions from the barely known and secret, from the discourse of the illicit, into the widely known, well publicized and generally advertised rhetoric of bourgeois elegance and convenience, promoting them as a sexual service for all women, single, married, straight, gay, prostitute or society matron.

To the extent such a social change might actually put a dent in the system of artificial heterosexual scarcity, I cannot guarantee; that all wolf-whistles or cat calls – other than Ben's historic and histrionic parody – will fall from our streets; but I *can* guarantee that their meaning, their hostile tenor (that is their content and form), will change radically, precisely as it becomes common knowledge among straight males that, in *this* town, you now have a statistically *much* larger chance of getting laid with a newly-met woman (because, even if she doesn't want to bond her life to yours forever but just thinks you have a cute butt, a nice smile, and something about you reminds her of Will Smith or Al Borland or John Goodman, and she has somewhere to take you) and the best way to exploit this situation of reduced sexual scarcity is probably *not* to antagonize random women on the street.

From the population problem to the lewd street comment, there are many reasons to promote public heterosexual sex on the model public gay sex has followed for years and, in one form or another, will likely continue to follow. But *if* we are going to do such a thing, it is only sensible to put its control into the hands of women and set it up for their safety and convenience from the start.

My active proposals do not extend to such utopian small-business sexual assignation hostels for women. Still, nothing in my argument precludes them.

What we must recall from our current theory, from our historical practice, is that such institutions and the resultant social contact practices they would develop and contour would no more overturn and rot our society than has alcohol, pop music, the novel, the opera, tobacco, the nightclub, any number of recreational drugs, make-up, men's clubs, tea-room sex among gay men, universal white male suffrage, lending libraries, comic books, black suffrage, women's suffrage, Catholicism, legal abortions, Protestantism, public education, Judaism, television, the waltz, coeducation, racial integration, jazz, the pin-up, the pornographic film, body piercing, bundling, taffypulls, tattoos, the fox trot, films, the theater, laws repealing the death penalty, beauty parlors, the university, laws preventing child labor, church marriages for the working classes – or any other social institution that is now, or was once, decried from one podium, pulpit, or another as the End of Civilization as We Know It. Such institutions are always-already within the social; indeed they *are* the social – and are not outside it: that is why they all require social intelligence in their administration. All are always-already in tension with other institutions: that is why they all have at one time or another required more or less vigilant protection as a set of freedoms.

10.4 Interclass contact conducted in a mode of good will is the locus of democracy as visible social drama, a drama that must be supported and sustained by political, educational, medical, job, and cultural equality of opportunity if democracy is to mean to most people anything more than an annual or quatra-annual visit to a voting booth; if democracy is to animate both infrastructure and superstructure – which is to say, the supports and stays that stabilize such contact must be judicially enforced and legally redressable. It is not too much to say, then, that contact – interclass contact – is the lymphatic system of a democratic metropolis, whether it comes through the web of gay sexual services, through the lanes of heterosexual services (and such gay and straight services include, but are in *no* way limited to heterosexual and homosexual prostitution!) – or any number of other forms which, by their very nature (standing in line at a movie, waiting for the public library to open, sitting at a bar, waiting in line at the counter of the grocery store – or in the welfare office – waiting to be called for a *voir dire* while on jury duty, coming down to sit on the stoop on a warm day, perhaps to wait for the mail, or cruising for sex), while in general they tend to involve some form of 'loitering' (or, at least, lingering), are nevertheless unspecifiable in any systematic way. (Their asystematicity is part of their nature.) A discourse that promotes, values and facilitates such contact is vital to a vision of a democratic city. Contact fights the networking notion that the only 'safe' friends we can ever have must be met through school, work or pre-selected special interest groups: from gyms and health clubs to reading groups and volunteer work. Contact and its human rewards are fundamental to cosmopolitan culture, to its art and its literature, to its politics and its economics: to its entire quality of life. Relationships are always relationships of exchange – semiotic exchange at the base, in a field where, as Foucault explained, knowledge, power and desire all function together and in opposition within the field of discourse. To repeat: contact relationships cannot be replaced by network-style relationships because, in any given network group, the social competition is so great that the price of social materials and energies exchanged is too high to effect emotional, if not material, profit. If we can talk of social capital, for those who enjoy a truly outrageous metaphor, while networking may produce the small, steady income, contact both maintains the social field of 'the pleasant' and provides the high-interest returns that make cosmopolitan life truly rich.

Notes

1. I would like to thank Bill Bamberger of Bamberger Books; Robert S. Bravard of the Stevenson Library of Lockhaven University; Barbara Cruikshank of the Department of Political Science and Don Eric Levine of the Comparative Literature Department, both at the University of Massachusetts, Amherst; and Peter Rheinhardt of the Department of Political Science at Williams College for reading and commenting on earlier versions of this essay. Needless to say, errors, overstatements, and idiosyncrasies are all my own.
   Portions of this essay were first delivered as the 1997 Kessler Lecture at the Center for Lesbian and Gay Studies (CLAGS) at SUNY Graduate Center in New York City.
2. Paul Rabinow, ed., *Michel Foucault: Ethics, Subjectivity and Truth, Vol 1 (Dits et écrits)*, New York: The New York Press, 1994, p. 654; Michel Foucault, *The Order of Things: An Archaeology of the Human Sciences*, New York: Pantheon, 1971, p. xi.
3. Jane Jacobs, *The Death and Life of Great American Cities*, New York: Vintage Books, 1961, pp. 98–111.
4. Astute as her analysis is, Jacobs still confuses contact with community. Urban contact is often at its most spectacularly beneficial when it occurs between members of *different*

communities. That is why I maintain that interclass contact is even more important than intraclass contact.

5. Marshall Berman, 'Signs of the Times: The Lure of Times Square', *Dissent*, Fall 1997, p. 78.
6. Louis Althusser, 'Ideology and Idological State Apparatuses', *Lenin and Philosophy*, New York: Monthly Review Press, 1971, p. 72.

2 GLOBALIZATION AND THE FORMATION OF CLAIMS

SASKIA SASSEN

The current phase of the world economy is in many respects discontinuous with the preceding periods.[1] This is particularly evident in the impact of globalization on the geography of economic activity and on the organization of political power. There is an incipient unbundling of the nation-state's exclusive authority over its territory. The most strategic instantiation of this unbundling is probably the global city, which operates as a partly de-nationalized platform for global capital. At a lower order of complexity, the transnational corporation and global markets in finance – with their cross-border activities and the new semi-private transnational legal regimes framing these activities – can similarly be viewed as instantiations. Sovereignty, the most complex form of national authority, is also being unbundled by these economic and other, non-economic practices, and by new legal regimes.

At the limit this means that the state is no longer the only site of sovereignty and the normativity that comes with it; further, it means that the state is no longer the exclusive subject of international law and the only actor in international relations. Other actors from NGOs and minority populations to supranational organizations are increasingly emerging as subjects of international law and actors in international relations.

In my reading, the impact of globalization on sovereignty has been significant in creating operational and conceptual openings for other actors and subjects.[2] The ascendance of a large variety of nonstate actors in the international arena signals the expansion of an international civil society. This is clearly a contested space, particularly when we consider the logic of the capital market – profitability at all costs – against that of the human rights regime. But it does represent a space where other actors can gain visibility as individuals and as collective actors, and emerge from the invisibility of aggregate membership in a nation-state represented exclusively by the sovereign.

I am trying to isolate here two strategic dynamics: a) the incipient de-nationalizing of specific types of national settings, particularly global cities, and b) the formation of conceptual and operational openings for actors other than the nation-state in cross-border political dynamics, particularly the new global corporate actors and those collectivities whose experience of membership has not been fully subsumed under nationhood in its modern conception, for example, minorities, immigrants, first-nation people, and many feminists.

Today's large cities emerge as strategic sites for these new types of operations. They constitute one of the nexuses where the formation of new claims materializes and assumes concrete forms. The loss of power at the national level produces the possibility for new forms of power and politics at the subnational level. In other words, as the nation, formerly the container of social process and power, begins to crack, a new geography of politics linking subnational spaces takes shape. Cities are the foremost instances of this new geography. The question that arises is this: what type of transnational politics is being localized in these cities?

Recovering Place

Including cities in the analysis of economic globalization is not without its consequences. Economic globalization has mostly been conceptualized in terms of the duality national-global where the latter gains at the expense of the former. It has also been conceptualized largely in terms of the internationalization of capital, and even then only in terms of the upper circuits of capital. Introducing cities into this analysis allows us to reconceptualize processes of economic globalization as concrete economic complexes situated in specific places. This contrasts with typical conceptions that understand communications and control as forces that efface the specificity of place. A focus on cities also decomposes the nation-state into a variety of subnational components, some profoundly articulated with the global economy and others not; it signals the declining significance of the national economy as a unitary category in the global economy. Even if this was formerly a unitary category constructed in political discourse and policy, it has become less of a fact in the last fifteen years.

Why does the recovery of place in analyses of the global economy matter, particularly when it is a question of place as constituted by major cities? First, it allows us to see the multiplicity of economies and work cultures in which the global information economy is embedded. It also allows us to recover the concrete, localized processes through which globalization exists and to argue that the multiculturalism one finds in large cities is as much a part of globalization as is international finance. Finally, focusing on cities allows us to specify a geography of strategic places at the global scale, places bound to each other by the dynamics of economic globalization. I refer to this as a new 'geography of centrality'. This is a geography that cuts across national borders and the old North-South divide, but it does so along bounded *filières*. It is a set of specific and partial, rather than all-encompassing dynamics.

Insofar as my economic analysis of the global city recovers the broad array of jobs and work cultures that are part of the global economy – though typically they are not marked as such – it permits me to examine the possibility of a new politics of traditionally disadvantaged actors operating in this new transnational economic geography. This is a politics that arises out of actual participation of workers in the global economy – whether factory workers in export processing zones or cleaners on Wall Street – but under conditions of disadvantage and lack of recognition.

The centrality of place in a context of global processes makes possible a transnational economic and political opening for the formation of new claims and hence for the constitution of entitlements, notably rights to place. At the limit, this could be an opening for new forms of 'citizenship'. The city has indeed emerged as a site for new claims, not only by global capital which uses the city as an 'organizational commodity', but also by disadvantaged sectors of the urban population, frequently as internationalized a presence in large cities as capital. The de-nationalizing of urban space and the formation of new claims by transnational actors, raises anew the perennial question, 'Whose city is it?'

This political opening contains both unifying capacities across national boundaries and capacities for sharpening conflicts within such boundaries. Global capital and the new immigrant workforce are two major instances of transnationalized actors that have unifying properties internationally and find themselves in contestation with each other within global cities. Such cities are the sites for the overvalorization of corporate capital and the devalorization of disadvantaged workers. Many of the disadvantaged workers in global cities are women, immigrants, people of color – men and women whose sense of membership is not necessarily adequately captured in national terms, and indeed often evinces cross-border solidarities around issues of substance. Both types of actors find in the global city a strategic site for their economic and political operations. Immigration, for instance, is one major process through which a new transnational political economy is being constituted, one which is largely embedded in major cities insofar as most immigrants – whether in the US, Japan or Western Europe – are concentrated there. In my reading, immigration is one of the constitutive processes of globalization today, even though not recognized or represented as such in mainstream accounts of the global economy.[3]

The ascendance of international human rights illustrates some of the actual dynamics through which an operational and conceptual political opening can be instituted. Ironically, international human rights, while rooted in the founding documents of nation-states, are today a force that can undermine the exclusive authority of the nation over its citizens and entitles individuals to make claims on grounds that are not derived from the authority of the state.

The Localization of the Global

Economic globalization, then, needs to be understood also in its multiple localizations, rather than only in terms of the broad, overarching macro-level processes that dominate the mainstream account. Further, we need to see that many of these localizations are not generally coded as having anything to do with the global economy. Many are embedded in the demographic transition evident in global cities, where – as I have noted – a majority of resident workers are immigrants and women, often women of color. In these cities one finds an expansion of low-wage jobs that do not fit the sanitized images of globalization, but are nevertheless demonstrably part of it. The consequent invisibility of these workers contributes to – 'legitimates' – their devalorization.

This can be read as a rupture of the traditional dynamic whereby membership in leading economic sectors contributes to the formation of a labor aristocracy – a process long evident in Western industrialized economies. 'Women and immmigrants' come to replace the Fordist/family wage category of 'women and children.'[4] One of the localizations of the dynamics of globalization is the process of economic restructuring in global cities. The associated socio-economic polarisation has generated a large growth in the demand for low-wage workers and for jobs that offer few advancement possibilities. This takes place amidst an explosion in the wealth and power concentrated in these cities, that is to say, in conditions where there is also a visible expansion in high-income jobs and high-priced urban space. 'Women and immigrants' emerge as the labor supply that facilitates the imposition of low wages and powerlessness under conditions of high demand for those workers and the location of those jobs in high-growth sectors. It breaks the historic nexus that would have led to empowering workers and legitimates this break culturally.

Informalization, another localization rarely associated with globalization, reintroduces the community and the household as an important economic space in global cities. I see informalization in this setting as the low-cost (and often feminized) equivalent of deregulation at the top of the system. As with deregulation (especially financial deregulation), informalization introduces flexibility, reduces the 'burdens' of regulation and lowers costs, in this case especially the costs of labor. Informalization in major cities of highly developed countries – whether New York, London, Paris or Berlin – can be seen as a downgrading of a variety of activities for which there is an effective demand, but the process creates an enormous competition for these positions, given the low entry costs and limited number of alternative forms of employment. Going informal is one way of producing and distributing goods and services at a lower cost and with greater flexibility. With the effect of devaluing the workers who produce them. In brief, it is women and immigrants who, for the most part, absorb the costs of informalizing these activities.[5]

The reconfiguration of economic spaces associated with globalization in major cities has had different impacts on women and men, and on male- and female-typed work cultures, on male- and female-centered forms of power and empowerment. The restructuring of the labor market brings with it a shift of labor market functions to the household or community. Women and house-holds emerge as sites that should be part of the theorization of the particular forms these elements in labor market dynamics assume today.[6] These transfor-mations contain possibilities, however limited, for women's autonomy and empowerment. For instance, we might ask whether the growth of informaliza-tion in advanced urban economies reconfigures some types of economic relations between men and women. With informalization, the neighborhood and the household re-emerge as sites for economic activity. This condition has its own dynamic possibilities for women. Economic downgrading through informalization creates 'opportunities' for low-income female entrepreneurs and workers, and so reconfigures some of the work and the household hierarchies in which women find themselves. This type of reconfiguration is more dramatic in the case of immigrant women who come from more tra-ditional, male-centered cultures.

A large literature exists to show that immigrant women's regular wage work and improved access to other public realms has an impact on their gender relations. Women are gaining greater personal autonomy and independence while men are losing ground in these populations. As these women gain more control over budgeting and other domestic decisions, they also acquire greater leverage in requesting help from men with domestic chores. Their access to public services and resources facilitates their incorporation into the mainstream society; often they become the family mediators of this process. Since it is likely that some women benefit more than others from these circumstances, more research and analysis will be necessary to establish the impact of class, education and income on these gendered outcomes.

There are two arenas where immigrant women are particularly active – in institutions for public and private assistance, and in immigrant/ethnic communities. The incorporation of women in the migration process strengthens the likelihood of settlement and contributes to a greater immigrant participation in community and state activism; they are also more likely to have to handle the legal vulnerability of their families by seeking assistance from public and social services. This greater participation of women suggests that they may emerge as more forceful and visible actors in society at large and may eventually also make their role in the labor market more visible.

It is possible to discern from the above a joining of two different dynamics in the condition of women in global cities. On the one hand women are constituted as an invisible and disempowered class of workers in the service of the strategic sectors constituting the global economy. This invisibility keeps them from emerging as whatever would be the contemporary equivalent of the 'labor aristocracy' of earlier forms of economic organization, when a low-wage worker's position in leading sectors had the effect of empowering that worker by providing the possibility of unionizing. On the other hand, the access to (albeit low) wages and salaries, the growing feminization of the job supply, and the growing feminization of business opportunities brought about by informalization, do allow women to alter their position in gender hierarchies.

Another important localization of the dynamics of globalization is found in the new stratum of professional women. Elsewhere I have examined the impact of the growth of top-level professional women in high-income gentrification in these cities – both residential and commercial – as well as in the reurbanization of middle-class family life.[7] What we are seeing is a dynamic of valorization that has sharply increased the distance between the valorized, indeed overvalorized, sectors of the economy and devalorized sectors, even when the latter are part of leading global industries.

A Space of Power

What makes the localization of the processes described above – even though they involve powerless and often invisible workers – strategic and potentially constitutive of a new kind of transnational politics is that this localization, the global city, is also the site of the valorization of the new forms of global corporate capital. Global cities are centers for the *servicing* and *financing* of international trade, investment, and headquarter operations. That is to say, the multiplicity of specialized activities present in global cities are crucial in the valorization, indeed overvalorization, of leading sectors of capital today. Global cities are production sites for today's leading economic sectors. This function is reflected in the ascendance of these activities in their economies. Elsewhere I have argued that what is specific about the shift to services is not merely the growth in service jobs but, more importantly, the growing service intensity in the organization of advanced economies: firms in all industries – from mining to wholesale – buy more accounting, legal, advertising, financial and economic forecasting services today than they did twenty years ago.[8] Whether at the global or regional level, urban centers – central cities, edge cities – are adequate and often the best production sites for such specialized services. When it comes to the production of services for the leading globalized sectors, the advantages of location in cities are particularly strong. The rapid growth and disproportionate concentration of such services in cities signals that the latter have re-emerged as significant 'production' sites after losing this role in the period when mass manufacturing was the dominant sector of the economy. Under mass manufacturing and Fordism, the strategic spaces of the economy were the large-scale integrated factory and the government through its Fordist/Keynesian functions.

Further, the vast new economic topography that is being implemented through electronic space is one moment, one fragment, of an even vaster economic chain that is in good part embedded in non-electronic spaces – *there is no fully dematerialized form of industry*. Even the most advanced information industries, such as finance, are installed only partly in electronic space. This is so even in industries that produce digital products, such as software designers. The growing digitalization of economic activities has not eliminated the need for major international business and financial centers and all the material resources they concentrate, from state of the art telematics infrastructure to brain power.[9]

It is precisely of because territorial *dispersal*, facilitated by telecommunication advances, that *agglomeration* of centralizing activities has intensified. What we encounter is not a mere continuation of old patterns of agglomeration but, one could argue, a new logic for it. Many of the leading sectors in the economy operate globally, in uncertain markets, under conditions of rapid change in other countries (for example, deregulation and privatization), and are subject to enormous speculative pressures. What glues these conditions together into a new logic for spatial agglomeration is the added pressure of speed.

A focus on the *work* behind command functions, on the actual *production process* in the finance and services complex, and on global market*places* has the effect of incorporating the material facilities underlying globalization and the whole infrastructure of jobs typically not marked as belonging to the corporate sector of the economy. An economic configuration very different from that suggested by the concept of information economy emerges. We recover the material conditions, production sites and place-boundedness that are also part of globalization and the information economy.

One of the proofs of the place-boundedness of the most powerful and globalized sectors of corporate capital is the major transformation now evident in financial centers. It might be interesting to decode some of the forecasts that such centers would inevitably decline as the result of globalization and electronic trading. Cities that were once major manufacturing centers did suffer inordinate losses, but major international financial and business centers – New York, London, Tokyo, Paris, Frankfurt, Zurich, Amsterdam, Los Angeles, Sydney and Hong Kong among others – have not. They have, however, experienced significant restructurings, partially because they have become linked to new cities, such as São Paulo, Buenos Aires, Bombay, Bangkok, Taipei and Mexico City. These new interurban links have further consequences for the subnational politics emerging from local instantiations of globalization.

The Future of Place in the Global Financial Market

The global financial system has reached levels of complexity that now require the existence of a cross-border network of financial centers to service its operations. This network differs from earlier versions of the 'international financial system'. In a world of largely closed national financial systems, each country duplicated most of the functions needed for its economy; collaboration between different national financial markets amounted to little more than the execution of a given set of operations in each of the countries involved: for example, clearing and settlement. With few exceptions, such as offshore markets and a few large banks, the international system consisted of a string of closed domestic systems.

The global integration of markets pushes towards the elimination of redundant systems and makes collaboration a far more complex matter, one which has the, perhaps ironic, effect of raising the importance of leading financial centers. Instead of each country having its own center for global operations, a leaner system is developing, with fewer national centers and more hierarchy. At the same time, national centers that do not become part of the global hierarchy are becoming more domestic in their orientation. London and New York, with their enormous concentrations of resources and talent, will continue to be powerhouses in the global network. They are still the leading exporters of financial services and typically part of any major international public offering – whether the privatization of British Telecom or of France Telecom. In the Eurozone a steep hierarchy is being put in place, with Frankfurt at the top, and a criss-cross of alliances among Frankfurt and the other major centers.

The 'international financial centers' of many countries around the world will increasingly fulfill gateway functions for the circulation in and out of national and foreign capital. The incorporation of a growing number of these financial centers is one form through which the global financial system expands: each country's center is the nexus between that country's wealth and the global market and between foreign investors and that country's investment opportunities. The overall sources and destinations of investment therewith grow in number. Gateway functions will be their main mechanism for integration into the global financial market, rather than, say, the production of innovations to package the capital flowing in and out. The complex operations will be executed by the top investment, accounting and legal services firms, through affiliates, branches, direct imports of those services, or some other form of transfer.

These gateways for the global market are also gateways for the dynamics of financial crises: capital can flow out as easily and quickly as it flows in. And what was once thought of as 'national' capital is now easily participating in the exodus: for instance, during the Mexico crisis of December 1994, we now know that the first capital to flee the Mexican markets was national, not foreign, and in the current flight out of Brazil of an estimated one billion US dollars a day by early September 1998, not all of it is foreign.

Because the globally integrated financial system is not only about competition among countries, we will see an increase in specialized collaborative efforts among these centers. Nobody would really gain if Tokyo or Hong Kong were to crash. The ongoing growth of London, New York and Frankfurt is in part a function of a global network of financial centers. Since its inception, Hong Kong has been a crucial intersection of different worlds, forever a strategic exchange node for firms from China to the rest of the world and from the rest of the world to China, as well as among all the overseas Chinese communties. Only if all investor interest in China were to cease would Hong Kong lose this historic role. Today it still has the most sophisticated concentration of advanced services after London and New York. As for Tokyo, it will continue to be a crucial cog in the system, given its enormous concentration of financial resources: one trillion US dollars in assets under institutional management and ten trillion US dollars in savings and similar accounts that are about to be deregulated. But a difference in the structure has been introduced, largely because of the recent financial crisis; this difference is described in Tokyo as the 'Wimbledon-effect', with reference to the fact that, while the court still belongs to them, the main players and winners are foreigners.

Finally, while electronic networks will grow in number and in scope, they will not eliminate the need for financial centers. Rather, they will intensify the networks connecting such centers in strategic or functional alliances, as was dramatically illustrated by the new link-up, announced in July 1998, between the stock exchanges of Frankfurt and London. Such alliances may well evolve into the equivalent of cross-border mergers and acquisitions of firms. Electronic trading will also contribute a radically new pattern whereby one market – Frankfurt's Deutsche Eurex, for example – can operate on screens in many other markets around the world.

The reason electronic trading will not eliminate the need for financial centers is that they combine multiple resources and talents necessary for executing complex operations and servicing global firms and markets. Frank-furt's electronic futures network is actually embedded in a *network* of financial centers. Financial centers cannot be reduced to their exchanges; they are instead part of a far more complex architecture and constitute far more complex structures within that architecture.

In the digital era: more concentration than dispersal?

The most striking evidence of the global financial industry is the extent to which there is a sharp concentration of the shares of many financial markets in a few financial centers.[10] London, New York, Tokyo (notwithstanding a national economic recession) regularly appear at the top *and* represent a large share of global transactions. London, followed by Tokyo, New York, Hong Kong and Frankfurt, accounts for a major share of all international banking. London, Frankfurt and New York account for an enormous world share in the export of financial services, while London, New York and Tokyo represent an enormous share in the global currency market. London, New York and Tokyo also account for over one third of global institutional equity holdings (as of the end of 1997, after a 32 percent decline in Tokyo's value over 1996). London, New York and Tokyo together represent 58 percent of the foreign exchange market – one of the few truly global markets – and with Singapore, Hong Kong, Zurich, Geneva, Frankfurt and Paris, they represent 85 percent of this market. Trading in all these cities takes place among banks using the same systems (either Reuters or EBS).

This trend towards consolidation in a few centers is also evident within
countries. In the US for instance, all the leading investment banks are concentrated in New York; there is only one other major international financial center
in this enormous country – Chicago. Sydney and Toronto have equally gained
power in continental-sized countries and have taken over functions and market
share from what were once the major commercial centers – Melbourne and
Montreal respectively. Similarly São Paulo and Bombay, which have gained
share and functions from Rio de Janeiro in Brazil and New Delhi and Calcutta
in India. One might have thought that these enormous countries could sustain
multiple financial major centers, but the facts indicate otherwise. In France,
Paris today concentrates larger shares of most financial sectors than it did ten
years ago, and once important stock markets such as Lyon have become
'provincial', even though Lyon is today the hub of a thriving economic region.
Milan privatized its exchange in September 1997 and electronically merged
Italy's ten regional markets. In Germany, Frankfurt now concentrates a larger
share of the financial market than it did in the early 1980s, and so does Zurich,
which once competed with Basle for power. This scenario is repeated in many
other countries, but what is already clear is that this pattern towards the
consolidation of one leading financial center is a function of rapid growth in
the sector, not of decay in the losing cities.

We are seeing, then, both a consolidation in fewer major centers across and
within countries *and* a sharp growth in the number of centers that become part
of the global network as countries deregulate their economies. São Paulo and
Bombay, for example, joined the global financial network after Brazil and India
deregulated, at least partly, their financial systems. This mode of incorporation
of cities into the global network is often at the cost of losing functions which
they had when they were largely national centers, insofar as the leading
financial, accounting and legal services firms enter their markets to handle the
new cross-border operations. In other words, the incorporation typically happens without a gain in the share of the global market they command, even
though they add to its total volume.

Why is it that, at a time of rapid growth in the network of financial centers, in
overall volume and in electronic networks, we have such a high concentration
of market shares in the leading centers? Both globalization and electronic
trading entail expansion and dispersal beyond that which had characterized
the confined realm of national economies and floor trading. Given this fact,
one might well wonder why financial centers are necessary at all.

Why do we need centers in the global digital era?

That major centers should continue to thrive is in a way counterintuitive, as is, for that matter, the existence of an expanding network of financial centers. The rapid development of electronic exchanges, the growing digitalization of much financial activity, the fact that finance has become one of the leading sectors in a growing number of countries, and that it is a sector that produces a dematerialized, hypermobile product, all suggest that location should cease to be relevant. In fact geographic dispersal would seem to be a good option, given the high cost of operating in major financial centers. Further, the last ten years have seen an increased geographic mobility of financial experts and financial services firms.

Geographic decentralization of certain types of financial activities, aimed at securing business in the growing number of countries being integrated into the global economy, has indeed taken place. Many of the leading investment banks have operations in more countries than they had twenty years ago. The same could be said for the leading accounting and legal services and other specialized corporate services. The pattern is also repeated for some markets as well. For example, in the 1980s all basic wholesale foreign exchange operations were in London; today these are distributed amongst London and several other centers (even though their number is far smaller than the number of countries whose currency is being traded).

There are, in my view, at least three reasons for the trend towards consolidation rather than massive dispersal. I developed this analysis in *The Global City*, focusing on New York, London and Tokyo; since then events have made this trend clearer and more pronounced.

i) First, while the new telecommunications technologies do indeed facilitate geographic dispersal of economic activities without losing system integration, they have also had the effect of strengthening the importance of central co-ordination and control functions for firms and, even, markets (let us remember that many financial markets have 'owners', are run by firms, so to speak, and hence also contain central management functions. Indeed for firms in any sector, operating a widely dispersed network of branches and affiliates and operating in multiple markets has made central functions far more complicated. Their execution requires access to top talent, not only within the firm but also, more generally, in the immediate milieux: in technology, accounting, legal services, economic forecasting, and all sorts of other, and often new, specialized corporate services. Major centers have massive concentrations of state-of-the-art resources that allow them to maxi-

mize the benefits of telecommunications and to govern the new conditions
for operating globally. Even electronic markets such as NASDAQ and
E*Trade rely on traders and banks that are located somewhere, with at least
some in a major financial center.

One fact that has become increasingly evident is that to maximize the
benefits of the new information technologies, it is necessary to have not only
an infrastructure but also a complex mix of other resources. Most of the
added value these resources produce for advanced service firms is as external
benefits. This means, basically, material and human resources: state-of-the-art
office buildings, top talent and the social networking infrastructure that
maximizes connectivity. Virtually any town can provide fiber optic cables, but
it is the other resources that make the crucial difference.

A second fact that is emerging with greater clarity concerns the meaning
of 'information'. There are, one could say, two types of information. One is
the datum: at what level did Wall Street close, did Argentina complete the
public sector sale of its water utility, has Japan declared such and such bank
insolvent? But there is also a far more difficult type of 'information', akin to
an interpretation/evaluation/judgement. It entails negotiating a series of
data and a series of intepretations of a mix of data, in the hope of producing
a higher order datum. Access to the first kind of information is now global
and immediate, thanks to the digital revolution. You can be a broker in the
Colorado mountains and have access to this type of information. But it is the
second type that requires a complicated mixture of elements – the social
infrastructure for global connectivity – which gives major financial centers a
leading edge.

You can, in principle, reproduce the necessary technical infrastructure
anywhere. Singapore, for example, has technical connectivity matching
Hong Kong's, but does it have Hong Kong's social connectivity? When
the more complex forms of information needed to execute major international deals cannot be obtained from existing databases, at whatever
price, then one needs the social information loop and the associated *de
facto* interpretations and inferences that come from sharing information
among talented, informed people. It is the necessity of this input that
has boosted the importance of credit rating agencies, for instance, which
interpret data. When interpretation is taken as 'authoritative' it becomes
'information' and is made available to all. The process of transforming
inferences/interpretations into 'information' takes quite a mix of talents
and resources.

In brief, financial centers provide the social connectivity which allows a
firm or market to maximize the benefits of its technological connectivity.

ii) Global players in the financial industry depend on enormous resources and this leads to rapid mergers and acquisitions of firms and strategic alliances among markets in different countries. Such mergers are taking place on a scale and in combinations few would have foreseen just three or four years ago. In the last year alone we have seen a whole new wave of mergers, notably Citibank with Travellers Group (which few would have predicted just two years ago), Salomon Brothers with Smith Barney, Bankers Trust with Alex Brown, and so on. This wave has been so sharp that now, when firms such as Deutsche Bank and Dresdner Bank want to purchase a US security firm, there is a lack of suitable candidates. Many analysts now think that mid-sized firms will find it difficult to survive in the global market against global megafirms such as Merrill Lynch; Morgan Stanley Dean Witter; and Goldman, Sachs. We are also seeing mergers between accounting firms, law firms and insurance brokers; in brief, firms that need to provide a global service. Analysts foresee a system dominated by a few global investment banks and about twenty-five big-fund managers. A similar scenario is also predicted for the global telecommunications industry, which will have to consolidate in order to offer state-of-the-art, globe-spanning services to its global clients, among which are the financial firms.

Will all of this mean the consolidation of a stratum of select financial centers at the top of the worldwide network of thirty or forty cities through which the global financial industry operates? Yes. We now also know that a major financial center needs to have a significant share of global operations to maintain itself as such. If Tokyo does not succeed in getting more of these operations, it will lose its standing in the global hierarchy despite its import-ance as a capital exporter. It is this same capacity for global operations that will keep New York at the top levels of the hierachy even though it is largely fed by the resources and the demand of domestic (though state-of-the-art) investors. This capacity will also allow Chicago to remain an important city despite the loss of some of its futures contracts.

Will the fact that there are fewer global players affect the spread of such operations? In my reading, not necessarily, but it will certainly buttress the hierarchy in the global network. For instance, institutional money managers around the world control approximately twelve trillion US dollars. The worldwide distribution of equities under institutional management shows considerable spread among a large number of cities that have become integrated into the global equity market, the result of a deregulation of their economies and the fact that 'emerging markets' have become attractive investment destinations in the last few years. Technimetrics, for instance, has estimated that at the end of 1997, twenty-five cities accounted for 83 percent of the world's valuation. These twenty-five cities also account for approximately 48 percent of the total market capitalisation of the world, which Technimetrics estimates at 20.9 trillion US dollars at the end of 1997. On the other hand, this global market is characterized by a disproportionate concentration in the top six or seven cities. London, New York and Tokyo together accounted for a third of the world's total equities under institutional management at the close of 1997. London and New York together account for well over half of the global currency exchange market.

These developments make clear a second important trend that in many ways specifies the current global era. These various centers do not just compete with each other: among them there is collaboration and division of labor. In the international system of the postwar decades, each country's financial center, in principle, covered the universe of necessary functions to service its national companies and markets. The world of finance was, of course, much simpler than it is today. In the initial stages of deregulation in the 1980s there was a strong tendency to see the relation among the major centers as one of straight competition between New York, London and Tokyo – the heavyweights in the system. But it was already clear then that there was a division of labor among them. What we are now witnessing is yet a third pattern: strategic alliances not only between firms across borders but also between markets. There is competition, strategic collaboration and hierarchy.

In brief, the need for enormous resources to handle increasingly global operations, in combination with the growth of central functions described under section (i) produces strong tendencies towards concentration and hence hierachy in an expanding network.

iii) National attachments and identities are weakening among these global players and their customers. The major US and European investment banks have therefore set up specialized offices in London to handle various aspects of their global business. Even French banks have set up some of their global specialized operations in London, a move that was inconceivable even a few years ago, and still not avowed in the national rhetoric.

Deregulation and privatisation have further weakened the need for *national* financial centers. The issue of nationality simply plays itself out differently in these sectors to the way that it did even a decade ago. Global financial products are accessible in national markets and national investors can operate in global markets. It is interesting to observe that, where investment banks used to split up their teams of analysts by country to cover a national market, they are now more likely to do so by industrial sector.

In *Losing Control?*, I described this process as the incipient denationalization of certain institutional arenas. I think such denationalization is a necessary condition for economic globalization as we know it today. The sophistication of this system lies in the fact that it only needs to involve strategic institutional areas – most national systems can be left basically unaltered. China is a good example. In 1993 it adopted international accounting rules necessary to engage in international transactions, yet it did not have to change much of its domestic economy in the process. Japanese firms operating overseas adopted such standards long before Japan's government considered requiring them. In this regard the wholesale side of globalization is quite different from the global consumer markets, in which success necessitates altering national tastes at a mass level. This process of denationalization will be facilitated by the current foreign acquisitions of firms and property in all the Asian countries in crisis. I would argue that the Asian financial crisis has functioned as a mechanism, at least partly, to denationalize control over key sectors of economies which, while allowing the massive entry of foreign investment, never relinquished that control.

Major international business centers produce what we could think of as a new subculture. The resistance to mergers and acquisitions, especially to hostile takeovers in Europe or to foreign ownership and control in east Asia, signal the existence of a national business culture somewhat at odds with the new global economic ethos. I would argue that major cities, and various international meetings and fora, contribute to the denationalization of the corporate élites. Whether this is good or bad is a separate question; but it is, I believe, one of the conditions for setting in place the systems and subcultures necessary for a global economic system.

Making Claims on the City

These processes signal that there has been a change in the linkages that bind people and places and in the corresponding formation of claims on the city. It is true that throughout history people have moved and through these movements constituted new places. But today the articulation of territory and people is being constituted in a radically different way, at least in one regard, and that is the speed with which that articulation can change. One consequence of this is the expansion of the space within which actual and possible linkages can happen. The shrinking of distance and time that characterizes the current era finds one of its most extreme forms in electronically-based communities of individuals or organizations from all around the globe who interact in real time and simultaneously, as is possible through the Internet and kindred electronic networks.

I would argue that another radical form assumed today by the linkage of people to territory is the loosening of identities from what have been their traditional sources, namely the nation or the village. This unmooring in the process of identity formation engenders new notions of community member-ship and of entitlement.

The space constituted by the worldwide grid of global cities, a space with new economic and political potentialities, is perhaps one of the most crucial spaces for the formation of transnational identities and communities. This is a space that is both place-centered, in that it is embedded in particular and important sites, and transterritorial, insofar as it connects sites that although not geograph-ically proximate are intensely connected. As I argued earlier, it is not only the transmigration of capital that takes place in this global grid, but people as well, both rich – the new transnational professional workforce – and poor – most migrant workers; and it is a space for the transmigration of cultural forms, for the reterritorialization of 'local' subcultures. It is an open question whether these spaces will facilitate a new politics, one going beyond the politics of culture and identity, even if partly embedded in them.

Another way of thinking about the political implications of this new transna-tional space is to consider the formation of new claims on the space. Has economic globalization shaped new claims? Major new actors are now making claims on these cities, notably foreign firms that have been allowed to do business in them. Foreign or international business people are among the new city users and they have profoundly marked the urban landscape. Their claim to the city is not contested, even though the costs and benefits they bring to these cities have barely been examined. These claims contribute to the incipient dynamics of denationalization discussed in the previous section, which though institutional, tend to have spatial outcomes disproportionately concentrated in global cities.

City users have often made immense claims on the city and have even reconstituted spaces within the city in their image: theirs is a *de facto* claim, which has never been made problematic. They contribute to the alteration of the social morphology of the city and to the constitution of what Martinotti has called the 'metropolis of the second generation', the city of late modernism.[11] But the new city of city users is a fragile one, whose survival and successes are centered on an economy of high productivity, advanced technologies and intensified exchanges.

On the one hand this raises a question of what the city is for international businesspeople – it is a city whose space consists of airports, top-level business districts, world-class hotels and restaurants, a sort of urban glamour zone. On the other hand, there is the difficult task of establishing whether a city that functions as an international business center does in fact recover the costs involved in serving as such a center: these costs involve maintaining a state-of-the-art business district and all it requires, from advanced communications facilities to top-level security and a 'world-class culture'.

Perhaps at the other extreme of conventional representations are those who use urban political violence to make their claims on the city, claims that lack the *de facto* legitimacy enjoyed by the new 'city users'. These are claims made by actors who have to struggle for recognition and entitlement in order to claim their rights to the city.[12]

There are two aspects in this formation of new claims that have implications for the new transnational politics. One is the sharp and perhaps sharpening differences in the representation of these claims by different sectors, notably international business and the vast population of low-income 'others' – African-Americans, immigrants, women. The second aspect is the increasingly transnational element in both types of claims and claimants. This signals a politics of contestation which, though embedded in specific places, in specific global cities, is transnational in character. At its most extreme, this divergence assumes the form of: a) an overvalorized corporate center occupying a smaller terrain and one whose edges are sharper than, for example, in the post-war era, which was characterized by a large middle class; and b) a sharp devalorization of what is outside the center, which comes to be read as marginal.

The question here is whether the growing presence of immigrants, African-Americans and women in the labor force of large cities is what is responsible for this sharp increase in inequality, as it is expressed in both financial and cultural terms. The new politics of identity and the new cultural politics have brought many of these devalorized or marginal sectors into the forefront of urban life; it has made them representable.

There is something that must not be missed here: a distinction between powerlessness and the condition of being an actor who nevertheless lacks power. I use the term 'presence' to name this condition. In the context of a strategic space such as the global city, the types of disadvantaged people described are not simply marginal; they acquire 'presence' in a broader political process that escapes the boundaries of the formal polity. This presence signals the possibility of a politics. What this politics will be depends on the specific projects and practices of various communities. Insofar as the sense of membership in these communities is not subsumed under the category of the national, it may open opportunities for a transnational politics centered in concrete localities.

Global capital has made claims on national states, and these have responded through the production of new forms of legality. The new geography of global economic processes, the strategic territories for economic globalization, had to be produced, both in terms of the practices of corporate actors and the requisite infrastructure, and in terms of the work of the state in producing or legitimating new legal regimes. These claims very often materialize in claims over the city's land, resources and policies. Disadvantaged groups, having gained presence, are also asserting claims, but these lack the legitimacy attached to those asserted by global capital.

There are two distinct issues here. The first is the formation of new legal regimes to negotiate between national sovereignty and the transnational practices of corporate economic actors. The second is the particular content of this new regime, which contributes to strengthening the advantages of certain types of economic actors and to weakening those of others.[13] There is also a larger theoretical/political question underlying these issues, which has to do with which actors gain legitimacy and which lose it.

In sum: Globalization is a contradictory space; it is characterized by contestation, internal differentiation, continuous border crossings. The global city is emblematic of this condition. Global cities concentrate a disporportionate share of global corporate power and are one of the key sites for its overvalorization. But they also concentrate a disproportionate share of disadvantaged people and are one of the key sites for their devalorization. This joint presence happens in a context where: 1) the globalization of the economy has grown sharply and cities have become increasingly strategic for global capital; and 2) marginalized people have found their voice and are also making claims on the city. This joint presence is brought dramatically into focus by the sharpening of the distance between the two. The center now concentrates immense power; a power that rests on the capability for global control and the production of superprofits. Yet marginal groups, notwithstanding their limited economic and political power, have become an increasingly strong presence through the new politics of culture and identity and an emergent transnational politics embedded in the new geography of economic globalization. Both sorts of actors – increasingly transnational and in contestation – find in the city the strategic terrain for their operations.

Notes

1. The notion of a global economy is increasingly used to distinguish the phase of the world economy that begins to emerge in the 1970s. It is characterized by the rapid growth of transactions and institutions outside the older framework of interstate relations. See, for example, James Mittleman, ed., *Globalization: Critical Reflections. International Political Economy Yearbook*, vol. 9, (1996).

2. Saskia Sassen, *Losing Control? Sovereignty in an Age of Globalization* New York: Columbia University Press, 1995.

3. For a full examination of these issues see my *Globalization and its Discontents* New York: New Press, 1998, Part One.

4. The economic significance of this new situation is worse than that secured by the Fordist contract which, through the family wage, veiled or softened the consequences of the economic relation.

5. Sassen, *Globalization and Its Discontents.*

6. See, for example, my *Losing Control?*

7. Saskia Sassen, *The Global City: New York, London, Tokyo* Princeton: Princeton University Press, 1991, chapter 9.

8. Saskia Sassen, *Cities in a World Economy* Thousand Oaks, CA: Pine Forge/Sage, 1994, chapter 4.

9. Telematics and globalization have emerged as fundamental forces reshaping the organization of economic space. This reshaping ranges from the spatial virtualization of a growing number of economic activities to the reconfiguration of the geography of the built environment for economic activity. Whether in electronic space or in the geography of the built environment, this reshaping involves organizational and structural changes.

10. Among the main sources of data for the figures cited in this section are the International Bank for Settlements (Basle); IMF national accounts data; specialized trade publications such as *The Wall Street Journal's WorldScope, Morgan Stanley Capital International, The Banker,* data listings in the *Financial Times* and in *The Economist,* and, especially for a focus on cities, the data produced by Technimetrics,Inc. Additional sources are listed in my *The Global City* and *Losing Control?*

11. Guido Martinotti, *Metropoli: La nuova morfologia sociale della città* Bologna: Il Mulino, 1993.

12. S. Body-Gendrot (*Ville et Violence* Paris: PUF, 1993) shows how the city remains a terrain for contest, characterized by the emergence of younger and younger actors. It is a terrain where the constraints and institutional limits placed on governments to address the demands for equity engender social disorders. Body-Gendrot argues that urban political violence should not be interpreted as a coherent ideology, but rather as an element of temporary political tactics that permits vulnerable actors to enter into interaction with the holders of power on terms that will be somewhat more favorable to the weak.

13. There are many questions here, from that of the legitimacy of the right to economic survival, to human rights, and the representativity of the state. I have discussed these questions more fully in *Losing Control?*, chapters 2 and 3.

3 'NEW URBANISM' AND ITS DISCONTENTS

DEAN MACCANNELL

The Other that we experience through [religion] is omnivalent. It is precisely what is called, in Christianity, the neighbor. It is a way to nullify extimacy; it grounds what is common, what conforms, conformity. It belongs fundamentally, as universal, to this conformity.

Jacques-Alain Miller, *Extimité*

Big Capital is currently in the process of pushing the United States' middle class closer together in high-density suburban developments and urban infill designed to resemble nineteenth-century towns. This movement is called the 'New Urbanism' or sometimes 'neotraditionalism'. The ideas for this kind of community planning have been around for a long time on the intellectual fringes in the ecological movement. Only in the last ten years has it captured mainstream attention.

There is more happening here than just a move uptown of a part of Environmentalism. For a start, an entire new 'class solidarity' is being marketed along with the physical amenities of 'New Urban' developments: 'shared values', a 'renewed sense of community', 'neighborliness', 'co-operation', 'closeness', and 'harmony'.[1] The first phase of the experiment has already been bought by eager new home owners at Seaside in Florida, Harbor Town in Memphis, Haymount and Carlyle in Virginia, Battery Park City in New York, Southport near Sacramento, and The Crossings in Mountain View, California. The boldest expressions of New Urbanism are Disney Development's town of Celebration in Florida and Steven Spielberg's Dreamworks town of Playa Vista in Los Angeles.

The New Urbanism can be seen – and this is one of the ways it sees itself – as a straightforward antidote to the kind of suburbs built after World War II. In the 1950s, low-density development effectively thwarted local control and discouraged lasting local intimacies. Major corporations freely transferred their executives to distant offices knowing they would find a home of equivalent value in a neighborhood where the social life would be at least as superficial as the one they just left. A certain level of intra-community hostility was supported as families were encouraged to build back-yard bomb-shelters and equip them with guns to ward off neighbors who had failed to prepare themselves for attack.

This is perhaps the least significant way in which, for the last fifty years, the 'politics of propinquity' has been driven by nuclear strategic considerations. Proletarian and subproletarian ethnic minorities have been jammed together with a few die-hard liberal professionals at ground zero. The conservative, white middle class has been distributed around the countryside in low-density suburbs.[2] This was horrendously uneconomical, requiring massive investment in highways and other infrastructure duplication, overdrafts of fossil fuel, the destruction of America's smallest farms, and so on.

But cost was no object as the United States reconfigured itself as an enormous defensive weapon, a nuclear military-demographic masterpiece, a society that could mask its racism as a certain casual bravado in the face of nuclear threat. Every time the Soviets built a new type of bomb, the United States built five new white suburbs and found new negative terms for inner-city existence: 'welfare cheats', 'gang related', 'drug infested', 'psychotic homeless', 'drive-by shooting'. If this is permissible as 'social consciousness', its unconscious would be a desire for a nuclear hit on the city. An attack by our enemy would solve all our worst problems. Of course, no sensible person could actually believe such a thing, but it was official United States policy.

Now we are entering an era wherein the 'politics of propinquity' is supposedly no longer warped by strategic concerns. Today, economics is the driving force. In the absence of nuclear threat, it is both more economical and ecologically correct to push the white middle class together. It always would have been except for the 'nuclear thing.' Now we hear enthusiasm for 'urban in-fill' and the New Urbanism from quarters where such ideas would have been unthinkable only ten years ago – banks, developers, and mainstream planners.[3]

The deep pathos of the New Urbanism is that its proponents do not see their plans as symptomatic of nuclear trauma. The town of Celebration's copyrighted logo is pure kitsch: 'a little girl with a ponytail riding a bicycle past a picket fence under a spreading oak tree as her little dog chases along behind.'[4] The entire ensemble is symptomatic of an unavowed desire to rewind the life of the people from the present back to 1945 and replay it as if it had not been lived under threat of nuclear annihilation. The Celebration logo reproduces the opening scene of the infamous 1950s civil defense film 'Duck and Cover': a boy happily riding his bike past picket fences in Anytown, US is hit by a nuclear blast. The phrase 'a sense of' – as in 'a sense of security', 'a sense of community', 'a sense of family values', 'a sense of involvement', 'a sense of mutual interdependence' – forcefully reminds us of the impossibility of living 'as if' the last fifty years could be erased from collective memory. Yet this impossible desire is precisely the aim of neo-traditionalism.

The Ahwahnee Principles

Two years after the Berlin Wall was taken down, just as the American people began to believe that they might not be vaporized in a nuclear holocaust, a group of architects, planners, community activists and lawyers got together at Ahwahnee Lodge in Yosemite and laid out a conceptual framework for the New Urbanism. Set forth in fifteen short, easy-to-understand points, the *Ahwahnee Principles* contain new language suggesting respect for the natural environment, but otherwise they are quite similar to the *Thirteen Points of Traditional Neighborhood Development* set forth earlier by Andres Duany and Elizabeth Platte-Zyberg, both of whom were at the Ahwahnee meeting.

The *Principles* are implicitly critical of the low-density suburbs developed after World War II. The New Urban, or neo-traditional neighborhood should have a discernible center. Most of its dwellings should be a short walk from the center. It should have a variety of housing, ranging from rental apartments to substantial single-family dwellings. Shops within walking distance (at the center or at the edge) should provide for the residents' weekly needs. The elementary school should be within walking distance for most children. There should be small playgrounds no more than 700 feet from every house. The houses should be set close to tree-lined streets and the streets should be narrow, slowing vehicular traffic and emphasizing the importance of pedestrian traffic and the pedestrian experience. Parking is located in the backs of the homes, accessed by alleys. The transportation corridors for motor vehicles, bicycles and pedestrians should be integrated, lighted, and otherwise designed in such a way as to encourage walking and bicycle use and discourage high-speed traffic. The natural terrain, drainage and vegetation should be preserved wherever possible. Community systems should be designed in such a way as to conserve water and energy and to minimize waste. Decision-making should be local and democratic. The single signifier of 'neo-tradition' is a generous, covered front porch.

Setting aside the sentimentality, there are several socially and environmentally sound design concepts contained in the *Principles*. Seaside is apparently one of the most successful planned communities in America. Duany and Platte-Zyberg have gone beyond the earlier position papers, suggesting that residents be allowed to build secondary structures in their backyards to be used as rental property or workshops. As often happens with a good idea, the heart of the matter seems to have gotten lost in its corporate interpretations. The only development to implement the secondary structures idea maintains a separate deed to the backyard shop, causing homebuyers to have to buy two pieces of property. For the most part, the history of the implementation of the *Ahwahnee Principles* has been a history of perversion.

Real estate developers instantly embraced the New Urbanism. Norman Blankman, writing in *Real Estate Finance Journal* remarks:

> Housing policy must be fundamentally altered. The single most important thing that should be done to bring affordable housing within reach for millions of people is to change zoning codes to permit more compact development. The first steps have been taken by a nationwide movement to reform US urbanism. Its principles are applied to a project proposed for Suffolk County, New York, which is an epitome of suburban sprawl. Calthorpe Associates prepared a master plan embodying neo-traditional principles. The plan provided on 840 acres the essential elements that a developer proposed on 2150 acres. The plan . . . establishes a strong sense of community.[5]

In every statement made on behalf of New Urbanism by developers and builders, expressions of concern for 'community' thinly veil broad hints about new ways to make profits.

Community solidarity and the new urbanism

John Gardner, writing in the 'Inaugural Issue' of *The Celebration Journal*, comments, 'The forces of disintegration have gained steadily and will prevail unless individuals see themselves as having a positive duty to nurture their community and continuously reweave the social fabric.' But what is meant here by 'community'? Gardner is not specific about the process of 'reweaving', and what exactly are those 'forces of disintegration'?

Emile Durkheim argued that pushing people together, or increasing population density and the social complexity of the community causes what he called 'greater moral density'. He writes:

> [T]here occurs a drawing together of individuals who were separated from one another . . . Hence movements take place between the parts of the social mass which up to then had no reciprocal effect upon one another. [Social relationships] consequently become more numerous, since they push out beyond their original boundaries on all sides.[6]

Durkheim goes on to say, in effect, the more complex the better, because a differentiated population is not in competition for the same resources. As the citizens 'perform different services, they can perform them in harmony'.[7] Thus, we might look to the New Urban community for creative coalition building on a local level, and improvements in participatory democracy, local self-definition and autonomy.

Historically, middle-class solidarity at the local level very often takes the form of obstinate resistance to the free play of large corporate interests: environmental activism, anti-development initiatives, consumer boycotts, food safety movements, subscription farming, local money, and so on. This is not the kind of citizen action the developers of New Urban towns have in mind when they invoke the various concepts of local solidarity. It is another, even opposing, kind of solidarity, a solidarity of consumer and corporate interests.

> Celebration will make its critical mark – for it breathes to life an intangible heritage, and that heritage is one of hope: a hope that large corporations can and will work with existing communities and local governments to accomplish great things, beneficial to both corporate life and to local entities.[8]

The corporate interpretation of the New Urbanism marks either the end of the twentieth century or the beginning of the twenty-first. Already there is talk that Disney will retreat from the field of town building, having discovered that they cannot 'storyboard' real life drama.[9] If Celebration is to be the last Disney town and not the first of many, as was initially claimed, perhaps it is because Michael Eisner, and not some neoleftist, was quick to see one of those pesky social contradictions that refuse to go away even after the fall of the Soviet Socialist Republic. How is it possible to create new middle-class neighborhoods supposedly founded on principles of ecological sustainability, civic involvement and so on, and at the same time neutralize in advance any convergence of people's interests which might frustrate the corporate definition of the citizen as pure consumer? The problems would go away if, and only if, the needs and desires of the citizen were precisely coincident with the goods and services produced by the corporation. But so far this is only a corporate utopian ideal.

Disney Democracy – Cause for Celebration?

In its currently unanalyzed state, the New Urbanism is fully shaped by the nuclear unconscious. Its politics are built around a nostalgic submission to the kind of absolute authority that replaced civic life during the nuclear age. From the very beginning, even before the first house was built, Celebration was mobilized against its citizens, against any possibility of meaningful citizen involvement. In all the official materials there is a compulsive emphasis on surface detail, and a corresponding vagueness when it comes to decision-making, governance, and so on.

> Celebration will surely be one of the most visible and potentially influential designs as we enter the next century, and it presents a subtle and complex reading of our future that many will find a welcome antidote . . . Celebration [is] new but tradition inspired . . . The architects decided to design some buildings to resemble large houses that had later been converted to apartments . . . Color, too was the subject of long discussion . . . Residential neighborhoods will have variety but a . . . neutral palate . . . The collection of favorite house types appropriate to Celebration led to a choice of six designated styles: Classical, Victorian, Colonial Revival, Coastal (raised cottage), Mediterranean and French (the last two giving spice to the mix). (pp. 37 and 41)

Alongside these remarks *The Celebration Journal* contains an article on the one-room school: 'older students taught younger students – there was a sense of mutual interdependence – today those same conditions can be recreated' (p. 19). Another article extols the virtues of picket fences 'just tall enough to keep in the chickens – and to keep small boys out of the petunias – but not so tall as to form an impediment to adult discourse' (p. 54). And yet another article explains the philosophy behind Celebration Health, the community HMO, a 'hospital without walls' that will reduce health care costs by accessing 'the gift economy' the 'untapped resource of thousands of volunteers' (p. 65).

Clearly what is being sold is not a two-hour celluloid fantasy but an entire fantasy life. And, by now, it is pretty widely known that not everyone who came to Celebration is having a good time. Some have expressed concern that Celebration is over-designed:

> [E]very last visual detail my eyes had taken in during my two-hour walk, from the precise ratio of lawn to perennials in the front yards to the scrollwork on the Victorian porches to the exact relationship of column, capital and entablature on the facades of every Colonial Revival, had been stipulated . . . I knew all that, yet now I felt it, too, and how it felt was packaged, less than real, somewhat more like a theme park than a town.[10]

And perhaps also like a graveyard. The shadow of death and its denial is a central theme which gives tension to many Disney products.[11]

Some residents are not happy that the town manager is a Disney executive and that conflict, even conflict over the Disney rules, is relegated to 'focus groups' run by professional facilitators hired by Disney. It seems that everyone tries to live comfortably within these rules, which require, among other things, white or beige window covering, no pick-up truck parking in the streets, only one garage sale per household in any given twelve-month period, and political expression limited to a single sign, no more than eighteen by twenty-four inches, posted no more than forty-five days prior to the election. Master planner and board member Robert A.M. Stern explains the rules:

> In a free-wheeling Capitalist society you need controls – you can't have community without them. It's right there in Tocqueville: in the absence of an aristocratic hierarchy, you need firm rules to maintain decorum. I'm convinced these controls are actually liberating to people. It makes them feel their investment is safe. Regimentation can release you.[12]

Stern's philosophical fatuity aside, he probably won't get much argument from the residents of Celebration. It is not as though he told them, '*Arbeit Macht Frei*.' These are, after all, surface matters, not much more intrusive than the required architectural details in the Disney pattern book.

But the 'one-room' schoolhouse is something else. At Celebration, it is not exactly 'one room', but several rooms, each modeled on the one-room school, that is, with grades one through six taught together. The planners were apparently not mindful that one-room schools in America were historically understood by those who attended them, and who taught in them, to be inferior to graded classrooms; that they were replaced by graded schools as soon as population density increased to the point that the community could afford education differentiated by age; that whatever virtues they may have had were dictated by necessity. The 'one-room school' concept is not based so much on a consideration of sound educational policy as on a desire for yet another nostalgic signifier of 'tradition'. It also, incidentally, prepares future citizens to live in arbitrarily configured, artificial social environments.

Ironically, this and some other features of the Celebration school (its insistence on using the discredited 'whole language' approach to reading) have deeply divided the residents of Celebration, giving us our first glimpse of postmodern politics at the neighborhood level. Instead of the usual political divisions between Democrats and Republicans, conservatives and liberals, and so on, Celebration is divided into 'Positives' and 'Negatives'. The Corporation was quick to label residents who complained about the school 'the Negatives' and the Negatives in turn labeled the Corporate organized supporters of the school the 'Positives', or sometimes the 'Pixie Dust Parade'. And how does the postmodern community deal with the Negatives? It encourages them to leave. Home buyers in Celebration must sign a contract promising not to profit from the sale of their homes within a specified time. The Corporation has informed vocal Negatives that it will not hold them to that contract if they take their profits and go quietly, that is, if they sign an agreement 'promising never to reveal their reasons for leaving Celebration'.[13]

On the side of the 'Positives' there is ample evidence that they could not be happier with the paternal set-up. A 'Positive' homeowner is reported to have responded to a question about the corporate form of government, 'Come on! Disney gives me a sense of security. They will insure a quality product and keep home values up.' Another defines Disney democracy: 'It is definitely a democracy because we can go to town hall and express our feelings. It's a very responsive government.'[14] A third remarks, 'If it was anyone other than Disney, we would never have done this. We just feel that they represent first class all the way. Anything they do is quality.'[15]

The panoptic house

A glance at the three house plans schematized in the Realty pamphlet, 'Welcome to Celebration', reveals one design element that is featured in all plans, independent of the price level of the house, namely: from the front door through the house and into the backyard, nothing obstructs one's line of sight. There are almost no architectural options that would allow one to move from room to room without being seen by someone presenting him or herself at the door. This has been remarked upon by architects as if it were some kind of design error.

> The [indoor] layouts make for great expanses of awkward space and such dubious innovations as downstairs master bedrooms off the dining areas of two-story homes. Robert A.M. Stern, the New York architect who is one of Celebration's master planners, described the interiors . . . as 'horrendous'.[16]

Rymer labels this a 'dissonance of surface and depth' between the inside and the outside of Celebration homes, but closer examination reveals a unifying logic: the panoptic style of house answers to a nostalgia for central authority that penetrates the most intimate details of life. It is designed to replace the unconscious. Perhaps because it does not require changes in local zoning laws, the panoptic house precedes the creation of entire 'new urban' towns. In the last five years the panoptic house has spread through virtually every new middle-class and upper-middle-class tract in America.

The panopticon domestic dwelling eliminates the possibility of discovering anything that might disconfirm the hypothesis of deep spiritual harmony. The entry hall has become the entire house. When one enters this space just beyond the front door, one has a sense of expansiveness. To the left is the 'living area'; just ahead, and up a step, is the 'dining area'; to the right, a large stairway leads up to a balcony that traverses the scene like a theater stage. The doors into the bedrooms are clearly visible just beyond the stage-balcony railing. Toward the back of the dining area, beneath the balcony, through expansive archways are the kitchen to the left and family room to the right, and still beyond through 'French' doors is the backyard. Never mind that each one of the functional spaces is smaller than its counterpart in the box-full-of-boxes suburban tract home built five years ago; it looks huge.

What is more important than the visual lie is the absence of any sacred center, any place of privacy, any place where some kind of local craziness might thrive unexamined by everyone who happens to come up to the front door. The hearth is not a hearth, but an opening in the living room wall covered with glass and surrounded by a thin veneer of natural material – slate, marble or limestone. There can be no sacred center, no place for being, because it is *all* center. This is a new kind of domestic space, without shadows, with nothing to be opened up by story or memory; it is a successful totalitarian attempt to remove habitability.[17]

The Threshold of Difference

The interpretation of the New Urban community and the panoptic house at Celebration and elsewhere constitutes a suppression, even an erasure, of human difference except as a (very) few demographic categories recognized by corporate community planners. This erasure takes the form of enforced, deep homogeneity, not just on matters of aesthetics, but on what constitutes proper authority, and even on the details of life beyond the domestic threshold. The panoptic house leaves no room for questioning the existence of homogeneous neighborhood standards, including those extending to the most intimate details of domestic life.

Neighborhood and subject before the new urban convergence

Neighborhoods as such are experienced from the outside. That is their essence. You can live next door to people for years, never cross their threshold or know their name, and still recognize them as being 'from the neighborhood'. If self-understanding is nuanced by imagined responses to neighborhoods and strangers who live in them, it is shaped by external signs, by documentary evidence. Viewed from their streets, each suburb, *barrio*, bourgeois urban enclave, tenement district; each place in the United States where people live side by side, easily lends itself to a totalizing experience of its visible elements, its surfaces.

There are exceptions – Houston's Third Ward, and beach and river-front communities – but overall, neighborhoods in the United States are supposed to exude socio-aesthetic homogeneity. Postmodern theory's assertions of depthlessness is in this respect suspiciously similar to official doctrine: that is, to representations of neighborhood advanced by banks, insurance companies and realtors, and to the enforcement of zoning ordinances, building codes, and laws governing public conduct. There has always been a moral structure to neighborhood representation, and this moral structure is very often linked to the definition of self.

When an individual enters a neighborhood, it is an occasion for a broad-based appraisal. Is the neighborhood safe or dangerous? Is its economic standing below, the same as, or above that of the visitor? Are the locals trusting, or suspicious and menacing? Is it too quiet or too noisy; too clean or too messy? Is the housing aesthetically appealing? Is the visitor comfortable around the people encountered there? Are there too few shops and services or too many? Even if this interrogation is conducted just outside the range of conscious thought, it is not about the neighborhood so much as it is about the visitor him- or herself. The New Urbanism rounds off the edges of all these questions in advance.

If the visitor can be said to have a self, it is composed in some measure of the answers she or he gives to these kinds of questions; answers that may be shaped as much by the desires and prior experiences of the visitor – and by the policies of banks, zoning departments, and so on – as by actual characteristics of the neighborhood. Thus both the self and the neighborhood first appear in the realm of the imaginary. A similar unconscious dialogue may occur when an individual is introduced to a new country or person, but *neighborhood* is among the most ubiquitous, accessible, and fine-grained progenitors of self. Micro-responses to neighborhood symbols and signs, to the range of public behaviors encountered there and to human difference, map being.

The apparent drive of the New Urbanism is to forge a vapid unity of self and place, unconstrained by history, seemingly unconstrained by what was once called 'the human'. At Celebration, the undoing in advance of any edge that might be capable of producing a human contour is accomplished by the creation of a 'backstory' for the town. Peter Rummel, president of Disney Design and Development, explained to Russ Rymer, 'One of the things we do particularly in imagineering, is we often create a story, a backstory. You write a whole mythology about something, and it helps you to stay true to your design of a show or a ride or whatever you are doing.' The mission of the Celebration

Foundation is to make the town 'feel like it has a tradition, even though it doesn't.'[18]

Michel de Certeau wrote that all urban space is built on broken pieces of the city's past, ultimately on the extermination of forests, of aboriginal inhabitants, of 'hidden places where legends live'.[19] He called the city a 'suspended symbolic order'. But it is clear that he did not think it possible for the urban to suppress its violent origins absolutely. He said 'haunted places are the only ones people can live in – and this inverts the schema of the *panopticon*.'[20] What de Certeau intended to suggest by this is that in a very real way the things and events buried in our neighborhoods, under our basements, are looking back at us. He refers to the relationship between the neighborhood and that which it suppresses as a kind of silent partnership – as 'stories in reserve'.

Let there be no mistake on this point: Celebration and every other New Urban community has its traditions, its 'stories in reserve', just like every other inhabited place on the face of the earth, but its 'stories in reserve' bear no resemblance to the 'backstory' provided by the real estate development company. The hidden places where legends live are the corporate back offices, and the all-but-forgotten heroes are Michael Eisner, Peter Rummel, Robert Stern and others.

The difference between the founding heroes of the New Urbanism and the other forgotten ancestors is attributable to the fact that the developers have gone to great lengths to produce a fiction of unity, one that blocks in advance the emergence of any human difference. There may always have been a collective desire for such styling clichés and affectations which would affirm an underlying sense of local neighborhood homogeneity. But until the emergence of the New Urbanism this desire had been attenuated by one of the most powerful extant social norms, that against unannounced and uninvited visits beyond the doorway or front hall of a home. Neighborhoods may have been marked by apparent unity, but the households were equally marked by extreme circumspection on the matter of identity, subjectivity and local practices. These latter were not neighborhood matters but domestic, and the uniqueness of this sphere has been protected by custom and law.[21] Such laws are a clear example of what is meant by the 'paternal metaphor': a symbolic function that allows us to replace the alpha male whose responsibility it was to defend 'his' women and children from any kind of intrusion.

Before the New Urbanism, neighborhoods, especially middle-class neighborhoods, strained to represent deep structural equivalences among local life forms (and here I am purposefully including plant life, animals, insects, and germs and viruses, because neighborhood moral integrity eventually references all of these). But there was an additional social contract to leave these forms

unexamined except under staged conditions – an invitation – or extreme
conditions – a subpoena, a search warrant. On the one hand there was the
assumption that people living next to one another ought to be deeply like one
another, and on the other hand there was an agreement not to test the
assumption of propinquitous moral homogeneity.

Cops

Some measure of the actual diversity of neighborhoods, and of domestic scenes,
in the United States is available on the television show, *Cops*. The neighborhoods on *Cops* are a New Urbanist's nightmare – the evil sibling of 'neo-
traditionalism'.[22] Watching *Cops* one learns that calls to domestic disturbances
often take the patrol officers into neighborhoods where tall weeds grow out of
cracks in the streets and sidewalks; that there are mobile home parks with
planned landscaping and temporary skirting around the base of the homes
between the floor-level and the ground; that there are other parks with no
plants, no skirts and the wheels still on the trailer, as if the entire neighborhood
is ready for a quick getaway.

Even if the neighborhood has a look of drab anonymity, it has a distinctive
'look' which, for better or worse, is recognizable to residents, cops and
outsiders. This overall appearance is grounded in a maze of local norms and
local meanings of pride, shame and limit, all of which is made manifest in the
forms and condition of the housing, the public spaces and the objects found
there. Are the lawn chairs and barbecues broken, rusted and fallen over, or are
they pristine? Are the garden hoses neatly coiled or snaking across sidewalks?
Are the street gutters filled with fast-food wrappers? Off to the side of the
action on *Cops* we see details of local practices which have unexpectedly become
a part of the scene of the action. Here, someone has converted an abandoned
right-of-way to a garden; there, the right-of-way has become a hangout for kids.
The look and feel of the place is manifest in the moveable stuff – pulsations of
human presence, accumulations of vehicles, the periodic movement to the curb
and back (or not) of garbage cans.

It would seem that very little work would be required to restore the fictional
moral unity of the neighborhood. But often, calling the police has the opposite
of the intended effect. Bill Nichols, who has made an important contribution
to the literature on 'reality TV', has commented specifically on *Cops*.[23] Nichols
suggests that *Cops* patrols 'the boundary of normalcy', that 'we are there on the
street with the cops', and that 'we share their point of view and subjectivity'.
What is intriguing about *Cops* is that this 'boundary of normalcy' is not always,
or even usually, set up around a part of the community that is openly taboo – a

brothel, a crack house, the scene of a murder. The boundary most often crossed on *Cops* is usually the interior of a neighborhood residence or the sanctity of a backyard, garage or tool shed. What *Cops* does nightly is to break the rule against sudden, unannounced penetration into deep domestic space. It is repeated exposure of domestic back regions that distinguishes *Cops* from other 'reality TV' shows.

After Lacan, Jacques-Alain Miller has suggested that racism and other forms of hatred for one's neighbors is based on a theft of enjoyment:

> We may well think that racism exists because our Islamic neighbor is too noisy when he has parties. However, what is really at stake is that he takes his *jouissance* in a way different from ours. Thus the Other's proximity exacerbates racism: as soon as there is closeness, there is a confrontation of incompatible modes of *jouissance*. For it is a simple matter to love one's neighbor when he is distant, but it is a different matter in proximity.[24]

One could argue from this position that the norm against uninvited visiting is designed to block this kind of jealousy, to prevent neighbors from witnessing one another's enjoyment, thereby permitting them to maintain the fiction of deep subjective homogeneity. The facts of intrusion suggest otherwise. Certainly differences in the ways of pleasure are revealed, but more often what one finds are differences in everyday, abject pain. The common denominator is *difference*: human difference which exceeds fictional imagination; difference that exceeds scientific finding now that sociology and anthropology have abandoned their mandate to describe us to ourselves. What is exposed on *Cops* goes beyond any representational conventions found in regular TV and motion picture neighborhood and domestic depictions.

Sometimes it is hot pursuit: a kid caught with a weapon or dope makes a break for it and is followed by the police and the cameraman into a neighbor's house, through the living room, the hall, the back bedroom, out the window, across the yard, over the fence. Often it is a domestic disturbance. In one episode, a seven-year-old boy refuses to leave his grandparents' home to return to the care of his mother and her boyfriend. The police find the mother and her boyfriend cowering in the street, complaining that the grandfather brandished a gun at them. The discussion over custody is brought into the grandparents' home, first in the living room, then in a back bedroom. Every square inch of the living room wall from floor to ceiling is covered with shallow shelves crowded with ceramic animals. In the bedroom there is a picture on the dresser that appears to be the daughter when she was younger. In the picture, she is wearing a white dress with red ruffle trim. The curtains on the bedroom windows are white with red ruffle trim outline. The feeling of unavowed madness is palpable. Certainly any sense of deep *petit bourgeois* homogeneity is rendered unsustainable.

A *Cops* segment shot in Kansas City begins with officers Mark Horkheimer and Tony White going to a house to serve a warrant. They knock at the door.

TW: 'POOlice!' (Long pause.) 'POOlice!'

Officer Horkheimer goes around the side of the house. White pushes on the front door and it comes open. He sticks his head in. The camera follows the line of sight inside the house; a scene of total disarray with furniture, clothing, utensils, packing boxes, in heaps and jumbles. In the middle of the mess, staring straight into the camera is a large, hostile pig. The pig breaks wind.

TW: 'Oh, that doesn't sound good.'

The officers call 'Animal Control' and begin interviewing the neighbors. They find a pretty girl about ten years old in the alley carrying a baby in her arms.

MH: 'Who's seen the pig before?' Has she seen the pig?
Girl: 'Yeah, I have.'
MH: 'What's goin' on with the pig?'
Girl: 'I don't know.'
MH: 'Does it ever come out and run in the street, or . . .'
Girl (interrupting): 'Yeah, it comes over here. My oldest brother, he was afraid, and he goes running home.'
MH: 'He goes and comes as he wants?'
Girl: 'Uh huh. There was a dog, too, with the pig. Sometimes they go out together.'
MH: 'So the dog and the pig run together?'
Girl: 'Uh huh. Sometimes they go out and sometimes they don't. But the dog ran away.'

Horkheimer rejoins White to compare notes

MH: 'Apparently the pig has been coming and going as it pleases and terrorizing the neighborhood with its buddy the dog. But the dog left the pig – like a divorce.'

This segment illustrates, among other things, the elasticity of the human capacity to normalize neighbors, no matter how different. There were a few smiles and puns, but the only discourse readily available treats the pig as an occasionally annoying neighbor, in a domestic relationship (in this case with a dog), a couple that 'comes and goes' and has their differences, as neighbors are wont to do. All of this would seem to substantiate Miller's thesis, except that everyone extended a kind of courtesy toward the pig – much more than occurs when human neighbors are upset with one another. The pig is the figure of excess, perhaps even excess enjoyment, routinely engaging in at least one of the seven deadly sins, and this particular pig lived up to its symbolic role. But everyone – cops and other neighborhood residents – was fully prepared to accept the pig as a kind of eccentric neighbor, not as someone (or something) to be despised for living a life of excess, for having a home just like theirs even though it was 'only' a pig.

Not every house or apartment in *Cops* is 'the same' as the one beside it, but they are ineffably *equivalent* in the moral totalization of the 'neighborhoods'. This moral homogeneity appears to be based on contractual and quasi-contractual agreements. This is not just a matter of demographics, of lending policies, zoning laws, residential inspection practices, and the like. And it is certainly not a matter of centralized rules governing the color of curtains, or parking for pick-up trucks. Local tolerance of disorder and noise levels, the appearance of front yards, behavior of children and dogs, even pigs, of what are taken to be 'appropriate' ways of appearing to be different, of the local limits of difference; all of this must be worked out between neighbors as a living agreement. It is precisely the human capacity to arrive at this kind of agreement with one's neighbors which has been denied by the New Urbanism.

When agreements break down, someone calls the cops. We know from *Cops* that these calls are often for banal delicts and infractions: a neighbor's dog poops in the yard; kids play on cars instead of in the playground; and so on. Across the United States there are countless variations on these agreements and much is made of these variations by realtors, residents and visitors. As a system of socio-cultural differentiation it has enormous integrity. The differences *between* neighborhoods in the United States are perhaps as great as have existed in any other time or place. But *intra*-neighborhood variation easily falls within Freud's 'narcissism of small differences'. The shirtless skinhead with jail tattoos on every visible part of his body does not stand out in the crowd that gathers for his arrest in his own neighborhood.

Not all the results have been exemplary, but the enormous variation of neighborhoods in America and local agreements on which this variation is based are the laboratories in which new cultural arrangements are being created by the people. The New Urbanism is opposed to naturally occurring cultural variation. One might go so far as to suggest that this is its reason for being.

The Mutation of 'Community'

What remains to be shown is the opposition between society and culture that opens the way for the construction of postmodern/New Urban/neo-traditional places. There are two kinds of 'significant' social relations or relations of human adjacency: *statistical* and *symbolic.* These two are not mutually exclusive, occupying at the same time the space or gap between people.

Statistical significance rests on the determination of frequencies of the occurrence of a characteristic or quality in the population. The determination of frequency requires the use of number, and number is based on the assumption of individuation. In this framework, a person, originally and in the first place, is not a part of a group. A person is an individual. All 'groups' are artificial, that is, statistical aggregates. Postmodern neighborhoods are aggregates based on specified ranges of household income, ethnicity and other selection criteria.

One cannot speak of the 'statistical significance' of the relationship between x and y unless x and y are conceived to be separate series. Statistics does not specify any direct relation between x and y, if any exists, only a co-relation. Any real relationship that might hold between conservative political beliefs and the rules requiring 'earth tone' exterior home colors in some Orange County neighborhoods (for example) cannot be specified statistically. What can be specified is the probable incidence of political conservatism (x) occurring by chance, compared to the probable incidence of earth tone exterior home colors (y) occurring by chance. When x and y co-vary and certain conditions of measurement and sampling are met that make it possible to assert that the observed incidence of x and y occurring *together* by chance is fewer than five times in 100, or one time in 100, their co-variation is 'statistically significant'.

In short, any causal connection that may hold *between* x and y is not relevant to statistical significance. Thus, *statistically,* we have neighbors who are like ourselves in several socio-economic particulars – skin color, income level, life stage, family size, and so on – without ever needing to *relate* to them beyond the polite exchange of clichéd platitudes. And so long as nothing upsets the balance of life in postmodern neighborhoods, the people living in them can pretend that the *statistically* significant relationships between them are also actually *socially* significant. They are held together by the bonds of consumerism. This could be called 'Yuppie Solidarity'.

The substitution of a statistical for a social relation is an administrative ideal, and as such it is the basis for the organization of increasingly large spheres of human life on both smaller and larger scales than neighborhood composition. For example, the content and timing of jokes in television situation comedies is based on a statistical analysis of the demographic characteristics of the population that is known to be flipping channels at the moment the joke is planned – the joke is written to hook and hold a significant proportion of channel surfers.[25] Every neighborhood that has been created as a part of a postmodern or neo-traditional 'housing development' is based on similar statistical analyses of the 'target market'. Let there be no mistake on this – the people who live in such developments do not necessarily see themselves as living in a bad joke. The people of '92707' live in housing tracts which pioneered the use of statistical models developed in the first place for electronic media audience analysis. They have adopted for themselves the slogan, 'Another Day In Paradise'.

Just because the statistical relation implies no actual connection between people does not mean that the people will refuse to value it. The statistical relation, perhaps because it contains nothing of the human, is jealously guarded by those who live it. Some of the sharpest conflicts in the postmodern world are over the presumed right to maintain a strict numerical definition of identity and the person: for example, the recent insistence by University of California Regents that 'minority groups' should not be given any statistical advantage in admission policies. A dominant pop philosophy of our current epoch summarizes its own position in the phrase 'looking out for number one'.

The *symbolic relation* specifies a human tie that is symbolically mediated, classically by language and contractual obligation. Both Freud and Durkheim provided accounts of symbolically mediated group formation wherein the function of other persons for an individual was to serve as model, object, helper or opponent. This should not be taken to suggest that symbolic relations are good (while statistical relations are bad). The symbolic tie is transparent to good and evil. It differs from the statistical relation in that *number* is not a basis for meaning or value. Two people can be connected via spoken language by thousands of symbols; and millions of people can be united by a single symbol.

There is, however, a point at which a fantasy form of the symbolic relation and the statistical relation converge. This convergence is precisely the principle governing relations with one's neighbors in New Urban developments, which continue to run smoothly according to corporate definitions of class solidarity, that is to say for as long as any real solidarity is effectively undermined. According to Freud (reading McDougall's *Group Mind*)[26] individuals in a group may have a common interest in a symbolic object, a similar emotional bias toward that object, and a degree of reciprocal influence – a contagion of emotions – which pleasurably carries them toward a single goal. Often it is a goal which none of the members of the group holds individually. This formation radically simplifies the range of possible outcomes for communication and joint co-operative activities that is inherent in the symbolic relation *and* in the diverse interests of the members of the group.

Freud points out that in groups that have *leaders*, the leader becomes the symbolic object of identification for the members of the group. Each individual narcissistically views the leader as the missing piece of his or her own ego. So long as they believe the leader fills in for their lack, they can love the leader and the group exactly as they would love themselves if only they were perfect and whole. So long as the leader appears to love all of them equally, every member of the group, even complete strangers, can believe themselves connected on a basic level, united by the same psychic lack which the group and its leader seems to fill. According to Freud, a 'primary group' (he also calls them 'artificial groups') is a number of individuals who have put the same object in the place of their ego ideals and have therefore identified themselves with one another in their egos. Thus, group solidarity based on the fantasy symbol that promises to complete the ego is just the flip side of envy. 'I want what you possess' has been 'democratized' to read, 'Everyone must be the same and have the same'.[27] This is also the postmodern/neo-traditional/New Urban ideal.

Postmodern neighborhoods may have administrators, even elected administrators, but they do not have leaders. An absence of leadership is one of their most distinctive features. We have seen that in Celebration, potential leaders are run out of town. So, on first examination they would seem to fall outside Freud's critique of artificial group formation. Or do they? I would suggest that the so-called neo-traditional, New Urban neighborhood *itself*, its demographic definition, aesthetics and paternal administration, replaces 'the leader' as the external fantasy object of ego-identification.

Let's go back to a symbolic neighborhood, one that has not been permitted to degenerate into a human aggregate, one that is not yet susceptible to psychic administration, the kind of neighborhood that appears on *Cops*. Within the symbolic-as-language, other people help, hinder, serve as positive and negative models, perhaps as 'pawns in the game of life'. Even a pawn in a language game retains more human potential than the highest ranking 'number' in the statistical or pseudo-symbolic relation that communicates only via career and consumer codes. Symbolic communication involves efforts to express oneself verbally and in other ways, calculated and naive moves to conceal expression, and strategic efforts to uncover information which others may wittingly or unwittingly hide. Culture guarantees *human* intelligence by not offering any guarantees on human interaction.

This kind of 'full communication', in Goffman's sense of the term, all but disappears in postmodernity. The New Urban development comes with guarantees. And the scope of the 'guarantee' now extends well beyond the boundaries of the New Urban community. Creative activities once requiring intense communication and risk for their accomplishment (for example, starting a successful small company, establishing democratic processes in a small community, or running a grass-roots neighborhood organization) are now done according to formulae. Success and funding depend on manuals, advanced degrees in non-fields (for example, 'Arts Administration'), how-to seminars, and hyper-specialized consultants for every defined stage in the process. Court-ship and seduction, once highly language-dependent activities, can now be accomplished by simply comparing resumés or otherwise providing proof that one has reached an acceptable level on an appropriate career track. If there is no courtship beyond a mutual disclosure of professional accomplishments and material possessions, biological reproduction can occur without there having been a sexual or other human relation. IBM inventor, Tom Zimmerman, is testing prototype wet wire data transfer devices so that when two people ('wet wires') stand close to each other in an elevator (let's say) or brush by each other in the street, or shake hands, they will exchange biographical or other facts stored on a credit-card sized chip in their wallets. 'Business cards', 'marital status', and so forth can be exchanged, to be downloaded later, just by rubbing elbows. Lacan's apocalyptic-sounding aphorism has in fact become a stated goal of postmodern medicine and reproduction in families headed by two pro-fessional adults.

Durkheim, and the sociology that is based on his work, did not believe that anything like this could ever happen. He thought that hyper-specialization in a complex division of social labor would ensure that human beings would always have to come together and negotiate their differences. He further believed that an evolving symbolic and legal order would serve as the singular medium for the negotiation of human difference. Durkheim understood that no individual is self-sufficient and that the symbolic order exists precisely to balance and mediate competing human needs under conditions of absolute interdepend-ence. More than this, Durkheim also believed that modern complex societies would exhibit strong *moral integration* because everyone would recognize their mutual dependence, at least at the level of a collective conscience.

This is perhaps the nicest theoretical picture that could have been devised for us. Unfortunately, the model of social complexity Durkheim provided is flawed. What he did not understand is an all too human tendency to abrogate, be blind to, abridge, and short-circuit interdependence, to ignore the rules of restraint that make life together possible.

In fact, the social circuit is, itself, designed so as to make possible a human blindness to the symbolic imperatives. In the simplest model of social complex-ity, person A and person C need not be related directly, but can be related through a third party, usually 'God'. If B is not a god, but merely a bureaucrat, he is able to keep the A:B relationship completely separate from the B:C relationship. In fact, his success as a bureaucrat is dependent on his ability to compartmentalize his relationships. A and C may be necessary in the division of labor, but their efficiency as specialists is predicated on their not having other than an abstract, instrumental relationship. If the boss (B's) supervision of C is affected by the fact that he worried about a complaint that A has threatened to file against him, that is, if A is *actually* influencing C, the system of differentiated roles and functional integration breaks down.

In actual situations governed by the principle of task specialization and functional integration, there is a necessary double effacement of both 'self' and 'society'. Functionally specialized and integrated workplaces, homes, neighborhoods, and so on, are of necessity composed of the absence of human relationships. Of course, human relationships may subversively occur there, but that is not what such settings are about. Thus, the secular division of labor in society was set up in the first place so that it might evolve into a kind of postmodern pretense of community. If it was a test, humankind is failing it.

It is sad to return to Durkheim's community, composed of every imaginable human type, with the realization that no one ever really *belonged* or had a place there, and that no one ever really *had* to enter into a relationship with anyone else, even those upon whom they were completely dependent. Hopefully, every postmodern individual will have a few human relationships made up on the spot for no apparent reason, even if structurally they can get along without them, that is, continue to misrecognize their mutual dependency. Hopefully some postmodernites will dream of making a difference instead of just *being* a difference. But these dreams can very quickly turn into bourgeois fictions of 'place', 'roots', or 'fame' that are routinely substituted for the missing links that might actually connect one person to others. The various postmodern fictional versions of the social relation masquerade as social life. This simply could not occur in a universe that was designed according to theoretical principles laid down by Durkheim, or even by Marx, to the extent that Marx believed the 'superstructure' to occupy an important supporting role.

A fiction of deep subjective unity at the neighborhood level cannot be based on possessions, whether these are material, mental or biological. Whenever assignment to a group is made on the basis of possessions, the group is designed to fall apart. Credentials are challenged, someone may claim to have more of the requisite possession or a better version of it. As soon as possession is the criterion, there is the possibility of a '*plus de jouir*' and the neighborhood devolves into hostility, as Jacques-Alain Miller suggests. Deep unity at the group level can only be based on shared *lack*. The basis for any spiritually homogeneous group is some *external* object that everyone desires and no one can have. Until recently, it was *security* in the face of nuclear threat that everyone lacked.

There are some historical groups for which it has been possible to specify the external missing object: security, the phallus, a healthy ego, 'agency.' In the postmodern world it cannot be specified – it is a phantom object that simply signifies lack, one's own lack and the same lack in the other. In the 1950s, lack was signified by the various guarantees of privacy. Uninvited visitors were not permitted beyond the threshold because they might see what the family did not have. So long as no unannounced visitor entered the private space of another, everyone could collectively maintain the fiction that they all were equally deprived of something. If any members of the group actually possessed the object rather than simply holding it as an ideal, the group would fall into jealous fighting over it. The norm against surprise visits permitted every family and other domestic unit co-operatively to uphold the fiction that no one has 'It', or possesses 'The Thing'. The norms of privacy also permitted every family to congratulate itself, if it wished, for secretly having It so long as they kept It sufficiently hidden to prevent anyone else from becoming jealous. Since no one knew what It was, any family would congratulate itself in this way, so long as no one would surprise them in their conceit.

In the 1990s lack is signified differently, by adherence to a small number of 'approved' surface details and by opening up domestic space for all to see. The entire home is visible from the front door and there is nothing to see. Everything is as in a stage-set. The entire design of the neighborhood is built around a fantasy guarantee of shared lack. The New Urban development precludes any possibility of unwanted intrusions into the back regions of the community – and the mind – by the simple expedient of eliminating any such space from the community.

The human prospect here is ultimately more horrifying than jealous racism, and could even produce a nostalgia for a time when a theft of enjoyment or a '*plus de jouir*' even in the 'other' was possible. The New Urban neighborhood realizes the impossible ideal of a solidary neighborhood in which *everyone* imagines themself to be *uniquely* in possession of the universal object of desire. In this way, they are, in fact, deeply spiritually homogeneous. They are collectively guilty because there is a gap or separation between the ego and its ideal. But they have all filled in the space of their guilt with the same fantasy of lack transformed into the appearance of a generosity of pure space painted white, a pure absence of being.

Notes

1. All invoked in the 'Inaugural Issue' of *The Celebration Journal* (Celebration, Fla: Walt Disney, n.d.)

2. Some historic evidence for this relationship between the bomb and the suburb is examined in my early paper, 'Baltimore in the Morning After,' *Diacritics* Summer 1984.

3. See, e.g., the 1996 Bank of America Position Paper opposing 'leap frog' development and low-density suburbs in favor of urban infill.

4. As reported by Russ Rymer in *Harper's Magazine*, October 1966, p. 67.

5. Norman Blankman, *Real Estate Finance Journal*, vol. 9, no. 4, 1984, pp. 70–74.

6. Emile Durkheim, *The Division of Labor in Society*, pp. 200–201.

7. Ibid., p. 210.

8. 'Editorial' in *The Celebration Journal*. (All further references to this journal will be from the editorial and will be made in the text.)

9. For a good discussion of the environment of corporate decision-making, see Jon Lewis, 'Disney after Disney', in Eric Smoodin, ed, *Disney Discourse*, New York, Routledge 1994, pp. 87–105.

10. Michael Pollan, 'Downtown Building is No Mickey Mouse Operation,' *The New York Times Magazine*, Dec. 14, 1997, p. 62. The same point was made earlier by Michael Sorkin in his 'Introduction', *Variations on a Theme Park*, New York: Noonday 1992.

11. For a fuller treatment, see my *Empty Meeting Grounds: the tourist papers*, New York, Routledge, 1992, pp. 74ff. Diane Ghirardo observes, along these same lines, that in his original plan for EPCOT (which was supposed to be a living community with real inhabitants, not just a theme park), Walt Disney stipulated that no older people would be allowed to reside there.

12. Reported in Pollan, 'Downtown Building is No Mickey Mouse Operation' p. 80.

13. Ibid., p. 76.

14. Ibid., pp. 80 and 81.

15. Rymer, in *Harper's Magazine*, p. 75.

16. Ibid., p. 70.

17. Brian Block has pointed out to me in conversation that this is the obverse of the experience reported by Michel de Certeau in 'Walking in the City', *The Practice of Everyday Life*, Berkeley: University of California Press, 1984, pp. 91ff.

18. Rymer, p. 18.

19. De Certeau, 'Walking in the City' p. 106.

20. Ibid., p. 108 (my emphasis).

21. At the individual level, and the level of the domestic establishment, these laws are designed to guarantee and protect privacy. The function of the same laws at the social level is to protect human difference. Structurally, it is very difficult to separate legal guarantees of individual privacy from guarantees of social difference, though the right is always trying to make this separation.

22. *Cops* is shot, edited, and presented in a 'real TV' format. According to the baritone male voice-over, the camera crew rides on patrol with 'the men and women of law enforcement' in cities and rural areas of every region of the country. At the beginning of each episode, a small block letter title in the lower left corner of the screen names the jurisdiction, e.g., North Boston or Lee County, Florida. The name of the officer in the car appears in the title space as he or she speaks about joining the force or about why he or she likes police work. Whatever the other messages of *Cops* may be, it is valuable, for the purposes of this paper, because it provides a unique, spontaneous glimpse of neighborhoods across the United States.

23. Bill Nichols, *Blurred Boundaries: Questions of Meaning in Contemporary Culture*, Bloomington and Indianapolis: Indiana University Press, 1994, p. 44.

24. Jacques-Alain Miller, 'Extimité', *Lacanian Theory of Discourse: Subject, Structure and Society*, ed. Mark Bracher, New York and London: Routledge, 1994, pp. 79–80.

25. Nick Browne has described this and similar strategies in 'The Political Economy of the Television (Super)Text', in *Television USA*, ed. Nick Browne, New York: Harwood Academic Publishers, 1994.

26. Sigmund Freud, *Group Psychology and the Analysis of the Ego, The Standard Edition of the Complete Psychological Works of Sigmund Freud*, London: Hogarth Press, 1955, vol. 18.
27. This transformation has been analysed by Juliet MacCannell in 'The Postcolonial Unconscious, or the White Man's Thing', *Journal of the Association for the Psychoanalysis of Culture and Society*, vol. 1, no. 1, 1996, especially pp. 30–31. She attributes the discovery of the structural relation of democracy to envy not to Freud, but to Rousseau.

II
BORDERLANDS

4 SAVE AS JERUSALEMS

ARIELLA AZOULAY

Jerusalem, as everyone knows, is the name of a city. But what this city is is difficult to say. There is an earthly city Jerusalem, and there is a heavenly one; a Jerusalem of stone and one of paper, a Jerusalem of iron and one of gold. There is a Christian, a Muslim, and a Jewish Jerusalem. Evidently Jerusalem is the capital of a Palestinian state, which is but a dream and a symbol of a national struggle; Jerusalem is also the capital of the State of Israel, which claims today to encompass all the other cities in one city 'united forever'.

Jerusalem is the name of a heterogeneous ensemble of spaces, events and meanings. This ensemble includes the struggle over the city's geographical and historical borders, its transformations along these two axes of time and space, the mapping of the city, the nature and structure of its urban networks – both physical and virtual, those that are contained within it and those that cross it and spread far beyond its geographical borders – and finally, the politics of naturalization and citizenship in and of the city. I will argue that any discussion of Jerusalem must encompass all these aspects at once and account for their interrelations. To understand the (human) reality of the city one must understand the (discursive) reality of its name, and through it ponder relations between maps and warfare, history and strategies of producing truth and subjectivity, concrete space and transcendent temporality. I will try to touch upon this complexity through a consideration of Foucault's conception of space and spatialization, focusing on the notion of heterotopia. I will relate this consideration to an analysis of the administration of Jerusalem's urban space, on the one hand, and to the work of two Israeli artists, Aya & Gal, which features an interactive map of one Jerusalem neighborhood, on the other.

During the thirty years of the Israeli occupation of East Jerusalem the organization of space and the distribution of representations in the public space of Jerusalem have been in the hands of one authority; one body has determined the rules of place, the rules according to which Jerusalem is governed and preserved as an archive of past and present. The occupation is also – always – an occupation of representations. Palestinians have been deprived of resources and political positions that would enable them to represent (their) past and produce and distribute images of (their) city. A recent demonstration of this fact was the year-long celebration of the supposed 3,000th anniversary of Jerusalem, organized by the municipal authorities with generous support from the state and Jewish organizations abroad. The entire event, the history it unfolded and the future it promised, was wholly biased, representing mainly the Jewish view of the city and eliminating the present national conflict. The opening ceremony took place in the Palestinian village of Silwan, located in the valley between the Old City and The Mount of Olives. A moment that was one of elation and joy for the Jews was one of intrusion and threat for the Palestinians, who protested at the end of the ceremony by flying balloons colored in black, green and red – the colors of the Palestinian flag. For a few ephemeral moments the Palestinians occupied a space in the city's heaven in which they could inscribe their own images and representations. But neither then nor now could they actualize their representations in a public space. The Palestinian residents of Jerusalem have no archive in which documents and images of their city's history can be compiled, stored, classified, and displayed at will, and there is no Palestinian agency that claims the authority for stating and enacting the rules for a Palestinian representation of the history of Jerusalem.[1]

This is a not uncommon description of the Palestinian situation in Jerusalem, and its importance for the political struggle against the many evils of the Israeli occupation of the eastern part of the city cannot be denied. And yet, politically useful as it may be, the description is questionable. One may ask, for example, what exactly is this space administered by the Israeli government, how homogeneous it is, and to what extent it is indeed governed and controlled by the Israeli authorities alone?[2] One may ask whether this description, just like those it seeks to replace, does not deny the heterogeneity of the different spaces gathered under the name 'Jerusalem' and reduce it to a homogeneous, single space – the national one. For if one considers Jerusalem only as a site of a national struggle, then it must follow the rules of this master narrative, that is, it must contain two distinct adverse positions and two possible ends, or 'solutions' – either a domination by one nation and the subjugation of another – whose traces in the city are wiped out, much like the remnants of an old tenant – or a partition of the city that actually doubles the national space.[3] I will try to show that in both cases the national space is made sacred and is privileged over all the other spaces of the city, in which there actually exist, or could have existed, complex interrelations irreducible to linkages between two parties external to one another.[4]

I will start with a short version of such a unidimensional history of an ethnic and religious space, which I will then try to reformulate differently. When the Arabs conquered Jerusalem in the seventh century, they had to remove vast quantities of accumulated garbage that covered the Temple Mount compound. They then built the El-Aksa Mosque on the site. The Crusaders conquered the city in 1099, slaughtered Jews and Muslims, removed all signs of Islam from the Temple Mount site, and transformed the Mosque into a Christian basilica. One hundred years later, Jerusalem was again purified when the Muslims returned and removed all crosses and symbols of Christian ritual. Descriptions of Jerusalem from the eighteenth century tell of a neglected city in ruins, overflowing with garbage. Extended Ottoman rule had neglected the acts of purification. Afterwards there was an Egyptian occupation, then Ottoman rule again, followed by British, Israeli, and Jordanian rule, each occupation accompanied by removal activities. The Israeli army conquered East Jerusalem, including the Old City, in the 1967 war. Immediately after the conquest of the Temple Mount, the Israeli army set about 'cleansing' the buildings and the minarets of Arab Legion soldiers, then vacated and razed an adjacent Muslim neighborhood. The David Tower Museum, founded in 1988, was the climax of a 'conservation' project that allowed the story of the city of Jerusalem, as written inside this museum, to be reconstructed via the removal of any details that might trouble the causal order justifying the occupation's continuation.[5]

But does the city exist only in one ethnic, religious or national space – does it really respond only to one history? The above description, which aims at banishing simultaneity and heterogeneity and imposing – each time anew – an image of hegemony, is not the only one possible; the following description restores some of what is lost by the former. Jerusalem's first museum – the Museum of the Greek Orthodox patriarchy – was established in 1858. In 1902, the Franciscan Museum was established in the Church of the Flagellation. In 1905, Bezalel's museum was established, with the goal of collecting Jewish cultural treasures from all over the world.[6] Indeed, this collection was the basis of the Israel Museum which opened in 1965. In 1923, the Supreme Muslim Council established the Islamic Museum. In 1938, the Rockefeller Museum was established in East Jerusalem, its main goal being to house archaeological treasures. Each of these museums represented its own point of view, a point of view that determined the rules of the place and its exhibits. The establishment of a museum marks a threshold consisting of treasure hoarding and control over the entrance gates with regard to what should be let in. But the museum is part of a discourse within and through which its status, position and authority are determined. The severe procedures of selection that a certain museum exercises reflect only the rules and constraints of the discourse within which it operates; rejected objects may still flourish outside this discursive space and its museal incarnation. When a museum participates in more than one discourse, it may allow more objects to pass though its space and employ multiple heterogeneous space-time frameworks: those which it crosses and those which it frames. This was the situation of the museums described above in 1948, at the time of the foundation of the Israeli state; they existed side by side in the space of simultaneity and heterogeneity.

The first description follows a 'sequential', diachronic pattern and presents the history of the city as a continuum of stories of occupation, defeat and domination. Each story replaces its predecessor and suppresses its claims to shape the city's present. The second description follows a spatial and rather static pattern and emphasizes certain privileged sites without the specific narratives associated with them. In the diachronic, sequential description, time and space are taken to be empty, homogeneous containers of events that the historian collects. In the spatial description, space and time are taken to be clusters of intersections, links and transmissions that allow the simultaneous coexistence of heterogeneous frameworks of spatialization and temporization (e.g. of the museum as a cultural site, of the objects and artifacts displayed in it, and of the visitors who pass through it).

The spatial description may be read, of course, as but another ring in the diachronic chain of domination stories, in fact as the culmination – and resolution – of the ongoing conflict, leading to a kind of urban harmony in which the peaceful coexistence of different points of view and competing positions is made possible. But such a reading would miss the essential difference between the two descriptions. The sequential pattern rests on a logic of detachment and purification – each new ring in the chain seeks to replace its predecessor and either removes or incorporates its traces into its new regime of identity. The spatial pattern, on the other hand, rests on a logic of simultaneity in the *present*, without governing the elements that comprise it.[7] In other words, subordinating the spatial logic to the logic of the sequential pattern eliminates the difference between the two descriptions, establishes the sequential pattern as a meta-narrative and imposes a homogenous conception of space-time.

It is for this reason that the spatial description is presented here not as the culmination of the sequential narrative, nor as its replacement. At most, the spatial description provides a sketch for an attempt to deconstruct the logic of the sequential description. Space, in the former description, is fragmentary, multiple, extends beyond the physical and the visible, and is never fully subject to domination by its masters, or even by those who claim to map and represent it adequately. Among the many subjects and objects that inhabit it, it also has an agency of its own. The spatial narrative proposes a grid, a network of interrelation, a structure of junctions in which not all possible passages and connections are manageable or controlable by a preconceived plan.[8]

The diachronic, sequential narrative exits within – but is not controlled by – the spatial description, as a possible link, another junction, a way out to another dimension, a passage to and from history, being always more *and* less than the story which unfolds it. Space is organized in many different ways, and it is impossible to describe it as a product of the acts and conscious intentions of urban agents – civilian, military or paramilitary – who claim to administer it. Space is not an object, a container, and these agents can never really become its master, for it is not written in the language of agency and authorship and does not respond to its syntax and semantics. Both space and the agents who use it are part of the networks in which they are enmeshed, in ways that undermine their professed identities and fool their explicit intentions, turning them all into knots of acted-upon-actions. I will try to exemplify this throughout this essay through the case of the 'Green Line', the borderline that tends to re-emerge when spatial agents try to wipe it out and to disappear when they try to re-inscribe it.

In November 1948 Israel and Jordan signed an armistice agreement and drew a dividing line. Both parties considered the line as a temporary concession and hoped that the political reality it created would soon change. At the talks, their representatives insisted on drawing the line with two different pencils. Abdallah El-Tal, the Jordanian, used a red pencil, while the Israeli, Moshe Dayan, used a green one.[9] The map was of small scale (1:20,000) and the two lines together had a certain width, which meant in reality a long stretch of no-man's-land, 60–70 meters wide and many kilometers long.[10] The line crossed streets and even houses, thus enlarging the area of friction and conflict between the two parties. The two leaders tried so hard to keep their agreements and disagreements in check, believing, so it seems, that they were capable of bringing everything under control, letting nothing evade their planning. Obviously, the result was just the opposite, and all along the dividing line there emerged an unexpected, unplanned area of conflict, that narrow and long no-man's-land created by the width of a pencil. It was as if the pencil had taken revenge on the hand that wielded it as an innocent, indifferent and ready-to-hand means of control. A year after the agreement, a fence was erected along the dividing zone. Neither of the parties liked the idea of such a conspicuous delineation of the border line, so the fence was officially named: 'a fence for the prevention of infiltration'. Infiltration had to be fought without a formal recognition of the transgressed boundary.

Foucault opens his essay *Of Other Spaces* with the assertion that the greatest obsession of the nineteenth century was *history*. The present period, adds Foucault, would perhaps be the epoch of *space*. 'We are in the epoch of simultaneity, we are in the epoch of juxtaposition, the epoch of the near and far, of the side by side, of the dispersed.'[11] In his various studies Foucault developed the concept of discourse as a criticism of conceptions of subjectivity and history, and endowed it with materiality, space and the structure of a network. Yet despite what he says in *Of Other Spaces* and in his various studies of the prison, the clinic and other heterotopic spaces, the spatial analysis Foucault conducts is confined *within* the temporal paradigm. The shift he describes as taking place from time to space, I contend, takes place within the framework of the first paradigm – historical time; it is this that makes it possible for him to present these two paradigms as successive. Foucault criticizes the discipline of history, which posed at its center a constituting subject, and stretches a comprehensive historic canvas of a different weave. He positions discipline, and disciplinary sites in particular, as the object of his research and writes their history.[12] Instead of a history of subjects, Foucault gives us a history of relations of knowledge and power, in which the subject is an effect or function.[13] It is true that this shift includes a spatialization of the subject and the creation of networks of relations, but such as are always given to observation, prediction and supervision; either from 'inside', from the supervisor's position, or from 'outside', from the historian's or critic's position.[14] The supervisor's or the critic's visual field remains homogeneous, its components can be placed together or projected on a single table, and the transformations that take place in it – including the breaks – are clearly seen. The visual field achieves its homogeneity by dint of being an intersubjective space of discourse and action; the power relations in this space are such that, at every point, any act of control may arouse resistance. It is one subject's position against that of another. The entire space is governed by subjects.[15] The network model of discourse in Foucault is achieved as a result of the conversion of intersubjective spaces of discourse and action. In this way, even when Foucault attempts to transcend the disciplinary site as a demarcated intersubjective space and develops the concept of discourse, he remains within the boundaries of discipline and history.[16]

Foucault's subject has undergone spatialization, and has been deconstructed into positions of addresser and addressee. But, in the last analysis, it acts, speaks, sees and is seen in an empty and homogeneous space-time – history's disciplinary site. History can be written, within and from this site, as the history of relations of knowledge and power, relations of governing and of being governed, of subjects by subjects. It was his critique of the discipline of history that led Foucault to spatialize the subject, the view and power, and to organize them within the framework of networks of relations (relations of power/ knowledge). The spatialization of power represents power as lacking a source; the spatialization of the gaze deprives it of a focal point. The spatialization of both together – meant to uproot the notion of origin and to speak instead of an entanglement of branchings lacking beginning or end – creates a network without a center, of relations between different points. But every point in the Foucauldian network of power-relations is a position that can only be grasped by a subject, and which in paradoxical fashion preserves, like a cell, the logic of force as stemming from a source and the logic of a focal gaze.[17] This position may enable the subject to regain his autonomy, which in this context means taking a point of view on the verge of the visual field without being a presence within it. But this point of view is a fantasy that exists only with regard to the virtual historical time-site, which forcibly fuses different perspectives into a single focus and attempts to manufacture for it a virtual visual field – the visual field of history – purporting to overcome the discontinuity and unruliness of both the view and the visual field in the modern epoch. This history is the history of spatial settings as produced in an historical time by subjects, as the realization of their plans, as the traces of their activities.[18]

Heterotopy (*heteros-topos*, other place/space), says Foucault,[19] is a social site designed for human activity, well demarcated, both spatially and temporally. It is characterized by a double logic of social space and the simultaneous coexistence of two or more spatial settings. Foucault mentions a few examples: the museum, the cemetery, the holiday village. These examples – closed and demarcated sites created by humans – prevent one from fully realizing the power of the heterotopic idea, for they restrict the concept to the point of view of sovereign subjects who define the rules of the game in heterotopic sites.

Heterotopy, I would like to argue, concerns the users of a site, not only its spatial organization. For in the heterotopic site, not only spaces may be multiplied – the simultaneous presence of the individual in these different spaces may be multiplied as well, for example, as a citizen in civic space, an address in virtual space, an outlet in a network, a body in a physical environment, and so on. Moreover, today heterotopy is not just a matter of well-demarcated sites. The whole world, or at least large portions of it, have become heterotopic. Heterotopic spaces are not mastered or administered by the subjects that inhabit them; their rules are not determined according to their will. If the world is heterotopic, or if being-in-space means being-in-heterotopic-space, going into and out of 'other' spaces is a matter of making and unmaking links and contacts, hooking or unhooking appliances, being in touch with someone, being exposed to the gaze of someone, being in reach of something.

Let us return to the passage from Foucault's *Of Other Spaces* concerning the transition between diachronic and spatial paradigms. This transition is itself described by Foucault in terms of the diachronic paradigm and the historicity it entails. Furthermore, Foucault reduces temporality to historical temporality and actually dissociates spatialization and temporization. His genealogical researches, which undermine the concept of historical time as an ahistorical container indifferent to the stuff it contains, still write the history of space within the framework of the diachronic paradigm. In *Of Other Spaces* he mentions some of the main stages in spaces' history without thinking about the spatial dimension of this history itself, once again assumed to be a homogeneous trunk in which some stuff – a variety of spaces in this case – is accumulated. But time is a rhizome that moves out in all directions, and the rhizome has no trunk, historical or otherwise.[20] One may domesticate some chunks of time and call them by names of periods and ages, divide them into centuries and decades, and yet each one of these chunks may possibly root itself in a different spot on the ground. The ground thus changes continuously and loses its coherency as these multiple temporizations cut through, cross, and interweave space in so many different ways. Space and time are always in the plural.

For Foucault, however, the history of time is still written in the singular. For this reason, perhaps, his analyses of social formations stopped at the disciplinary society. Disciplinary society is characterized by sites well demarcated by a single, recognized and visible borderline in which a single geographic and architectural space is shared by all the participants in the power relations. In the second half of the twentieth century these sites still exist and flourish, of course, but due to new technologies and new economic and geopolitical relations, they have been woven into and crossed by a variety of other spaces, shared differently by different inhabitants of the site. In these new spaces mobility, for example, is not measured by the ratio between travelling time and travelled distance but by other means, for example the ratio between time and the number of links crossed and created, or by the ratio between a site's surface and the intensity of temporizations that cross it. The forms of space-time in the late twentieth century are characterized above all by new and intense means for the temporization of space and spatialization of time (for example, access to air time for reaching more listeners in a wider zone, or access to historical time through visits to 'historical sites' or digging deeper into the ground of archaeological sites).

Gilles Deleuze touched on these issues in a short essay, *Postscript on the Societies of Control*. There he described the new social formation that replaces the disciplinary society in the West, briefly mentioning its new spatio-temporal dimensions: 'Control is short-term and of rapid rates of turnover, but also continuous and without limit, while discipline was of long duration, infinite and discontinuous. Man is no longer man enclosed, but man in debt.'[21]

Mastery and domination are not inscribed in space, and physical borders are no longer a main mechanism of control: man is no longer enclosed. The boundaries of domination have become complex and undetermined, they are disseminated everywhere, and yet they are mostly invisible. The seemingly inevitable link between a physical and a conceptual limit has been loosened, and the positioning of an individual in any particular place in social space is no longer necessary. Man has become 'man in debt'. Debt may be disseminated over different spatio-temporal frameworks and, one may add, it is not physically associated with the one who is in debt (as it was the case when man was enclosed), but is only linked to his or her address in so many virtual and non-virtual spaces. In such a world, it is not only time and space that are multiplied and fragmented, the individual herself is fragmented and multiplied according to the number of spatio-temporal frameworks within which she is linked. The individual does not act upon a world, but is part of an action of which she is never the source and for which her organs – hand, eye, mouth – are not means for a purpose, or expressions of her subjectivity, but links in anonymous chains of action – reaction. Together with many other instruments and objects, hand, mouth, and eye enable the functioning of systems – observation, communication, production – which in their turn make these organs effective and useful to the individual to whom they supposedly belong.[22] A short discussion of the hand and its spatial environment will serve here as an example.

The hand is a link in a network; it belongs neither to a sovereign citizen nor to an instrument that is supposed to serve him or her. It is the hand of the neturalized[23] citizen, the heterotopic-citizen, the one who becomes a citizen of liminal zones, of intermediate spaces, of passages; a citizen in passing, that is, one who is always in the process of becoming a citizen. The heterotopic citizen tries to create an intermediate environment 'inside' the networks of social interaction, knowing all too well that there is no place 'out there'. The heterotopic citizen lives in the immanent tension between two elements that structure the field of social action. On the one hand, the position of the subject within a defined field of discourse and action that allows one to judge and act with a certain authority and claim to knowledge; these are remnants of the disciplinary society. On the other hand, the unavoidable intertwining of the subject's acts within conflicting networks of interaction that lie beyond his or her control, undermining his or her plans and intentions and constantly robbing his or her actions of their meaning.

When this is the nature of our most basic spatial condition, the spatial inscription of socio-political demarcations, boundaries and borders cannot be presented any longer in terms of territory and territorialization, at the very least not *only* in these terms. Nor can the individual be 'contained' within the space occupied by his or her body. The limited space of one's body is multiplied in these 'other spaces', it is represented or has correlates in these spaces. But all these spaces are always somehow 'out of joint' – there is no exact overlapping, no one set of spatial coordinates that contains them all. These other spaces are populated with persons, bodies, objects, instruments and appliances; they are interwoven in different, partly intersecting and partly unrelated networks of speech, vision and interaction. And in the constant shifts and transitions among these spaces the hand provides the ticket, the license, the right of passage; it serves as a gatekeeper and a bridge; it crosses and builds distances; in short, it allows space to become spatialized.

When the concept of heterotopia is applied not only to space but also to those who use it, it becomes possible to overcome that constituting subject of which Foucault tried to rid us in order to escape the strictures of historical discourse. Extending the notion of heterotopia to include space users, and taking the hand as an agent that escapes the logic of subjectivity, one is able to deconstruct the claim of the national-constituting-subject in the city of Jerusalem. Let us follow different hands through the urban space of this city.

Before the conquest of East Jerusalem, the parties to the conflict recognized the armistice line, usually called the Green Line, as an international boundary only *de facto*, but never *de jure*; their city was one and whole, only it was temporarily and brutally divided. In June 1967 the Israeli army crossed the Green Line between Jordan and Israel and conquered East Jerusalem (along with the rest of the West Bank).[24] The unrecognized borderline was unilaterally erased by Israel and ever since, the entire city has been in Israeli hands, which have alone taken charge of all its municipal affairs. Shortly after the war, in defiance of international law, Israel annexed East Jerusalem along with other territories surrounding it. After June 1967 the Green Line was systematically erased from all official maps and gradually disappeared on the ground as a result of massive urban development. Erasing the line was the form of its inscription, and massive urban building projects were soon planned and performed in order to erase further what the initial erasure had inscribed. It was only when Israel tried unilaterally to erase the borderline that the city became divided for the first time in consciousness – not only on the ground – and a dividing line that both parties recognized – the one in order to wipe out its traces, the other in order to re-establish it – was inscribed.

Following the occupation of East Jerusalem in 1967, and as an expression of its claim to sovereignty over the entire city, Israel annexed the occupied part and granted its 66,000 Palestinian inhabitants the status of permanent residents, giving them the option of becoming its citizens. They only had to swear allegiance to the Jewish State, the political incarnation of the Jewish national subject. Not surprisingly, very few Palestinians (no more than 2,000) have accepted this 'generous' offer of a change of sovereignty and quick naturalization. As a result of this act of 'unification', the city was again divided into classes of inhabitants. Most Palestinians are no longer citizens of their own city. Their status as permanent residents was – and still is – conditional: Palestinians who leave the city for a long period for purposes other than education lose their right to live there (B'tselem 1997). This right is conditional upon the Israeli law of immigration that grants them the status of permanent residents. Legally, they have become foreigners who immigrated to their own birthplace and their right to stay there is not automatically granted to their children. Thus the unified city is based on a system of nationalist apartheid in which the non-Jewish residents are systematically discriminated against in terms of rights, housing, urban and economic development, and education.[25]

The ambivalence and indeterminacy of the Green Line, which divided the city between 1948 and 1967, embodied the heterogeneity of the city and the fact that it inhabits heterogeneous spaces and times which can neither be reduced to a single geopolitical space nor contained in a single historical span. This conflict was inscribed onto the surface of the city and its resolution was visibly postponed. Direct confrontation between the hostile parties was deferred, allowing for a certain co-existence between conflicting fantasies and narratives. The different heterogeneous segments of which the city consists – national, religious and ethnic groups, forms of life, collective memories and dreams – were not forced into a hierarchical system and no primacy could have been granted to any of them.

Such a hierarchical system was, however, an inevitable consequence of the Israeli occupation and annexation of East Jerusalem and of the official, imposed unification of the city. The hierarchical system has been maintained within a fixed demographic framework. A special governmental committee for the development of Jerusalem found in 1973 that the population ratio was 73.5 percent Israeli Jews to 25 percent Palestinians, and the official policy of all Israeli governments since has been to maintain this ratio by various means.

Massive development of Jewish neighborhoods and Israel's legal administration
of the city have created a continuous, if fragmentary, Jewish area in and around
the city and have cut deeply into the Palestinian settled areas, shattering the
Palestinian presence in and around the city into isolated fragments.

There are three main mechanisms for maintaining this population ratio, as
well as the Zionist image of Jerusalem:

a) *Cartography.* The Israeli sovereign draws the city maps and uses cartography as a means of maintaining its demographic 'balance'. The annexation of
East Jerusalem and its surroundings incorporated as much land as possible
for future Jewish development and as few Arab suburbs as possible. Later
changes in rather flexible municipal boundaries served to bring more Jewish
neighborhoods into the city. Today there are 411,000 Jews and 166,000
Palestinians who live within the jurisdiction of the city of Jerusalem. But a
different map, which would have taken into account the dynamics of Palestinian life in and around the city and the geographical reality in the Palestinian
sections of the city, would have yielded a very different demographic ratio.

b) *The legal apparatus* The conditional residency granted to the Palestinians
enables the Israeli authorities to control the demographic composition of the
city on an almost daily basis.

c) *Planning and housing* The ratio of new housing for Palestinians as
opposed to Israelis is 1:8. Palestinians are much more often denied permission
to build than Israelis. Between 1967 and 1995, 64,000 apartments were built in
Jewish neighborhoods (half of them on confiscated land that mostly belonged
to the Jordanian government) and only 8,000 for Palestinians.[26]

The Israeli occupation and administration of Jerusalem is based on a misleading
ambiguity between representations (maps, statistical tables) and the represented objects (the urban space, population). On the one hand, the occupation
regime uses the clean, objective language of scientific discourse, and assumes
its distinction between objects and their representations. On the other hand,
the same regime takes a very active part in the production of both the
represented objects and their discursive representation, as if there were nothing
to distinguish between them.[27] When the data gathered 'in the field' do not
yield the desired map of Jerusalem, the map changes; when the reading of the
map yields data that smack too much of apartheid, the data change. Jerusalem
too, that most metaphysical of all cities, has witnessed the loss of the clear
metaphysical distinction between the original and its simulacra, between territory and map, between the 'thing itself' and its representation.

But this is not a result of the fragmentation of the visual field and of the field of action or of the dissemination of the forces acting in Jerusalem. On the contrary, it is the result of Israel's domination and over-determination of these fields of vision and action. What seems for a moment a postmodern practice of representation – a free and open market of identities, territories, maps and narratives, a real fair of simulations – appears upon closer scrutiny to be the result of conscious manipulation of the data, the map and the territory, of rigid control of the different markets, and of massive intervention in the various practices of exchange. Israel administrates the city to fit its desired map, and it draws the maps so as to fit its desired city. As a result 70,000 out of the 170,000 Palestinian permanent residents find themselves living in suburbs outside the official territory of Jerusalem, and they are gradually losing their status of residency.

At the basis of Israel's illegal policies in Jerusalem lies the faith that the Israeli state and its agents are at one and the same time an incarnation of a universal principle of transcendent subjectivity and the most powerful expression of one particular national subject. Israeli governments have acted and spoken as the sole legitimate representative of the Jewish people and its holy city. They have acted as if they believed that the world, history and their neighbors are but clay in the hands of the potter, the Israeli sovereign – as if they could impose their will on reality and mold it single-handedly to their own view. 'Let there be no Green Line,' they have declared, 'let the city be united', and the divided city has become one. Jerusalem thus becomes the arena for the manifestation of two aspects of subjectivity: on the one hand, the subject as origin and expression of mastery over others; on the other hand, subjectivity as self-mastery and self-determination. Presented from the perspective of this double subjectivity, the Green Line appears as a scar in the heart of the Holy City, and the city itself as an entity that has existed continuously, with no interruptions, throughout 3,000 years of history. The city has sometimes been desolate, of course, in ruins, and fifty years ago it was divided, but there has always been one discrete entity, they claim, which has undergone destruction and division. But the Israeli attempt to present a unified city never succeeded in erasing completely the real and imaginary line that still exists in some other spaces separating two hostile communities, two peoples – conquerors and conquered.

So many hands have a stake in the city of Jerusalem; so many people and groups are fighting to get their hands on the city, to manipulate its past and future, digging its ground to find new data to support these conflicting claims, reconstructing the evidence and preparing themselves, and their city, for the Day of Judgement. These hands intermingle with and interfere in the work of others who build energetically and destroy, no less energetically, what others (and they themselves) have built. These hands draw maps, open some paths and close others, inscribe some dividing lines and erase others. Above all, they try to mold the city's image and superimpose it on all other competing images.[28] These latter hands are an extension of a national subject, acting as if there may never be another chance to do whatever is not done today in this city where time stretches to eternity. And almost all this work is being done in the name of a *past* and for the sake of a certain *future*; in a diachronic time conceived as a homogeneous, empty container in which events are chained uninterruptedly from the depths of the past to the most distant future.

But what about the *present?* When one cares only for the past and the future, the present tends to disappear. If one were to ignore for a moment both the past and the future, this hectic urban scene I have just described would suddenly be emptied of all national and religious narratives and the transcendent subjects that animate it. One would see the city as a multiplicity of heterogeneous spaces and irreconcilable points of view. All one can see are busy hands, gentle and violent actions, rapid, seemingly arbitrary changes in the city's surface: people working, travelling, staying home, surfing the Internet, turning on their televisions, zapping from station to station, watching a local network, then a global one, shopping at a shopping center, getting stuck in traffic jams, sitting in a bar or a coffee house, visiting friends, going to the movies or to the theater. These sites of social life change from area to area, from neighborhood to neighborhood, they differ among themselves and not only according to the great division of the city between East and West Jerusalem.

The way the Israeli occupation divides the city is not unambiguous. Today the city seems to function as a single urban unit. For the innocent, or ignorant, eye, the few checkpoints manned by a few policemen and soldiers scattered here and there on the outskirts of Arab neighborhoods, as well as the ruins of some old military posts, are the only visible, often misleading witnesses to the Green Line. But these checkpoints need to be looked at more closely. As a symbol of the passage from the Jewish part of the city to the Arab one, they defy Israel's policy of unification (though Jews and Arabs clearly have different access to and mobility through these checkpoints). For the purpose of security they are quite ridiculous, since the imaginary dividing line may be crossed at numerous other points. The national logic of unification creates 'security reasons' and the need to control the passage from the Arab to the Jewish part of the city, but too strict a control contradicts the unifying imperative. In fact, the checkpoint is a symbol of paradox for the Israeli domination over Jerusalem, where the unifying efforts only deepen the dividing forces that resist unification. Recently, a possible ethnic solution to the paradox began to be tested by Israeli authorities: an ethnic purification of the city ('the silent transfer'; see below). Such a purification would enable the peaceful coexistence of the spatial and (Jewish) sequential narratives of the city; once the city becomes entirely Jewish it will be possible to subject the spatial narrative to the sequential – national – one, to transform Jerusalem into 'Jerusalem – a city united forever'. In the meantime, however, the checkpoints function as filter. Various spaces leak through the holes, however; link into other spaces, escape all efforts at unification – diachronic or synchronic.

The refugee camps on the city's outskirts no doubt bear witness to the most difficult, brutal and painful aspects of the occupation in the urban space of Jerusalem (they are also the camps of which Jews who inhabit the western part of the city are least aware). On the other hand, in the seams of the city, in neighborhoods like Pat and Beit-Tzaffafa, the differences between east and west are barely visible, especially for those who are not residents of these areas. A visitor may mistake the Arab houses of Beit-Tzaffafa for the villas of the occupiers, and the eight-story building project in neighboring Pat for the housing estates of the occupied. As a matter of fact, the difference in height is just one more example of the evils of the occupation – highrise construction is permitted only in Jewish neighborhoods; the Palestinians must solve their problems of density and overpopulation in other areas, outside Jerusalem.

The professed policy of the Israeli state since 1967 has been to turn Jerusalem into a Jewish city. The unification of the city is no political utopia meant to serve all parties involved. Its aim has not been to build bridges between hostile nations and religions. It is, rather, a unilaterally metaphysical fantasy projected by Israelis onto thousands of years of Jerusalem's history. But the city is harsh and stubborn; it does not respond in kind.

The 'Jewification' of Jerusalem follows a logic of 'catch as catch can' – every area under the city's municipal jurisdiction which has not yet become Jewish is a target for a second conquest that would make it Jewish, or at least more Jewish than it is now.[29] The 'Jewification' of the city, which is closely related to its unification, seeks to enlarge the Jewish area of the city at the expense of the Palestinian and thus gradually homogenize the entire urban space, imposing on it a national-Jewish identity. But the practice of 'catch as catch can' yields opposite results. Instead of expanding the homogeneous Jewish area, it creates more and more heterogeneous areas, which are complex and fragmented, containing more zones of friciton and conflict. The entire city has become riddled with enclaves. Israeli authorities imagine themselves to be the subject and master of the city, responsible for the production and management of its space and its borderlines, capable of administering mobility, routes of passage, movement of populations, patterns of construction and modes of exchange (of instruments, artifacts, smells, news, weapons, health, friendship and love).[30] But despite all the means and measures of control, surveillance and repression at their disposal, which serve to keep the Palestinians in a kind of a third world enclave, circulation and exchange take place constantly in ways that defy the nationalist rules set by the Israelis.[31]

The circulation of goods, messages, images and people takes place in 'other spaces' that are not necessarily subject to the rules of the national space determined by the Israeli authorities. Apart from and besides the authorized routes, communication, circulation and exchange take advantage of the many loopholes scattered all along the borderlines in Jerusalem. These loopholes are not accidental gaps but the very stuff of which those lines consist. Because of the presence of these loopholes, the border may interpellate all its users with a double message: 'respect me' and 'transgress me'; it may declare at one and the same time: 'here is a border' (discriminating between Israelis and Palestinians) and 'there is no border' (for the city is united and welcomes all its residents alike). This Janus face of the border appears in the national space, but also in economic, educational and other daily spaces. Israeli authorities act as if they believe themselves capable of controlling which face of the borderline will appear where and when. But borders have lives of their own and their users different ways of using and abusing them. Thus, for example, Israel has built Jewish neighborhoods as enclaves in the midst of Palestinian areas in an attempt, step by step, to accumulate more and more urban territory, hoping that somehow the new enclaves will form a new border. But the rapidly growing Jewish enclaves have turned the Palestinian neighborhoods, too, into enclaves that continue to spread (through mostly illegal construction of new houses) and often trespass borderlines, erasing some and inscribing, or threatening to inscribe new ones.[32] Whereas Jewish neighborhoods were supposed to purify the national space, fortify it, and demonstrate Jewish sovereignty in it, they often serve opposite ends. Instead of purifying space, they only emphasize its heterogeneous nature; instead of fortifying it, they create more areas of friction and increase the threats to the safety and well-being of those who dwell in and around them; and instead of demonstrating Jewish sovereignty, they create more opportunities to challenge and question the claim of the sovereign.

Straightforward Jewification seems politically impossible under the present circumstances. As the urban space is planted with as many Jewish spots as possible, the neat division of the city between Jews and Arabs collapses. Israel's policies have brought Jerusalem to the verge of a spatial unification of such a heterogeneous kind that no transcendent temporality is able to chain it in a consecutive chain, no single narrative can contain it, and no political subject can master it. Unification – if one still wants to use this word – takes place through numerous links and a constant weaving and unweaving of knots in an undefined network that escapes the rule of all authority.

The question that remains, however, is this: doesn't a reading of the city that seeks to interpret the present as an ensemble detached from the past and from the subjects who claim to act in its name and define its representation, not itself produce just another limiting narrative? Isn't a reading that obliterates the past similar to one that obliterates the present? The first thing to be said is that no reading strategy, however successful it may be, can on its own homogenize the heterogeneity of the city. Having made this point, it is important to stress that between the two strategies there is a radical difference. The first, spatial and 'presentist' strategy, which reads the city as a heterogeneous multiplicity of relations (economic, political, religious, ethnic), completely ignores the claims of nationalism. This strategy is self-defeating: instead of *recognizing* the existing heterogeneous multiplicity and conceiving the national narrative as one element among others, it seeks to eliminate unwanted elements and *produce* an abstract, 'better' multiplicity. Thus the present is endowed with an abstract heterogeneity that ignores nationalism, its embodiment, and its role in urban life and space. This abstraction actually works to create a new chain in the sequential narrative in the form of a multiple spatialization that would be the new historical agent driving the old national subject off the stage. But even if it were to be triumphant, the spatial strategy has neither the means nor the motivation to eliminate the national subject, the many forms of its narrative, and its various agents.

The second, more common strategy, is the one enacted by the Israeli government. The heterogeneous multiplicity of the city is made subject to the Jewish national narrative, to the mechanism of its exclusions, and to the constraints of its temporality, which stretches from antiquity to eternity and is constructed in cycles of destruction and redemption. Within this framework, Jerusalem is 'a city united forever', temporarily spoiled by elements that introduce divisions and fractions. Unity is understood as 'united under Jewish sovereignty', and the threatening elements are interpreted accordingly, in nationalist and ethnic terms. Dividing elements are impure elements and they must be removed.

A few years ago, Aya & Gal, two Israeli artists who live and work in Jerusalem, launched the project of *neturalization*. Neturalization does not take place in a state, does not involve laws of immigration, and is not related to national identity; in short, it goes against the conventional laws of naturalization. The procedure that baptizes one a citizen of a nation-state is, first of all, a means of determining the identity and status of the individual and his or her relation to the political sovereign. Neturalization is, on the contrary, a *process*, not a procedure; it exists for the duration of this process and does not strive to achieve any end. Alluding to Deleuze, one could say that Aya & Gal's neturalization is an act of the order of *becoming*, not of *being*; in fact it actually consists of an active denaturalization. Through this process, one intentionally becomes a stranger in known, common situations, strips oneself of one's identity, or navigates one's way in purposefully strange, ready-made environments, in which one exercises a gradual accommodation. Neturalization deconstructs or better, dissolves, the unity and seeming coherence created by a dominating point of view – the point of view of the national subject, for example. It places one between different regimes of power and knowledge, exposing the bold stitches with which the dominant regime tries to hold together a heterogeneous reality. Aya & Gal's project, I should add, is in no way a practical proposal, a politically conscious attempt to come to terms with the problem of naturalization in general or with the civic status of Palestinians in Jerusalem in particular. Nevertheless, it can easily be related to these problems, and to the specific situation of Jerusalem. Speaking about their work, Aya & Gal have said: 'Schematically, the neturalized-citizen lives in two separate worlds. The act of neturalization puts him in a liminal position, which he could not hold in any other way. He becomes a neturalized-citizen when he dons the suit. But it can be any form of separation, although *separation* isn't exactly the word. We are not attempting to disconnect him from this world, but neither is there any attempt to fix him in the other world he's being offered. The intention is to place him for a moment in a non-territorial position, it being unclear where the world begins and where it ends, and what his data are.'

One day, Aya & Gal's neturalized-citizen got into an automobile. His body was encased in a layer of skin made of latex. He embarked on a drive around the YMCA tower in Jerusalem, one of the more elevated points in the city's center. The car rolled through the streets of some neighborhoods of West Jerusalem, an area that has become the heart of the city since the 'urban surgery' performed by Israel after 1967. The car moved like a spider in the middle of its web around the tower which enjoys a panoptic view of the city.

There was one neturalized-citizen sitting in the car that morning. He sat in the driver's place, a place usually intended for sovereign citizens trained by the state to drive through its streets, the place of a person deemed worthy to navigate on his own, choose direction, have intention. But the place of the citizens is in fact only the place of an accessory which, when put in its place, can propel the car and drive it properly. The state has forged this accessory – a free, yet obedient citizen – in its factory but hasn't yet cast it inside the automobile. The automobile sets out on its way only after the citizen has sat in his place. Inside the car that toured Rehavya that morning sat a different sort

'drive round the YMCA tower'

of citizen – a neturalized one. His sensory environment was dulled by a layer of
latex and honed by the electronic eye that saw for him. A video camera
attached to the steering wheel documented every turn, every stop. On sharp
turns the neturalized-citizen's legs were captured by the camera lens in an
overview, looking down from the steering wheel. The video camera functions
as the eye of the automobile; the neturalized-citizen, with eyes in his head but
with his head covered in latex, uses the camera as his own eye. This original
journey became the basis for the creation by Aya & Gal of an interactive map
which later became, in turn, an invitation to spectators (users of the interactive
map) to become neturalized. This invitation is addressed to anyone who uses
the map. As the artists put it: 'The neturalized-citizen operates all intersections.
When you watch a movie you watch somebody else doing something. When you
touch the mouse it's as if you've shut the car door and driven off. You are
inside the network, you and the network are one and the same thing, whoever
comes to see becomes part of it, whether he wants to or not.'

Aya & Gal projected their interactive map of Rehavya's streets in the YMCA
tower, and later in the Documenta X in Kassel. The spectator is invited to enter
a sealed space, sit down and take hold of the mouse; she then sets out on a

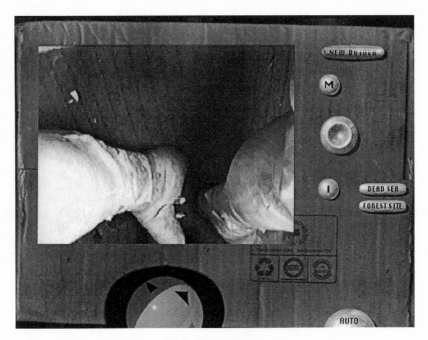

'neturalized citizen's legs'

journey of navigation. She is invited to become neturalized for a moment, in
the network of streets, while driving by means of a mouse. The seeing car
provides her with new fields of vision and never allows her to assume the
position of a detached spectator. For, the interactive map projected on the wall
is the opposite of a territorial advantage (a 'view from above', for example), a
means of control over space. In this map, the overhead view from the tower is
replaced by the systematic view of the photographed map, which has been
composed of hundreds of segments filmed by the video camera while driving
through the city streets. The drive is guided by a conventional city map in
which a hierarchical dimension is emphasized: a panoptic view at the center,
not far from the prime minister's residence, and a vertigo-like drive in the
streets that surround it. The transposition of the drive from the video to the
interactive map was mediated by a different sort of non-hierarchical map, made
entirely of strings of numbers. It is these numbers that enable one to drive
through the intersections and road junctions. Each number signifies an intersection, or an encoded link between several intersections, and thus all intersections in the numerical map are linked equivalently to all other intersections.
'The project at the YMCA is another type of observation', Aya & Gal argue:

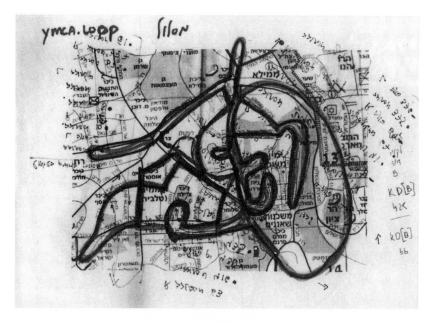

'interactive map'

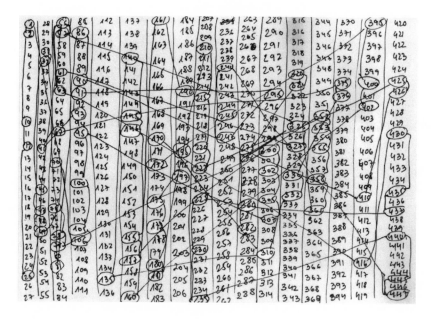

'strings of numbers'

Let's assume that a spy takes the CD of the interactive map to Syria and wants to
identify the escape routes from the prime minister's residence, located in this area. He
can do it interactively. He can decide that he wants to drive left. You film a movie, scan
the information, and the question is how you splice it and organize his navigational
possibilities. From an innocent movie of the streets of Rehavya, such as any tourist
could take, it can turn into top secret information. The way in which it's arranged
turns it into an interactive map that had better not fall into the Syrians' hands; it's
already in the same class as an aerial photograph.

The hand is an important part of the body. It is an agent of action, an
instrument for the realization of one's will and intentions. The hand is not
conceived as a free agent, of course, its activity is 'in the hands' of the one
whose hand it is, its master. The hand is a unique manifestation of its master's
identity, personality, social status and manners an expression of his or her inner
nature. For two centuries at least, this same hand has also supposedly represented its master as a legal person, equal to others, and expressed his or her
right to be represented as such. For more than two centuries, in Europe at
least, this hand has reached out every once in a while to the voting booth and
given expression to its master's reason and free will, his ability to make a
reasonable decision;[33] this is the hand of the citizen. In modern political
systems voting has become the main instrument of political representation, and
the citizen's hand has become the material seat of his or her political freedom.
The voting citizen is a subject who gives expression – by means of a simple,
handy gesture – to his or her inner, private will, thus turning it into a public
voice.[34] Together with the eye that sees and the mouth that speaks, the hand
takes part in the interplay between interiorization and exteriorization, subjectivity and citizenship, freedom and equality.[35] But the hand, whether it belongs to
a citizen or to an illegal resident, to a sovereign or to a subject (*subjectus*), does
not simply belong to its master. The hand (and the same goes for the eye or
the mouth, of course) is a mediating agent of actions whose origin and end lie
far beyond the control of its master, the one who acts. The hand is an
instrument for the realization of working-plans inscribed in the networks of
interaction and communication and in other instruments of all kinds distributed around civic, geopolitical and virtual spaces. The hand is not a free agent
and not the obedient agent of a free subject. It is controlled by different
networks and various objects, continues their work, prolongs or extends them,
and signals their presence. The hand is almost always a necessary organ of a
certain instrument, an important switch in a network. When the modern citizen
appeared a few centuries ago, the hand was still a major organ in the use of
force. Today most (western) citizens keep their hands near their pockets,
manipulating buttons and plastic cards, moving them timidly and politely

among instruments in a very limited area, yet reaching very far indeed. With a slight move of a hand so many gates open wide, vast distances are bridged, and foreign worlds become accessible. Yet once inside the webs of techno-science and the networks of the media-market, that same mighty hand is interpellated, constrained, and manipulated by powers far beyond its control. But one thing is clear: there are no subjects in this web, transcendent or otherwise, no sovereignty either.

The industrial revolution and later technological developments created new conditions for the hand's movements and activity, transforming the spatial relations within which it is entangled. Once an organ for carrying objects in space, the hand has become hooked to vehicles, an organ of transportation and commuting in real and virtual spaces. The hand has become capable of taking on acts and roles once associated solely with the leg, freeing the entire body for all kinds of new activities. Means of transportation have been improved to such an extent that distance and travel time leave less and less an impression on the body and mind of the travelers. Our daily environment is filled with instruments ready to hand, designed for ever more controlled and precise movements. Gadgets of all kinds interpellate the hand, call upon it to operate them, and through them to activate the entire systems to which they are hooked. The hand has become the servant of two masters: the person of whose body it is an organ, and the networks of interaction and communication to which it is hooked through all kinds of instruments.

This double mastery over the hand deconstructs sovereign subjectivity, liberates us from the interiority of the subject and from the tyranny of the truth of the self. This opens the possibility of an *interactive* freedom sustained by continuous acts of reverse naturalization: 'Usually', say Aya & Gal, '[the position of] the spectator [in art, in culture] has no interactive dimension. The spectators just see everything through their eyes. Seeing is completely detached from action. The neturalized-citizen has an interactive dimension, but he is generally blind. The blindness stems from the fact that he is never sure in which space he is present. He is in a transient position. Neither here nor there.'

In postmodern, multiple space, every place can be located in countless maps, pictures and networks. Every point in 'real' space is in principle locatable in other spaces of at least two different types: those in which it is represented (by means of photos, maps, and so on) and the virtual spaces of interaction and communication that place it alongside other points, connect it to or separate it from them. Real or virtual, a place in postmodern, multiple space is nothing more than a connection and crossover point from place to place.

These spaces of interaction and communication cannot be reduced to a given physical territory; they are not coterminous with any such territory, nor do they cancel it out. Technology has destroyed the metaphysical conception of place as possessing value, essence, meaning, and a peculiarity of its own. It is possible to argue that the French Revolution balanced the damage to the metaphysics of place to a certain degree by inventing the citizen. The citizen is an address – and an intersection – in the virtual space of the republic. If the citizen is an address, man is the one who lives there. The Man within the citizen ensures – according to the metaphysics of the sovereign subject and its modern state – that this address will not remain a virtual one. Man ensures the metaphysical rights of the citizen: to be the possessor of an essence, value and peculiarity, to be the origin of acts of interaction and communication, to be the source of their meaning and value. The invention of the citizen was in fact the invention of a new place – the human being. In the *Declaration of the Rights of Man and of the Citizen* the citizen is defined as someone who is supposed to defend the human being, his natural rights and his liberty by means of membership in a sovereign political community. For its part, the humanity of man provides the citizen with an anchor for his universal pretension, the pretension to possess rights and experiences that cannot be abrogated by the political order. The man that finds expression in the *Declaration of the Rights of Man and of the Citizen* is a 'natural' human being, whose body is his own property, who has a right to his body. He is endowed not only with freedom of movement and speech, but also with freedom to operate the instruments at his disposal. Rights ascribe concrete acts and alienable objects to an inalienable transcendent subject. Hence the person who dwells in this body and operates these instruments conceives of them as alien, subject to his or her authority. The freedom to operate and the desire to make use of instruments merge in the regime of a subjectivity that is beyond the world of appearances.

The concept of man mediates between the citizen as an address in virtual space, and the individual, concrete place in real space. The citizen's possessions – the body being his or her real estate – are a real place that in principle cannot be appropriated. Assets can be replaced in accordance with market conditions, but the body is unique as the fixed irreplaceable residence of the sovereign citizen. This place, and the space in which it is planted, compete with the virtual space in which the citizen is only an address, an intersection, and a crossover point. There are thus at least two orders of space involved here: a growing movement toward the colonization of the individual and the world takes place in both. Each makes a claim to totality and denies or ignores the other. The entire world turns into a heterotopic space.

Aya & Gal's neturalization project reinterprets the concept of heterotopy in a way that distances it from the examples provided by Foucault, yet follows his logic more closely. There can be no heterogeneity of time and space as long as the human being remains their sovereign and continues to occupy a homogeneous territory. The heterotopic dimension of the world is a daily occurrence that takes place at surface level, in the abrasive meeting between spaces, in the emergence of new configurations. Heterotopic neturalization takes place on the boundary between places. It is an act of individuals that only seldom exceeds the boundaries of private action, to take place entirely in that undefined space that is open in principle to everyone and in which each individual is nothing but an address. This work of Aya & Gal is another attempt – perhaps as hopeless as its predecessors – to escape homogenizing and arbitrary networks of exchange and communication without falling into the closed world of the subject and the spaces managed by the State and its apparatuses.

I am not trying to suggest that the world of techno-science, with its virtual spaces, random events and inevitable catastrophes, is necessarily superior to the modern world in which identities are fixed and pinned to nationalities and territories. Nor would I agree to the meta-narrative implied by such a suggestion, especially not to its *either-or* logic. I have assumed that the postmodern resident of diverse spaces is always already here and there, and that a unified, coherent world has been lost forever. Always serving two masters or more, we may at best navigate our way between different spaces, resisting all temptation to stick to the one and disregard the other(s).

And Jerusalem? Jerusalem must be de-naturalized. It must be allowed to be what it really is: a complex of irreconcilable spaces, a real heterotopy. One should free it from the hold of this or that transcendent, national subject. The sanctity of the city must turn into one more value of exchange in its many heterogeneous economies, a code for one more map of sites and itineraries. The condition for all this is, of course, the termination of the Israeli occupation and the granting of citizenship to its Palestinian residents. This citizenship should be equal, *de jure* and *de facto*, to the one to which Israelis, who share the same geographic and urban space with them, are entitled. But how would this solution be attained?

If this citizenship were Israeli, this would mean that Palestinians would have to acknowledge the Israeli occupation and accept the status of a minority in a Jewish State. If it were Palestinian, assuming that a sovereign Palestinian state emerges, the apparatus of Israel, the nation-state that has generated the occupation, would simply be doubled and inscribed in two apparently separate, yet entirely nationalized, urban spaces. The establishment of a Palestinian state that would grant citizenship to the Palestinian residents of Jerusalem, which seems a more feasible solution, would probably solve the 'national' problem within the national space, but no other. The separation of the two national entities would probably blur for some time the concrete links between the different spaces gathered within the two national spaces. From a minority, the Palestinians would become a majority in their own state and they would be sovereign and autonomous in shaping their own identity.

But is this solution, which most Palestinians and the Israeli left are striving to bring about, an adequate remedy to the question of identity? Or is it actually a poison which will trap the Palestinian people for many decades to come in the space of a nation-state ruled by the drive to remove ethnic heterogeneity and achieve national homogeneity? This remedy is poisonous insofar as it requires Palestinians to call upon themselves, in the name of their transcendent, national identity, to close the passages to the spaces in which they have managed to become integrated during thirty-one years of Israeli occupation. The remedy is dangerous insofar as it requires Palestinians to cut their links to those networks in which they have managed to become intertwined, despite all the restrictions that have been imposed upon them by Israeli authorities. The separation into two nation-states resembles surgery on a body, a more or less traumatic but nevertheless isolated event, after which most systems gradually recover and get back to normal functioning.

It is highly plausible that after such geopolitical surgery, that is, after the foundation of an independent Palestinian state, the systems of power and networks of economic, political and social relations would return to their 'normal' oppressive functioning in the local, national and international spaces. The Palestinians would remain a minority dominated and exploited both economically and politically – only now they would be governed by two rather than one cluster of state apparatuses and their inferior position *vis-à-vis* the Israelis, with whom they would still be entangled, would be reproduced. The Palestinians who push for this solution, the establishment of a separate nation-state, are responding to what Deleuze and Guattari have called the 'national axiom',[36] which is part of the system of the majority, and as Deleuze and Guattari formulate it, seeks 'to accord the minorities regional or federal or statutory autonomy, in short to add axioms . . . this operation consists in translating the minorities into denumerable sets or subsets, which would enter as elements into the majority, which could be counted among the majority.'[37] In other words, even if a Palestinian state were to be created and the territory under Israeli control divided, it would still be appropriate, at least for some time, to think about hierarchized relations between a national majority and a national minority within the single space of national existence.

Another conceivable, though less realistic, possibility is for Israel to give up its definition of itself as a Jewish nation-state and become 'the state of all its citizens', Arabs no less than Jews.[38] But even then the threat of new and renewed colonial and postcolonial forms of domination would frame the

Palestinians in a third-world enclave inside Israel and reproduce their inferior position in the many virtual spaces opened to Israelis in recent years by the hi-tech industry and its transnational corporations. The new conditions would not emerge *ex nihilo*; they would transform present conditions in a way that would only intensify and emphasize the ugliness and injustice, which thirty years of Israeli critique of the occupation have disguised because it was so utterly restricted to the national space.

Those who have hoped to purify their national space from 'foreign' elements that are not 'natural' to it would be surprised to find the excluded elements shaping from the 'outside', even more powerfully, perhaps, that which has remained inside. And those who have hoped to end the occupation by making nationality one (negligible) component of citizenship, instead of deriving citizenship from nationality, would lose the position from which it would be possible to resist the future exploitation and oppression of Palestinians.[39] These would surely continue in a new integrated state, for the latter would be even more integrated into the global economy, and its minorities would resemble third-world immigrants in the metropolitan slums of the West even more than they do now.

Therefore, utopian or dystopian as the two political solutions mentioned above may sound, they still do not automatically mean emancipation or redemption, for there will always remain those other spaces in which one becomes entangled in opaque networks no one will ever control. Thirty years of occupation – or fifty or a hundred, depending on how one counts – are imprinted in the Israeli-Palestinian space, and in all those 'other spaces' of the region. The traces of these years cannot be removed by a single political act or event – path-breaking, heroic – or momentous as it may be. The creation of a Palestinian state would not yield an 'authentic' Palestinian existence or a 'purified', more enlightened Israeli one. The various forms of occupation imprinted in the spaces of this region must be taken into account by every political vision and act and must be reorganized in order to reduce the evils they produce more or less systematically. Reducing all spaces and networks to the framework imposed by two unified, but all too similar, homogeneous national spaces, dominated by two quite similar national utopias, would not help in achieving this goal. Instead we need to create as many heterotopic sites as possible and allow them to thrive at every juncture and point of passage where human bodies are or can be linked. We must 'assert the power of the nondenumerable, even if that minority is composed of a single member. That is the formula for multiplicities. Minority as a universal figure, or becoming-everybody/everything.'[40]

Notes

1. This is a general and generalizing claim. It characterizes the condition of the Palestinians as being deprived of their own place, which means, among other things, the archive as a possible Palestinian place. The fact that there may be some archives in which documents about the Palestinian past are stockpiled does not contradict the exclusion of Palestinians from the archive as a possible place of their own. See also my discussion of the structural subjugation of the Palestinian narrative to the Zionist one in 'Clean Hands', *Documenta X: The Book*, vol. 3 Ostfildern: Cantz, 1977. On the archive as place, see Jacques Derrida, *Archive Fever; A Freudian Impression*, trans. Eric Prenowitz, Chicago: University of Chicago Press, 1996. For the conflict between Israelis and Palestinians over the organization of the public space and collective memory, see Azmi Bishara, 'Between Place and Space: On the Palestinian Public Space', *Studio*, no. 37, 1992. Bishara relates the exclusion of Palestinian traces from Israeli public space to the Zionist ideology of 'rejection of the Jewish Diaspora'. The Diaspora Jew and the Palestinian are two 'Others' whom the Israeli Zionist discourse systematically excludes.
2. This paper is an attempt to think about Jerusalem outside and against the binary logic imposed by the occupation, which necessitates a seemingly clear-cut opposition between conquerors and conquered, unification (imposed by the conquerors), and partition (demanded by the conquered and a few among the Israeli left). As two opposed political solutions, unification and partition demonstrate an adherence to a sacred national common space. Those who enforce a united city are ready, if not willing, to continue the oppression and discrimination against the Palestinian residents in the name of a sacred Jewish national space. Those who struggle for the partition of the city have as their goal a Palestinian nation-state with its own sacred national space. Instead of this binary logic, I will try to describe the city as a complex mesh of networks, spaces and times, which are not given to any clear-cut binary division. The political demand to put an end to the occupation is not abandoned, but the conception of the occupation as an entity with clear-cut 'ends' is questioned.
3. On Landau's exhibition in Jerusalem, especially the video documenting her drive in a garbage truck from the Israel Museum to the garbage site in the Palestinian village of Tel-Azaria see Azoulay, 'Clean Hands'.
4. The distribution of means and opportunities to create other spaces or to link into existing ones is not equal among Israelis and Palestinians. For example, a precondition for links to, and mobility within, globalized spaces is the modernization of physical space, which has usually taken place only when and where this space has been nationalized, or at least has become an object for the administration of a nation-state. Without a nationalized space of their own, the Palestinian access to the spaces of globalization is restricted and mediated through different Israeli agencies. Masao Miyoshi ('A borderless world?', *Documenta X: The Book*, 1997) points to the continuity between old forms of colonialism conducted by different nation-states and postmodern forms conducted by trans-national corporations. Even if these corporations call into question the very idea of the nation-state, they can emerge only within its framework. See also in this context Saskia Sassen's analysis of the way the global economy is anchored in postmodern, highly developed metropolitan centers ('Global Cities and Global Value Chains', *Documenta X: The Book*).
5. The history on display in the museum at the moment completely ignores the partition of the city in 1948 and the Jordanian control of the city for nineteen years. The city is presented as a site and object of conflicts among the three monotheistic religions, while the national struggle over the city recedes into the background and is de-politicized. For more on this point, see my 'With Open Doors: Museums and

Historical Narratives in Israel's Public Space', in *Museum Culture*, Minneapolis: Minnesota Press, 1994.

6. The aim of the Betzalel Museum, as in other Zionist museums etablished in the first half of the century (for example, the Ein-Harod Shrine), was to gather 'the treasures of Jewish culture' of all times and places. The construction of the realm of knowledge and objects does not differ in principle from similar constructions taking place within the framework of the history museum. However, in a way that reminds one of the classification of animals in Borges's Chinese Encyclopaedia, one of the categories, 'the Zionist Museum', tries to include the entire table of categories and threatens to undermine its logic of classification. See Foucault, *The Order of Things: An Archaeology of the Human Sciences*, New York: Vintage, 1994.

7. See Benjamin's discussion of space and the present: 'History is the Subject of a Structure Whose Site is Not Homogeneous, Empty Time, but Time Filled by the Present of the Now [*Jetztzeit*]', *Illuminations*, ed. Hannah Arendt, trans. Harry Zohn, New York: Collins, 1973.

8. The distinction drawn here is indebted to the one formulated by Gilles Deleuze and Felix Guattari (in *A Thousand Plateaus: Capitalism and Schizophrenia*, trans. Brian Massumi, London: Athlone Press, 1988, between smooth and striated space.

9. On drawing the border line, see Meron Benbenisti, *Jerusalem – A Place of Fire*, 1996, in Hebrew.

10. Alongside this accidental no-man's-land, there were other no-man's-lands that were created intentionally, territories in regard to which the parties agreed not to agree, that is, it was agreed to postpone the division. Thus the map of division actually reflects the reluctance of the two sides to come to terms with the division of the city.

11. Michel Foucault, 'Of Other Spaces', *Diacritics*, vol. 16, no. 1, 1986, p. 22.

12. Discipline is described as the collection of practices of subjection to rules, supervision and monitoring, of bringing to justice, of application of authority, of delimiting boundaries – and in general as the modern game between subject, power and truth. Discipline – in both senses, indeed, as the disciplining of knowledge and as the disciplining of the self by the self and others – became institutionalized, according to Foucault, in the form of a regime of discourse in the modern epoch.

13. On the spatialization of the subject in Foucault, see Adi Ophir, 'Michel Foucault and the Semiotics of the Phenomenal', *Dialogue*, vol. 27, 1994.

14.. For more on history and critique in Foucault's texts, see my 'Sign from Heaven: Murder in a Moonlit Arena', *Theoria ve Bikoret*, vol. 9, 1997, in Hebrew.

15. For example, those that design the ultimate in control structures–the panopticon–in which even the observers are observed in turn, or that build walls to prevent masturbation, or provide cover for it.

16. When discipline comes to rest in the individual, when it is networked over the entire social space and exhibits more and more phenomena that can no longer be observed at the physical site of the confined institution, Foucault turns to history to reconstruct the shattered visual field. History, that is the homogeneous and empty container in which the discourse is unfolded, and which reveals the breaks that have occurred in it, provides Foucault with a sort of virtual disciplinary site as well as a point of view that both establishes it and is established by it. This disciplinary site is not a closed unit of space, or alternatively a place of confinement; it is a virtual and homogeneous unit of time and space: 'When the constituting subject is got rid of, the subject itself must be got rid of, that is arrive at an analysis which may account for the constitution of the subject in the course of history. And this is what I term genealogy, that is a form of history that accounts for the constitution of the knowledges, fields of discourse, domains of objects, etc., without relying upon the subject' (Foucault, *Dits et Ecrits III*, Paris: Gallimard, 1994, p. 147.)

17. These branchings are nevertheless reflected within boundaries given to observation and control, within mutable relations of power, that exist in the tension between

potential power and effective power, legitimate power and arbitrary power, the seen and the unseen.

18. On a point of view on space and a blind spot within it, see Azoulay, 'Sign from Heaven'.

19. Foucault 'Of other spaces' *Diacritics* vol. 16, no. 1, 1986

20. The notion of the rhizome is borrowed, of course, from Deleuze and Guattari.

21. Gilles Deleuze, 'Postscript on the Societies of Control', *October* 59, 1992, p. 6.

22. In *Discipline and Punish* Foucault speaks about handwriting as an apparatus for the constitution of subjectivity. For more on the hand, the eye, and the mouth as instruments and their role in the construction of subjectivity, see Azoulay, 'Sign from Heaven'.

23. The word 'neturalize' and its derivatives has been coined as a combination between 'network' and 'nature' by Aya & Gal in relation to their work. Quotations from the artists, unless otherwise noted, are taken from as yet unpublished interviews with them.

24. 'Temple Mount is in My Hands' shouted the commander of the conquering unit into his field radio, coining an idiom that has become a symbol of the Israeli conquest.

25. Much effort is invested in maintaining or inventing the Jewish 'character' of the city, especially in building new Jewish neighborhoods all around the eastern part of the city. In the last year there have been discussions on several plans for the development of Jerusalem, all of which support the Israeli policy of Jewification of the city. Speaking before architects about the annexation of an undeveloped area on the western outskirts of the city for the purpose of building new Jewish neighborhoods there, Mayor Ulmart reiterated this policy: 'We have to influence the patterns of growth in the city so that they would fit the desired character of the city': the 'desired character' meaning maintaining its Jewish majority, of course.

26. The data are taken from the reports of B'tselem, an Israeli organization for human rights in the occupied territories (B'tselem report 1995, *Policy and Discrimination* [in Hebrew]) and from the daily press.

27. The Israeli policy and plans for the development of the city have always given preference to political considerations over urban ones. The construction of new neighborhoods immediately after the Six Day War was planned in order to eliminate the traces of the Green Line; the annexation of new areas all around the city was planned to make possible rapid growth of the Jewish population; the ongoing discrimination in the allocation of construction permits to Arabs and Jews has been a clear attempt to force Palestinians to leave the city.

28. The hectic work being done in Jerusalem is only partly overt. Much of it is clandestine, concealed from the public eye. Some hands work gently, others are violent, but everyone seems very busy, and everything seems awfully urgent. Everything must be done before it's too late; before further urban development takes place, or before too many Palestinians infiltrate the city, or before more land is confiscated by the Israeli authorities, or before the peace talks resume, or before the next war, or before the Messiah comes.

29. 70 square km have been annexed to Jerusalem since the Six Day War (B'tselem, 1995).

30. The description presents a more complex picture of the relation between occupiers and occupied without, however, erasing the differences between Arab and Jews in their ability to move through and to multiply spaces created by the Israeli occupation. The entire urban infrastructure in the Palestinian sections is conspicuously less developed than that in the Jewish sections, and the gap keeps widening. But the multiplication of spaces is not merely a result of a more or less developed infrastructure.

31. The border Israel imposes on the Palestinians does not function according to the intentions of its authors; it acquires new meanings and functions through the interpretations given by those who use it. Conceived as a means to limit, it actually

functions as an amplifier of production; instead of closing more tightly the gaps in the boundaries separating Jews and Palestinians, it creates ever more and new gaps; and instead of consolidating governmental control, it dilutes it.

32. See Faisal Husseini's plan to strengthen the city's eastern ring, which is like a negative of the Israeli plans for the same area. Israel is capable of blocking Husseini, of course, while the reverse is not true, and yet Israel's capacity to implement its plans does depend, among other things, on Palestinian reactions to those plans.

33. *His* ability first, the rich before the poor, and only later *her* ability; the ladies came last.

34. In assemblies as well as in voting booths, by raising one's hand, casting a vote in the ballot box, or pushing a button, the hand expresses an inner will and a public opinion, taking part in the decision-making, in the process of collective self-determination, and in the formation of the general will.

35. The hand of the Israeli citizen is the hand of the sovereign. The sovereign – as defined by Agamben – is he who dominates and imposes the law on the outside, on the other, on the abnormal, on the exceptional; he who demarcates, determines the threshold, distinguishes the excluded from the included (see Georgio Agamben, *Homo Saccer: Sovereign Power and Bare Life*, trans. Daniel Heller-Roazen, Stanford: Stanford University Press, 1998. In distinction, Palestinian hands are not like this. Theirs do not represent their 'owners', the persons to whom they belong, as legal persons equal to others, as citizens who have the right to be represented. At most, the Palestinian hand is an overt expression of the origin and identity of the one to whom it belongs. It is a means in the hands of the Israeli sovereign, who may use fingerprints for the purpose of identification and identity as the mark and cause of discrimination. Palestinians' hands are not part of a space in which identities are determined according to what one does, but according to one's origin. In Jerusalem, a Palestinian hand may remain 'within the law' if it is the hand of a manual worker who serves others, or it may transgress the law in protest and rebellion by throwing stones or Molotov cocktails, brandishing posters, or drawing graffiti on walls.

36. This is the same axiom that guides Israel's policy toward illegal immigrants and guest workers. Israel uses guest labor in order 'to free itself' from its dependency on Palestinian workers, thus severely damaging the already weak Palestinian economy. 200,000 workers have joined the Israeli labor market in the last three years. They are deprived of almost any rights and their work conditions are worse than in any other labor-importing democracy.

37. In the words of Deleuze and Guattari: 'Once again, this is not to say that the struggle on the level of the axioms is without importance: on the contrary, it is determining.' (Gilles Deleuze and Felix Guattari, 'The Included Middle', *Documenta X: The Book*, Ostfildern: Cantz, 1997, p. 470).

38. That Israel should become the state of all its citizens is a recent leftist slogan. But most people on the left who use it have only Israeli-Arab citizens in mind, and not the Palestinians under Israeli jurisdiction (who are supposed one day to have their own state alongside the State of Israel). The call for one democratic and secular state, which will truly be the state of all its citizens, has been renewed lately by some Palestinian intellectuals, such as Edward Said and Gada Karami.

39. On nationalism and citizenship see, for example, Etienne Balibar, *La crainte des masses*, Paris: Galilee, 1997.

40. Ibid, p. 470.

5 ALGERIA, FRANCE: One Nation or Two?

ETIENNE BALIBAR

Algeria, France: one nation or two? The wording of this question is clearly provocative, since the answer is 'obvious'. Who then would want to reopen the question of independence, or 'review' the meaning and effects of the War of Algerian Independence? And yet, at a time when, on both sides of the Mediterranean, voices are being raised to state that Algeria and France are not sufficiently separate, to express regret that they are not really 'two' (that is, that neither is truly 'one': Algeria still too 'French' or Gallicized, France already too 'Algerianized'), is not such a provocation necessary? And if the spatial-temporal, or socio-temporal, idea of an irreversible *duality* were the mark, not of a 'decolonization', but of a persistent 'colonization of history'?

Because of what is currently happening in Algeria, we wonder what the history of Algeria had been 'before and after France', 'before and after independence', but just as importantly we should wonder about the history of the 'French people' and of the state in France – 'before and after Algeria' – for France today was made (and doubtless is still being made) in Algeria, with and against Algeria. These are questions without simple answers, and perhaps we are in the process of asking them for the first time. In them can be seen the return of a certain repressed, as well as the business of a *generation*, an essential aspect of our conjuncture.

Neither colonization nor decolonization is being written off, on the contrary: they are the very substance of this reflection. They are at the heart of the problem of 'the meeting of gazes'. Can we rethink Franco-Algerian history in an *isolated* way, and *a fortiori adversely*? Certainly not. Or can we rethink it in an *identical* fashion? No more easily. Doubtless reciprocity corresponds to neither one nor the other of these extreme modalities. What then is reciprocity? Jacques Rancière has told us: to speak of the relation of France to Algeria is to speak first of all of the relation of France 'to itself', to the *alterity* it carries within itself and, for the most part, denies.[1] It is thus to pose the problem of a dis-identification, without which there can be no democratic politics. For Rancière, as for me, precisely because of our nationality, it is difficult to cross over to the other side. But should it not be done, here and now? To speak of the relation of Algeria to France, then, will also be to speak of the relation of Algeria to its own interior alterity, and of its necessary 'dis-identification'.

Once again, however, can these discourses of dis-identification – by which each tries to liberate itself from the identity that imprisons it in order to recognize its own inherent alterity – be *one single discourse*, or at least a *common discourse*, a *shared discourse*? We must discover the mode of reciprocity not in the abstract but within actual painful experience. This does not mean that there is not also a completely *general* problem: that of the internationalism of our time. If we speak, as Derrida did recently, of a 'new internationalism', what will its language be?[2] Classical internationalism had recourse to the idea of 'class consciousness', which was supposed to cross frontiers. Others, militants or intellectuals, sought to forge a language common to all peoples (significantly christened *Esperanto*). All these attempts to constitute a meta-discourse, a superior conscience, a 'neutral' vehicle, have more or less failed, precisely because they did not adequately take into account the specificity of situations and conflicts. Nevertheless, without an answer to the question of how internationalism expresses itself, the latter simply has no place. I would like to suggest here that it must begin with innovative conceptions of the historical correlations between nations, and of the very relation of history to the nation-form, in its current form.

What then are we to learn from the history of Algeria and France, the singular relation designated by these names, about the concept of 'nation', its uses and limits? When I first began considering these questions, I only wanted to clarify an element of hypothetical truth, the one that resides in the violent schisms of appurtenance (and haunts such deadly phrases as 'French party' in Algeria or 'Maghreb invasion' in France). It is not so much a matter of wondering if these two nations form but one or are in reality two, as it is of wondering if each is in itself 'one' or 'two' – which is as relevant for France as it is for Algeria.

These questions seem to be objectively posed, which is a function of the singularity of the Franco-Algerian relation, even if this relation is not historically unique. After all, we could and should wonder if Great Britain and Ireland, or

Germany and Austria, form 'one nation or two', and in each case there are reasons for taking either side. A few years ago, René Gallissot used in this context the expression 'Franco-Algerian hybrid', an interesting phrase but one that does not fully satisfy me.[3] I believe that another image is possible to represent the nonseparation or nonexclusion of two historic entities: not that of 'hybridity', which is still too fluid, not confrontational or dialectical enough, but the more abstract figure of a *not-whole frontier*, what contemporary geometricians call a 'fractal'. What must be questioned is the idea that the dimensions of national appurtenance can necessarily be represented by whole numbers, like 'one' or 'two'. It must be suggested, then, at least by way of numerical allegory, that Algeria and France, taken together, do not make two, but something like *one and a half*, as if each of them, in their addition, always already contributed a part of the other.

If Algeria and France taken together absolutely do not make two, it cannot simply be because they share a common population, even if this fact is important. There are a fair number of bi-nationals, actually or virtually recognized (that is, who could easily become or again become so at the price of minor changes in legislation). But this particularity brings us back to a more general question. Arithmetic is in fact an essential aspect of the nation-form itself, or of the constitution of the nation-state. Nations *count* or *number* themselves based on their political unity and certain 'identifying characteristics' or 'unary characteristics' (*traits unaires*, Lacan), whether these be a matter of cultural or historic landmarks or of founding events. At the same time they count the individuals who 'belong' to them. Such is precisely the origin of *statistics*, that is, of a 'science of the state', which was originally called 'political arithmetic'. Still more importantly, through the processes of subjectification that have already been mentioned here, nations assure that those who are supposed to belong to them (and who are entered into the census as such) count themselves as one of the set of citizens.

This institutional reality cannot be evaded. It translates state influence into history. One thing I wish to say however (and I will return to it again when raising the question of citizenship) is this: we cannot leave it at alternatives of form: *either* adopt the state's point of view, *or* ignore it, pretend frontiers do not exist, belong only to the past. We cannot not count individuals and groups as the state does, based on this institutional account. And yet it is just as often said that we cannot always count in a simple, 'whole' fashion. There are situations of uncertainty: often when at a certain historic moment a maximum of certainty was sought and proclaimed, it produced a 'forced' object.

That is why the present situation in France and Algeria compels us to re-examine all the possibilities of imbrication as well as isolation. We must ask ourselves at what moment certain possibilities were imposed to the detriment of others, and why they were privileged. During the 'Algerian War', Germaine Tillion published with Editions de Minuit a book some may recall: *Les ennemis Complémentaires.*[4] This expression did not have unanimous support; it preserved or promoted the idea of a unity being divided into two even as it promoted the idea of a duality being fused into one, according to which long-term evolution was envisaged, on both sides of the Mediterranean.

All the nationalists of different sides – purely and simply, those who recognize and defend the primacy of the nation in politics – have naturally privileged the figure of division into two. They are not all in the same camp, and certain among them are particularly interesting here. We can find a remarkable illustration of this position in Raymond Aron's book, *La tragédie algérienne* (Paris, 1957). Because Aron, in his political philosophy, at that time as throughout his life, has been a believer in the necessary identity of the state and of the nation, he thinks that Algeria and France, if not forming 'one', must necessarily make 'two'. Consequently, he says so.

Internationalists have adopted the most complex positions, not to say the most ambiguous. During the 'war without a name' (to take up the expression Bertrand Tavernier used as the title of his film:[5] a war that no one has been able to designate – from the French point of view, at least – either as a 'foreign war' or as a 'civil war', that is, either as stemming from a duality or as dividing a unity), this question was certainly debated. Finally, however, decolonization has taken us from the false simplicity of one to the false simplicity of two, has restored in sum the equation of citizenship and nationality that is so deeply inscribed in the French tradition. Many among us nevertheless ask ourselves if decolonization did not mark the beginning of this tradition's decline. Because we could not institute interdependence or institutionally arrange interpenetration, we have returned to impossible isolation.

At this point you would be entitled to ask me why I use exclusively the term *nation.* I am tempted to answer by stating the paradox itself: because this term is the most equivocal of all. The same could not be said of *people.* I don't believe that any of us would be tempted to say that the 'Algerian people' and the 'French people' form but one. We will be all the less so as we become more conscious of the internal multiplicity proper to each; nor will we be tempted to say that Algeria and France form or could form one single state. They are two peoples and they are two states, each of which is relatively sovereign, independent as states today are able to be. But it is not certain that they are exactly two nations.

At a time when – on both sides – we would like to cut France from Algeria and Algeria from France, that is, to 'complete' the process of 1962 that was revealed, in a sense, as not open to completion, we perceive that it is no longer possible. Less so than ever. That is why I always return to the same question: do we have ways to conceptualize such a situation that do not turn it into a 'review' of history: neither an 'incomplete decolonization', nor a return to the well-known thesis of Algeria as an 'emerging nation' more or less haunted by the ghosts of the French Empire?

It would be necessary, to be rigorous, to examine here several questions regarding peoples: people as a social and political category; the constitution of state-sanctioned hegemonies; reciprocal nationalisms and nationalist couples. I shall briefly mention just three hypotheses.

The first is that the Franco–Algerian couple, with the resulting effects of identification and rivalry, is in its way as decisive for our contemporary history as is the Franco–German couple. This is due to the exceptional figure which the imperial trace assumes here. So even though today the world is witnessing the eclipse of the imperial figure of the nation, I don't believe, in the case of Algeria and France, that the decolonization of 1962 sufficed in itself to bring on this decline. With a good thirty years behind us, we begin to see more clearly to what extent the imperial form was necessary to the constitution of the Western nations, and consequently what was significant about decolonization and the recognition of new nations. In Algeria, we were dealing with an extreme situation whose existence was completely denied. By declaring the Algerian territory a 'French department', France denied its imperialist domi-nation of it, to the point of denying the existence of those it dominated. Which was translated not just into the forms of discrimination with which we are now familiar, but into a veritable cultural eradication.

But the fact that the nation was formed as part of the empire means that the empire remains part of the nation for a long time after physical and juridical separation. This is seen in particular today by the way in which multiculturalism in the Algerian, as well as French, social space is denied and repressed by administrative and cultural politics. The phenomenon is certainly not symmet-rical – no more than colonization itself is – but it exists on both sides, so in the Franco–Algerian couple we find first of all the persistent trace of this mutual appurtenance of nation and empire, this ineradicable 'remainder' of national imperialism with the state organizing itself as a domination.

My second hypothesis is that we are retroactively living, a generation later, the consequences of the crumbling of this form of sovereignty. Immediately the question arises whether there can be nations that are not empires, even in a fictive fashion. A few years ago, such a question would have seemed incongru-ous: we would have asserted instead that authentic nations liberate themselves from the form of the empire. New nations, in what has been called the 'Third World', have in fact tried to constitute themselves as anti-imperial nations. They have not escaped the necessity of becoming imperialist at their own level, even on a smaller scale. There is in fact an Algerian imperialism. As for former colonialist nations, they have not ceased to perpetuate in their own midsts forms of ethnic and cultural discrimination, while at the same time they have been reformulating their claim to be bearers of the universal on a worldwide scale. They have become imperialist nations without an empire. That is doubtless what is in the process of being undone. This possibility disappears, however, to the profit, not of a formal equality between the nations of the world, such as the United Nations Charter ideally codifies it, but of new relations of interdependence and hegemony which still remain to be defined.

This leads us to my third hypothesis, concerning the notion of *frontier* and the very particular figure it assumes in the case of France and Algeria. I would be tempted to say that it is the Franco–Algerian ensemble itself that is becoming a 'frontier', obviously a very broad and complex one, irreducible to the theoretical line of demarcation between autonomous sovereignties. The encounters and conflicts that come into play there have significance for the entire Mediterranean space. It is what we could call a *world-frontier*, as Braudel and Wallerstein have spoken of *world-economy*.[6] All the frontiers in the world are not like those of the *world-wide* frontiers, that is, the economic-cultural frontiers where north and south overlap, at once like types of societies and economies and like types of antagonistic civilizations (in this instance, the 'difference' between European-ness and Arab-ness, following the Christian–Muslim divide).

Then to what are we witness at this expansive line of which France and Algeria are part? Not to a simple relation of adjacency, a relation between neighbors, more or less close according to the time period, but to the intensification of a permanent double constraint: the necessity and impossibility of separating these two ensembles. Which translates into the multiplication of paradoxical individualities, in search of a political recognition that is always more indispensable and always more difficult: formerly the 'Muslim French person', now the 'French Muslim'.

Far indeed from definitively dissociating France and Algeria, the 'world-frontier' that reunites them constrains them to occupy together a confrontational position on the very line of the frontier. Now we can observe the singular signification of heritage, the retroactively produced results of colonization and decolonization within French as well as Algerian society. Algeria is irreducibly present in France as is France in Algeria. On either side, the 'foreign body' is all the more impossible to eliminate as it is not due solely to physical presences,

but also to memory and the constitution of identity; each being affected by an
interior difference, an essential noncontemporaneity to itself.

This noncontemporaneity is found again at the heart of the key institutions
that operate the representation of society in the state and, reciprocally, the
'nationalization' of society by the state. First on the side of *language*: the politics
of language and the place of different languages in public space. The question
is which is the most visible political language in Algeria, not only because it is
striking to note the extent to which French remains the vehicle there of
popular demands and intellectual projects, but because there is in permanent
operation a reference to a sort of ideal Frenchness (or republicanism, sometimes christened 'Jacobinism' or 'secularism'). But I believe there is also a
latent question of the place of the Arab and of Arab-ness in the French public
space. The influence of the Arab on the evolution of popular language (that of
the '*banlieues*', or suburbs) is an indication, but the question of the place of the
Arab – and the culture from which she or he is indissociable – in teaching and
in intellectual life is also eventually raised (as a book such as Alaon de Libera's
Penser au Moyen Age brilliantly bears witness).

Even more than the question of language, the question of familial structures
and genealogies is fundamental. They seriously blur the distinction between
public and private spaces at the same time as constituting a challenge to
administrative practices. Earlier, Abdelwahab Meddeb has used the striking
expression 'genealogical interruption' to describe a certain impossibility of
finding one's identity in Algeria today. I would pose the reciprocal question:
how is genealogical interruption overcome, or sutured? It is first of all through
'private' means, insofar as innumerable Franco–Algerian families have been
constituted, with their double 'neighborhood'. That is precisely their 'identity'.
It is not very comfortable, but already it carries political consequences. We
mustn't underestimate the violence of certain of these consequences, which
contribute to the fueling of nationalist tension, in the south of France
especially. It is the culmination of a double repression: on the one hand, the
transfer of populations at the end of the War of Independence, on the other,
the progressive integration of immigrant work. The fact remains that France
and Algeria, in all social classes, share larger and larger families (they *divide*
them, and they *share* them).

The problems are considerable, as we know, for the families themselves –
whether it is a matter of housing, of education, or of relations with the
administration and the police – but they are perhaps just as considerable for
the state. Raison d'Etat is the great reducer of complexity; that is, from
multiplicity to unity. It manifests a violence of its own in a continual tendency

to carve up families, as we see every day in interminable and sordid stories about the securing or denial of visas and 'papers'. Thus the primacy of politics is reaffirmed, but at a very high symbolic price, which is a certain moral de-legitimation of the nation-state. For the nation-state must constitute in the imaginary a sort of large family. It is confronted with its own limits from the moment it can no longer present itself as an enveloping unity within which the family is instituted, recognized and protected. It will be necessary one day generally to revise the way in which 'private' structures are implicated in the reproduction of any 'public' institution.

As for the question of language, doubtless the possibility of developing private ties across frontiers calls for concrete analyses, 'micro-sociological' or 'micro-political'. We cannot forget for all that that these analyses are presented in a global context of the re-examination of economic inequalities and the relativization of national sovereignties, in the north as well as in the south, as demonstrated more than ever by fierce power struggles (let us not forget the Gulf War). Should we not at least ask how this context determines the form of 'cultural' confrontations? It is particularly important if we wish to say a word about the place and role of Islam within the Franco–Algerian ensemble.

Which aspect should appear to us here as the principal one? Is it Algeria's traditional Islam-ness, insofar as it is a *particularism*, which colonization brutally repressed, indeed attempted to annihilate, and that today threatens to return? Is it the persistent *discrimination* that Islam is always subjected to in the French public space (for which Edgar Morin invented the provocative but pertinent expression 'Catholic secularism' [*catholaïcité*[7]]), and which doesn't fail to determine in Algeria a certain perception of France? Is it not also, on the contrary, a certain *universalism*, or a certain way of acceding to universalism *through Islam*? It would be based, obviously, on the *particular* representation of the universal and of the nation that Islam historically gives itself. But it would have nothing to do with overly simple images of particularism and traditional-ism (always marked by the prejudice Edward Said called *orientalism*).

Our friend Mohamed Harbi, among others, has strongly insisted on the idea that present-day Islam is not a simple step backward to a pre-modern religiosity.[8] In any case it cannot be reduced to that. It is more a form of politicizing the religious within the global crisis of the modernization process. Now, the crisis of the nation-form and of its proper models of 'civility' are obviously part of this. In this point precisely are knotted certain alliances that are surprising, but which nevertheless should be taken completely seriously: notably the one made between Islamic fundamentalism and a certain technological and scientific progressivism. As opposed to the stereotype of 'obscurantism', there is a tendential unity, in certain cases at least, between the aspiration to entry into technological globalization, and the claim to Islam as a universalist ideology. In Algeria such an alliance can fuel the denunciation of the 'French party', or of its own confinement within the French space and the French imaginary. That is not explained by sociological generalities about intellectual pariahs nor by the specific history of the Arabization of teaching and administration. Better to think today about the fashion in which collective transnational identities, which can generally be called alternatives to Americanization, try to locate themselves in the context of globalization. At this conjuncture, a certain Islamism at least would be not so much the substitute or to supplement traditional nationalism as a new way of laying claim to universality in the face of the dominant, necessarily 'exclusive', European or Western, figuration of universality.

That would doubtless be quite a brutal and disagreeable way for many of us to highlight the element of particularism that inhabits the Western presentation of universality. Things must be made clear: I am not looking here to rally the idea that human rights are a 'Western invention'. I would suggest, rather, the inverse: in a certain way of referring to Islam, there is also a claim for human rights and for their universalization, the intrinsic contradictions of which only ever lead to another contradiction: the appropriation of the universal, the monopoly of interpretation that Western powers have arrogated in the matter. The global ideological scene is in no way one of conflict between universalism and particularisms. Rather it is the scene of conflicts between fictive universalities, antagonistic claims to universality, and conflicts within universalism itself.

All the questions that I have just attempted to pose apropos of the nation, language, the family or genealogy, religion and universality, concern equally the question of the frontier; they constitute its very complexity. We do not have a clear enough idea of what a frontier is, or our ideas about it are less and less clear, because frontiers are *de facto* more and more complex. The frontier is doubtless not *the same*, depending on whether we see it from the north or from the south. But what I am trying to say here is that, in the case of Algeria and France (and perhaps in other cases), those two gazes that meet have been internalized one by the other, and so in some sense internalized within the frontier itself.

That leads us to ask, in conclusion, about the conditions under which the relation of the frontier to political space is being transformed. I don't believe that citizenship will be completely detached from national appurtenance. There is no more citizenship without a state than there are politics without a state; now the idea of a supranational state or of a state without frontiers is not really on the agenda. On the other hand, that of transnational institutions is a searing reality. The question is whether it is the statist notion of nationality that imprisons and conditions citizenship, or if, in a measure to be determined, citizenship overflows the boundaries of nationality and relativizes it. Where and for whom could it do so? On what conditions can a new citizens' institution allow us to satisfy these two contradictory requirements: that of the right to difference, and that of the right to differ from difference?

For my part I am convinced that this is possible only if the Franco–Algerian couple (or the historical coupling) becomes one of the privileged stakes of our political reflection and practice. Paradoxically, that also means that it ceases to involve a purely dual relation, a face-to-face where each assumes in turn the benevolent and malevolent figure of the other. French and Algerians do not have only to 'dis-identify' from themselves and from their imaginarily closed history, but to dis-identify from their 'couple'. That is why it is so important to inscribe this discussion within the perspective of globalization. It is all the more necessary in that the frontier we are discussing here, and that we ourselves constitute, is no longer solely an administrative, economic or cultural frontier, or one between the principles of civilization. It has become the frontier (or one of the frontiers) of violence. At a moment when, for many Algerians, it is vital to circulate freely between the two countries, and even to arrange their existence across the frontier, many French people see the frontier as a way of keeping outbursts of violence at a distance. They tend to imagine the fortification of this frontier as a condition of their security and of politics itself. It is a particularly dangerous illusion, but is also particularly difficult to combat.

In opposition, then, I will plead for an anti-violent politics (what I call a 'politics of civility') while maintaining that the proliferation of extreme violence, which kills politics and democracy as well as people, is also, in large measure, the result of state-run border patrols and the segregation of populations, by reinforcing the impossible imperviousness of frontiers. Instead of a police conception of the frontier, a political conception and practice of the frontier are needed. The frontier must be placed within the field of politics so that it is no longer on the margins, out of reach of all contestation or control, all reciprocity, but rather in the center, in the same way that individuals and groups today live now on one side, now on the other, and in this way straddle its line.

How to assure that this non-democratic institution *par excellence*, which is itself never collectively monitored, but serves to monitor individuals and populations, becomes a stake in a politics whose modalities of use and transformations can be negotiated? This is one of the fundamental questions at present. And as it is in the privileged form of the Franco–Algerian couple that we encounter it, it is also in this form that we must confront it. In this way the very general idea of a 'Mediterranean space', designating not so much a history or a culture as a meeting point and point of permanent conflict between histories and cultures, can again become the horizon of a project of civilization.

Translated by Adele Parker

Notes

1. Jacques Rancière, 'La cause de l'autre', *Lignes*, no. 30, February 1997, pp. 36–49. 'Algeria, France: One Nation or Two?' was first published in this same volume of *Lignes*.
2. Jacques Derrida, *Spectres de Marx. L'État de la Dette, le Travail du Deuil et la Nouvelle Internationale*, Paris: Editions Galilee, 1993, ch III. Translation by Peggy Kamuf, *Specters of Marx: the State of the Debt, the Work of Mourning, and the New International*, Routledge: New York 1994. See also *Cosmopolites de Tous les Pays: Encore un Effort!* Paris: Editions Galilee, 1997.
3. René Gallissot, *Misère de l'antiracisme. Racisme et identité nationale, le défi de l'immigration*, Paris: Editions Acantère, 1985.
4. Translation by Richard Howard, *France and Algeria: Complementary Enemies*, New York: Knopf, 1961.
5. *La guerre sans nom*, 1992; in English, *The Undeclared War*.
6. The phrase is found throughout the work of Fernand Braudel; see *Civilisation Matérielle, Économie et Capitalisme*, Paris: Armand Colin, 1979. Translated by Siân Reynolds, *Civilization and Capitalism, 15th–18th Century* (3 vols), London: Collins, 1981–84. See also Immanuel Wallerstein, *The Modern World-System* (2 vols), London: Academic Press, 1974–89.
7. *Catholicité* + *laïcité*: the term suggests that either the Church has become completely secular, identified with the state, or that the republican secular institutions, such as the national school system, are but another religion.
8. Mohamed Harbi, 'L'emprise du sujet collectif', *Lignes*, no. 30, pp. 33–36.

III
URBAN GUERILLAS

6 REASONABLE URBANISM

ROSALYN DEUTSCHE

Neil Bartlett's beautiful novel *Ready to Catch Him Should He Fall* is a love story whose main characters include two men and a city.[1] The lovers are Boy and O (short for The Older Man), and, as these names suggest, the couple has the quality of an allegorical image, evoking an entire world and history of homoerotic relationships. The city is London, which, like the story's human characters, is larger than itself. Bartlett portrays it as a city of Eros: setting of love, object of love, and site of encounters with exquisite strangers – the passing strangers that Walt Whitman, celebrating the urban nature of gay life and the erotic nature of urban life, called 'lovers, continual lovers'.[2] One might say of Bartlett's London what Apollinaire said of Paris,[3] that it was created by love. For Eros is not only the thematic content but also the driving force of the narrative, at least the comprehensive Eros that, for the Greeks, surpassed passionate attachment to one's own things and inspired the search in life for the good and the just.

Ready to Catch Him Should He Fall can, then, be read as a story – a myth really – about ethics, justice and urbanism, where 'urbanism' refers, in a broad political sense, not simply to the way of life of those in urban areas but to our manner of living *together* in the city. This is the story, from a novel rich in stories, which I will read and weave together with certain strands of urban theory. My main purpose is to question two phenomena that currently threaten democratic urbanism. One consists of the moralistic attitude and the animus against rights and equality that dominate public discourse in cities throughout the United States, including New York – the city where I live. The other is the prevailing framework of urban debates, which sets up a division between a homogenizing and a particularistic politics, either relativizing differences by encompassing all people within a complete social totality, or asserting absolute differences in the form of auton-omous group identities. Neither position interrogates the exclusionary oper-ations that simultaneously affirm and prevent the closure of identity; neither makes its exclusions available for contestation. Common to both is an orienta-tion toward protecting those who are like 'us'. This framework makes no room for a politics tied to the capacity for what Emmanuel Levinas calls 'non-in-difference to the other', a capacity he considers 'the essence of the reasonable being in man'.[4] Secondarily, I use Bartlett's novel to explain why I believe that attempts to understand what a *reasonable* – rather than *moralistic* – urbanism might mean are impeded by a tendency among critical urban scholars to limit urban reality to that which can be fully seen or known and to relegate anything else to the realm of the merely, even dangerously, fictional.

Bartlett's London is not only an amorous city but also a menacing one. Gay men and other outsiders – immigrants, blacks and ethnic minorities – are knifed, beaten, arrested, and verbally abused in the city's public spaces nearly every night. Accounts of these attacks punctuate the story, like gathering clouds. They refer to actual incidents of homophobic and xenophobic violence in London. But they also create a mental landscape for the reader that recalls scenes in classical myths or in Handel's 'magic operas', when an approaching earthquake, thunderstorm or some other natural or – what in this case amounts to the same thing – supernatural event warns a community of danger, portend-ing great disasters or highly marvelous happenings. What danger hangs over London in *Ready to Catch Him Should He Fall?* Put schematically, my answer is this: the fact that members of certain social groups are treated as detestable strangers with no 'right to the city' – the phrase, to which we shall return, is, of course, Henri Lefebvre's – and are, as a consequence, threatened in the city by its 'rightful' citizens, places the city itself in peril.

An anonymous narrator tells most of the story in the form of a memoir, performing a role akin to that of Socrates in the dialogues of Plato. The novel invites this comparison with classical tradition in its opening paragraph, as the narrator sets the scene and introduces the characters, beginning with Boy:

> This is a picture which I took of him myself. He was so beautiful in those days – listen to me, *those days*, talking like it was all ancient history. It's just that at the time it all seemed so beautiful and important, it was like some kind of historical event. *History on legs*, we used to say; a significant pair of legs, an important stomach, legendary . . . *a classic of the genre. Historic.* Well it was true, all of it.[5]

Ancient history, legendary, a classic of the genre – three times he alludes to the antique world. In addition, the story recalls a particular classic of the genre:

Plato's *Republic*, one of the serio-comical dialogues that Mikhail Bakhtin calls 'the novels of their time'.[6] According to Bakhtin, the early serio-comical genres distinguished themselves from the epic by portraying 'the subject of serious literary representation . . . without any distance, on the level of contemporary reality'.[7] The serio-comical story is explicitly memoirist. Told as a belated narrative, it places its author on the same temporal plane as the events he recounts, bringing him into a 'zone of contact' with the depicted world.[8] At the same time, it brings both the text and the distant past it portrays 'into contact with the spontaneity of the inconclusive present'.[9]

In this novelistic spirit, Plato's *Republic* and Bartlett's *Ready to Catch Him Should He Fall* examine civic life. Both depict quests for justice in the city, interrogate conventional morality and the nature of love, and 'found' imaginary cities, though, to be sure, quite different ones. Both take the form of a story within a story, which is told in a conversational style by a narrator who, as J. Hillis Miller writes about Plato, 'probably made the whole thing up anyway'.[10] Bartlett's narrator says as much. A few pages into an eyewitness account of Boy's first appearance on London's gay scene, he equivocates: 'Actually, I am not sure that I was there on that night of his arrival'.[11] Toward the end of the book, after describing a final photograph of the lovers, he says, 'Oh how I wish there really was a picture like that for me to give you' (p. 310). At such moments he calls attention to the role of desire in narrative, to the inseparability of memory and fantasy, to his status as an authorial image rather than the actual author, and, above all, to his story's artifice. Yet he neither breaks its spell nor disqualifies it as a reference to reality. On the contrary, he insists that 'it was true, all of it'.

Does the fact that he is lying make the story unreal? Or, as Oscar Wilde asks in 'The Decay of Lying', one of his own Socratic dialogues about art, is 'lying' – the term that Wilde favored over 'imagination' – the only way to make a story real?[12] More to the point of this essay, does the ambiguity about fiction and reality expressed by Bartlett's narrator mean that the urban space to which his story refers is 'unreal'?

Today, many critical urban scholars would no doubt answer 'yes', especially those reacting against the strong influence that cultural theories of representation have exerted on urban studies over the last two decades. Cultural critics have treated discourses as social spaces and social spaces as discursive constructions, and insisted that both imply a human subject, calling into question the foundations that mark off the boundaries of established spatial categories. Against these ideas, certain neo-Marxist geographers have issued a call to order in spatial thought, trying to maintain a traditional division between what they call 'material' or 'concrete' space, on the one hand, and 'metaphorical' or 'discursive' space, on the other. They designate the first 'real', the second 'unreal'.[13] Frequently they add the adjective 'social' to the 'material' and 'concrete' pole of the division and in this way place discourse outside the social world. The social/nonsocial division in critical urban theory repeats an opposition that critical social theory has traditionally drawn between political and non-political, public and private, space. Ultimately, the argument is this: concrete, material or real – that is, social – spaces are proper objects of political struggle; metaphorical, discursive or unreal – that is, non-social – spaces divert attention from politics. Like other inside/outside dichotomies, the concrete/metaphorical space polarity stabilizes the identities of the political and the non-political while making it seem as though these identities are discrete entities that stabilize themselves.

What exactly do these geographers mean by 'concrete space'? Their definitions can be bewildering, testifying to an underlying disavowal that categories of social space are themselves socio-spatial productions. One thing is clear, however: they do not simplistically equate concrete space with the physical space of the built environment. Indeed, a major achievement of radical geography, which emerged in the late 1960s as a critique of what Lefebvre calls 'traditional spatial knowledge', was its refusal to detach spatial forms from social relations. Geographers and other spatial theorists defined urban space as the materialization of social processes and urbanization as the spatial component of social change, arguing that transformations in spatial organization are not the effect of inevitable evolutions – natural, supernatural, social or technological – but go hand in hand with the restructuring of the oppressive social relations of capitalist society. Space is socially produced and therefore political. Traditional spatial knowledge supports existing power relations by endowing spaces with proper uses that seem dictated by natural or objective truths. It engages in and conceals 'the politics of space'. The neo-Marxist spatial critique investigated the socioeconomic conflicts that produce seemingly coherent spaces.

During the same period, changes taking place across a host of disciplines began challenging the social theory that informed radical geography. These changes included: the assertion that social reality is not independent of language; the calling into question of the orthodox Marxist idea that society is governed by a single, economic antagonism; the proposal, first made by Ernesto Laclau and Chantal Mouffe, that society, in the sense of a closed entity, is 'impossible' insofar as it is constituted by an outside that not only affirms, but also threatens its closure;[14] psychoanalytic notions that social space is entangled with the psychical processes of the human subject; and feminist explorations of the role played by totalizing images of social space in producing and maintaining masculinist subjects, whose orientation toward completion represses differences.

Often, geographers themselves helped bring about these changes, enlarging the critique of spatial politics so that it now extended to, among other things, the power relations that structure the space of geographical knowledge. In short, scholars explored the spatial politics of the discourse about spatial politics and investigated the production of the space of politics itself.[15] But some geographers tried to steel Marxist geography against innovations in the conceptualization of space by shoring up the real/unreal space dichotomy and an equally rigid subject/object division. In this way, 'objective', external space was safeguarded from contamination by its 'subjectivization' in other disciplines.

Still other geographers, perhaps inadvertently, go a step farther. They not only polarize discourse and reality or the spaces to which discourse refers, but also take it for granted that the field of discourse – of uses of language – can itself be so divided, calling certain *conceptions* of space material, hence real, and others metaphorical, or unreal.[16] With this slippage, they couple 'real space' with 'real language' and imply that both must be protected from the supposed 'distortions' of figuration – of, that is, 'unreal', or metaphorical, language. Indeed, this protective attitude, though not explicitly stated, is embedded in the assumptions underlying a great deal of the literature about real and unreal space. Many geographers use the adjectives 'real', 'concrete', and 'social' interchangeably to designate a space they construe as the materialization of oppressive economic relations, which in turn unify emancipatory political struggles that are presupposed to be independent of discourse. They presume, in other words, that real political space is extra-discursive and that real political discourse uncovers and analyzes this space, while unreal discourse ignores it and so colludes with oppression, endangering real politics, real space and real discourse. Demanding a literal use of language, these authors beg the question of reference and, in the name of order, breed confusion. For what they forget is that space 'itself' never speaks directly through discourse, and what they refuse to avow is that to say this is not to deny the existence of a world external to thought but, rather, to acknowledge that in the field of representation, as Bakhtin points out – in appropriately spatial terminology – 'the boundaries between fiction and non-fiction . . . are not laid up in heaven'.[17]

It is precisely the laying down of boundaries – in the social world, not heaven – that is at issue when Bartlett's narrator exposes the artifice of his story while insisting upon its truth and, in so doing, raises important questions about reference: how does a story refer and thus give us access to reality – in this case, urban reality? Is the text's relation to reality measured, as in the simplest realist model, by its references to an urban world that can be seen or, if invisible, understood? Is 'urban space' the ground rather than the effect of a discourse that not only knows its object but also knows itself? As in all boundary disputes, the stakes in debates about these questions are political. How and by whom are the boundaries of reality established? What and who are forced into unreality, which political struggles are abandoned as unreal, and, most important, how do epistemologies that treat their exclusions as self-evident fortify their realities against democratic contestation? While urban critics sometimes invoke the simple realist model of reference in unmasking the political conflicts that produce seemingly harmonious spaces, it is important to remember that the model itself can be a powerful political tool, masking its own identity as representation, devalorizing whatever challenges its mastery, and depleting reality of that which cannot be made fully visible or known.

There are of course more complex ways to think about reference. Cathy Caruth, in an essay about the relationship between texts and reality, counters the accusation that deconstruction is unconcerned with reference. Deconstruction, she says, does not do away with, but offers a different model of reference. Caruth approaches reference as a response to realities that cannot be encountered from a position of full understanding. Reference refers to 'the ways in which texts render legible those realities that may not be available to preconceived notions of language and the world'.[18] A case in point, one that concerns urban reality, is *Ready To Catch Him Should He Fall.* The novel presents a topography of London, mapping empirically identifiable features of the city's physical and social landscapes – specific monuments, buildings, and parks – as well as generalized but recognizable spaces of homosexual culture and homophobic violence. But cityscapes have features that are not so easily mapped. These include, as Henri Lefebvre writes, the residua of earlier people and events: 'Nothing disappears completely . . . nor can what subsists be defined solely in terms of traces, memories or relics. In space, what came earlier continues to underpin what follows. The preconditions of social space have their own particular way of enduring and remaining actual within that space'.[19] 'What came earlier' often survives in physical form, as ruins, traces or preserved objects. For Lefebvre, however, social space cannot be extricated from the 'mental space' of the human subject. That which is empirically observable he calls 'spatial practice', designating that aspect of social relations that is materialized in the organization of physical space. But spatial practice is only one facet of social space. Another is 'representational space', or space as psychologically 'lived'.[20] Both are 'moments' in what Lefebvre famously calls 'the production of space'.

Insofar as ruins or traces are objects of meaning, what came earlier is inseparable from the relationship the human subject in the present has to them. Spatial practice thus exhibits the same combination of spatial immediacy and temporal anteriority as the serio-comical memoir with which I have associated Bartlett's book. The sense of 'what came earlier' provoked by spatial practice also resembles what Roland Barthes calls the '*having-been-there*' quality of the photograph, the type of visual image that Bartlett's narrator repeatedly longs to show us and makes the object of the reader's desire.[21] In the absence of physical traces, however, what came earlier may persist solely in the subject's psychical relationship to spatial practice. Moreover, what came earlier came only in relation to what did *not* come earlier, what *might* have come, and what has not *yet* come. Social space thus eludes mapping inasmuch as it contains these events that never 'took place' as phenomenal happenings. Indeed, Michel de Certeau contends that it is just such events that produce 'space'. He proposes that any 'place' – which is to say, any clearly demarcated, seemingly coherent interior that serves as a base for managing relations with an outside – contains such events, which destabilize it, no matter how solid and univocal it appears.[22] Bartlett, as we shall see, mobilizes dreams, memories, hopes, repressions, and possibilities that interrupt and put into question the city's present existence, troubling it from the moment of its founding. Are these 'unreal?' Is narrating them not an act of reference? Is the 'truth' of the city separable from what might have been and still might be true? How do we refer to a reality-in-the-making, a making that is, moreover, directed toward no known ideal but is, precisely, unknowable?

For Bakhtin, this is the reality to which fiction refers. When the novel, departing from the conventions of the epic, placed the author in the field of representation and made contemporary reality its starting point, the past world to which the novel referred was opened to history.

> Every event, every phenomenon, every thing, every object of artistic representation loses its completedness, its *hopelessly finished* quality. . . . No matter how distant this object is from us in time, it is connected to our incomplete, present-day, continuing temporal transitions, it develops a relationship with our unpreparedness, with our present. But meanwhile our present has been moving into an inconclusive future. And in this inconclusive context all the semantic stability of the object is lost; its sense and significance are renewed and grow as the context continues to unfold.[23]

Further: 'Reality as we have it in the novel is only one of many possible realities; it is not inevitable, not arbitrary, it bears within itself other possibilities'.[24]

A past brought into a present, which by its very nature demands continuation and moves into a future; a reality that contains other possible realities; a quality of 'unfinish' that is the condition of hope: these features characterize the city of London in *Ready to Catch Him Should He Fall*. The book refers to a space – and is itself such a space – inhabited by 'the force of what is not known . . . the powerful effects of the ill-understood and the not-yet-known in human experience',[25] by that force which founds every reality.

The problem of reference opens onto the tension between 'revealing' and 'creating' that is inherent in mapping, writing or any means of representing the cityscape. J. Hillis Miller argues that the very term 'topography' contains this tension. Topography has two dictionary definitions: first, the representation of a landscape using the conventional signs of a system of mapping, and, second, that which is mapped, the landscape 'as such', with no reference to representation. Discourse about landscape frequently elides the difference between the two, but the relationship of the first to the second is never direct: 'The landscape 'as such' is never given, only one or another of the ways to map it'.[26] While critical urban theory often maps the oppressive social relations hidden by traditional spatial knowledge, the social landscape revealed by alternative maps is also never given 'as such'. Alternative maps – which are different from critical maps – also conceal events, especially those that cannot be assimilated to phenomenal reality and that, because they do not take the form of identifiable entities, cannot be mapped but only narrated. Are these narrations, then, untrue? Lynne Tillman, in a superb essay on Bartlett's work, answers this way: 'Fiction's "truth" is verisimilitude, an appearance of truth, of likelihood'.[27]

What inhabits the topography of London in *Ready to Catch Him Should He Fall*? If, as I have suggested, the spirit of the *Republic* haunts Bartlett's London, it is only one of many spirits, a whole crowd of books and plays, musical and literary forms, artists and writers that populate the novel and the city it depicts. Prominent among this spectral group is Oscar Wilde, whose imprisonment in 1895 for indecent behavior with men, precipitated by his affair with the young Lord Alfred Douglas, is remembered and reimagined in the book. In a way, Bartlett undoes Wilde's fate; he gives O a Boy worthy of love, their relationship turns out well, and the lovers prevail over the city's homophobic moralism. The very title of Bartlett's book alludes to Wilde, who is described in the first few lines of Richard Ellman's classic biography as 'refulgent, majestic, ready to fall'.[28] The evocation of Wilde also embeds the novel more firmly in the Greek context. Wilde admired Plato and mimicked the dialogue form in his own essays. What is more, Wilde, like Socrates, conducted 'in the most civilized way, an anatomy of society, and a radical reconsideration of its ethics',[29] and this interrogation of conventional morality led each man to his trial and downfall.

'Haunts', however, is not quite the right word to describe the relationship between *Ready to Catch Him Should He Fall* and the *Republic*. It would be more accurate to say that Bartlett breathes life into Plato's dialogue. This act of animating Plato exemplifies the trope of 'prosopopoeia', a term that also reaches us from the Greeks. Following Paul de Man, the literary theorist Kenneth Gross defines prosopopoeia as 'the often hallucinatory figure by which poets lend a voice, face, or apparent subjectivity to things in themselves inanimate, absent, or lost – the wind, a dead child, a past self, an ideal of liberty'.[30] Apart from Bartlett's specific resuscitation of the *Republic*, his very use of prosopopoeia raises the spirit of Plato. Plato's dialogues are narrated by Socrates who, when Plato wrote them, was already dead, and therefore, as Miller writes, the dialogues are one extended prosopopoeia.[31]

Miller makes this point in an essay about Plato's *Protagoras*. He demonstrates how the dialogue at once uses and comments on prosopopoeia. In the dialogue, Socrates recounts his encounter with Protagoras. While narrating the meeting, he twice quotes Homer's *Odyssey*. Both citations are from the account of Odysseus's visit to the underworld. Miller argues that, in quoting Homer at the point where Socrates meets Protagoras, Plato places Socrates's entire narrative under the aegis of Odysseus's visit, which is 'the original myth on which all prosopopoeias depend or of which they are miniature imitations'.[32] When Plato repeats the myth told in the *Odyssey*, a myth that, incidentally, is also a subtext of the *Republic*, he directs the reader's attention to prosopopoeia, which, says Miller, may be 'the fundamental poetic power' and 'is certainly the power that makes narrative possible'.[33]

> All prosopopoeias are visits to the underworld. They depend, in a shadowy way on the assumption that the absent, the inanimate, and the dead are waiting somewhere to be brought back to life by the words of the poet or orator.[34]

Miller links prosopopoeia to ethical responsibility: by following his argument and bringing it together with ideas about democracy, freedom and rights, we can illuminate the way this literary figure bears on issues of urbanism.

To begin with, Miller connects prosopopoeia to ethical thought and action and to struggles against forgetfulness by maintaining that in acts of prosopopoeia a writer assumes 'the responsibility the living have to the dead'.[35] Moreover, responsibility informs not only the act of storytelling but also that of reading, in which the reader ascribes 'a face, a voice, and a personality to those inanimate black marks on a page'.[36] He continues: 'The moment no one, anywhere, is reading Plato, all the figures in his dialogues will die again'.[37] Prosopopoeia is therefore a way of telling stories and of keeping stories and people alive.

Past events, stories and people are not simply in danger of being forgotten, however, but, as Walter Benjamin famously warns, of being remembered in a manner that turns them into 'a tool of the ruling classes'.[38] Throughout history tradition has been constructed as the tradition of the victorious, burying what Benjamin calls the 'tradition of the oppressed',[39] which is to say, the tradition of fighting against oppression. Tradition ceaselessly falls prey to a petrifying conformism, and, 'Only that historian will have the gift of fanning the spark of hope in the past who is convinced that *even the dead* will not be safe from the enemy if he wins'.[40]

Miller's discussion of prosopopoeia is part of his broader theory of 'the ethics of reading', a phrase which refers to that aspect of reading in which the reader opens herself to something unknown, responds to a call in a text, and, further, takes responsibility for the effects of her act of reading.[41] Responding differs from, indeed interrupts, understanding. For reading is ethical when we expose ourselves and answer to the other – an other that is not a transcendent entity but something which manifests itself precisely as that which is not an object for understanding. Emmanuel Levinas names this other 'the face', a term that designates the other human being who both looks at and 'concerns me', who matters 'to me as someone for whom I am answerable'.[42] Ethical responsibility appears then when certainty disappears. It emerges with the proximity of the face – not that which is literally near to me but that which addresses itself to me as something that is 'not mine' and which therefore disrupts a world construed as an object for the 'self'. Responsibility is incompatible with moral discourses that posit unassailable, substantive grounds of the norms they seek to enforce. Rather, it presses us to interrogate conventional morality, and, in this way, resembles Sin, about which Wilde wrote that, 'In its rejection of the current notions about morality, it is one with the higher ethics'.[43]

Like responsibility, democracy is also constituted by uncertainty. Claude Lefort, in his generative work on democracy, argues that the bourgeois political revolutions of the eighteenth century shifted the site of power. The monarchical state referred its sovereign power to a source outside society – God or Supreme Justice – a transcendent source that also guaranteed social unity. With the *Declaration of the Rights of Man*, however, state power derives from 'the people;' it is located within the social. But with the abandonment of references to a transcendent ground of power – with 'the dissolution of the markers of certainty' – references to an unconditional ground of the social order disappear as well. We are exposed to others, but the 'basis of relations between *self* and *other*'[44] is indeterminate. Put differently, indeterminacy exposes us to others and, with this exposure, democracy is invented. While the markers of certainty legitimated absolute power, their dissolution legitimates debate about what is socially legitimate and what is illegitimate. Because the ground of our common-ality is uncertain, has no fixed point, no external guarantee, it is open to interrogation through the declaration of rights, a process in which the meaning and unity of society are perpetually negotiated. Social questions may well be decided and conflicts settled, but to be democratic society itself must remain an unsolved problem.[45]

With the collapse of the ground, the social world becomes an enigma and slips from the grasp of the subject. The image of social space as an object totalized by a substantive foundation, an object that transcends partiality and is independent of all subjectivity, positions the subject as the external point of complete or, more often, potentially complete knowledge. Democratic society does not, however, present itself as an object for the subject. The removal of its ground pluralizes society – not by fragmenting it into self-contained, conflicting groups, but by making it incompletely knowable and therefore 'not mine'. Far from dividing a substantially unified humanity – which is a frequently expressed fear – the collapse of the ground makes us what Levinas calls 'reasonable' human beings, beings who are defined by the capacity to be 'non-in-different to the other'.[46] And since the dissolution of the markers of certainty is simultaneous with the founding of the rights of man, these rights imply a 'consciousness of the rights of the other, for which I am answerable'.[47] Demo-cratic rights can then be understood not simply as the freedom *of* the self but as freedom *from* the self, 'from its egotism'. Through this non-indifference of the one for the other, 'the justice of the rights of man takes on an immutable significance and stability, better than those guaranteed by the state'.[48] Levinas's conception of rights casts doubt on an ethics that would link rights to the unified identity of a political group, such as the nation-state, since this would only sanction indifference. As Julia Kristeva points out, a national political conscience normalizes the notion of foreigners, which it defines as 'people who do not have the same rights as we do'.[49]

With the idea of non-indifference, we can again take up the discussion of Bartlett's novel and of ethical reading, whose prerequisite is precisely the capacity to respond to a world that does not belong to me, in which *I* am a foreigner. Tillman captures this connection beautifully: 'The resistance to reading fiction may be a refusal to enter into another world, a strange place, where one must suspend one's own world, which may be ignored. A novel speaks: This is a world not of your making'.[50] *Ready to Catch Him Should He Fall* tells us a story of a strange place – the city – in order to speak for those with no voice of their own, even, as I shall propose, in defense of their rights.

Bartlett animates Plato, just as Plato rejuvenated Socrates, who has been seen as the first philosopher 'to call philosophy down from the heavens and set her in the cities of men'.[51] Yet this invocation of the origins of political philosophy signals no adherence to substantive notions of the good society, no simple nostalgia. *Ready to Catch Him Should He Fall* deals with *contemporary* urban–political issues, specifically those that began to threaten London in the 1980s, when an aggressive homophobia surfaced as an emblematic urban problem. This problem has manifested itself in moralizing anti-sex campaigns, legislation aimed at censoring pornography, a censorship system that, as Simon Watney writes, 'regards all references to homosexuality as such to be intrinsically indecent and/or obscene',[52] and the press's construction of homosexuality 'as an exemplary and admonitory sign of Otherness . . . in order to unite sexual and national identifications amongst readers over and above all distinctions of class, race and gender'.[53] The violence that erupts at key moments in Bartlett's London encapsulates these threats. But there is another striking feature of the cityscape, another danger that has occasioned and legitimated homophobia and which, though never named, may lie at the secret heart of the novel – the AIDS epidemic that began to devastate London in the 1980s, as it did so many other cities.

Boy and O walk all over this city. They meet when Boy finishes a journey so exhausting that it seems as though he has wandered out of the past and across vast territories. He arrives at The Bar, where O, another 'man with a past' (p. 68), is a regular patron and where much of the novel takes place. In a way, Boy's arrival is a homecoming. The narrator, a longstanding denizen of The Bar, describes it as a very strange place that 'to us' was 'as normal as home' (p. 23). Run by Mother, who helps educate Boy about gay history and culture, The Bar is both a shelter from the homophobic city and itself a kind of city (a metropolis or mother-city), one in which gay men can walk, have sex, get engaged, be promiscuous, and dance all night without fear, subject only to 'our own rules' (p. 30). The Bar is a fictional amalgam of different types of spaces – bars and sex clubs – in which gay men have developed a public culture. In The Bar, gays, who live in what Bakhtin, writing about medieval carnival, calls a 'two-world condition', have 'built a second world and a second life outside official-dom'.[54] Evoking the rituals of play associated with both carnival folk culture and modern urban traditions of gay male performance, Bartlett's narrator describes dramas that are staged each night at The Bar against painted backdrops representing foreign countries. Sometimes Mother feels that the men under her care need a more drastic change of scenery and she redecorates the whole place to look like another city: Amsterdam or Paris or just London – 'our own dear city' – in an earlier era (p. 27). But whichever city The Bar resembles, 'whatever city we were all supposed to be in', one element remains constant: the ceiling, painted black and inlaid with hundreds of tiny lights forming constellations. 'And on a good night', says the narrator, 'the stars would seem to brighten; if you looked up it was like a clear winter's night in the city' (pp. 28–9).

Outside The Bar is a homophobic city of fear; inside, a city of homoerotic refuge. Yet Bartlett cancels the opposition as much as he affirms it. While The Bar is a city nested within London, London is also nested within The Bar. The Bar is big and 'contained in a way the streets of the whole city, there were men there from all the different parts of it' (p. 33). And while The Bar permits a kind of eroticism prohibited in the city, it also brings the eroticism of urban space – wanderings, chance meetings, encounters with strangers, dark corners, public intimacies, bodies coming together and moving apart – into its interior. The Bar reiterates and transforms the features of the city so that, as Henry Urbach writes about gay sex clubs, 'once contested sites are voided of homophobia to become enclaves of queer sexual practice'.[55] Toward the end of *Ready to Catch Him Should He Fall*, the conditions of The Bar prevail in the larger city when, in a carnivalesque reversal, traditional socio-spatial hierarchies are suspended for a single night, and Boy and O walk freely through the streets of London.

Boy appears on the threshold of The Bar like a herald of this marvelous event. 'Boy was truly beautiful, when he came to us', recalls the narrator, 'I can see him now standing there in the door' (p. 15). At the exact moment of Boy's arrival, a man from The Bar is stabbed four times in the city outside. Only later does the narrator connect the two events. First he describes Boy and, immediately afterwards, a second image: 'I have this postcard depicting an allegorical figure of Strength'. The figure 'is naked like a statue' and 'in the palm of his raised, right hand he holds out to you a miniature city, complete with dome, bridges and towers, the freedom of which he is offering you and which he has promised to protect' (p. 15). The narrator compares Boy's beauty to that of a civic statue watching over a city. Perhaps the description was inspired by Wilde's homoerotic and ethical fairy tale *The Happy Prince*, in which a gilded and bejeweled statue of a prince perched on a hillside 'high above the city' is overcome with sorrow at the inequality and misery he sees. Aided by a male swallow, with which he falls in love, he is able to alleviate the sufferings of the oppressed by giving away his gold and precious stones.[56] In addition to painting a picture of Boy, Bartlett's passage about the statue gives us an image of the novel's own activity, of the way it, too, will protect the city's freedom. Like *The Happy Prince*, the passage is an example of 'ekphrasis', the literary description of a real or imagined work of visual art. *Ready to Catch Him Should He Fall* contains numerous ekphrases. Indeed, the entire book is ekphrastic: it begins by describing Boy's photograph and ends with a phantasmagoria of images of Boy, O, Mother, and all The Bar's inhabitants in a variety of cities that have been liberated from totalitarian or tyrannical regimes. Like prosopopoeia, ekphrasis transfigures objects, submitting the inanimate artwork 'to languages of . . . conversion'[57] or to conversions wrought by language. Ekphrastic texts do not uncover original, unchanging meanings of art objects. They rediscover the fact that political struggles constitute the meaning of an object. Ekphrasis thus figures the way in which ideas, language and images are reanimated – through practices of use.

Among the silent, immobile objects that can be brought to life and lent a voice through ekphrasis and prosopopoeia are the things of the city – buildings, monuments, streets, parks and the built environment as a whole. Midway through *Ready to Catch Him Should He Fall* something astonishing, though not miraculous, occurs: the clouds that have been gathering over London break, and, in the ensuing storm, the city speaks. It happens at the climax of Boy and O's courtship. On this night, Mother has staged a play at The Bar. The *dramatis personae* are: The Son (Boy), The Father (O) and The Lover (also played by O). In the play's final scene The Son defies The Father and runs off to Paris with The Lover.[58] The curtain falls and then rises again at midnight. Gary, The Bar's pianist, strikes twelve notes as Mother steps onto the stage, leads Boy and O toward the footlights, and joins their hands 'in public'. 'And that was it,' recounts the narrator, 'I had tears in my eyes, and they were engaged' (pp. 167–68).

Shouts, applause, and a joyous, drunken celebration follow, drowning out the thunderstorm that has struck London. The storm's proportions are epic; it nearly wrecks the city. But it also interrupts the city's violence. No gay men are attacked that night. Moreover, London becomes the setting of a drama, which, like that performed inside The Bar, publicly announces and commemorates the male couple's love. As the narrator puts it, 'the city itself had celebrated O and Boy's engagement, but in the strangest fashion' (p. 168). As the storm hits the city's power lines, extinguishing streetlights and illuminated clocks, time is suspended and the theatre darkened. The statues of London begin to move and talk. Their speech is operatic, stretched to the expressive limits of the human voice.

> They beckoned to each other, their arms upraised against the winds in benediction, exhortation, jubilation; and when the rain finally came, just before morning, the stone and metal of these limbs, which had become warm, almost as warm as flesh, in the heat of the long summer day and evening, seemed to take on a sort of life. Of course none of the statues was actually seen to move; that would have been a miracle; but as the rain fell they seemed, though immobile, to live. The Temple dragon in the Strand mewed a clear poison which dripped from under his forked tongue. The great, stupid, sleeping lions in the square drooled saliva and seemed about to rise and roar; a kind

of clear blood ran down the blade of the uplifted scimitar with which the Allegory of
Fortitude protected her naked child from the snake pinned beneath her foot at the
Aldwych; there was so much blood it ran over the handle of the scimitar and down
over her wrist. The wings of the Victory alighting atop the arch at Park Lane found a
wind for once adequate to their size, weight and fury; her horses reared at the
lightning and were lathered in sweat. On the parapet of the cathedral at Ludgate, St
Agatha expressed a single drop of milk from the nipple of her stone breast. And on
churches, tombstones, banks and derelict theatres, all the angels of London wept; tears
dripped down their metal cheeks and trickled from under their stone eyelids. Since
their faces did not move, their reasons for crying on this occasion remained hidden
. . . Michael, Prince of all the city's angels, wept on the porch of St Peter, Cornhill.
And above them all the great golden figure on the Old Bailey, Justice herself,
blindfolded and armed just as Love is armed and blind, Justice herself was seen to
move; she rocked and swayed in the storm (pp. 169–70).

This is the most elaborate and overt prosopopoeia in *Ready to Catch Him Should
He Fall*. Like the earlier description of the postcard of a civic statue, the passage
about the storm has affinities with *The Happy Prince*. In Wilde's story a statue
also weeps, and the swallow that loves the prince at first mistakes his tears for
rain. And like Wilde's fairy tale, Bartlett's thunderstorm scene epitomizes a
recurrent literary fantasy: 'the dream of the moving statue', which Kenneth
Gross analyzes in his book of the same name. The salient characteristics of
statues are silence and immobility, yet they have, Gross argues, the power to
transfigure the spaces they share with us. Indeed, it is the very silence of statues
that makes them sites of contest, though silence can also serve as an image of
'what seems to exist outside the deformations of human language'[59] and is
therefore *incontestable*. While the fantasy of their animation turns statues into
literal figures of speech – figures that speak – it, like ekphrasis, also 'turns our
attention away from the artifact itself and toward the complex act of reading it'
(p. 142). The fantasy thus emphasizes the figurative, rather than literal, nature
of language. Perhaps this is one reason that signs of life in statues can be
frightening and are frequently warded off by countervailing fictions of stability.
'Works of sculpture are such solid wishes,' says Gross, 'or vehicles of a wish for
things that *are* solid', that they 'are more than usually subject to the fate that
threatens any work of figuration – that of becoming literalized' (p. 198). The
insistence on literalism kills statues – by, paradoxically, rendering them statu-
esque – just as, in Miller's words, it 'strikes language dead'.[60] Conversely, the
dream of the speaking and moving statue can keep alive not only the statues
but also language, and, particularly in the case of civic statues, the cities we
inherit.

This capacity for revitalization depends not only on the content but also on
the form of the statues' speech. Bartlett makes it clear that his statues are

neither literally alive nor animated from within: 'Of course none of the statues was actually seen to move; that would have been a miracle; but as the rain fell they seemed, though immobile, to live'. The scene is realistic, though it does not purport to convey meanings inherent in the external world, in things themselves. Rather, it dramatizes the emergence of meaning at the object's surface, its point of contact with an outside.

Bartlett thus avoids the danger to which the urban theorist Raymond Ledrut alerts us: making the city speak 'in such a way that it will seem as if the city itself were speaking'.[61] In a 1973 essay, *Speech and the Silence of the City*, Ledrut combines semiological and sociological analyses to investigate the city as a signifying practice. How, he asks, are the things of the city made meaningful? How, that is, do they learn to speak? The answer depends in turn on what we mean by 'the city'. Ledrut rejects the technocratic notion that the city is a spatial framework created *for* users by powers that surpass them, and suggests that 'the city is truly the city' only insofar as it is an environment formed by users.[62] It is 'an object charged with meaning by . . . the use men make of it'.[63] To make the city speak in a way that makes it seem as if the city itself is speaking is to give the impression that the organization and uses of urban space are dictated by the objective needs of a uniform society. This has the effect of erasing the operations that produce urban meaning by claiming that a pregiven reality can speak for itself. For Ledrut, as for all critical urban scholars, the city is more than the built environment. But he does not defetishize the city by revealing the socioeconomic relations materialized in space only to refetishize it by fixing its meaning in these relations. Rather, Ledrut implies that the built environment is a city only insofar as it is a term in a relationship with a subject.

Bartlett also restores the subject to the city. The fantasy he weaves of speaking statues works not so much to supply a lack as to release the statues from a spell – a state of petrifaction – that has been cast over them to avoid the apprehension of a lack, of, that is, their incompletion. His statues are civic monuments. More than figures *in* the city, they are figures *of* the city, images of the city as a social form. Like the Florentine statues analyzed by Mary McCarthy in *The Stones of Venice*, the statues of London might be viewed as 'formalized civics lessons' and 'even a group of ideal stone citizens'.[64]

Throughout history, political revolutions have demolished such symbols, as when the Paris Commune toppled the Vendôme Column, calling it 'a permanent insult to the vanquished by the victors'.[65] Does the monument scene in *Ready to Catch Him Should He Fall* join this tradition of political iconoclasm? Yes and no. On the one hand, the thunderstorm that shakes the statues in a celebration of gay love has the vehemence of a rebellious political force that, like the Commune, challenges the authority the monuments represent. Also like the Commune, the storm contests urban geography, challenging the exclusionary operations of a city that leaves certain social groups – in the first case, workers, in the second, gays – with few 'expectations of space'.[66] The storm undoes an urban space in which, to borrow de Certeau's words, 'there is no longer any alternative to disciplinary falling-into-line or illegal drifting away, that is, one form or another of prison and wandering outside the pale'.[67]

On the other hand, where the Vendôme Column commemorates imperialist conquest, Bartlett's statues are figures of saints, angels, Fortitude and 'above them all the great golden figure on the Old Bailey, Justice herself'. And the storm that makes them tremble and weep is allied *with*, not *against*, them. Historically, of course, such sculptural figures have legitimated conquest, transposing it into a civilizing mission. But the animated statues of *Ready to Catch Him Should He Fall* perform differently. In the first place, the thunderstorm scene is set within a story that has the quality of a fairy tale, one of the fictional forms that, according to Freud, makes strangeness less real, less threatening, and therefore less susceptible to rejection or conquest.[68] In *Strangers to Ourselves*, Julia Kristeva brings Freud's investigation of the unconscious – what she calls the 'small truth' that there is foreignness within us[69] – and of the uncanny feeling of strangeness – which Freud defined as 'that class of the frightening which leads back to what . . . is familiar'[70] – to bear on ethico-political concerns about living with others in a contemporary world characterized by an unprecedented mixing of 'foreigners', a term Freud does not use.[71] The archaic, narcissistic self, Kristeva argues, constructs 'the strange' by projecting 'out of itself what it experiences as dangerous or unpleasant in itself'.[72] One form of uncanny projection is the creation of doubles: statues, for example. The strange, then, is the product of repression, which never fully succeeds. Kristeva suggests that encounters with people from foreign countries or societies can provoke confrontations with our own foreignness, our own unconscious. We at once reject and identify with the foreigner, and this ambivalence troubles our sense of boundaries, of being itself.

Freud speculates that the obvious, generalized artifice of literary forms such as the fairy tale eliminates the reader's uncertainty about whether what is strange is real, 'whether things . . . regarded as incredible may not, after all, be possible'.[73] In the fairy tale, strangeness is not uncanny since it is set in an imaginary space that seems definitively separated from reality. Strangeness becomes less familiar, more acceptable, even pleasurable, and we can confront it, which is to say detect it in ourselves, with less apprehension. For Kristeva, consciousness of our own otherness is the precondition of 'being *with* others'[74] without either expelling them or obliterating them by transforming them into ourselves: 'The foreigner comes in when the consciousness of my difference arises, and he disappears when we all acknowledge ourselves as foreigners, *unamenable* to bonds and communities'.[75] Kristeva reserves the term 'foreigner' for a person who is not a citizen of the nation in which she resides. But her analysis can, I think, apply to other groups that, diverging from social norms, interrupt the image of society as a unitary, organic whole – ultimately an idealized self-image. Any 'disruptive' group can appear as the actualization of early, fantasized dangers to the integrity of the self. Bartlett's thunderstorm scene, in which civic monuments come to life and speak on behalf of non-normative sexualities, can be read as a theatricalization of the stranger, which, like the fairy tale, offsets the impulse to conquest that such monuments often represent.

A second way in which the thunderstorm scene differs from traditional political iconoclasm is that instead of destroying the statues it gives them a role in the ethical, political and historical education of a troubled city. It casts them as democratic citizens – actors in a contest over the meaning of the urban community they symbolize and the ideas, values, customs and beliefs they allegorize. It is no accident that the scene reaches its climax with the 'move-ment' of Justice on top of the Old Bailey, the courthouse where in 1895 the statue witnessed a different scene as the first trial of Oscar Wilde opened, also with a theatrical air: 'There was the sense that a great legal battle was to be fought, and a crowd watched the arrival of the principals'.[76] It is not by chance that in Bartlett's rewriting of the scene Justice is aligned *with*, rather than *against*, Love.

Like most civic monuments, Bartlett's statues signify power, but on the night of the thunderstorm they also signify the right to question the basis of power. They mutate into democratic monuments. As Lefort argues, democracy is 'inspired by a demand for freedom which destroys the representation of power as standing above society and as possessing an absolute legitimacy'. This demand 'has the effect of challenging the omnipotence of power',[77] which can no longer appeal to a substantial basis. Bartlett's statues could not make this demand for freedom were they, too, not liberated from the assumption that 'they have a self-presence or transparency alien to the domain of the figura-tive'.[78] For just as the indeterminacy of society is the starting point of democratic politics, just as the question at the heart of democratic society makes it possible to question society, so the indeterminacy of works of figuration – in this case, of the things of the city – opens them to subversion and resignification. All monuments, to vary an idea from Alois Riegl, are 'unintentional'[79] – open to their own historicity and to unintended meanings. Iconoclasm is inscribed within their very being.

The scenes in which weeping citizens – men and monuments – publicly celebrate Boy and O's love assume their poignancy in the context of a homophobic society where non-standard intimacies are denied, denigrated and violently attacked. One night, on their way to The Bar, Boy and O are threatened by a group of homophobic men. Overcoming his fear, O protects Boy. As in the folk tradition of carnival, when the destruction of fear turns everything into gaiety, and light replaces darkness,[80] the lovers join a crowd assembled for a public ritual in which the city is lighted for Christmas. They walk and dance together freely until dawn. 'For this one night they went out', Bartlett has said, 'and instead of the world being the city where you're walking down the street, after just having made love, and someone says to you "Queer" – and that's it, it's all taken away from you. In *Ready* the reverse happens, the city is turned into a carnival, and for once the city seems to be operating on their laws'.[81] After this incident, Mother closes The Bar and in the book's penultimate scene the narrator imagines a third magical transformation of the city – 'one final picture' he ardently wants to show us (p. 312). In this image, Mother stands with Boy and O on a stage in a public square, 'against the backdrop of some grand historical event' (p. 310), and speaks the opening words to 'All of Me', the love song she had sung repeatedly on the stage in The Bar:

> Your goodbyes,
> Left me with eyes that cry,
> How can I go on, dear, without you?

At this point, 'from the great crowd comes rising the whispered chorus, a great, strong, slow, gentle sound, everyone now holding up a candle or just a hand or a photograph of a person who couldn't be here tonight' (p. 312). This account summons up images of the candlelight vigils held for AIDS victims in London and other cities in the 1980s. Coupled with the book's less overt references to AIDS – for example, when the narrator compares Boy to an allegorical statue, he says that 'it is him who will attend our funerals' – this scene makes it possible to read *Ready to Catch Him Should He Fall* as an extended prosopopoeia which lends a voice to, among others, those silenced by AIDS.

The fantasy of the moving statues, in which the figures of the city celebrate the survival of Boy and O's relationship and of the collective gay world that fostered it, throws into relief the city's actual reaction to AIDS: punitive policies against its victims, moralistic indictments of homosexuality – and, by implication, of those who have died – harassment of gays in public places, and restrictions on gay sexual culture. The statues come to life at a Benjaminian 'moment of danger',[82] when the city is employing images of the dead to overpower tradition with sexual conformism – in addition to the political and economic conformism about which Benjamin wrote. At this moment, memories 'flash up',[83] including the memory of Wilde, reminding us that today's victors descend from those who nearly a hundred years ago, in the highest moral tone and calling on the 'common sense of indignation',[84] condemned Wilde. Seizing hold of this memory, 'fanning the spark of hope in the past', Bartlett uses the symbols of civic tradition to wrest it from the victors. His monuments re-enter a dialogue with 'the tradition of the oppressed' and therefore with history, including the history of the search for justice in the city, a search stretching back to the classical tradition that makes up the past of the monuments themselves.

Placed within the tradition of the oppressed, the statues' speech does more than publicly announce Boy and O's love or protest the cruelty of a moralizing, heteronormative culture. It also declares rights, itself a kind of prosopopoeia, since claiming rights keeps democracy alive. Patricia Williams, describing how the discourse of rights animates oppressed peoples, who at the same time give life to the notion of rights, compares rights to alchemical transformations:

> Give to all of society's objects and untouchables the rights of privacy, integrity, and self-assertion; give them distance and respect. Flood them with the animating spirit that rights mythology fires in this country's most oppressed psyches, and wash away the shrouds of inanimate-object status, so that we may say not that we own gold but that a luminous golden spirit owns us.[85]

Williams's alchemy of rights, poetically distinguished from interests, resembles Hannah Arendt's notion of 'a right to have rights'.[86] Discussing the long history of struggles against oppression that have been framed as demands for new rights, Lefort asks: 'Are these various rights not affirmed by an awareness of right without objective guarantees, and equally with reference to publicly recognized principles which are partly embodied in laws and which must be mobilized in order to destroy the legal limits that restrict them?'[87]

Bartlett's monuments set rights in motion, for each new rights-claim repeats the initial democratic demand for a 'public inscription of freedom and equality'.[88] Democracy depends on this continual revitalization since the lack of guarantees that is its condition means that in declaring rights we do not lay claim to something that belongs to us by nature. More radically, in referring power to society, the democratic invention relocates rights from a transcendent to a political realm. The declaration of rights generates democracy, and rights themselves are invented only when they are declared. They are coextensive with, not prior to, politics so that democracy affirms what Balibar calls 'a *universal right to politics*',[89] the right to engage in struggle by . . . declaring rights.

This entanglement of rights and politics undermines distinctions between the rights of man – the supposedly private, non-political individual – and the rights of the citizen, that person whose activity connotes politics. Balibar writes,

> The declaration of the rights of man and the citizen is a radical discursive operation that deconstructs and reconstructs politics. It begins by taking democracy to its limits, in some sense *leaving* the field of instituted politics ... but in order to mark, immediately, that the rights of man have no reality and no value except as political rights, rights of the citizen, and even as the unlimited right of all men to citizenship.[90]

The radical discursive operation contains an ambiguity. On the one hand, the invention of democratic rights is tied to the logic of the unified political group or nation, separating 'man' and 'citizen' and naturalizing the assumption that some people have fewer rights. On the other hand, the declaration erodes the citizen/man distinction by politicizing rights and expressing 'an essential limitlessness characteristic of democracy'.[91] While social questions are decided, none can be forever excluded from politics. The problem of society can never be finally settled. Therefore the rights of man imply conflicts over attempts to gain respect for *different* rights.

Bartlett's monuments intervene in such conflicts. Exercising the right to constitute and question – to constitute by questioning – the social order that they represent, they publicly claim liberties for gays: the right, say, to walk in the city or the right to a publicly accessible sexual culture. In so doing, they no longer present themselves as either 'ideal' or 'stone' citizens. Unlike the citizens posited in classical theories of the public sphere of citizenship, they do not claim or aspire to the status of abstract, impartial beings that, upon entering the public sphere, transcend race, gender and sex and remain untouched by history and undivided by an unconscious. They cast off the pretense, inherent in the ideal of the abstract citizen, of sexlessness that every normalization of sexuality protects. As sexualized actors in the public sphere, the statues awaken from their confinement to what Lauren Berlant calls 'dead citizens': beings that, like certain common metaphors–her example is 'the legs of a table' – have become 'so conventionalized as to no longer seem figural, no longer open to history'.[92]

Although Bartlett's monuments divest themselves of abstract personhood, they do not assume the alternative disguise of a specific, fundamental identity. They do not, that is, retreat from public space, the sphere where, in the absence of a prepolitical 'basis of the relation between *self* and *other*', we negotiate social identities and the identity of society.[93] But while the rights the statues claim have no ground in an *essential* human nature, they do lay claim to *universality*, if by this we mean that they demand an equal right to politics for all people.[94] The civic statues demand precisely this equality and this freedom,[95] proclaiming on behalf of non-normative sexualities 'the right to the city', to use Lefebvre's famous phrase.

What kind of rights claim is this, which has inspired urban social movements and compelled the attention of critical urban theory but still remains so loosely theorized? For some time now, radical urban scholars, following Lefebvre, have invoked the right to the city against the capitalist domination of space. Some equate opposition to capitalist space with the defense of so-called 'authentic' owners and uses of space. The Paris Commune has been described, for example, as an exercise of the right to the city, defined not only as the contestation of spatial exclusion but as the reclamation of space by its proper owners – in this case, the workers of Paris – or as a step toward restoring an originary spatial wholeness, a true identity given by the 'use-value' of space. Major aspects of Lefebvre's theory support this interpretation, especially his conception of power, which ultimately reduces oppressive social relations to those of class and of a state in the service of capitalism, and, further, his references to a once integrated, non-alienated socio-spatial condition.

In a different vein, urban scholars invested in dividing metaphorical and concrete spaces often claim Lefebvre's mantle. Linking material space with real politics, they loosely associate both with struggles for the right to the city. Explicitly or implicitly, they suggest that debating the discursive construction of space or investigating the spatial politics of discourse ignore – and thus prevent us from engaging in – struggles over the right to the city. The argument, though rarely articulated in any clear fashion, is this: theories about the politics of subjectivity in discourse, images and representation, divert attention from, and are therefore complicit with, social oppression and violence.[96] Yet once we ask what kind of claim is made in declaring 'the right to the city' and once we pose the question *in a democratic manner* – which is to say, once we dispense with appeals to external guarantees of meaning – we have to acknowledge that the answers we propose depend on our images of the city and of rights, and this in itself erodes the dichotomy between social-concrete and metaphorical-discursive spaces and, with it, easy divisions between real and unreal politics.

How can we formulate an ethical and emancipatory conception of the right to the city that does not appeal to proper owners and users of space? A right to the city that does not idealize traditional city spaces as 'authentic' and dismiss new spatial arrangements as unreal, thus abandoning them as new spaces of political action? It is possible to locate in Lefebvre support for this other formulation. For while he sometimes deploys a vocabulary of 'restoration', he also contends that the right to the city is not a return to traditional cities but a right 'to appear on all the networks and circuits of communication, infor-mation, and exchange'.[97] Far from a right to something known but not yet achieved or a naturally given right of which one has been dispossessed, the right to the city is 'a right in the making',[98] a right to urban society, to, that is, a heterogeneous and non-segregated social space[99] of 'encounter' and 'simultaneity'. Lefebvre claims the right to the city against the suppression of this form of society, and for him the democratic character of a regime can be measured by its attitude toward 'urban freedoms'.[100]

Reinventing the concept of the right to the city is the task of another essay, but the urgency of this undertaking is increasingly apparent in cities such as New York, whose conditions distressingly resemble those of Bartlett's London. In making rights inseparable from democratic urbanism, the notion of the right to the city challenges the ease with which those who are hostile to rights now present themselves as guardians of urban life. For hostility toward rights is a hallmark of moral crusades, which are guided by the precept that today's urban problems spring from a decline in adherence to conventional moral values.[101] In New York, this moralizing attitude is currently embodied in campaigns to improve 'the quality of life', a term that has become the centerpiece of public discussion about the city, though its genealogy in urban discourse awaits critical investigation. Since the early 1990s, policy intellectuals at the conservative Manhattan Institute have promoted a 'quality-of-life' agenda at élite conferences and in their magazine *City Journal*.[102] In 1993, Rudolph Giuliani, influenced by the Institute and building on the foundation laid down during the Reagan–Bush–Koch years, adopted the term as the slogan of the first of his successful mayoral campaigns, and his administrations have mobilized it to legitimate authoritarian policies. They equate quality-of-life initiatives with the imperatives of urban comfort, beauty and utility – all considered to be benign and to lie outside the limits of the political. Within this framework, interrogating notions of 'comfort', 'beauty', and 'utility' becomes tantamount to repudiating them. Questioning their deployment signals an embrace of discomfort, ugliness and dysfunction, which, by the very nature of things, endanger the city.

Quality-of-life initiatives have of course been criticized, often on the ground that they trivialize urban problems. But actually they have deadly serious effects. Residents made homeless during the 1980s by changing employment patterns, cutbacks in social services and city government's support of real estate interests, are now removed to undisclosed locations. People apprehended for quality-of-life violations are likely to be arrested if they do not live in the neighborhoods in which they commit their offenses. Public space is increasingly controlled by the housed residents of neighborhoods and conceded to corporations, real estate and non-accountable entities representing private profit, such as Business Improvement Districts. And the conditions of gay public life are endangered:

Times Square is being redeveloped into a family entertainment area; the Hudson River piers, a refuge for gays, where 'we can hold hands without being harassed',[103] are fenced off for redevelopment; gay bars and dance clubs are harassed and closed; and in 1995 a new zoning law was passed, which threatens to eliminate the vast majority of legal sex businesses in Manhattan, businesses that have long provided public venues for gays to meet in a homophobic city.[104] The zoning law restricts sex businesses to remote – frequently unusable – sites, makes them less visible by limiting the size, placement and illumination of signs, and isolates them by allowing no adult business within 500 feet of another.

In these circumstances, certain gay writers, such as Gabriel Rotello, author of *Sexual Ecology: AIDS and the Destiny of Gay Men*, have recently blamed urban gay sexual culture for causing AIDS and continuing to spread HIV infection.[105] In contrast, the organization Sex Panic! was formed in 1997 both to promote safer sex and, taking a stand against the city's quality-of-life campaign, to defend the right of gays to a publicly accessible sexual culture.[106] Sex Panic! takes the position that sex businesses have been major sites of safer sex education and that higher rates of HIV transmission will result from trying to cope with the complexity of human sexual behavior by sorting it into a few moral categories, encouraging shame, and, in Walt Odets's words, taking 'no account of the reality of the gay men most susceptible to HIV infection, the young ones' who are exploring their sexuality.[107] Arguing against Sex Panic!, Rotello claims that while he does not necessarily support quality-of-life regulations, they do not specifically target gays since they are applied almost universally.[108] This is a mistake. It is true, as Rotello says, that New York's quality-of-life campaign benefits real estate – this is one of its principal functions. Gays are not isolated victims. But this increases, rather than mitigates, the danger of making common cause with sanitizing crusades. In *Ready to Catch Him Should He Fall*, Mother takes a different approach when she urges the men in The Bar to understand the connections between homophobic, xenophobic and racist violence.

It is also true that the presumption of unanimity embedded in the singularity of the term 'quality of life' gives the impression that the regulations apply equally to all residents. But in fact they are only neutral on their face and fall with disparate impact on different social groups. For instance, the criminalization of sleeping, bathing and urinating in public has little relevance for housed New Yorkers. Likewise, as the queer theorist Michael Warner points out in a 1995 essay, *Zones of Privacy*, gays are particularly vulnerable to initiatives such as the new zoning bill since, with few publicly accessible resources, they have constructed a shared world largely through sex businesses: 'Extinguish sexual culture, and almost all *out* gay culture will wither on the vine'.[109]

In claiming the right of gays to a public sexual culture against the city's attempts to privatize sexuality, *Zones of Privacy* diverges sharply from the more familiar arguments for sexual liberties based on the right to privacy. Warner places his claim under the rubric 'the right to the city', which, however, he mentions only in passing, without elaborating its meaning. Nonetheless, his use of the term is consistent with and even enlarges on Lefebvre's notion. Warner affirms the right to a public sexual culture against the power of city government and real estate to isolate and exclude gay sexuality. Similarly, Lefebvre invents the right to the city to challenge the segregating and isolating ambitions of the state and private enterprise. Although Warner invokes the right to the city as the right of access to pregiven spaces, he does so while posing the question of what an urban space is and, in answering, moves closer to Lefebvre's explanation of the right to the city. 'The *right to the city*', says Lefebvre, 'legitimates the refusal to allow oneself to be removed from urban reality by a discriminatory and segregative organization'.[110] Warner observes that the zoning bill isolates, hence privatizes, sexual culture by mandating three changes in the organization of sex businesses: from concentration to dispersal, from conspicuousness to discretion, from residential to remote sites.[111] Where Warner maintains that the zoning bill promotes a particular vision of urban life, Lefebvre might conclude that, by virtue of its isolating strategies, it suppresses urban life. In the end, Warner agrees. He argues that the zoning scheme advances an ideology of neighborhood that defines urban space as a community of shared interest based on residence and property, and he asserts that this ideology is anti-urban: 'Urban space is always a host space. The right to the city extends to those who use the city. It is not limited to property owners'.[112] For Lefebvre, of course, the right to the city does not extend to, but is declared against, private property ownership. Still, Warner's proposal is in keeping with the spirit, if not the letter, of Lefebvre. Calling the city a host space is similar to defining urban life in terms of 'encounter' and 'simultaneity'. True, Warner's rejection of neighborhood control may contradict Lefebvre's support of community self-management, and, more important, the categorical nature of Warner's dismissal seems politically counterproductive. In failing to differentiate among neighborhoods on the basis of, say, their socioeconomic and racial character, to take account of historical contingencies, including the legacy of environmental racism, or to give any weight to people's attachment to the places where they live, Warner disregards the possibility that under certain circumstances struggles for neighborhood control may resist, rather than support, spatial domination. In no way, however, does this obviate the question he poses. In New York today 'neighborhood' is deployed to evict homeless people from the city, deprive gays of public venues, and support social service cutbacks. Jane Jacobs's famous celebration of

neighborhood in *The Death and Life of Great American Cities*[113] is cited ubiqui-
tously, not, as she intended, against urban renewal and anti-urbanism but
against heterogeneity and the rights of others and, as Jacobs was accused of
doing, to treat the city 'as an organization for the prevention of crime'.[114] In
this situation, there is reason to take very seriously the ways in which the
discourse of neighborhood, far from saving the city, threatens urban life, and
may even be unneighborly.

Historically, of course, defending neighborhood has hardly been the only
way of challenging sociospatial power. Michel de Certeau, for one, proposed
something different: 'walking in the city', this is, using space to elude the
discipline imposed by urban development. If Lefebvre's 'right to the city' is at
odds with current invocations of neighborhood, it is compatible with de
Certeau. Consider *Ready to Catch Him Should He Fall*. The book declares a right
to the city that might be interpreted as, precisely, the right to walk in the city.
Walking is a recurring motif in the novel, and as the object of a rights claim
might refer to literal freedom of movement for gays – no insignificant demand,
indeed, as Bartlett makes clear, a matter of life and death. If, however, we
approach the city as a form of society, the right to walk in the city assumes
broader and more radical implications. What happens, for instance, if we define
the city not as a city of neighborhoods but as, in de Certeau's words, an
'immense social experience of lacking a place', an experience brought about
by 'the moving about that the city multiplies?'[115] The right literally to walk in
the city then becomes part of a more comprehensive freedom, the freedom to
use the constructed spatial order in a way that not only actualizes but also
transforms it. De Certeau likens walking in the city to figurative uses of
language. Both drift from the proper meanings of the spatial systems within
which they operate – urban and linguistic. Both introduce tension and differences and found within those systems 'a legitimate *theater* for practical *actions*
... a field that authorizes dangerous and contingent social actions'.[116] Both
take the risk of creating a public space.

Bartlett's drama of the moving statues, which I have read as a figure of
democratic urbanism, animates the city by walking and animates democracy by
declaring rights. The two practices converge in the 'right to the city'. We might
now reanimate this right – modifying, perhaps discarding, some of Lefebvre's
ideas and articulating them with ideas from other sources – to assert it against
the cruel and unreasonable urbanism that currently travels under the slogan
'the quality of life'. Proponents of this urbanism treat those who diverge from
moral norms as representatives of the city's 'outside' and adopt punitive
measures against these outsiders, remaining indifferent to the possibility that,
to paraphrase Oscar Wilde, one of moralism's saddest victims, 'the habitual

employment of punishment' may brutalize a city as much as the occurrence of crime.[117]

Notes

1. Neil Bartlett, *Ready to Catch Him Should He Fall*, New York, Dutton, 1990.
2. Walt Whitman, 'City of Orgies' and 'To a Stranger', in Francis Murphy, ed., *The Complete Poems*, London: Penguin Books, 1975, pp. 158–60.
3. Guillaume Apollinaire, 'Voyage à Paris', in *The Selected Writings of Guillaume Apollinaire*, New York: New Directions Books, 1971, p. 200.
4. Emmanuel Levinas, 'The Rights of Man and the Rights of the Other', in *Outside the Subject*, trans. Michael B. Smith, Stanford, California: Stanford University Press, 1994, p. 124.
5. Bartlett, *Ready to Catch Him*, p. 11 (emphases and ellipsis in the original). Subsequent references to this book appear in parentheses in the text.
6. Mikhail Bakhtin, 'Epic and Novel: Toward a Methodology for the Study of the Novel', in *The Dialogic Imagination*, trans. Caryl Emerson and Michael Holquist, Austin: University of Texas Press, 1981, p. 22.
7. Ibid.
8. Ibid., p. 28.
9. Ibid., p. 27.
10. J. Hillis Miller, 'Face to Face: Faces, Places, and Ethics in Plato', in *Topographies*, Stanford, California: Stanford University Press, 1995, p. 58. Miller is discussing Plato's *Protagaras*.
11. Bartlett, *Ready to Catch Him*, p. 16.
12. Oscar Wilde, 'The Decay of Lying', (1889), in *De Profundis and Other Writings*, London: Penguin Books, 1954. In this dialogue, which is filled with Wilde's characteristic paradoxes and serious word play, the character Vivian says: 'There is such a thing as robbing a story of its reality by trying to make it too true'. For Richard Ellman, 'The Decay of Lying' defines art's function as making 'a raid on predictability'. Ellman, *Oscar Wilde*, New York: Random House, 1984, p. 304.
13. For examples of the real–unreal distinction in recent discourse about geography, see Gillian Rose, 'As if the Mirrors Had Bled: Masculine Dwelling, Masculinist Theory and Feminist Masquerade', in Nancy Duncan, ed., *Bodyspace: Destabilizing Geographies of Gender and Sexuality*, London and New York: Routledge, 1996, pp. 56–74.
14. Ernesto Laclau and Chantal Mouffe, *Hegemony and Socialist Strategy: Towards a Radical Democratic Politics*, trans. Winston Moore and Paul Cammack, London: Verso, 1985.
15. See, for example, Doreen Massey, 'Flexible Sexism', *Environment and Planning D: Society and Space*, vol. 9, 1991, pp. 31–57; Meaghan Morris, 'The Man in the Mirror: David Harvey's 'Condition of Postmodernity',' *Theory, Culture and Society* 9, 1992, pp. 253–79; Mark Wigley, 'Theoretical Slippage: The Architecture of the Fetish', in Sarah Whiting et al, eds., *Fetish*, Princeton: Architectural Press, 1992, pp. 88–129 and 'Lost and Found', in Laura Kurgan and Xavier Costa, eds., *You Are Here: Architecture and Information Flows*, Museu d'Art Contemporani de Barcelona, 1995, pp. 171–85; Gillian Rose, *Feminism and Geography: The Limits of Geographical Knowledge*, Minneapolis: University of Minnesota Press, 1993; Derek Gregory, *Geographical Imaginations*, Oxford: Blackwell, 1994; Rosalyn Deutsche, 'Men in Space', 'Boys Town', and 'Chinatown, Part Four? What Jake Forgets about Downtown', in *Evictions: Art and Spatial Politics*, Cambridge MA: MIT Press, 1998, pp. 195–253; and Victor Burgin, *In/different Spaces: Place and Memory in Visual Culture*, Berkeley: University of California Press, 1996.

16. Neil Smith makes this slippage in 'Contours of a Spatialized Politics: Homeless Vehicles and the Production of Geographical Scale', *Social Text* 33, 1992, pp. 54–81. For a critique of the division between real and unreal space, that sees it as an attempt to maintain a hierarchical sexual division, see Rose, 'As if the Mirrors Had Bled'.

17. Bakhtin, 'Epic and novel', p. 33.

18. Cathy Caruth, 'Introduction: The Insistence of Reference', in Cathy Caruth and Deborah Esch, eds., *Critical Encounters: Reference and Responsibility in Deconstructive Writing*, New Jersey: Rutgers University Press, 1995, p. 1.

19. Henri Lefebvre, *The Production of Space*, trans. Donald Nicholson-Smith, Oxford: Blackwell, 1991, p. 229. Originally published as *La production de l'espace*, Paris: Anthropos, 1974. For a psychoanalytically informed discussion of the ways in which urban and cultural theorists have formulated the relationship between social and psychical space, see Burgin, introduction to *In/Different Spaces*, Berkeley: University of California Press, 1996, pp. 1–36.

20. Ibid., pp. 38–39. Lefebvre's social space contains another moment, which he calls 'representations of space', referring to the conceptual abstractions of technocratic planners that dominate space.

21. Roland Barthes, 'Rhetoric of the Image', in *Image, Music, Text*, trans. Stephen Heath, New York: Hill & Wang, 1977, p. 44.

22. Michel de Certeau, 'Spatial Stories', in *The Practice of Everyday Life*, Berkeley: University of California Press, 1984, p. 117.

23. Bakhtin, 'Epic and Novel', p. 30 (emphasis added).

24. Ibid., p. 37.

25. Caruth, 'Introduction: The Insistence of Reference', p. 6.

26. Miller, 'Face to Face: Faces, Places, and Ethics in Plato' p. 6.

27. Lynne Tillman, 'That's How Strong His Love Is', in *The Broad Picture: Essays*, London: Serpent's Tail, 1997, p. 105.

28. Ellman, introduction to *Oscar Wilde*, p. xv.

29. Ibid., p. xvi.

30. Kenneth Gross, *The Dream of the Moving Statue*, Ithaca: Cornell University Press, 1992, p. 150.

31. Miller, 'Face to Face: Faces, Places, and Ethics in Plato, p. 74.

32. Ibid., p. 72.

33. Ibid., p. 71.

34. Ibid., p. 72.

35. Miller, 'Face to Face: Faces, Places, and Ethics in Plato', p. 75.

36. Ibid., p. 74.

37. Ibid., pp. 74–75.

38. Walter Benjamin, 'Theses on the Philosophy of History', in *Illuminations*, ed. Hannah Arendt, trans. Harry Zohn, New York: Schocken Books, 1969, p. 255.

39. Ibid., p. 257.

40. Ibid., p. 255.

41. J. Hillis Miller, *The Ethics of Reading: Kant, de Man, Eliot, Trollope, James, and Benjamin*, New York: Columbia University Press, 1987.

42. Emmanuel Levinas, 'The Rights of Man and the Rights of the Other', pp. 124–25.

43. Wilde, 'The Critic as Artist', (1891), in Richard Ellmann, ed., *The Artist as Critic: Critical Writings of Oscar Wilde*, Chicago: The University of Chicago Press, 1968, p. 360.

44. Claude Lefort, 'The Question of Democracy', in *Democracy and Political Theory*, trans. David Macey, Minneapolis: University of Minnesota Press, 1988, p. 19.

45. It is a very common error for critics to conclude that poststructuralist ideas about uncertainty and democracy preclude the possibility of decision-making rather than obligate us to decide.

46. Levinas, 'The Rights of Man and the Rights of the Other' p. 124.

47. Ibid.

48. Ibid., p. 125.

49. Julia Kristeva, *Strangers to Ourselves*, trans. Leon S. Roudiez, New York: Columbia University Press, 1991, p. 103.

50. Tillman, p. 105.

51. Cicero, *Tusculan Disputations*; quoted in Jacob Howland, *The Republic: The Odyssey of Philosophy*, Twayne's Masterwork Studies No. 122, New York: Twayne Publishers, 1993, p. 10.

52. Simon Watney, *Policing Desire: Pornography, AIDS and the Media*, Minneapolis: University of Minnesota Press, 1987, p. 17.

53. Ibid., p. 98.

54. Mikhail Bakhtin, *Rabelais and His World*, trans. Hélène Iswolsky, Bloomington: Indiana University Press, 1984, p. 6. Originally published as *Tvorchestvo Fransua Rable*, Moscow: Khudozhestvennia literatura, 1965.

55. Henry Urbach, 'Spatial Rubbing: The Zone', *Sites* vol. 25, 1993, p. 95.

56. Oscar Wilde, 'The Happy Prince' (1888), in *Complete Fairy Tales of Oscar Wilde*, New York: Signet Classic, 1990, pp. 9–22. I would like to thank Jeff Nunokawa for bringing this story to my attention.

57. Gross, *The Dream of the Moving Statue*, p. 142.

58. Mother's play, like the novel as a whole, can be read in part as a reworking of Wilde's life, which here ends happily. For instance, The Son's love for The Lover overrides his obedience to The Father, unlike that of Lord Alfred Douglas to whom Wilde wrote from prison: 'Your hatred of your father was of such stature that it entirely outstripped, overthrew, and overshadowed your love of me'. (Wilde, De Profundis, in *De Profundis and Other Writings*, London: Penguin Books, 1954, p. 126.) There is another Father in *Ready to Catch Him Should He Fall* – Boy's father, one of the book's major characters. He is a fantastic character, both Boy's 'real' father and, as Bartlett puts it, 'that patriarchal father who forbade me to be who I am'. (Bartlett, quoted in Lynne Tillman, 'That's How Strong His Love Is', p. 110.) He comes to live with Boy and O, nearly destroys their relationship, and dies cradled in Boy's lap.

59. Gross, *The Dream of the Moving Statue*, p. 147 (subsequent references to this book appear in parentheses in the text).

60. Miller, 'Faces, Places, and Ethics in Plato', p. 73.

61. Raymond Ledrut, 'Speech and the Silence of the City', in M. Gottdeiner and Alexandros Ph. Lagopoulos, ed., *The City and the Sign: An Introduction to Urban Semiotics*, New York: Columbia University Press, 1986, p. 121.

62. Ibid., p. 122.

63. Ibid., p. 120.

64. Mary McCarthy, *The Stones of Florence*, New York: Harcourt Brace Jovanovich, 1963; quoted in Gross, *The Dream of the Moving Statue* p. 175.

65. Catulle Mendès, *Les 73 journées de la Commune*, Paris: E. Lachaud, 1871, pp. 1149–50; quoted in Kristin Ross, *The Emergence of Social Space: Rimbaud and the Paris Commune*, Minneapolis: University of Minnesota Press, 1988, p. 5.

66. de Certeau, 'Spatial Stories, p. 130.

67. Ibid.

68. Sigmund Freud, 'The 'Uncanny',' in *Writings on Art and Literature*, Stanford: Stanford University Press, 1997, p. 223.

69. Kristeva, *Strangers to Ourselves*, p. 182.

70. Freud, 'The "Uncanny"' p. 195.

71. Kristeva writes: 'It is through unraveling transference – the major dynamics of otherness, of love/hatred for the other, of the foreign component of our psyche – that, on the basis of the other, I become reconciled with my own otherness-foreignness. . . . Psychoanalysis is then experienced as a journey into the strangeness of the other and of oneself, toward an ethic of respect for the irreconcilable' (p. 182).

72. Ibid., p. 183.
73. Freud, 'The "Uncanny",' p. 227.
74. Kristeva, *Strangers to Ourselves* p. 192.
75. Ibid., p. 1 (emphasis added).
76. Ellmann, *Oscar Wilde*, p. 444.
77. Claude Lefort, 'Human Rights and the Welfare State', in *Democracy and Political Theory*, p. 31.
78. Gross, *The Dream of the Moving Statue* p. 198.
79. Alois Riegl, 'The Modern Cult of Monuments: Its Character and Its Origins', *Oppositions* vol. 25, Fall 1982, pp. 21–51. In this 1903 essay, Riegl uses the term 'unintentional monument' to designate the work of art or architecture that becomes a landmark of history only after its creation and is thus assigned a new role in new circumstances. Riegl distinguishes the unintentional monument from the 'intentional monument', which is built from the start as a permanent commemoration of a historic event or person. My use of 'unintentional' differs from that of Riegl, since I am suggesting that both kinds of monuments are in some sense 'unintentional'. But this idea is also implicit in Riegl's argument, which, as Kurt Forster points out, fundamentally undermines the belief that architectural monuments possess stable meanings. Forster, 'Monument/Memory and the Mortality of Architecture', *Oppositions* vol. 25, Fall 1982, pp. 2–19.
80. Bakhtin, *Rabelais and His World*, pp. 39–41.
81. Bartlett, quoted in Tillman 'That's How Strong His Love Is', p. 111.
82. Benjamin, 'Theses on the Philosophy of History', p. 257.
83. Ibid.
84. Justice Sir Alfred Wills, quoted in Ellman, *Oscar Wilde*, p. 477.
85. Patricia J. Williams, *The Alchemy of Race and Rights: Diary of a Law Professor*, Cambridge MA: Harvard University Press, 1991, p. 165.
86. Hannah Arendt, *The Origins of Totalitarianism*, New York: Harcourt Brace & Company, 1948, p. 296.
87. Ibid., pp. 261–62.
88. Etienne Balibar, 'Rights of Man' and 'Rights of the Citizen:' The Modern Dialectic of Equality and Freedom', in *Masses, Classes, Ideas: Studies on Politics and Philosophy Before and After Marx*, New York and London: Routledge, 1994, p. 49.
89. Ibid.
90. Etienne Balibar, 'What Is a Politics of the Rights of Man?' in *Masses, Classes, Ideas*, pp. 211–12.
91. Ibid., p. 211.
92. Lauren Berlant, 'Live Sex Acts (Parental Advisory: Explicit Material)', in *The Queen of America Goes to Washington City: Essays on Sex and Citizenship*, Durham and London: Duke University Press, 1997, p. 60.
93. For discussions of contemporary debates over the meaning of the 'public sphere', see Bruce Robbins, 'Introduction: The Public as Phantom', in Bruce Robbins, ed., *The Phantom Public Sphere*, Social Text Series on Cultural Politics 5, Minneapolis: University of Minnesota Press, 1993, pp. vii–xxvi; Nancy Fraser, 'Rethinking the Public Sphere: A Contribution to the Critique of Actually Existing Democracy', in Craig Calhoun, ed., *Habermas and the Public Sphere*, Cambridge: MIT Press, 1992, pp. 109–42; Thomas Keenan, 'Windows: Of Vulnerability', in Robbins, ed., *The Phantom Public Sphere*, pp. 121–41; Rosalyn Deutsche, 'Agoraphobia', in *Evictions: Art and Spatial Politics*', Cambridge: MIT Press, 1996, pp. 269–327.
94. Etienne Balibar draws a distinction between extensive and intensive universalism. 'In the extensional, denotative sense, the universal is what addresses all people . . . in order to encompass them in a single whole and arrange them under the same 'law', which in this way *neutralizes* or *relativizes* their differences. . . . But more profoundly, the concept of the universal has an intensional, connotative significance: this is what *equality* (and equal freedom, equal dignity) proposes in symbolic and

practical terms for all people, regardless of their differences. This intensive universality can only result from shared interests and practices'. 'Critical Reflections',
Artforum, vol. 36, no. 3, November 1997, p. 101.

95. In 'Rights of Man and Rights of the Citizen', Balibar fuses the two in his term
'equaliberty', which expresses the idea that freedom and equality are one and the
same.

96. Jacqueline Rose makes a similar point about the theory/social reality dichotomy in
relationship to ideas about psychoanalytic theory and sexual violence. She argues
that writers such as Wilhelm Reich and Jeffrey Masson draw a rigid opposition
between inside and outside, which corresponds to a second opposition between the
psychic and the social. These writers locate violence strictly in the external world of
social reality and suggest that psychoanalytic theory ignores this reality. For example,
Masson says that Freud ignored sexual violence against women and so handed
women over to that violence. Rose claims that these writers are arguing that the
theory itself causes death and violence and, further, that the inside/outside, psychic/
social oppositions they draw support a third opposition – that between psychoanalytic theory and politics. This conceptual framework, which Rose criticizes, resembles
that used by urban scholars who, as I indicate above, suggest that psychoanalytic,
poststructuralist, or various other theories, which they group under the rubric
'postmodernism', ignore the violence that produces and takes place in real social
space. See Rose, 'Where Does the Misery Come From? Psychoanalysis, Feminism,
and the Event', in Richard Feldstein and Judith Roof, eds., *Feminism and Psychoanalysis*, Ithaca and London: Cornell University Press, 1989, pp. 25–39.

97. Henri Lefebvre, 'The Right to the City', in Eleanor Kofman and Elizabeth Lebas,
eds., *Writings on Cities*, London: Blackwell, 1996, p. 195. Originally published as *Le
droit à la ville*, Paris: Anthropos, 1968.

98. Ibid., p. 179.

99. Ibid., p. 180.

100. Lefebvre, *Le droit à la ville*, p. 100.

101. For a typical statement of this position, see Fred Siegel, *The Future Once Happened
Here: New York, D.C., L.A., and the Fate of America's Big Cities*, New York: The Free
Press, 1997, especially chapter 14, 'The Moral Deregulation of Public Space'.

102. See, for instance, 'New York Views', *New York: The City Journal*, vol. 1, no. 1, Autumn
1990, pp. 2–3 and *The City Journal*, vol. 2, no. 2, Spring 1992, a special issue on 'The
Quality of Urban Life'. In conjunction with this issue, the Manhattan Institute
sponsored a conference on the quality of life, where 'Giuliani could be found seated
in the audience . . . scribbling notes'. (Janny Scott, 'Turning Intellect Into Influence:
Promoting Its Ideas, the Manhattan Institute Has Nudged New York Rightward',
New York Times, May 12, 1997, B3) Note that by 1992, the journal had dropped 'New
York' from its title, perhaps reflecting its nationwide influence: 'Despite its focus on
New York, the Manhattan Institute has had its greatest influence in other cities'.
(Tom Redburn, 'Conservative Thinkers are Insiders', *New York Times*, December 31,
1993, B2).

103. Quoted in David Bahr, 'As Piers Close, Gay Protesters See a Paradise Lost', *New York
Times*, September 14, 1997, Section 13, p. 6.

104. See Allan Bérubé, 'A Century of Sex Panics', in *Sex Panic!*, 1997, pp. 4–8.

105. Gabriel Rotello, *Sexual Ecology: AIDS and the Destiny of Gay Men*, New York: Dutton,
1997.

106. 'A Declaration of Sexual Rights', statement by the National Sex Panic Summit,
November 13, 1997.

107. Walt Odets, letter to the editor about *Sexual Ecology*, *The New York Times Book Review*,
June 22, 1997, p. 4.

108. Gabriel Rotello, 'An Open Letter to Sex Panic', *Lesbian and Gay New York*, August 4,
1997, p. 16.

109. Michael Warner, 'Zones of Privacy', unpublished paper, 1995, p. 22. Warner's paper

was written prior to the City Council's passage of the zoning amendment and the court challenges it has since undergone, but the questions Warner raises remain highly relevant to debates about the meaning of the urban.

110. Lefebvre, 'The Right to the City',
111. Warner, 'Zones of Privacy', p. 14.
112. Ibid., p. 24.
113. Jane Jacobs, *The Death and Life of Great American Cities*, New York: Vintage Books, 1961.
114. Lewis Mumford, 'Home Remedies for Urban Cancer' (1962), in Donald L. Miller, ed., *The Lewis Mumford Reader*, Athens: The University of Georgia Press, 1995, p. 191.
115. de Certeau, *The Practice of Everyday Life*, p. 103.
116. Ibid., p. 125. It is worth noting in our context that for de Certeau the poetics of walking makes urbanism inseparable from eroticism. He argues that spatial practice is a way of undoing the dominant spatial order and of moving into something different. It originates in the child's differentiation from the mother's body and repeats the move toward the other initiated by this childhood experience.
117. Oscar Wilde, quoted in Ellman, *Oscar Wilde*, p. 495.

7 THE COMPULSION TO REPEAT FEMININITY

LAUREN BERLANT

When, in *Landscape for a Good Woman*, Carolyn Kay Steedman renders
her mother's desire for the good life, she tells a story about the class-
related bases of desire, a desire whose animating force produces
migration, marriage, the management of knowledge, the manipulation
of money, and the marginality of children.[1] In this cluster of movements
and positionings, desire is something that makes you restless, defensive,
and ambitious; it propels you toward an elsewhere that, you imagine, will
offer you a fresh start, a new horizon of possibility and fewer economic
impediments. In this view, desire merges the intimate ambitions of your
life narrative with the economic ones, while pushing back the demons of
a burdensome past.

The co-production of intimacy and economy opens up for Steedman
other modes of meaning that have less to do with the linearity of moving
stories than with the circularity of static signs. Here the subject's life is
made not from movement, but from relations to *things*.[2] Addressing the
ways commodity cultures work to organize fantasy, Steedman suggests
that the cultivated appetite for things both tempers and temporalizes
desire by attaching it to concrete and potentially attainable objects,
fixing people in thing-oriented circuits of repetition that promise a life
of something like sublimity, but without its risk or pain.

Many women of the postwar era, for example, identified the pleasures
of their ideal world with beautiful fabrics, beautiful hands, beautiful
clothes and good food.[3] In advance of class security, Steedman's mother
is said to turn in on herself for practice, performing the feeling of
freedom she dreams of in the cultivation of her body and the bodies
around her, from managing familial programs of culinary discipline to

working as a manicurist for an élite class of fashion model. The body, Steedman writes bitterly, is what the powerless work on when they have nothing else:[4] a certain skirt and certain foods can overwhelm the scene of imaginable satisfaction where feminine aspirations for belonging are concerned. This constellation of need conventions has enabled a quasi-literal reading of the social to gain popular legitimacy, such that the things and practices of self-discipline identified with women's desires came themselves to seem evidence of the good life's propriety and good value.

Steedman means to expose here more than a tendency toward feminine fetishism: she suggests that these conventions of the beautiful object convey a less-enunciated desire for a world that can sustain families, love and dignity and that can overcome the economic strain and shame that working people experience in their effort to reach that plateau of satisfaction, the unanxious space and time of attainment that is the 'good woman's' fantasy.[5] All of the work and all of the moving, monitoring and accumulative fussing that go into survival as well as the reconditioning of the social body are also tactical moves in yet a third kind of space, where one wants to feel protected by an aura of plenitude and invulnerability like that which radiates from one's ego ideal or the experience of 'social standing'. The mother's fantasy is, more simply, for her life to become a space of perfect time *where that change has already happened.*

Steedman uses the artifice of the landscape to describe the interpretive devices people invent to make sense of their disjointed realities: the landscape form provides a clue to understanding how the contradictions of capitalist culture become liveable, desirable – or at least endured. This process is literalized for Steedman in the Lowry landscape that her mother hangs, of a mill town in northern England. Steedman puzzles that her mother would display a world from which she had fled and hidden, as though she wished after all to acknowledge what she had abandoned for the project of uplift. No doubt the mother's motive is derived in part from nostalgia's ghosts; but given Lowry's celebrity as the *auteur* of a fading Britishness in the popular artworld of postwar England, this landscape turns the detritus of her past into cultural capital, augmenting her claim to be, after all, the *thing* of her own fantasy.[6]

The substitutions Steedman's mother makes confuse by not being confusing enough. Somehow the drive to inhabit a metropolitan space where financial and cultural networks make ingots of opportunity available for the feverish taking is embodied in the national iconicity of the landscape form; somehow the hot complexity of a sexuality and a marriage that are not uniquely marked by secrets and shaming is imagined in the normative register of proper femininity and 'decent' class aspiration. The stress and compromise of life in metropolitan zones are translated into an imaginary space of absolute value that is never, or not yet, lived, and the violence of intimacy under economic and sexual inequality is perceived through the vaseline veil of an ideology that locates real love in a temporal tangent where it is protected from the *frottage* of the everyday. In *Landscape*, women and the working classes speak through desires for a good life that shows no wrinkles, tears, or bruises: the good life is an absolutely good object because in it desire is fixed up with a form that liberates everyone from acknowledging the circuitous route it has taken to its resting – or is it restive? – place.

This essay is interested in pursuing the forces that overorganize fantasy into conventional forms, scenes of improvisation and negotiated contradiction that come to be taken for granted as rules for living. The normative or prescriptive dicta about what constitutes the proper content of fantasy are sustained by their articulation as the moral responsibility of individuals. But what happens when the forms that have stood for virtue, value and social intelligibility generally are seen to have exhausted their unifying function? For example, the nation and the family have long provided a linked image of unity in liberal political regimes as well as in the registers of daily life: yet currently it is said that economic and intimate practices have surpassed these forms, such that they no longer organize or describe the world of power, knowledge and desire. I want to query the notion that to move past the form is to witness its breakdown, whether that form is the nation or sexual difference. I want to push back at the trend in critical theory to substitute new metacultural figures[7] – the hybrid subject, the metropole, the global – for the old ones, for by changing the content of the emergent subject of history we can merely replay the desire to know and to administer its proper forms.

In *Landscape for a Good Woman*, the metacultural forms that are noted for their traffic in the universal – the nation-form and sexual difference – come into contact with practices and spaces that are noted for their unwieldy and shifting improprieties – the city and sexuality. The city is the place where economic and cultural membership are negotiated, while the nation is the space where the law is sanctioned and persons gain value as citizens; likewise, sexuality is the practice where ambivalence prevails, while sexual difference organizes identity and all sorts of other taxonomies into proper locations. Yet these distinctions are only apparent, are they not? Using as its point of departure Steedman's concerns about the formal logics of national–capitalist subjectivity, this essay will replay them in a novel contemporary to it, Fay Weldon's *The Life and Loves of a She-Devil*. *She-Devil* takes on the desire to believe in the truth of form in its explicitly aversive attachment to generic femininity. Like *Landscape*, Weldon's novel plays with geopolitical and literary form to ask whether the destiny of femininity is to desire and therefore to reproduce itself as a conventional scene of failure. Both texts also reopen the question of feminism's difference from femininity, which has to do with the overvaluation of individual struggle at the expense of social relations of force, from exploitation and the discipline of law to the institutions of intimacy. As these are texts from the early 1980s, the lag between their critical concerns (socialism vs capitalism, sexual liberation vs patriarchy) and the geopolitical ones that animate contemporary questions of capitalism, nationality, subjectification and subjectivity can become an opportunity to interfere with the fantasy that a better form (of analysis, as of being) will solve the problem of living.

The 'So What?' Question

How do we begin to parse an imaginary that occupies unsettled spaces but reads the world as a fantasy thing, a city that leads to a landscape? We might begin by thinking about substitution as a form of repetition. Christopher Bollas describes the space of optimism a new object of attachment organizes as a 'transformational environment'.[8] Extending Winnicott's notion of the transformational object into a more properly scenic mode, Bollas argues that when someone recognizes a new attachment she is, as always, seeking to desire herself in the desire she elicits from another: this is not a self that already exists but one that the 'transformational environment' of the new object will help to bring into being. New attachments signify a desire for a change that cannot be produced by reason, intention or will: yet this desired change, embodied in the other, will simultaneously fabricate the desiring subject's fantasy of what she will be as the story of what she already is, while also confirming the self-ambivalence of which her desire to change is evidence.

Steedman's mother learns to seek transformational environments and to accumulate evidence for her goodness within regimes of normative ideology that link intimate desires to political realms of social membership, and self-development to the assimilation of norms. To remain endowed with the virtually legislative power of normativity, the fantasy or theory of a particular identity must be literalized in practice. To sustain optimism for the project of the feminine good life in the practical world, spaces are required where the labor of producing a better self can take place. In *Landscape* it is the city that functions as the central place for the production of the 'soft subversions' subjects generate to negotiate capitalist hierarchies of value.[9] Felix Guattari argues that under capitalism subjects are reduced to a 'microfascism' of the body, a masochism or a pleasure disorder that subjugates consciousness in self-directed fixations, which distort the subject's perception of her generic place in regimes of structural subordination. The subject is reduced to manufacturing history as a story about herself and begins to embroider her conventionality with consoling and conventional signs of uniqueness. Agency becomes diluted into incremental acts in the capitalist cityscape; time is absorbed into a space that only slowly registers effects.

These distinct but proximate temporalities render ordinary living relatively oblique to the flow of communication and capital that moves along rapidly in the metropole's networks.[10] In the intervals, one can learn to cloak those aspects of class history whose exposure would obstruct the public heights one aims to scale by accumulating capital, whether cultural or economic.[11] Steedman charts her mother's appropriation of a prosthetic life through the story of her migration from one city to the next. In London she uses her non-cosmopolitanism, her anonymity and genericness as camouflage, thus enabling her ideal self to emerge unmarked by its unpleasant past. To her, the city is an economic space where life can be contingently carved out, but it also grants a space of opportunistic loss and instrumental proliferation where the will can be exerted against the strain of history's determinations, just as women's sartorial and bodily habits can seem to eclipse history's distinguishing marks.

This particular desire for a dehistoricizing abstraction, which coded class ascension through feminine style, emerged in conjunction with a shift in national policy regarding British class hierarchy. The post-World War II generation extracted a promise from the state that the rebuilding of Britain would mean the fuller inclusion of all classes of citizen in the nation's resources. The so-called Welfare State expanded: but the political impact on working-class subjects of its redistributive program was not necessarily progressive.[12] Over time Steedman's mother became righteously conservative, identifying not with the lot of the laboring classes but with an aspiration to *feel* free from structural impediments the way she imagined the élite must feel. She desired to embody the best of 'culture.' Following Enoch Powell and others nostalgic for the eminence of Imperial Britishness, she adopted a patriotic nationalism, with its codes of xenophobia and racism, to give shape to what lay in the way of this freedom. Along with feminine bodily discipline, which provided a form of public consent to the values of the visibly superior proper world, these normative forms and practices of citizenship were crucial to sustaining the mirage that her 'I' was both particular and (potentially) universal: unique, superior, typical, law-abiding, and unfettered where need be.[13] While exploiting the cityscape to cultivate her aspiring brand of uniqueness and conventionality, her attachment to proper form impeded the development of a critical relation to the very conditions of national economic, sexual . . . and gendered subordination that produced her anxieties and induced her to work for a gratifying future in the first place. The body and the nimbus of intimacy it generates became the archive or the hoard that she could spend in order to fabricate a world that would confirm the power of the feminine thing, her fantasy. Meanwhile, the body magnetized the activity of consciousness, so that its destiny seemed also to be the destiny of the nation. In this context, the centrality of the city to fantasy's enactment gets lost in the roar of the universal.

To the degree that Steedman uses her mother's life to exemplify the fantasies that characterize women of the post-war working classes, it would be unwise to read this as a story about the ways they used commodities to express what would otherwise be critical theory. Instead, commodities are cast as an aesthetic solution to the complexities of social relations, an understanding of the aesthetic that Steedman places at the center of her class analysis of regimes of subjectivity. Clothing styles and norms of bodily performance are managed by individuals, who negotiate social membership through them. Meanwhile, she argues, one's sense of place and expectations for agency are profoundly influenced by the narrative genres in which subjectivity is conventionally represented: for the middle class, the psychoanalytic case study; for the working class, social history; for children, fairy tales; for citizens, political speeches.

This list of subject-producing genres is surprisingly incomplete. Although *Landscape* is mainly about women – it is Steedman's own story told as the unhappy extension of her mother's unfulfilled one, as well as about the uneven devolvement of gender's costs and privileges on men and women of different classes – its argument that class locates gender and sexuality in history does not articulate its analysis with an appraisal of the technologies through which women come to imagine femininity and the institutions of intimacy as the solvents that neutralize class and other modes of seemingly indelible located-ness. In the universalizing fantasy of the feminine, femininity is a type of natural law, a general mode of being that women can express, or a regulatory site of propriety to which they should aspire: its genre, however, is not the tablet of law but the book of love.[14] Capitalism uses romance to give content to fantasy, borrowing the commodity's aura of magic autonomy to locate the ordinary in a thrillingly unknowable story. In turn, romance narrative, high and low, is a machine for gendering women in the feminine, measuring the horizon of expectation about what life ought to bring (the love of X): if the value of the feminine present is symbolized in *things*, the good life's good future occurs through love's extension, its repetition into institution.[15] The genres of 'women's culture' market the love plot as the key to women's survival and optimism, as well as their estimate of their place in history.

In this sense love marks the bottom line in the project of feminization. Disciplinary ideologies and desire's unruliness merge in a romantic quasi-sublime: the repetition of the scene of failure and overcoming at the heart of romance plots structures the pleasure of the anxiety of competence to the feminine that is, according to Jacqueline Rose, femininity's ur-plot.[16] Just as the love plot erases its complexity on the way to its (generically inevitable) resolution, so too the multiplicity of forces articulated around femininity itself takes shape as crisis and, at the same time, must adapt to a normative form of fantasy that also plays as a universal. Identification with genericness figures here as an act of citizenship, a loyalty oath to the intelligibility of the social.

This association of the feminine with the capitalist nation is rooted in the political moment at which Steedman writes *Landscape for a Good Woman*. In contrast to the post-war prosperity that helped to shape Steedman's mother, the context for much of Steedman's own critique is left-wing politics after 1968, especially socialist feminism. Some central claims and tactics of the movement are expressed in the way *Landscape* tracks the double narrative of mother and daughter across national, sexual, and class divisions to bolster the claim that challenging the institutional and subjective effects of patriarchy requires dismantling traditional divisions and hierarchies of knowledge as well as those of the state, capitalism, the family and the law; and that a simultaneous revolution in sexual practices, institutions and ideology will further liberate feminine desire from its identification with emotional and domestic service economies. A socialist, sexual, and conceptual liberation would be required to disorganize the normal world, freeing persons from their destinies within the 'real' of subordination and exploitation.[17]

While tacitly endorsing these views *Landscape* also suggests that by presuming the universality of feminine subjectivity and desire, feminist psychoanalytic thought of the period participated in the normative work of maintaining femininity's generic status, in large part by diminishing the importance of class and national politics to the histories and futures of women. Yet Steedman cannot fully reject psychoanalytic configurations of gendered subjectivity – in part because the strategy of her text is to respect the different genres of subjectivity that represent the real for different categories of person; and in part because the compulsion to repeat the abjection to norms of sexual difference is the fundamental condition Steedman narrates, as it historically arbitrates the way class, racial, and national relations are lived. Against her will, she inherits this feminine location, along with the Oedipal mommy-daddy-me story that so frustratingly refuses to go away. The 'So what?' that functions as the epitaph to her mother's and her own life at the end of *Landscape* is meant to be a rhetorical question about the value of all these details, these species of feminine and feminist literalism.[18] But the very taken-for-granted triviality of women's lives reanimates the question about what the 'what' is that repeats the feminine attachment to the feminine attachment.

I want to reconsider this question about the compulsion to repeat femininity. 'So what?' asks about the centrality of the logic of cliché to the popular understanding of the feminine; it queries the 'pseudo-activity' of feminine genres, which produce narratives that seem to risk transgressing the structure of cliché while all along posing threats as conventional as any happy ending, any blue sky or love song.[19] This does not mean that the threats to fulfillment are mere mirages, but that frequently the drama of their overcoming requires disguising their conventionality. In *She-Devil*, the conventions of romance are so intensified that they generate an aura of stop-time in the continuously anxious present of feminine identity: yet the constancy of this anxiety has a timelessness to it as well, such that the sense of treading water or drowning in the present can also mark the pleasure and even the comfort one might derive from the most painful repetition.

At this level of generality it must be asked whether femininity is simply the ur-example of the routinization of all identity in national-capitalist culture; whether the articulation of commodity logic with psychoanalytic notions of attachment, ambivalence and repetition specifies women historically in modernity; or whether there is something irreducible, though not trivial, about the feminine; period. Yet these phrases are not quite right, since they are too absorbed in a project of reading that seeks identity's true shape. My task is to turn the compulsion to repeat femininity into the problem the essay addresses, rather than reconfirming that the always incomplete process of feminization can open up spaces for subversive kinds of improvisation, negotiation and change. 'So what?' can be read as a response to this claim, as well as a demand to account for the clichés of desire and complaint that constellate around feminine and feminist fantasies, a demand to come to some conclusion other than the one in which the pains women take to remain attached to the pleasures of the feminine undertaking seem inevitably like femininity itself.

The Life and Loves of a She-Devil is about love and femininity in ordinary life.[20] It locates the 'ordinary' in the lives of women of the British white middle-classes, whose minds are said to be distinguished and disfigured by the pressure they experience – by their desire – to reproduce an intimate life marked by conveniences of longing and estrangement. As in many historical romances, the novel uses a love triangle to universalize its image of personhood. But here the text is knowing about the libidinal tricks such formalism plays. Like Steedman's, a British feminist book from the 1980s, *She-Devil* also speaks critically of women's relation to love, locating it within the political economy of feminine suffering under global and patriarchalized regimes of intimacy and labor. Neither text deals much with the post-imperial racial struggles that marked the Britain of their own moment: crises in the political economy of sexual difference operate solely on a white national and familial axis. That the default image of proper femininity is white and upwardly mobile cannot be overemphasized.

At first it will seem that the novel locates the merger of women with femininity and femininity with love plots in satires of their normalizing institutions, discourses and desires. Yet by the end of the book, as so often happens, political knowledge drops out of the narrator's consciousness and, once again, it is only the personal sphere that is susceptible to radical change. 'Since I cannot change the world, I will change myself', the She-Devil resolves (p. 206). The personalization of politics helps her, but only somewhat, to neutralize the question about form faced by any critical thinker: what happens after you withdraw your attachment and adaptation to the collective objects, sites and ways of living that have for so long organized your knowledge of the world – for example, the nation-form and sexual difference? Is the potentially transformative value of new objects of desire and spaces of agency – hybridity, globalization – a therapeutic illusion held out as promise by the ultimately conservative, because repetitive, economy of fantasy?

The first-person narrative of *She-Devil* responds to this question by testing what it would take to destroy the conditions of feminine sub/abjection. The She-Devil's first tactic is unsurprising: she attempts to destroy the compulsion to identify with the fantasy of normal love. The second aim conjoins a critique of both feminine and feminist projects: *She-Devil* queries the belief that will, consciousness or reason can save women from desiring the iconic world that normal love maps out. It is an argument for the centrality of the unconscious for a materialist feminism and for deconstruction. Accordingly, alternate chapters are composed in two strikingly different registers – the satirically-slanted but acutely rendered language of the romance novel and the rage of feminist realism. That is, two forms of realism, the feminine and the feminist, signify different representational approaches to the desire for control that any mode of realism signifies. These modes struggle internally throughout the narrative to vanquish the undervaluation of women and the overvaluation of consciousness that produce the forms of desire and criticism that women have been compelled to repeat, with love.

'I sing a hymn to the death of love.'

Here is the novel's story. It is written in the voice of a woman named Ruth, who is hampered by many things: very tall, very fat and abjectly ugly, she has a hairy mole on her face that makes her not only very hard to look at, but also repulsive to imagine. Ruth is a product of a working-class environment in which feminin- ity is especially overvalued as a vehicle for class aspiration. Rejected by her family for her bodily anomaly and the ungainly personality formed around it, Ruth moves through her youth isolated, graceless and inarticulate. As she ages, her physical strength becomes her only valued attribute: she is a good worker, not a good woman, and work makes a place for her in the world. At her first job as a switchboard operator her competence depends on her body's suppression.

Ruth's depression about her bodily destiny is so complete that one cannot even call what she achieves 'survival': it is more simple than that, a not-stopping. When the book opens she is a suburban mother of two hateful children whose adulterous husband, 'Bobbo', an accountant, calls Ruth 'his best friend', which means in practice that she gets to hear detailed accounts of his affairs. Bobbo marries Ruth to spite his mother (and because Ruth's huge body, in the dark, is a comfort to him), but he soon realizes that such a deviant-looking creature will hold him back in his quest for success. Ruth tries to make a Victorian-style suburban world for Bobbo, but who she is visibly stains all that she does.

Under these circumstances, it is not surprising that Ruth is also, in her spare moments, an addicted reader of romance novels. She especially fancies those written by Mary Fisher, a novelist whose graced personal life is said to enact the fantasies and theories her novels weave, demonstrating by example that romance is both utopia and a reality that can be lived if a woman gives herself over to making beauty. Not just on her body: her language must be luscious, and she must create an exquisite home and landscape: 'Mary Fisher lives in the High Tower', writes Ruth at the beginning of nearly half the chapters: she lives on a rugged cliff near the 'surging' sea, 'where the new morning sun glances over hills and valleys and trees ... She is a woman: she made the landscape better' (p. 231). To Fisher and to Ruth (and implicitly, to all participating readers of the romance) the contrapuntal and material relation between reading and living suggests the value of the romance form to women: it is a tacit map of how to use fantasy to shape living, from the space of dreams to the landscape of the everyday. But because of what she looks like and what she cannot do, Ruth must separate fantasy from reality. Consuming Mary Fisher's novels with the insensate avidity of a bulimic, Ruth's compulsive pleasure is also a kind of knowledge – not of reality, but of her distance from the feminine world: 'I need to know the geographical detail of misfortune' (p. 4).

Ruth's love of the generic is a mirror of her failure at every aspect of it. Since her body has always been her destiny, providing no consoling mirage for the anxiety that is femininity, this might have been the end of the story of Ruth, and she suggests that an aerial photo of Eden Grove, her suburb, would show her as an irregular blob lumbering through a harmonious landscape. But then Bobbo becomes Mary Fisher's accountant as well as her lover. Ruth's first response to this crisis is traditional. To keep alive the fantasy of love's beautiful form, Ruth moves through the usual stages of feminine re-seduction – straining to cook beautiful meals, to dress elegantly, to speak pleasingly, and to disappear when she fears that she is on the verge of 'ugly and discordant' excesses and improprieties that may produce discomfort (p. 7). Unfortunately, Ruth's desire makes her spill the food, tear the dress, trip, pout, speak and cry at all the wrong places and times. Eventually, Bobbo decides to leave her. He encourages Ruth to get a job. Repeatedly, she says, 'but there are no jobs' (pp. 39, 48). He considers her pathetic, clumsy, ugly and dull-witted. 'You speak in clichés and talk in clichés' (p. 19).

But during the couple's final fight, there is a sea-change in Ruth's consciousness. Humiliated in front of Bobbo's parents, Ruth locks herself in the bathroom. Angrily, he declares, 'You are a third-rate person. You are a bad mother, a worse wife and a dreadful cook. In fact I don't think you are a woman at all. I think what you are is a she-devil!' (p. 41). Then, quietly, there is 'a change in the texture of the silence' that emanates from her (p. 41). Ruth embraces the hysterical gravity of her new appellation: it releases her from the world of feminine cliché.

Soon after Bobbo leaves, Ruth gives the children money to go to McDonalds, burns down her suburban house, and deposits the kids at the romantic 'High Tower' where Mary Fisher and Bobbo live; she disappears from her old life and identity and takes on the project of living as a She-Devil, a being of Nietzschean master proportions who uses her wisdom, bodily strength and will to build a world that suits her. To be a She-Devil means not only to live beyond the rules of normativity, but to go beyond sexual difference.

A she-devil is supremely happy: she is inoculated against the pain of memory. At the moment of her transfiguration, from woman to nonwoman, she performs the act herself. She thrusts the long, sharp needle of recollection through the living flesh into the heart, burning it out. The pain is wild and fierce for a time, but presently there's none. (p. 163).

For Ruth, this is a theoretical, practical and sexual transformation into the negative. The homeopathy of self-inflicted pain derived from the incineration of her memory (the memory of desire) numbs the general pain of failure at competence to femininity: but what is there for desire/identity when what was there for it is expelled?

No longer contracted to femininity, Ruth sees nothing at all utopian about the stabilizing fantasy of gender – it is one of the lies of romance.[21] This does not mean that she becomes postsexual, or denies the fascination and desire that sexuality (especially heterosexuality) organizes – quite the contrary. Ruth's response to her marital betrayal is to embark on a life of sexual adventure: every intimate contact she makes is triggered by her ability to become the sexual object her lover needs in order to feel confirmed in the world, which places her paradoxically in the feminine position of absolute power over the lover's grandiosity. Her failure to be feminine releases its power to her – but only in the event that love and desire not be part of the story, which is instead a story about power, about other routes to the feeling of plenitude and unconflictedness that love in a heterosexual family had never delivered to her.

Giving her lovers the gift of her fearlessness and her repudiation of sentimentality, Ruth receives from them access to modes of being she cannot produce through will alone – money, safe space, influence and bodily transformation. An expert reader of the diseases of subjectivity sexual normativity creates, she acts instrumentally on behalf of anger and hate, the purifying pain that defeminizes: 'I want to give hate its head', she says (p. 43). Each personal conquest she makes also advances her aim to destroy the institutions that keep women addicted to love and to the intimate scenes of their subordination: this means blighting the adulterous couple, along with 'the world of judges and priests and doctors, the ones who tell women what to do and how to think' (p. 120).

To do this she moves from Eden Grove to the city. As for jobs, she makes a discovery:

> There is always a living to be earned doing the work that others prefer not to do. Employment can generally be found looking after other people's children, caring for the insane, or guarding imprisoned criminals, cleaning public rest rooms, laying out the dead, or making beds in cheap hotels . . . There is always, as governments are fond of saying, work for those who want it. (p. 110).

She migrates from job to job, working in pseudo-domestic and semi-private arenas as a nanny for poor women, a nurse for the insane and the aged, and a maid for the privileged. In each job she takes on a new name, a new *vita*, a new history: Vesta Rose, Polly Patch, Molly Wishant, Marlene Hunter. In the city, it is presumed, women are hidden and in hiding, even when they are on the street or at work. Their zone of privacy is portable, labile: they make an intimate scene wherever they go. Yet in the metropole femininity is also put at risk constantly, in its proximity to bargaining and exploitation: this is to say that the putative universality of the feminine (as a space of activity) is marked by the difference between 'negotiating' alterity to survive only just and negotiating it with the kind of symbolic capital that makes femininity feel like an aspiration rather than a name for negativity. In *She-Devil* the city is a place of constant instrumental activity, but not a space of revolution.

The She-Devil works the ambiguous relation between threats to and the fulfilment of the fantasy in this next stage of her life. While working in a prison under the name 'Vesta Rose', for example, the She-Devil takes on as a lover 'Nurse Hopkins',[22] another misshapen and inassimilable woman whose sexual gratitude produces a political consciousness ('Women like us must learn to stick together' [p. 119].) and sexual pleasure that bind her to 'Vesta' for life. After a bit of time passes, Ruth persuades the nurse to leave the prison with her – ' "Out there in the world," said Ruth, "everything is possible and exciting" ' (p. 120). This seduction persuades the nurse to bankroll 'Vesta Rose', an agency for 'women shut away in homes performing sometimes menial tasks, sometimes graceful women trapped by love and duty into lives they never meant, and driven by necessity into jobs they loathe and which slowly kill them' (p. 120).

Once in the metropolitan world, saving women's lives through non-domestic labor becomes the lovers' manifest aim. 'The agency specialized in finding secretarial work for women coming back into the labor market – either from choice or through necessity – women who had good skills but lacked worldly confidence after years of domesticity. Those who signed on with the Vesta Rose Agency would receive retraining in secretarial skills and what Ruth called "assertiveness training" ' (pp. 121–122). The agency merges employment with self-help, as well as with a quasi-socialist understanding of the degrading aspects of the household economy. Merging this comprehension with the logic of the company town, Vesta Rose offers to the women it employs many extra life-sustaining services – and for a substantial fee: day care, laundry, shopping and cooking, for example. Thus while minimizing the contradictions of the double shift, the agency actually bolsters the domestic service economy in which femininity operates as an ideology promoting the aura of the labor of love. These happy and competent workers become known proudly as 'Vesta Roses'. They are intensely loyal to their leader.

In migrating to the city, then, Ruth creates jobs and supportive economic and emotional public spaces for women. Vesta Rose is so successful that within six months Ruth's women are posted all over the city, in every low-level white-collar working environment that counts – courts, jails, hospitals, schools and financial institutions. The geography of her misery turns into a fantasy space, a city produced by women's collaborative work and emancipated will. But Ruth has an ulterior purpose. She takes a spare key she had kept from the marriage to go to Bobbo's office at night, and shifts funds from his clients' accounts to the joint checking account they still maintain. Some months later Bobbo's office calls – he needs a typist. Vesta sends Elsie Flower to him – a Mary Fisher clone, 'little and sweet in looks', who 'bowed her neck as she bowed her mind, as if forever expecting some not altogether unpleasant blow to fall' (p.124). Bobbo, a sexual profligate, seduces Elsie, and Ruth, on hearing this, encourages the girl to fall in love with him and to tell him so. When Bobbo predictably dumps her, Ruth uses Elsie's rage to exact further revenge. She exposes him to Mary Fisher in a detailed letter with photographs; and, knowing the books of the business as well as she was trained to do, she (plus another Vesta Rose employee who works in Bobbo's bank) helps Vesta to transfer monies from his account to a Swiss bank account, making it seem as if Bobbo has embezzled the funds for his own purposes. The She-Devil notes the sum – $2,563,072.45 – as she notes many figures: her revenge on Bobbo requires mastery of his craft, plus even more precise accounting of who suffers love and how much it costs. Bobbo soon gets arrested. To exacerbate his pain, Ruth ingratiates herself with the Judge who hears Bobbo's case: she becomes his maid, his advisor, and his s/m slave, with the result that Bobbo is given a cruelly harsh sentence.

Ruth also revenges herself on Mary Fisher by getting Fisher's mother expelled from her nursing home and returned to Fisher's house. Obliged to care for the sarcastic and vocal aged woman and the jailed Bobbo's anarchic children, Fisher is dragged down into the muck of practical femininity she had previously dedicated herself to avoiding, which means disillusionment in the everyday and in the project of making a life as beautiful as a romance novel. As a result, she can no longer write romances. Her sublime estate decays. Her fingernails become jagged. Her friends desert her. Her publishers complain that her texts now alternate jarringly between romance rhetoric and housewife realism. Her only pleasure is in her sexual thrall to Bobbo, with which she loses contact on his imprisonment. Creatively disabled, with an imprisoned lover and no longer believing in feminine will, Mary converts to Catholicism and tries to let faith sustain her. At this point Ruth completes an affair she is having with a priest, and persuades him to go to save Mary Fisher's soul: they too have a sordid and sadistic affair until, at last, Mary Fisher contracts terminal cancer, which she and the priest both think she has brought on herself for her sins.

Ruth's revenge on those who were once her objects of unambivalent desire is only part of her She-Devil aim, however. Once Bobbo and Mary Fisher are taken care of, Ruth prepares to come to America. Here unfolds an aspect of the plot of which we have previously only seen glimmers. As she begins to embezzle money in London, she also embarks on a project of dental surgery, which involves a very painful filing away of every other tooth in her mouth; she then goes to a plastic surgeon and asks him to shorten her jaw and to give her new teeth, on behalf of what she calls 'the first step to the New Me' (p. 162). Her doctor even tells her excitedly that she 'will be making facial history!' (p. 175), which costs $1,761. Then Ruth goes to a plastic surgeon who 'believes in the power of intimacy' (p. 177), and when he asks her what she wants, she says she 'want[s] to look up to men'. This daunting task involves the reconstitution of her body through amputation and prosthesis: she reshapes her nose, her lips, her eyes, her hairline, and then chops six inches off each of her legs. The model for these changes is a picture of Mary Fisher that Ruth rips from the back of one of her novels: and in this Ruth is merely taking to an extreme what ordinary women are taught to do when consuming other women visually, that is, segmenting the female body into ideal erotic parts, and presuming that their sum would produce an erotically pleasing totality, a version of femininity that is both utopian and ordinary.

The doctors, overwhelmed, confused and in love with Ruth for having such big desire and such faith in them, turn Ruth into a simulacrum of Mary Fisher. The novel goes into excruciating detail about the procedures performed on her body: the skimming of fat from beneath the skin, the use of lasers to burn away scars, the hacking off of thick leg bone, and other acts of sculpting that involve gentle verbs like 'tucking', 'pinning', 'trimming', bracing', and the experimental one, 'heat-sealing' (pp. 207–208). This litany of detail is not expressed in the registers of pornography or fetishism. It is written in the dead, scientist language of accounting: $110,000 for the face, $300,000 for the body, $1,000,000 for the legs. Ruth takes no pleasure in the physical pain, nor sees herself as heroic for enduring it, but views it as a way of focusing and mastering the pain she has otherwise confronted in her life. Indeed, she says that it cleanses her by diverting the mental pain she so long suffered for her failure to be beautiful. Now, mentally a She-Devil and no longer a woman, Ruth is post-operatively physically a woman, in all the usual feminine senses. In transsexual terms, she is a monster-to-woman post-op.

After Ruth has healed, and sealed the new reality that extends from her new body, she returns to England for Mary Fisher's funeral. She buys and refurbishes the romantic high tower, but distorts the beautiful landscape in which Mary Fisher had crafted it; she re-hires Garcia, Mary Fisher's servant and lover, but now she treats him as a slave, in terms of both labor and sex. Finally, she reclaims from prison a now broken and overmedicated Bobbo and takes him back to the high tower, where he abjects himself to her for the rest of his days. She takes many lovers in front of him, and makes just as big a show of rejecting as accepting them: she tortures Bobbo with her lack of need for him, or for anyone, even her children, who have re-entered the working class. The right of refusal, Ruth emphasizes, is what defines the She-Devil. 'I want to be loved and not love in return ... the future lay in refusing men rather than submitting to them' (pp. 43, 232). In contrast, the feminine woman thinks that her world depends on the success of her improvisations around the realities men make for them: Mary Fisher the romance writer softened these scenes by insisting that romance is woman's realism, and that the harsh realities of capitalism, property, exploitation, sexual alienation and domestic inequality can be transcended through pastoral fantasy and a commitment to maintaining and living the beauty that fantasy can fold into the everyday of intimacy.

It is on this point, the articulation of fantasy with the material relations of the everyday under global capitalism, that we began our exploration of what it might mean to interfere with the conventions of desire's formalism and the compulsion to repeat, to defetishize our attachments to *kinds* of things – a particular body, body politic or body of knowledge. *The Life and Loves of a She-Devil* narrates a process of formal interruption in the flows of capital, the clarity of gender and the utopia of (hetero)sexuality by the She-Devil herself: but the logic of desire that solicits content with these normative forms – whether suburban, national or heterosexual – is never terribly unsettled. When Ruth transmigrates into the Mary Fisher prosthesis she switches her bodily destiny, but changes nothing about the ways identity congeals a bodily destiny within a type.

In this regard *She-Devil* demonstrates how easy it is to forget the impersonality and conventionality of those forms of identity that organize collective and personal fantasy and self-understanding. Central to that forgetting is the overvaluation of subjects, bodies and subjectivity to the stories we have learned to tell about history and power. In *She-Devil* 'genre' stands as the aesthetic trace of the wish for the simplification of universality, reminding us that rhetorical convention strongly organizes the shape of the subject's desire for social belonging and social value. Style and species, which merge whenever we talk about 'genre' texts, give the gift of appropriateness to the subjects who desire to consume their 'law': like a good citizen, the reader is 'free' within the law of genre to pre-experience the flow of unconflictedness dreamed of elsewhere than in the genre's horizon of expectations.

It would not, however, suspend the compulsion to repeat the pseudo-adequate relation between desires and their forms simply to eject 'the subject' from our analysis because her desires are so powerfully on the side of the law of (world-ordering) form; nor would a turn to retelling history from the standpoint of transpersonal systems – capitalism, nationality, heterosexuality –

disable the reality-effect of the conventions and monuments that allow the subject to feel organized within them. The current solutions to this critical desire, the conjunctural models of 'reiteration', 'negotiation', or 'practice', do bring to bear a productive consciousness of the lack of fit between conventions of structural determination and subjectivity, but weigh in too heavily on the side of the subject's temporality and sense of agency, and overvalue the way power/law *appears* to the subject, as though there operated no misdirection in the system to produce absorbing mirages, maps of social orderliness, or tricky conventional images of the good life – somewhat like the dream of standard sizes for women promised by the department store.[23]

I have tried to demonstrate the urgency of this conundrum by reading the book at hand as a case. I began with psychoanalysis to say something about a limit: the formalism of desire is a hardwired fact of life, but more importantly and experientially, a consciousness-shaping ideology-effect. (This suggests not universal support for social norms, but a common sense of their indexicality.) The nation-form and the fetishes of racial and gendered identity whose interarticulation is shielded by their formal separation can be projected back from an imagined future as archaic formations, as they already currently are by theorists of the postnational and hybridity. Meanwhile the normative process of disciplining people into their generic taxonomies remains, and we know the rest: after great pain, a formal feeling comes. The question is which formal feeling, what conditions its conventional zone of reference and consolation and under what conditions and in what kinds of space would it be possible to delaminate the radiant form from the desire that organizes it, makes it a *thing* of fantasy?

The Life and Loves of a She-Devil takes on the formalism of desire – its alternately consoling and aversive condensation in the fetishistic object – and its relation to normativity. Central to the translation of the form to the norm is the *scene* that enables the subject to experience her subordination to proper type as also a feeling of a freeing uniqueness. In *She-Devil*, as well as in the political contexts from which it speaks, the spaces of metropolitan capital and geopolitical fantasy provide the architectonic of modernity that both staples her to the identity form with which she is burdened and frees her to occupy the nooks and crannies of abstraction and universality. These relations describe more than the paradox of the General Will: under capitalist regimes of law in which property is the condition of symbolic mobility, individuals are free only to the degree that they appear to generate value within the rules of the proper or the normal. Otherwise, they are all too palpably vulnerable to the discipline of the state and the morality of proper social reproduction it engenders.

In *She-Devil*, the flow of capital and people through houses and across cities and oceans does show us other routes of meaning lived in ordinary life by people who manage survival in non-normative ways. But as these ways are forged under the pressures of precarious lives, they do not constitute redemptive *models*. Meanwhile, for women (and other migrants) the violence of intimacy with the law (of desire) is liveable because of the temporalizing promises of love, femininity and heterosexuality, those most ruthlessly *locating* of institutions that are at the same time vehicles for identifying with a version of personal history that transcends the materiality of the present.

The She-Devil's own story suggests, nonetheless, that consciousness, or paying attention to the proliferation of anomalies, does not reorganize life: recognition or redescription of a thing does not entail its destruction or transformation. If there is such a thing as a 'sad fact', it is that gender and nationality mark the space of an ever-attenuating optimism that the law (institutions, apparatuses and norms) might be reworked, re-seduced or reformed so that what is given is toxic but does not remain so but becomes untraumatically or incrementally obsolete over the long haul. (I take this to be the dream of liberalism.) I must close dissatisfyingly, then, by reconsidering the fortunes of desire across the three ur-forms we have been tracking – the nation, the gendered body and literary genre – without concluding anything about their future from the 'lesson' of their backstory.

The Nation-Form

In the beginning, before she raised hell and earth, Ruth understood as a fact of life the suffering of women across many terrains, both national and cosmopolitan ('Women in Korea and Buenos Aires and Stockholm and Detroit and Dubai and Tashkent, but seldom in China, where it is a punishable offense' [p. 46]); the superexploitation of women globally and at home and in the unliveable jobs at the bottom of the heap; the need for women to pool their knowledge and resources in order to refuse to be banalized into the silenced spaces of reproduction. But, significantly, however, the internationalist feminist/socialist-tinged structural view of the novel's first half drops out when Ruth leaves for the United States. In England the reduction of women to body and feeling became sickening to her, and so she embarked on a pilgrimage to agency that involved refuting the compliant form, encouraging women to enter the exciting present-tense world of public value (through labor, travel and agentive sex) – and only then did we see her instrumentalizing those women for her own private ends.

When Ruth migrates to America she leaves her gender utopianism behind.

She goes there to lose her body, her history and political consciousness: she arrives to assume the freedom of the sovereign individual, who thinks that her mind, her will and her control of capital by rights should make a new world on the model of her new body which, as an unnatural thing, is the closest a body ever comes to being an abstraction. What happens instead, after all her plotting, is that she loses her optimism for anything but the repetition of the negativity she knows.[24]

The novel is a melancholic form that signals its pleasure in these kinds of loss, for its procedure is to abandon most of what it shows through the proliferation of detail, scene and movement: failures of possibility are what make the novel dramatic. In *She-Devil* the loss is signified by the pilgrimage to 'America', a place dedicated to the ascendency of generic/normative individuality over any other national story, whether about capitalist processes or other paradoxically-related matrices of contingency, determination and identity in collective life.

'America' enables the cancellation of Ruth's socialist knowledge, and here, as so often, its loss folds the violent forces of money and property back into stories of the body and the intimate sphere. How much of this effect of narrative self-erasure is a performance of the compulsion to repeat, in which the love plot, nationality and capitalist triumphalism represent the conventionalized forms of fantasy? Is this narrative overvaluation of the subject's emergence from a complex field of detail inevitable, because reading produces subjects, not acts, and because the classic pedagogy of the novel represents changes of mentality on the same scale as it represents social redemption?

Ruth's tactic suggests that if a subaltern aims for survival in the mode of liberal individuality her desires can indeed find ways to negotiate or refunction ongoing systems of normativity – she can condense her entire being onto the body's hieroglyph, passing as well-adapted when necessary. But the minoritized subject who wants to live throughout the entire range of her personality (without closeting its bigness in the shell of a body) pays a huge cost if she also seeks a *representation* of it, in the nation or through surgery: the fictive totality of universalism and particularity requires the subject not to believe, but to act *as if* her autonomous individuality and her generic identity are the same thing, the simultaneous fulfillment of her omnipotent fantasy (mastery *of* the world) and her desire for belonging (mastery *by* it). The formalism of the liberal nation produces hierarchies of abstraction around identities: meanwhile, they deliver the bribe of a free and complex mentality to the citizen, who can develop any consciousness she wants so long as she declines to interfere with the pleasure/order her readable body creates for everyone else.

The Body

In the beginning of *She-Devil*, Ruth is a mute, abject shell who has no positive impact on the world. At the end she has a shell of dead cells (a beautiful body) that protect her from showing feeling. On the other hand, by taking on as a bodily project the urge for 'self-creation', Ruth endows her conscious self with a form of superpersonhood that subordinates everyone who encounters her. She-Devils, she says, absolutely refuse to assume the redemptive-pedagogical position of generic femininity. There is no trace of cyborg-style optimism here. Indeed, she calls herself a failure for being unable to change any body of land, water or language apart from her own (p. 231).

Could the postoperative Ruth teach, if she wanted to, a story that is not about failure? Does it turn out that the horizon of possibility the fantasy world femininity provides is the *only* material she has? In the space between her new bodily ego and the scarred traces of her historical one, she riffs on the feminine in yet a third way, derived from her knowledge of what it has cost for her to survive her fantasies. Would saying what she knows from the new body that refuses historical knowledge leave her nothing, no potential for pleasure, no possible life narrative, no resources of self-development? Ultimately, neither the nation, the city, the body nor sexuality are redemptive sites for her, as they have been for others: in *She-Devil*, as in *Landscape*, where women are concerned there is no privacy, only exposure; and survival comes only to those who can find prosthetic protection in the museum of normativity.

At this juncture, then, the compulsion to repeat femininity is the only condition of Ruth's life narrative: a return home that should be impossible but isn't, because the compulsion to repeat *is* femininity, the impossibility of breaking attachments and of experiencing self-sovereignty as such. Yet to say this is not to finish with the question of history past and future, for different women enter their gendering differently; and the form that expresses the animating attachment is not an inevitable resting or organizing place for that attachment.

This is where politics and ideology critique re-enter. The body is the only screen on which Ruth exists to the world, because she is female – it is the determining economy. All her gestures of refusal can come only after the consent to her femininity and the fantasy it sustains *for others* organizes desire. Despite the explicitness of her masquerade, it reminds her and everyone who sees her of romance, the vanquished ghost: as a mnemonic of the compulsion to repeat a never-experienced sublime, it demonstrates once again that your libidinal position is not yours, but a content that the world has given you to suffer and to fantasize through by calling it 'individuality'. It is also the portable limit you carry around, the very sign of the conventionality of your desire.

Genre, Gender, Nation

In this essay, genre stands as something like a conventionalized symbolic, an institution of culture whose modern translation through the commodity form affixes it with both genericness and a uniqueness derived from the particularity of its distinguishing details. Genre also figures the nameable aspiration for discursive order through which particular life narratives and modes of being become normalized as the real, the taken-for-granted. Romance, with its negotiation of desire and institution (marriage, reproduction, property, dynasty, nation) is in the not-strange-enough position of being identified intensively with both the fantastic unreal and the real that constitutes what 'a life' should be, especially for women. Thus, along with the rules of social membership that seek to saturate the political with the nation-form, genre establishes the place of reading in the production of normative law. But what does it mean to think about subjectivity as literalized in the law of genre?

As histories of the middle-class novel have long attested, the genre concept generally presumes a reader's competence in textual conventions: a competence not necessarily linked to a plot or setting as such, but to modes of causality, desire, enigma and affective response associated with that setting. To be competent in a genre is therefore to be cultivated as a certain *kind* of subject, a type. The association of different kinds of subject with different categories of represented desire in turn leads to a popular culture organized around types who are characterized by interior and exterior habits and narratives that are said to flow out of them in invariably recognizable ways. Read from within the law of genre, these kinds of fictional subject literalize their desire in acts and identities. It is as though both the narrative and the persons within it take on the form of cliché, a proposition repeated until it takes on truth value, a truth that is repeated until its resonance dies, a phrase that converts into a ghost of meaning, a tough transparency. This aura of the taken-for-granted around genre's institutionality (its common law, established by precedent) suggests the power genre-fictions have to mediate identity normatively, to cast proper identity as the seed out of which an imaginable future inevitably springs.[25]

Even the most blazingly generic texts are a mix of aesthetic elements (the western's coupling with romance, or the historical novel's articulation of melodrama, epic tropes and documentary verity, for example): yet it is also the case that generic conventions work according to an implicit contract that guides reading toward appropriateness. The instabilities of genre are thematized in the threat any text poses *not* to fulfill its contract to produce satisfaction: and if readerly *enjoyment* is played out in the narrative obstacles to or deferral of an anticipated resolution, the possession of and by that end is also a stabilizing attachment for the consumer.[26] The death of pleasure foreshadowed in *jouissance* remains central to the capacity to endure it. This dialectic is crucial to the compulsion to repeat.[27] The conventionality of this dialectic in love plots has been crucial to the reproduction of femininity and heterosexuality.

The Return of the Repressed: Pleasure

This raises very post-68 questions about the value narrative pleasure might come again to have in the formation of critical cultures and consciousness. In the 1970s the translated notion of pleasure that also went by *jouissance* (as first incited in the US by Barthes and Sontag), articulated a liberatory aim, much as the feminist movement reconceived sexuality as a site that demanded and would provide a new, revolutionary sensorium. Currently, that mode of critical pleasure through reading has been replaced by a professional incitement to make readings engage with material practices through ethnography and history, in part to repudiate the implied universality of interpretation set forth in the early manifestos. Still, I remain enchanted by the critical potential of pleasure/knowledge.

Sheila Rowbotham argues that feminism has had two phases: the emancipatory one of suffrage that produced juridical and cultural enfranchisements and the liberationist one of the'68ers, which tended to see history as a *Bastille* from which subjects need liberation.[28] For Barthes as later for Foucault, pleasure was the least public and least rationalized of practices. On this repetition, perhaps, the hierarchy of mentality – rationality, will, consciousness, affect, fantasy – over material determinations can be shaken up, not on behalf of the body's or practice's superior freedom but on behalf of thinking the thought of pleasure as a thought about cathexis and its apparent opposite, ambivalence.

The commonsense understanding of ambivalence emphasizes its negativity: uncertainty, obscurity or relentlessly assertive doubt. But, like pleasure, which can be rephrased as the compulsion to repeat an attachment that one likes, doesn't like or feels neutral about, ambivalence is, in its strongest versions, a pulling-apart or antithetical attraction that cannot be overcome by synthesis, will or better reason. The usual solution to the conundrum of ambivalence is to temporalize the intensified fraying the concept suggests: to understand it as a crisis that can first be fixed by attachment to a new form from which one can then be liberated until the next crisis, and so on. In contrast, the pleasure concept involves understanding that the feeling of freedom is not freedom, pleasure not pleasure, disavowal not repudiation, but ways we have learned to identify knowledge and sensation. They are maps to causality but not the truth about it. In this sense, the forms that codetermine crises of self and the pleasures of social intelligibility can be seen as transformational: in liberal culture love and the nation are the ur-types of the forms that have become saturated by their content, which makes it harder to see the fantasy motives for which they once seemed a solution and for which, like many a neurotic symptom, they may no longer work. The risk one takes with pleasure is not to presume, as the She-Devil does, that a better form will release one from the pressure of fantasy and the optimism of discontent.

The concept of the transformational environment describes why people enter new attachments, given what they know about the attenuation of the old ones: Bollas suggests that the new attachment expresses a subject's desire to change, but not traumatically (which would render the subject impossible). But the transformational environment is a way in which the attachment to form speaks against itself, as the subject's (or a mass's) desire to move beyond whatever is dead or deadening rubs up against the comfort that the form's stability brings. It may wish to accrue history like a dustball, a mystic writing pad, or a self-reproducing story, but it also signifies an aggressivity toward the scene of history.

This essay is not written in the self-help genre or with an eye to providing a conceptual solution to the lure of absorbing ideologemes. *She-Devil* shows us that the whole business of history and personality drags around behind us forever: the weight of its content produces the forms of resigned privatization so often called 'realism'. This is one example of the destruction produced by the redemptive promises of desire ideology (that new instances of it will save you from it) and the wishful thought that consciousness can prevent mistakes in the forging of attachment (as though knowing can protect the subject from being duped into the hope that a new good object is the end of the story of desire and the actual fulfillment of fantasy). To intervene in the pleasures of heteronormative romance and the nation-form involves dismantling their capacity to make old stories and practices look new and revolutionary while discrediting the restlessness and skepticism of the subjects who also desire them; the pleasure concept enables a post-prosthetic critical engagement with those aspects of conventionality that claim to provide the better law, rule or lexicon that will protect you from a traumatic engagement with the harsh and cutting world. In *She-Devil* the project of homeopathic cutting up involves leaving the city, going to America, and becoming an individual there. Individuality, that deracinated grandiosity of being, enables Ruth to live the iconic life of the landscaped subject – but because she remembers what her body cannot show, the visible life is anchored by a melancholic one, which involves staying at home with the brilliant anger that she can only express masochistically, in the fold between the mind's wildness and the body's conventionality. To the degree that the compulsion to repeat this condition supports the formalist romance in its political, intimate and intellectual senses, it is this plot, the plot of optimism for the iconic *thing*, that must go in for radical surgery.

Notes

1. Carolyn Kay Steedman, *Landscape for a Good Woman: A Story of Two Lives*, Newark NJ: Rutgers University Press, 1986.
2. *Ibid.*, p. 23.
3. *Ibid.*, pp. 27–47.
4. *Ibid.*, p. 141.
5. *Ibid.*, pp. 7–8, 110–114.
6. See Chris Waters, 'Landscapes of Memory: Art and Everyday Life in Postwar Britain', *Ideas* Vol. 5, no. 1 (1997), no page nos.
7. I take the metacultural concept, a unifying term linked to the universalism of liberal society, from Greg Urban, *Noumenal Community: Myth and Reality in an Amerindian Brazilian Society*, Austin TX: University of Texas Press, 1996. On its relation to national sexuality in particular see Lauren Berlant and Michael Warner, 'Sex in Public', *Critical Inquiry* 24, Winter 1998, pp. 547–566.
8. Christopher Bollas, 'The Transformational Object', in *The Shadow of the Object: Psychoanalysis of the Unthought Known*, New York: Columbia University Press, 1987, pp. 13–29.
9. Felix Guattari, *Soft Subversions*, ed. Sylvère Lotringer, trans. David L. Sweet and Chet Wiener, New York: Semiotexte, 1996. Guattari's argument throughout is that 'soft subversions' are a central means of pseudoindividuation provided for by the capitalist project of 'semiotic subjectification'. 'There is a microfascism of one's own body, of one's organs, the kind of bulimia that leads to anorexia, a perceptual bulimia that blinds one to the value of things, except for their exchange value, their use value, to the expense of the values of desire' (p. 11).
10. This essay's observations on the post-'68 European metropole (especially in Britain) are largely derived from: Elizabeth Grosz, 'Bodies-Cities', in Beatriz Colomina, ed. *Sexuality and Space*, Princeton NJ: Princeton Architectural Press, 1992, pp. 241–253; Doreen Massey, *Space, Place, and Gender*, Minneapolis: University of Minnesota Press, 1994; Saskia Sassen, 'Identity in the Global City: Structural and Economic Encasements', in Patricia Yaeger, ed. *The Geography of Identity*, Ann Arbor: University of Michigan Press, 1996, pp. 131–151; Nigel Thrift, *Spatial Formations*, London: Sage, 1996. See also Hall, *The Hard Road to Renewal: Thatcherism and the Crisis of the Left*, London: Verso, 1990.
11. Meaghan Morris, 'Great Moments in Social Climbing: King Kong and the Human Fly', in *Sexuality and Space*, ed. Beatriz Colomina, Princeton NJ: Princeton Architectural Press, 1992, pp. 1–51.
12. See Thrift, *Spatial Formations*.

13. Slavoj Žižek, 'The Spectre of Ideology', *Mapping Ideology*, ed. Slavoj Žižek, London: Verso, 1994, p. 21.

14. A central subtext for this engagement with love plots and the law is Jacques Derrida, 'The Law of Genre', in *Jacques Derrida: Acts of Literature*, Derek Attridge, ed., New York and London: Routledge 1992, pp. 221–252.

15. Although *Landscape for a Good Woman* is organized around the intimate upheavals in the natal family, sexuality is not a topic in this book. Steedman depicts her family members as aggressively isolated from each other because of the instrumental ruthlessness of their desires, and yet where mothers and daughters are concerned this atomization is experienced as a violent boundarilessness forced on the daughters: this presumption even further isolates 'gender' from sexuality. As a result, its institutions, practices, and contradictions are taken for granted – because they are simultaneously too banal and too overwhelming. I have written about this elsewhere: on Steedman (with Toni Morrison and Michelle Cliff) '68 or Something', *Critical Inquiry* 21, Fall 1994, pp. 124–55; additionally, 'Intimacy: A Special Issue', *Critical Inquiry* 24, 2, Winter 1998, pp. 281–88.

16. See Jacqueline Rose, *The Haunting of Sylvia Plath*, Cambridge MA: Harvard University Press, 1991.

17. For histories of the left/feminist conjuncture in post-'68 Britain see Angelica Bammer, *Partial Visions: Feminism and Utopianism in the 1970s*, New York: Routledge, 1991; Naomi Black, *Social Feminism*, Ithaca: Cornell University Press, 1989; Barbara Caine, *English Feminism, 1780–1980*, New York: Oxford University Press, 1997; Dennis Dworkin, *Cultural Marxism in Postwar Britain*, Durham NC: Duke UP, 1997; Barbara Epstein, *Social Protest and Cultural Revolution: Nonviolent Direct Action in the 1970s and 1980s*, Berkeley: University of California Press, 1991; Stuart Hall, *The Hard Road to Renewal*, London: Verso, 1990; Donna Landry and Gerard MacLean, *Materialist Feminisms*, Cambridge MA: Harvard University Press, 1993, Sohnya Sares, Anders Stephanson, Stanley Aronowitz and Fredric Jameson eds., *The 60s Without Apology*, Minneapolis: Minnesota Press, 1984, especially Stanley Aronowitz, 'When the New Left was New', pp. 10–43 and Ellen Willis, 'Radical Feminism and Feminist Radicalism', pp. 91–118; Sheila Rowbotham, *A Century of Women: the History of Women in Britain and the United States*, New York: Viking, 1997.

18. Steedman, *Landscape for a Good Woman*, p. 144.

19. Theodor Adorno, *Critical Models*, trans. Henry R. Pickford, New York: Columbia University Press, 1998, p. 291.

20. Fay Weldon, *The Life and Loves of a She-Devil*, New York: Pantheon, 1983. All future references will be contained within the text.

21. One might argue that the pronoun 'she' is inappropriate for the She-Devil, who becomes not-woman when she delaminates herself from the love plot. She/it would seem appropriate, since while her dramatic monologue is written from a post-gendered position, Ruth's specular femaleness and sexuality serve as instruments throughout the novel. But in English 'it' describes a thing, whereas Ruth is simply no longer conventionally gendered. Moreover, as I will suggest, the deployment of the will against taxonomic norms does not unmake one's intelligibility within those norms (here of gender): indeed, the She-Devil's negativity and critical consciousness cannot separate her *enough* from the feminine. Here Weldon predicts central dicta of Judith Butler's arguments in *Gender Trouble* and *Bodies that Matter*. Both authors presume that sexual difference (as the figure of species clarity in general) is a back-formation of heterosexuality that serves its claim to emanate from nature; and both tend to see sexuality in discursive terms, which means that radical conceptual transformations of gender and sexuality tend, in their texts, to be represented *as such* on the body and in practice. I read this as entirely continuous with a traditional tendency to overvalue consciousness and intentional agency as sources of social change, along with a particularly feminine-identified norm that wants to literalize scenes of sexual instability and resistance in representations of them. See *Gender*

Trouble: Feminism and the Subversion of Identity, New York and London: Routledge, 1990 and *Bodies that Matter: On the Discursive Limits of 'Sex'*, New York and London: Routledge, 1994. See also Joan Copjec's argument against Butler's tendency to presume a mimesis between linguistic and practical shifts in *Read My Desire: Lacan Against the Historicists*, Cambridge MA: MIT Press, 1994, pp. 201–211.

22. In *She-Devil*, the US film version of the novel, this lesbian relationship is entirely wiped out, available for reading only through the casting of the lesbian-identified actress Linda Hunt as Nurse Hopkins.

23. Here I am not arguing with the main thrust of Homi Bhabha's view of *negotiation* in *The Location of Culture*, New York and London: Routledge, 1994, insofar as it sees the term as present in *theoretical* events that disable the compulsion to reproduce in analysis the taken-for-granted antinomies and contradictions one finds in practice (pp. 25–26 ff). On the other hand, in Bhabha as in Butler (see note 20) there is a slippage between the theoretical commitment to change thought through the critical deployment of will, and a sense that iteration in general, as an inevitable practice of making meaning, offers 'opportunities' to transform the destiny of a concept or a problem.

24. Elizabeth Bronfen argues, in contrast, that Weldon's hyperbolic deployment of tautology, the uncanny, and other modes of comic repetition disconfirms what she calls the 'patriarchal' norms of the compulsion to repeat femininity. See ' "Say Your Goodbyes and Go" Death and Women's Power in Fay Weldon's Fiction', in *Fay Weldon's Wicked Fictions*, ed. Regina Barreca, Hanover and London: University Press of New England, 1994, pp. 69–82. This general view about the angrily transgressive nature of 'women's' comedy is detailed in Regina Barreca, *Untamed and Unabashed: Essays on Women and Humor in British Literature*,' Detroit: Wayne State University Press, 1994, pp. 11–33.

25. Common law is not prescribed by statute, but finds its shape in a jurist's reading of precedent. The juridical concept is *stare decisis*, and the conventions that guide the discovery of precedent contribute mightily to the law's conservatism, its bias toward reproducing the customary or the proper. Patricia Williams considers the effect of this process of 'undue literalism'. See *The Alchemy of Race and Rights: Diary of a Law Professor*, Cambridge MA: Harvard University Press, 1991, pp. 3–14, 141–2. Fredric Jameson's work on genre in *The Political Unconscious*, Ithaca: Cornell University Press, 1981 converges with common law logic in its explication of genre as institution, a history of uses that refer to each other and establish conventional horizons of expectation that are frequently articulated as the proper. This characterization, in turn, articulates with Jacques Derrida's, 'The Law of Genre.' Derrida's text works questions of counterauthority that move between the lines of the law/*récit* to talk about the inevitable agitation (or 'madness') produced by juridical fantasies of broken law: this early text is realized in his more recent 'Force of Law: The "Mystical Foundations of Authority"', in *Deconstruction and the Possibility of Justice*, eds. Drucilla Cornell, Michel Rosenfeld and David Grey Carlson, New York: Routledge, 1992, pp. 3–67, esp. 61–63.

26. Žižek works through the non-mimetic relation between abjection and sovereignty in *The Metastasies of Enjoyment: Six Essays on Women and Causality*, New York and London: Verso, 1994, pp. 89–112.

27. Leo Bersani, *The Freudian Body: Psychoanalysis and Art*, Columbia: Columbia UP, 1986. Bersani's argument was anticipated by Roland Barthes, *The Pleasure of the Text*, translated by Richard Miller, introduction by Richard Howard, New York: Hill and Wang, 1975, pp. 14, 19, 20, 26, 41–46, 55–57.

28. See note 15.

8 THE TOMB OF PERSEVERANCE: On *Antigone*

JOAN COPJEC

Greek tragedy is the term we commonly use to refer to it, but it would be more accurate to say *Attic* or *Athenian tragedy*, since it was *only* in the city-state of Athens that this aesthetic form was nourished and thrived. Yet not even this correction sufficiently discloses the intimate relation that bound this particular city to this particular form, for tragedy was not simply founded in Athens (between 534 and 530 BC) and there declared dead (by Aristotle, in 414 BC), it also reached out a hand to help invent the very city that invented it.[1] As Jean-Pierre Vernant has argued:

> [Athenian] tragedy is contemporary with the City [Athens] and with its legal system . . . [W]hat tragedy is talking about is itself and the problems of law it is encountering. What is talking and what is talked about is the audience on the benches, but first of all it is the City . . . which puts itself on the stage and plays itself . . . Not only does the tragedy enact itself on stage . . . it enacts its own problematics. It puts in question its own internal contradictions, revealing . . . that the true subject matter of tragedy is social thought . . . in the very process of elaboration.[2]

That is, not only did the Athenians insert themselves into their tragic dramas – as Chorus members, who judged the actions of the protagonists in the same way as the tribunal of citizens in the audience was judging the unfolding tragedy against others performed for the same contest – they also posed, through their tragedies, the juridical and ethical questions they were currently confronting in actuality.

But if the form of Athenian tragedy is so local, tied not only to a specific place, a particular and precisely dateable time and a unique set of social problems, it would seem, then, according to the historicist-relativist thinking of our day, to offer nothing that might help us think through the juridical and ethical issues raised by the modern city. In fact, to begin a consideration of contemporary urban issues with a reference to Athenian tragedy is automatically to brand oneself with the sin of anachronism. I propose, however, that the question should not always be, 'How can we rid ourselves of anachronism?', for it is sometimes more relevant to ask, 'What is its significance?' How can we account for the temporal nomadism of figures from the past? And, in this context, how is it possible that the drama of Antigone still concerns us?[3]

The simplest initial response would be to point out that German Idealism *resurrected* Antigone at the beginning of our own era and refashioned her as the paradigmatic figure of *modern* ethics. Hegel, Schelling and Hölderlin all wrote with deep fascination about this young Athenian woman, and it is their fascination that commands contemporary interest in her.[4] Voicing, undoubtedly, the sentiments of his colleagues as well as his own, Hegel proclaimed *Antigone* 'one of the most sublime, and in every respect most consummate works of human effort ever brought forth.'[5] Despite this transhistorical judgement, however, before the moment of German Idealism, the play had not received any special attention and had, in fact, been relatively neglected. It was only after paeans such as Hegel's began to revive the play that it became a major reference point of ethical speculation, including that of Kierkegaard, Brecht, Anouilh, Irigaray, Derrida and, of course, Lacan. In 1978 *Germany in Autumn*, a compilation film produced by nine New German Cinema directors, was released. Focusing on questions of a family's right to bury its dead and citizens' rights to rebel against their government, the film loosely associated actions taken by the Red Army Faction and the Baader-Meinhof terrorists against the German state with Antigone and Polynices's rebellion against Creon and the city-state of Thebes. More recently, Straub and Huillet's release, in 1992, of their film version of Brecht's adaptation of Hölderlin's translation of Sophocles's *Antigone*, has demonstrated that the legacy of German Idealism's retrieval of Antigone lives on. If our interest in her is an archaism, then it is a peculiarly modern one. What concerns me is less the historical conditions that reawakened interest in *Antigone* (the Hellenistic bent of German Idealism has been amply explored) than the play's susceptibility to a rereading in the modern context (how is it possible to resurrect such an old drama?); for this issue is closely linked to the ethical issues raised in the play.

My approach to these issues begins with a single re-reading of *Antigone*, or, more accurately, a rereading of a prior re-reading: Lacan, in *The Ethics of Psychoanalysis*, reinterprets Sophocles's play by challenging Hegel's interpretation in *The Phenomenology of Spirit (P)*. Though later, in the *Philosophy of Right*, Hegel will read the play straightforwardly as a modern drama of ethical action, in the *Phenomenology* he reads it as a tragedy belonging to an earlier moment which he describes (perhaps metaphorically) as that of the Greek city-state; at this moment the opposition between the universal and the particular, the state and the family, human and divine law, man and woman cannot be practically overcome. Hegel argues that classical Greek society held the two poles of these oppositions together, in a precarious equilibrium, through *custom*, which provided the community with a concrete unity. But when any decisive action was taken, this equilibrium collapsed into real and irresolvable conflict. Through the ethical *act*, the ethical *community* was dissolved, for the act

> initiates the division of itself into itself as the active principle and into the reality over against it, a reality which, for it, is negative. By the deed, therefore, it becomes guilt. . . . And the guilt also acquires the meaning of *crime*, for as simple, ethical consciousness, it has turned towards one law, but turned its back on the other and violates the latter by its deed.[6]

Only *inaction*, then, can remain innocent in the Greek polis, every *act*, insofar as it decisively chooses one pole of the opposition, one law, over the other, renders the actor guilty. This inevitable and tragic result is, according to Hegel, the very point of these dramas in general and of *Antigone* in particular, for there each protagonist, each ethical consciousness

> sees right only on one side and wrong on the other, that consciousness which belongs to the divine law sees in the other side only the violence of human caprice, while that which holds to human law sees in the other only the self-will and disobedience of the individual who insists on being his own authority. (para. 466).

Hegel here effectively argues that Antigone ('that consciousness which belongs to the divine law') and Creon ('that which holds to human law') are, in their very decisiveness and intransigence, *both* guilty, both in the wrong, insofar as they both abandon or alienate one principle through the very act of embracing its opposite. Acting on behalf of a particular individual, her brother, Antigone betrays the community and terrorizes the state, while Creon acts on behalf of the city-state and thus sacrifices Polynices and the values of the family.

Lacan attacks the deep undecidability of this reading in order decisively to side with Antigone, praising hers as the only real, ethical act in the play and condemning the actions of Creon as crimes. In this reading it is *only* Creon who, through his actions, renders himself guilty. This is not to say that Antigone's implacability goes unnoticed by Lacan; he is as strict as Hegel is in observing the raw, untamed and uncompromising nature of Oedipus's daughter's rebellion. 'The nature of the girl is savage, like her father's, and she does not know how to bend before her troubles', is what the Chorus says of her, and Lacan is quick to agree.[7] But as a psychoanalyst – and here we catch a glimpse of the difference between psychoanalysis and philosophy or psychology – he does not read the *behavior* of each of the protagonists, he defines the *structure* that gives meaning to their acts. Thus, while Antigone and Creon may be equally stubborn in the performance of their duties, this stubbornness, according to which fantasy structure it enters, admits of a fundamental distinction that Lacan will use to ruin the symmetry Hegel so carefully constructs.

In *Three Essays on the Theory of Sexuality*, Freud warns us not to conflate *Fixierarbeit*, which is an inexplicable fixation that persists despite every external attempt to dislodge it, with *Haftbarkeit*, 'which is perhaps best translated by 'perseverance' but has a curious resonance in German, since it means also 'responsibility', 'commitment' '[8] It is this distinction, made by Freud, which lies behind and undergirds Lacan's insistence that Antigone, and she alone, is the heroine of Sophocles's play; her *perseverance* in carrying out the burial of her brother is ethically different from Creon's *fixation* on enforcing the statist prohibition against his burial.

How Freud is able to distinguish between these two kinds of act is what we will have to determine, but Lacan gives us a clue when he refers to them as separate effects of 'the individual libidinal adventure' (*S VII*, p. 88). Whatever else needs to be said about the distinction, it is clear from this that it cannot be drawn without taking into account the *sexual* being of the subject who acts. The reason Hegel's reading has received so much feminist attention is precisely because it seems to be attentive to this issue insofar as it foregrounds the sexual difference between the play's main protagonists. But this difference turns out to be, in his reading, only a gender or biological difference, not a sexual one; that is, Antigone and Creon enact a division of labor which is defined sociologically, according to the spaces they are allowed to inhabit and the roles they are encouraged to assume, given their biology. In fact, Hegel consciously aims to *avoid* sex as far as possible, which is why he chooses to focus not on the husband/wife, but on the brother/sister relation. This relation, he says, provides a truer or 'unmixed' picture of the difference between the sexes insofar as it excludes sexual desire. This positing of a family relation free of libido is problematic to begin with – Freud and Foucault have both, in different and definitive ways, exposed the family as a hotbed of desiring relations – but it is absolutely stupefying in light of the fact that the family in question here is Oedipus's – no stranger, then, to the taint of incest – and the Greek text, which loads Antigone's references to her brother with libidinal overtones, never lets us forget this. There is, then, in this section of *The Phenomenology*, I would venture to say, no sex and no sexual difference, properly speaking, and this has the effect of leaving the notions of work and act undisturbed, unproblematized by sexual enjoyment.

According to Freud, however, between sex or libidinal satisfaction and work there is a permanent antagonism that threatens work (or the act) with extinction. As he notes in *Civilization and Its Discontents*, 'No other technique for the conduct of work attaches the individual so firmly to reality as laying emphasis on work ... [which is] indispensible to the preservation and justification of existence in society ... And yet ... work is not prized by men. They do not strive after it as they do after other possibilities of satisfaction.'[9] By rethinking the notion of work through that of pleasure, Freud opens Aristotle's distinction between the *act*, in all its rarity, and mere *action* to a redefinition in which what matters is the kind of relation each maintains toward sexual enjoyment. If the avowed ambition of the *Ethics* seminar is to remove the discussion of ethics from 'the starry sky' and place it where it belongs, 'in our bodies, and nowhere else', that is, if its ambition is to define an ethics of the *embodied* subject, then its crucial first step is to foreground the relation between work and the body as the site of pleasure, in order to distinguish the act of Antigone from the action of Creon on this ground.

Before embarking on an analysis of these relations, it will be useful to take a look at Hegel's reading from a different perspective, one that will eventually complicate the notion of pleasure. What makes Antigone and Creon equally guilty, in Hegel's eyes, is the fact that in choosing one course of action they thereby lose something that is not merely expendable, but that sustains, or is the necessary condition of, the very thing they choose. Antigone and Creon act on behalf of the particular and the universal, respectively, but since there is no particular without the universal, and vice versa, each choice ends in a betrayal of that in the name of which it is made. Thinking, of course, of Hegel, Lacan termed the either/or structure of such choices the '*vel* of alienation' and cited the mugger's offer, 'Your money or your life', as illustration of its lose/lose possibilities.[10] Once the choice is offered, you're done for – no matter which alternative you take. Between these terms, clearly the only real choice is life, but from the moment of your decision, yours will be a life severely limited by the loss of your wealth.

Now, it would seem that the revolutionary slogan, 'Freedom or death', offers a choice with the same alienating structure. If you choose freedom and thereby lose the threat of death, you have no way of demonstrating your independence of the life situation, as Hegel argued in his essay on 'Natural Law'; that is, you have no way of demonstrating that your choice is free. So, in this case the only real choice is death, since it alone proves that your choice has been freely made. But once this decision is taken, you lose all freedom but the freedom to die. This is what Hegel called the 'freedom of the slave'.

If you attend closely, however, you will notice that the second or *ethical* choice does *not* conform to the first. The description of the first choice as a mugging is meant to underscore what's at stake here; it suggests that this particular choice is a game played entirely in the Other's court. Stumbling into its preprogrammed scenario you, its victim, might have been anyone at all, and you must react, if you are rational, in a purely formal way, by making an *analytical* judgment, and surrendering your purse. Kant's moral law, 'Act in such a way that the maxim of your action may be accepted as a universal maxim', would be sufficient to get you through this urban dilemma; it would prescribe the correct choice. But this only underscores the problem with this statement of the moral law: it still imagines a choice prescribed by law, however formal it may be, and reduces the notion of the *universal* to that of the *common*. (*S VII*, p. 77) In this case, everyone must act in the same way, but 'must' loses its ethical connotation, since it is now guided by, rather than bereft of, external sanction.

In the second example, however, by choosing, one does *not* automatically lose what is not chosen, but *wins* some of it, instead. Lacan attributes the difference between the two examples to the appearance of death in the second; it is through the introduction of the 'lethal factor', as he puts it, that the revolutionary choice opens the possibility of an act about which it is improper to say that it sacrifices freedom, loses it to the structure of alienation. The choice of death gains freedom. This point is utterly incomprehensible unless one assumes that the death one opts for in the second example is not the same one that is avoided in the first. That is, at the point at which death intersects freedom – which is to say, at the point at which it intersects the *subject* – it ceases to be conceivable in literal or biological terms. The authority for this observation is, again, Freud, who argued that death is for the subject only 'an abstract concept, with a negative content.'[11] For this reason it does not enter psychoanalysis as such, but only in an altered form, via the death drive. We must assume, then, if we are speaking of the embodied rather than the abstract subject, that what is at issue in the intersection of freedom and death is not biological death, but the death drive. It is to the latter that we owe the possibility of an ethical act which does not alienate freedom nor incur additional guilt. More specifically, it is to *sublimation* – which is the only means of satisfying the drive – that we owe this possibility.

My argument, in sum, is that Lacan attacks Hegel's argument by (1) sexualizing work, and (2) debiologizing death in an effort, in both cases, to corporealize the ethical subject. I understand that this appears to open a contradiction: to declare ethical action, as such, a sublimation appears to purify it of the body and pleasure. But this apparent contradiction will eventually be dispersed as we come to show that 'sublimation is not, in fact, what the foolish crowd thinks . . . [it] doesn't necessarily make the sexual object disappear – far from it' (*S VII*, p. 161).

Immortality in the Modern Age

Let's turn our attention, finally, to the act of Antigone. What precisely does she do? Hegel's version is this: she buries her brother, Polynices, in order to elevate him to the status of 'imperishable individuality'; she makes him 'a member of the community which prevails over . . . the forces of particular material elements . . . which sought to . . . destroy him' (*P*, para. 452). This is Lacan's version: 'Antigone chooses to be . . . the guardian of criminal being as such. . . . [B]ecause the community refuses to [bury Polynices, she] is required . . . to maintain that essential being which is the family *Ate*, and that is the theme or true axis on which the whole tragedy turns. Antigone perpetuates, eternalizes, immortalizes that *Ate*. (*S VII*, p. 283) The two versions may appear to be roughly equivalent, but one significant difference (which will lead us to observe others) is Lacan's introduction of a word that draws attention to a notion, which not only Hegel, but the entire modern period is loath to look at too directly or closely, a notion that has, since the Enlightenment, become more obscene even than death; this is the notion of immortality. What does it mean to 'immortalize *Ate*'? In modern times, it is not only the Greek word *ate*, but also *immortalize* that strikes us as anachronistic.

Yet, although one would have expected the notion of immortality to perish completely, to become a casualty of the Enlightenment's secularization of reason and the dissolution of its links to the past, the truth is more complex. For, while officially we moderns are committed to the notion of our own mortality, we nevertheless harbor the secret, inarticulable conviction that we are *not* mortal.[12] Indeed, as Hans Blumenberg (*B*) announces in his monumental book, *The Legitimacy of the Modern Age*, not only does the idea of immortality not disappear, it is even 'pushed forward by Lessing, Kant, and Herder to the point of the idea of reincarnation.'[13] And in his essay, 'The Death of Immortality?' Claude Lefort (*L*) similarly exposes the insistence of the notion of immortality within the modern period, remarking that 'after the Bonapartist *coup d'état* in the middle of the last century . . . the question of immortality [took on] . . . a political import. Astonishing as it may seem to us, in order to be a true republican, a true democrat, or a true socialist, one either had to deny or affirm a belief in immortality.' (*L*, p. 256) Blumenberg and Lefort both stress that this notion is not a simple hold out from a superseded past, the survival in the present of an old religious idea, it is, rather, a product of the break from our religious past. But though they concur generally on the need to differentiate the classical from the modern notion of immortality, they are at odds on the question of how the distinction should be made.

According to Lefort's account, the classical notion named a kind of mortal ambition to participate in everlastingness through the accomplishment of great works or deeds, although the deed itself was not thought to have any chance of enduring, ultimately. Since every human effort was conceived as time-bound, none could hope to elevate itself above the temporal flux in order to install itself within the timeless realm of eternity. Thus, while the deed could win for its doer some measure of *immortality*, it could not win *eternity*, which meant that it was worth relatively little. The modern notion of immortality benefits from the collapse of our belief in an eternal realm. Where formerly every deed (the active life, in general) was thought to fail insofar as it was unable to elevate itself *out of time*, into eternity, in modernity the deed was reconceived as affording the possibility of transcending historical time *within* time. This is what is new; this idea that the act could raise itself out of impotence, or out of the immanence of its historical conditions, without raising itself out of time. It is at this point that the act – or work – took on a value it could not have had in the classical era. The valorization of work helped to forge, Lefort argues, a new link between immortality and 'a sense of posterity'. (*L*, p. 267). The great social revolutions at the end of the eighteenth century may have severed all ties with the past, but they did so, paradoxically, in order to establish a permanence in time, a durability, of human deeds, that was not possible previously. In other words, the 'sense of posterity' took place across a historical *break*; what was thus brought forth was 'the idea of a conjunction between something that no longer exists and something that does not yet exist' (*L*, p. 270).

In the argument Blumenberg presents, the notion of posterity is not linked to that of immortality, but instead opposes or replaces it. His argument is embedded in a larger one, which states that the attainment of complete knowledge by any individual has, in the modern age, been rendered strictly inconceivable. Within modernity, knowledge is objectified through scientific *method*, which means that it ceases to be a matter of individual *intuition*; that is, methods of objectification transform the process of acquiring knowledge into one that extends infinitely beyond the cognitive compass, and even ambition, of any single enquirer. Along with this objectification, the sheer speed with which knowledge comes into being, is superseded and discarded as useless, threatens to turn the curious into functionaries of the process of knowledge and render the possession of it irredeemably fleeting and incomplete. For these reasons, no individual, only a generational series of them, can become the subject of modern knowledge.

It is in order to clinch this argument that Blumenberg introduces Ludwig Feuerbach's notion of immortality. According to Blumenberg's summary, Feuerbach 'extracted the anthropological core' hidden within our notion of immortality, to produce the following definition: 'immortality extrapolated as the fulfillment of theory is the product of the difference ... between the "knowledge drive," which relates to species man, and its unsatisfied actual state in the individual man' (*B*, p. 441). In other words, once the rapid and conspicuous progress of modern knowledge makes the individual's limited share in this progress unbearable, the notion of immortality arises as a way of healing the wound between the species and the individual, of assuaging the structural dissatisfaction that emerges from their difference. A kind of error of prolepsis, immortality negates history in order to posit a *spatial* beyond where the future is already waiting to bestow itself on the individual. This error is *modern* because its anticipation of reward is based on the perception of the actual, temporal progress of man rather than on the presumed munificence of an eternal being; it is *mistaken* in that it unjustifiably converts some as-yet-unrealized temporal progress into a spatial paradise.

To correct this mystification, Feuerbach argues, man needs to *surrender* the notion of immortality and confront the finality of his own death. This will allow man, unimpeded by otherworldly distractions, to concentrate his energies into the pursuit of his 'knowledge drive [*Wissenstrieb*]', which is, for him, a *biologized* curiosity, through which 'the interests of the species are imposed on the individual as an obligation, but through which at the same time the individual lays claim to a counterinterest' in his own happiness. (*B*, p. 444) What this says, in brief, is that only the species is able to accomplish the destiny of man and this destiny is man's happiness on earth. The knowledge drive – which Feuerbach also calls the 'happiness drive' – aims at happiness by seeking to know not the answers to metaphysical questions, but only those things that will help satisfy the material needs of man; it thus places man within the co-operative machinery of the human pursuit of knowledge without reducing him to a mere cog, since this machine is specifically designed for *his* earthly benefit, for the benefit of his mortal existence.

While these conclusions are Feuerbach's, one looks in vain in the discussions of Kant and Freud that precede and follow this one in *The Legitimacy of the Modern Age* for some word of dissent from Blumenberg. One encounters instead the dubious implication that there is a *continuity* among these thinkers on the notion of the knowledge drive. If anything, Feuerbach is shown slightly to improve on Kant, for the former not only takes over the latter's position – that there are certain suprasensible ideas which are unsuited to human reason, which we cannot and should not strive to know – he also removes the last vestiges of the spatial metaphor of limits still discernible in Kant. Feuerbach thus allows us to view reason's limits as purely temporal; he teaches us finally that man has no 'supernatural knowledge drive' (*B*, 442). And though Freud's knowledge drive [*Wissentrieb*] is presented as similar to Feuerbach's in many respects, we are warned that in the study of Leonardo da Vinci, Freud does not pay sufficient attention to 'the historical conditions affecting [Leonardo's] individual biography'. (*B*, p. 452)

The distortions this continuity thesis precipitates are considerable; I will cite only the most basic. Kant's solution does not, as Blumenberg alleges, wipe out the tension between self-knowledge and salvation, or the immanent and transcendent destinies of the subject; quite the reverse. For, in Kant, the suprasensible is not simply eliminated from the realm of knowledge and thought, as it is in Feuerbach; it is instead retained as the very condition of thought. That is; no thought *without* the suprasensible. As far as the criticism of Freud is concerned, that he does not dwell on Leonardo's historical conditions is no indication of a weakness in his theory, but of its positive contribution. For Freud, the knowledge drive is bound up with the solution of sublimation, the problem being to explain how thought manages to escape compulsion and inhibition, or: how it escapes being a mere symptom of its historical conditions.

So far I have argued that the difference between Lefort and Blumenberg (or Feuerbach, since on this matter no discernible distance separates commentator from the author on whom he comments) hinges on the fact that Lefort links immortality and posterity while Blumenberg opposes them. But there is another crucial difference that affects their respective notions of posterity, which also turn out to be dissimilar. The conjunction of immortality with posterity, in Lefort, takes place through a notion of singularity, which is absent in Blumenberg.[14] Here is Lefort's most concise statement: 'The sense of immortality proves to be bound up with the conquest of a place *which cannot be taken*, which is invulnerable, because it is the place of someone . . . who, by accepting all that is most singular in his life, refuses to submit to the co-ordinates of space and time and who . . . for us . . . is not dead'. (*L*, p. 279)

Someone dies and leaves behind his place, which outlives him and is unfillable by anyone else. This idea constructs a specific notion of the social, wherein it is conceived to consist not only *of* particular individuals and their relations to each other, but also *as* a relation to these unoccupiable places. The social is composed, then, not just of those things that will pass, but in relation to these places that won't. This gives society an existence, a durability, beyond the changing make-up of those relations and the things that come to fill it. If, with the collapse of eternity, the modern world is not decimated by historical time, it is because this unoccupiable place, this sense of singularity, knots it together in time. Singularity itself, that which appears most to disperse society, is here posited as the modern social bond. Not only this, but another paradox seems to define it; singularity is described both as that which is 'localized in space and time' (*L*, p. 270) and as *universal*, as that which refuses the co-ordinates of space and time, which endures throughout time. (Quite clearly, *singularity* is distinct from *particularity*, which is also localized, but which we commonly and rightly associate with things that fade with time and distance, with the ephemeral, things that do not endure.)

This notion of singularity, which is tied to the *act* of a subject, is defined as *modern* because it depends on the denigration of any notion of a prior or superior instance that might prescribe or guarantee this act. *Soul, eternity, absolute* or *patriarchal power*, all these notions have to be destroyed before an act can be viewed as unique and as capable of stamping itself with its own necessity. One calls *singular* that which, 'once it has come into being, bears the strange hallmark of something that *must be*', and therefore cannot die. (*L*, p. 279). The *must* of this sentence – and thus the immortality of the act – is dependent on its *not* being determined by contingent historical conditions. Significantly, this notion of singularity, which gives rise to our obscure, one might even say *unconscious* sense of immortality, is associated by Lefort with the writer, that is, with sublimation.[15] For, my thesis is, that it is through the psychoanalytic concept of sublimation that we will be able to clarify exactly how singularity is able to serve as the modern social bond.

However incomplete the notion of sublimation remains at this point, it is nevertheless clear that it is *meant* to function as a bond. So, the immediate question becomes: what allows Feuerbach to do without it? Or: what *blocks* the emergence of any sense of singularity or temporal immortality in his theory? Recall that Feuerbach entertained (and rightfully rejected) only a *spatial* concept of immortality, no temporal version of the notion (whereby one could conceivably transcend time *within* time) presented itself to him as it does to Lefort. Why not? What Feuerbach sets out to do is to eliminate every trace of transcendence by incarnating the notion of eternity in the finite and forward movement of time, that is: in progress. Yet, as we have already suggested, the elimination of eternity presents a unique problem for the modern age; it risks the dissolution of society in a temporal vat. Something has to endure, it would seem, for progress to be even conceivable. In fact, Kant made this very argument, '[I]nfinite progress is possible . . . only under the presupposition of an infinitely enduring existence . . . of . . . rational being.' But while he offered this argument in defense of the postulate of the immortality of the *soul*, commentators have pointed out that what his argument actually requires, if it is to make any sense, is an immortal *body*.[17] Feuerbach tacitly acknowledges the

problem, as well as the corporeal requirement for its solution, in his proposal
of a notion of posterity, or of an infinite *succession* of bodies – which nicely
avoids the seemingly self-contradictory notion of an immortal *individual* body.

The nub of this solution is sheer and continuous succession. None of the
bodies by themselves possesses or actualizes immortality in the way the body of
the monarch was thought to do during the *ancien régime*, for example. Succession alone allows the individual enquirer to be taken up and included within
the whole without limits of humanity and saves society from the pulverization
of time. This solution also soothes the structural insatisfaction, the unbearable
gap, between the individual, whose share of progress is minuscule, and posterity, which 'possesses in abundance' the happiness the individual seeks. Finally,
this solution allows one to argue that the limits of human knowledge are merely
temporal and thus capable of being overturned.

The Death Drive: Freud's Thesis on Feuerbach

Feuerbach is right to want to snatch life back from eternity in order to insert it
into historical time. The problem is, however, that for him, this insertion means
that life is only conceivable in biological terms, that is: as *finite*, or as defined by
its temporal limit: death. His description of the relation between the human
individual and his posterity resembles, one could say in this context, Aristotle's
description of an animal's relation to its species, which relation, Aristotle
argues, renders the animal eternal, a part of ever-recurring life: 'Nature
guarantees to the species their being forever through recurrence [*periodos*], but
cannot guarantee such being forever to the individual.'[18] But the irony such a
comparison would entail (with Feuerbach's taking *flight from* eternity only to
settle on a definition of life that *depends on* it) is ultimately undone when we
stipulate that by the *biological definition of human life* we refer not *simply* to its
reduction to some ahistorical 'animal dimension', but rather to a conception
of bodily life that is specifically modern – and problematic.

To which conception do we refer, and why is it problematic? At the end of
his essay, 'Critique of Violence', Walter Benjamin isolates this conception when
he mentions with disdain the familiar proposition that 'higher even than the
happiness and justice of existence stands existence itself.' Judging this belief in
the sacredness of life itself, that is, in the sacredness of 'bodily life vulnerable
to injury by [our] fellow men,' to be 'false and ignominious', he speculates that
it is probably of recent origin, 'the last mistaken attempt of the weakened
Western tradition to seek the saint it has lost in cosmological impenetrability.'[19]

In *Homo Sacer: Sovereign Power and Bare Life*, Giorgio Agamben follows up on

Benjamin's suggestion and tracks the emergence of this dogma, wherein *bare* life, or life itself, is deemed to be sacred. While in classical Greece, *bios* (a *form* of life, or way of living, defined within the political sphere) could be, and systematically was, distinguished from *zoe* (the simple *fact* of life, common to animals, men and gods), in modern society, he argues, *bios* and *zoe* became conflated, making bare, biological life *the* matter of modern politics. Agamben thus adopts Foucault's thesis that in the middle of the nineteenth century – or, at the 'threshold of biological modernity' – natural life began to be the primary concern of the state and, as a result, politics, as such, was transformed into *biopolitics*. With the development of the 'life sciences', the old 'territorial state' (in which power asserted itself through the possession and control of geographical territory), gave way to the 'state of population' (in which power reigns less over land than over life itself): 'the species and the individual as a simple living body become what is at stake in a society's political strategies.'[20] It is against this backdrop that Feuerbach's notion of the biologically-based 'happiness drive' must be understood; it is in this context that its political profile assumes its ominous shape.

It must be said, however, that for all his bandying of the *term*, Agamben is surprisingly inattentive to the *notion* of bare life. This is undoubtedly because, according to his own argument, bare life is barely distinguishable from the power that defines it, and it is primarily the latter that interests him. His references to Foucault are therefore limited to *The History of Sexuality* and *Dits et Ecrits*, where the focus is primarily on strategies of modern power, rather than on the emergence of the biological definition of human life or, as Foucault puts it, the conceptual 'bestialization of man'. Faulting Foucault for failing to demonstrate how political techniques and technologies of the self ('by which processes of subjectivization bring the individual to bind himself to his own identity and consciousness and, at the same time, to an external power'[21]) converge to produce that form of 'involuntary servitude' which characterizes the modern subject, Agamben is himself guilty of the same failure, as well as another. For, by not inquiring further into the biological definition of life, he is unable to explain how the modern form of 'sovereign power' is able to sink its roots so thoroughly – so *inexhaustibly* – into bare life. In fact, it never seems to occur to him to ask, 'What is it about this definition of life that allows power to assume such a capillary hold over it?'

Though not offered as a response to this question, an answer might have been extrapolated from *The Birth of the Clinic*, particularly from the chapter 'Open Up a Few Corpses', where Foucault fittingly characterizes biological modernism as a 'mortalism'.[22] Placing the French physiologist Bichat in the

conceptual vanguard of this modernism, Foucault describes the former's inno-
vation thus:

> [I]n trying to circumscribe the special character of the living phenomenon Bichat
> linked to its specificity the risk of . . . death – of the death which life, by definition,
> resists. Bichat relativized the concept of death, bringing it down from the absolute in
> which it appeared as an indivisible, decisive, irrecoverable event: he volatilized it,
> distributed it throughout life in the form of separate, partial, progressive deaths, deaths
> that are so slow in occuring that they extend even beyond death itself.[23]

The 'medical gaze' of which Foucault speaks throughout *The Birth of the Clinic*,
the gaze, in Agamben's terms, of sovereign power, is an eye that sees death
everywhere immanent in life, sees everywhere this threat to life, and finds in
this very ubiquity the excuse for its own insidious and equally ubiquitous
control. To the exact extent that life becomes defined by death, is permeated
by death, it becomes permeated by power.

To return to Benjamin's formulation, from the nineteenth century on, '*bodily
life*' is defined essentially as *that which is 'vulnerable to injury'*, by processes of
disease as well as by our fellow men. To measure the novelty of this notion,
Benjamin asks his readers to reflect on the fact that this essential vulnerability,
which we now choose to label *sacred*, bore in antiquity the mark of *guilt*.[24]
Human life has always been known to be vulnerable to disease and death, of
course, but only in the nineteenth century did this vulnerability become
sacralized, by the discourses of power, as its essential aspect. Agamben, however,
departs from Foucault and Benjamin by seeing this notion of bare life not as a
rupture with previous thought but as the culmination of a gradual solidification,
throughout history, of the link between life – conceived (perennially, it would
seem) as that which is subject to death – and sovereign power. Thus, when he
declares, for example, that '*Not simple natural life, but life exposed to death (bare life
or sacred life) is the originary political element*', it is in the midst of a discussion of
Roman law, which is in this sense not so different from that of the modern
legal-juridical order.[25] His inattention to the concept of bare life, to the
specificity of the modern biological notion, leaves Agamben free to assume that
there is basically nothing new in it, that life has always been defined by death.

'Politicizing Death', the penultimate chapter of *Homo Sacer*, opens with a
reference to a 1959 study of what two French neurophysiologists termed *coma
dépassé* [overcoma], a degree of coma, or of death's incursion into life, involving
a much greater loss of vital functioning than that which had previously been
allowed to pass for life. The argument of the chapter is that advances in life-
support technology have led medical science to redefine death by pushing its
limits beyond those set by earlier standards. And as the limits of death are

extended, so the argument goes, so too are the reaches of sovereign power, which now begins to decide on the fate of a new class of citizens, the 'neomorts', or *faux vivants*, that is, the new 'living dead', over which power assumes a unique sort of control. What Agamben is in no position to observe, however – since the culprit, in his analysis, is nothing less than Western metaphysics itself – is that this recent extension of life beyond the cessation of its vital functions and the consequent increase of state power are *not* the latest increments of a centuries-old process, but the result of a redefinition of death that took place (not in 1959, but earlier; not at the dawn of Western thought, but later) in the middle of the last century. As we have already noted, Foucault, for one, has convincingly shown that it was with the emergence of the life sciences in the nineteenth century that death began to be conceived not as an absolute and unique event, but as a multiple phenomenon, immanent in life, dispersed through time, and extending 'beyond death itself'.

Agamben wants to indict Western metaphysics for the high crimes of biopolitics (in his narrative, it is the Nazi concentration camp that replaces the city as the paradigmatic socio-political unit of this politics) because, he argues: by the way in which it isolates its proper element – bare life – biopolitics reveals its fundamental collusion with the metaphysical tradition. That is to say, he views the positing of *bare life* as strictly equivalent to the positing of *pure Being* insofar as both issue as responses to the encounter with an 'unthinkable limit' beyond which these elements are then supposed to dwell, 'indeterminate and impenetrable'.[26] It is, according to this analysis, the logic of the supplement, or of the exception – which has been in place *ab urbe condita* – that led to the camps. Divisions may have flickered momentarily in the classical City; Antigone may once have rebelled against Creon, but these divisions and that rebellion were doomed from the start by the logic of exception that nourished sovereign power. And now, 'we no longer know anything of the classical distinction between *zoe* and *bios*, between private life and political existence, between man as a simple living being at home in the house and man's political existence in the city.'[27] Moreover, the current models by which the 'social sciences, sociology, urban studies, and architecture . . . are trying to conceive and organize the public space of the world's cities without any clear awareness that at their very center lies the same bare life . . . that defined the biopolitics of the great totalitarian states of the twentieth century', are in danger of simply *perpetuating* this politics of bare, bodily – or bestial – life.[28]

In fact, it is impossible to imagine – not only for the reader, but for Agamben himself, whose final pronouncements are irredeemably bleak – a model that would *not* risk perpetuating this politics. The problem, of course, is *Homo Sacer*'s totalizing, presentist analysis, which retroactively rediscovers the source of biopolitics at the origins of Western thought and is unable to contemplate any rupture within its tradition. The reason he does not ultimately adopt the position shared by Benjamin and Foucault – that the notion of bare life and the practices of biopolitics are of recent origin – is because he mistakes the specific limit of death for 'the' (unspecified) limit encountered by Western metaphysics, in general. Yet, though death in general is not a new idea, the notion, introduced by the biological sciences, that *death is immanent in life, and not simply its external limit*, is. New, too, since the nineteenth century is the link between the *finitude of man* (which the notion of bare life names) and his just-forged *freedom*. It is this link that any theory of biopolitics, of the way it gets man to place his freedom in the service of his servitude, would need to investigate. That this task has so far been largely neglected is the consequence of the sticky fact that we are ourselves still the dupes of this logic, victims of this dogma of bodily finitude, or of bare life. In a recent interview in *Artforum*, Alain Badiou makes this very point:

> The real romantic heritage – which is still with us today – is the theme of finitude. The idea that an apprehension of the human condition occurs primordially in the under-standing of its finitude maintains infinity at a distance that's both evanescent and *sacred* . . . That's why I think the only really contemporary requirement for philosophy since Nietzsche is the *secularization of infinity*. (my emphasis)[29]

Stated thus and affixed to Benjamin and Foucault's disparaging analyses of the modern sanctification of bestial life, this statement strikes one as a long overdue correction of certain contemporary commonplaces. Yet its judgement will remain out of reach to cultural theorists as long as they continue to misrecognize bodily finitude as the sobering fact that *confounds* our Romantic pretensions. For these theorists – for whom limits are almost always celebrated, insofar as they are supposed to restrict the expansionism of political modernism and its notions of universalism and will (this is only slightly a caricature) – the body is the limit, *par excellence*. But even those willing to entertain Badiou's point will probably find it difficult to abandon their interest in the body at this juncture or to imagine what a 'secularization of infinity' might mean.

What is needed, however, is not an abandonment of interest in the body, but a rethinking of its notion. This rethinking need not entail a radical reinvention, for, in truth, another notion of the body was developed long ago, precisely as a challenge to the one offered by the (bare) life sciences. The notion to which I refer is that proposed by psychoanalysis, where the body is conceived not, as in these sciences, as the seat of *death*, but as the seat of *sex*. That is, contrary to Foucault's claim, the sexualization of the body by psychoanalysis does not participate in the regime of biopolitics, it opposes it. Borrowing Badiou's phrase, one could put it this way: through its definition of the sexualized body, psychoanalysis provided the world with a secularized notion of infinity. Or: the concept of an immortal individual body, which Kant could not quite bring himself to articulate, becomes thinkable in Freud.

Notoriously, Freud's conclusion, stated in *Beyond the Pleasure Principle*, was that *the aim of life is death* – which seems on the face of it to contradict my argument. That is, Freud's theory appears to have been in tune with the bio-theory of the day, insofar as it places the death drive at the very core of life and its various ambitions. Not flinching from this conclusion, even buttressing it by arguing that for Freud there are no life drives, that *all* the drives are death drives, Lacan nevertheless calls into question that simplistic interpretation of the death drive which perceives it to be merely an explanation for the choice of death or unhappiness by the subject. Why do people commit suicide or act against their own interests? Because they are led by the death drive to do so. If this were all there were to it, the concept would not have met Freud's own avowed standards. Confronted with a proliferation of drives invented to account for almost every activity ('the drive to collect things', 'the drive to build', and so on), a querulous Freud insisted that a concept which did nothing more than assign a substantialized cause to a specific, known effect, and added nothing new to our knowledge, was an empty, useless thing. While one of the effects of the death drive *may be* the 'free' choice of death, this is by no means its only or even assured result.

The paradoxical Freudian claim that the death drive is a speculative concept designed to help explain why life aims at death, in fact, tells only half the story; the other half is given in a second paradox: the death drive achieves its satisfaction by *not* achieving its aim. Further, the *inhibition* that prevents the drive from achieving its aim is not understood within Freudian theory to be due to an extrinsic or exterior *obstacle*, but rather to be part of the very *activity* of the drive itself. The full paradox of the death drive, then, is this: while the *aim* (*Ziel*) of the drive is death, the *proper and positive activity* of the drive is to inhibit the attainment of its aim; the drive, *as such*, is *zielgehemmt*, that is, it is inhibited as to its aim, or: sublimated, 'the satisfaction of the drive through the inhibition of its aim' being the very definition of sublimation. Contrary to the vulgar understanding of it, then, sublimation is not something that happens to the drive under special circumstances, it is its proper destiny. Lacan summarizes this whole complex argument by referring to the death drive several times in the *Ethics* seminar as a 'creationist sublimation'. Significantly, in *The Four Fundamental Concepts* . . . , in the midst of his discussion of the drive, Lacan quotes the following Heraclitean fragment, appropriating it for psychoanalysis: 'To the bow (*bios*) is given the name of life (*bios*) and its work is death.'

(*S XI*, p. 177). The Greek pun is emphasized in order to place the proper accent on life, as it were. Life may be joined here to death, but not, we will soon see, in the same way it is in biopolitics.

Historically situated at the very 'threshold of biological modernity', as a contemporary of Bichat and the rest, Hegel considered Antigone's act from the point of death. Her deed, he argued, concerns not the living, but the dead, 'the individual who, after a long succession of separate disconnected experiences, concentrates himself into a single completed shape, and has raised himself out of the unrest of the accidents of life into the calm of simple universality.' (para. 452). That is, Antigone's act may be considered ethical, in Hegel's terms, inasmuch as it involves universal being rather than a particular aspect of it, and it concerns universal being inasmuch as it is undertaken on behalf of a dead and therefore completed being. A problem arises, however, because the universality, or completeness, brought by death is merely *abstract*: it is the product of a natural, biological process, not of a self-conscious subject. Antigone's task, then, is to redeem her brother from this first, biological death and this abstract universality by consciously performing a 'second death' through her act of *burial*. She must complete for her brother the reflexive circuit of self-conscious life which he, whose life has been finally shaped by death, can no longer accomplish himself. But what is it she is able to reflect back to him, except his own particularity, his own corporeal finitude, now *consecrated* by her act, raised to the dignity of 'universal individuality', which can only mean here a communally recognized individuality? Polynices is by this forever entombed in his own 'imperishable individuality', his own imperishable finitude. In this way bare, bestial life, has been dignified, rendered sacred; Hegel's analysis, supposedly an account of classical ethics, turns out to betray more than a little the thinking of his own day.

For Hegel the fault – the reason Antigone's act is ultimately as compromised as Creon's and results in the sacrifice of universality for the sake of particularity – lies with death. It sunders the journey out from the journey back, divides the circuit of self-reflexivity into mere biological or bodily life (a 'mere existent', in his vocabulary), represented by the *corpse* of Polynices, and a bodiless act, purged of desire; the body, divorced from the deed, appears, in Hegel's discussion, only as dead. And the act is powerless to do anything more than enshrine corporeal finitude. In Lacan's estimation the fault lies with Hegel's ceding too much to biological death, his reduction of the fact of human embodiment to the inevitable fact of death. Indeed, the whole of *The Phenomenology* is structured as a successive series of attempts to master bodily finitude and death, which has at this historical moment, according to Philippe Aries's massive study, been newly rendered obscene.[30] Henceforth, death must be 'civilized', taken up and transformed from the unique and traumatic event it once was to a normal and ongoing part of life. But this means that life itself becomes 'finitized', 'mortalized', and infinity – which is thus maintained at a distance (to recall Badiou) – taunts life with its shortcomings.

Once again: Lacan's interpretation turns on his recognition that the body is, rather, the site of infinity, of immortality, and his substitution, as we have said, of the 'dialectic of the bow' – of the death drive, which sexualizes the body – for the dialectic that enfolds death in life. These are the corrections that lead him to describe Antigone's deed not as the bestowing of 'imperishable individuality' on her brother, but as an 'immortalization of the family *Ate*'. But what does this difference signify in regard to Antigone's relation to the dead, to her familial past, or to the City? And what does it signify, to return to the terms of an earlier discussion, in regard to the relation between the '*individual organism*', which may be looked at, as Freud put it, 'as a transitory and perishable appendage to the quasi-immortal germ plasm bequeathed to him by his race', and the *species*.[31] Finally, how can our argument – that Lacan reconnects body and act, the very terms Hegel's analysis sunders – be reconciled with the Freudian argument that sublimation pries the act – whether it be a physical act or the act of thinking – from the body's grip?

Let us begin at the most basic level: death, and only death, is the aim of every drive; this is the Freudian proposition. Where the aim of the sexual *instinct* (which is to be found only among animals) is sexual reproduction, the aim of the *drives* (which Freud sometimes calls the *libidinal drives*) is death.[32] This means not only to say that there is *no* original life instinct directing the subject outward toward an other of the species for purposes of copulation, but also that there is nothing directing him/her toward the outside world for reasons of simple curiosity, as Feuerbach believed, for example. There is no drive impelling the subject toward any sort of fusion with others, toward 'vital association', which would allow 'the community of [subjects to] survive even if individual [subjects] have to die', a notion Freud dismisses as the 'Eros of the poets and philosophers'.[33] Freud categorically claims that '*there is unquestionably no universal instinct toward higher development*'; we must, then, definitively reject the 'benevolent illusion' that there is among men a drive toward perfection or progress. (*Beyond*, p. 40; my emphasis). But before thoughts of Schopenhauer's philosophy ('death is the "true result and to that extent the purpose of life"') spring to mind and lead us astray, we must recall that the involuted death drives are described by Freud as working *against* the teleology of a system such as Schopenhauer's and as winning for the subject 'what we can only regard as potential immortality'. (*Beyond*, p. 40) How so?

Directed not outward and forward, but back, the death drive aims at the past, at a time *before* the subject found itself where it now is, embedded in time and moving toward death. What, if anything, does this backward trajectory, this flight from biological death, uncover? It will surprise many to learn that Freud does not answer this question in the negative, 'Nothing!', but argues, in effect, that the drives discover certain ' "necessary forms of thought" . . . that time does not change . . . in any way and [to which] the idea of time cannot be applied.' (*Beyond*, p. 28) Freud employs the abstract language of Kant in order to assent to the philosopher's thesis regarding the conditions of the possibility of thought, which are not subject to temporal alteration or decay. These conditions cannot be absorbed, then, within the temporality of thought itself, they represent the immanent limits of knowledge that mere progress will never overturn. But Freud does more than simply assent to the 'Kantian theorem that time and space are "necessary forms of thought"'; he substantially rethinks these forms *and* their sources.

In brief, the Kantian conditions or forms of thought are given their equivalent, in psychoanalysis, in *the objects of the drive*. What are these objects and from where do they come? First, it must be made clear that the objects are *not* the aim of the drive, *that*, we have argued, is death – or, as Freud alternatively says: 'the restoration of an earlier state of things', a state of inanimation or inertia. (*Beyond*, p. 37). Now, this state exists, according to the theory, only as a retrospective illusion, never as an actual state; but its purely mythical status does not prevent it from having had a long history. Plato's Timeaus, for example, long ago recalled for us a similar inanimate past when the earth, created as a globe and containing all things, had no need of sense organs or, indeed, of organs of any kind: '[T]here would not have been any use of organs by the help of which he might receive his food or get rid of what he digested, since there was nothing that went from him or came into him, for there was nothing besides him.'[34] Psychoanalysis, it is well-known, rewrites this mythical state as the primordial mother-child dyad, which contained all things and every happiness and to which the subject strives always to return.

If this were the end of it (and unfortunately, too many think it is), the death drive would be a pure will to destruction or a 'will to nothingness', in Nietzsche's sense of the term. For, since this original state is mythical, the search for it is vain and would, through its endless and unsatisfiable pursuit, result in the annihilation of heaven and earth; the death drive would always inevitably end in death, in suicide and devastation. But this forgets two essential facts: (1) that there is no single, complete drive, only partial drives, and thus *no realizable will to destruction*; and (2) the second paradox of the drive, which states that the drive inhibits, as part of its very activity, the achievement of its aim. Some obstacle – the *object* of the drive – necessarily emerges to *brake* the drive, to curb it, thus preventing it from reaching its *aim*. Lacan gives to these obstacles the name *objects a*; they are, as it were, simulacra of the inanimate or pure object state. *Object a* is, however, the general term, specifically these obstacles are called *gaze, voice, breast, phallus*; in other words, they are given the names of bodily organs. In its condensed and commonly expressed form, the argument is, then, that the objects of the drive are the various organs of the body, but this does not yet explain how these objects can be viewed as equivalent to Kant's 'necessary forms of thought', nor how they *curb* the drive, act as obstacles to its full realization.

If we continue to translate Timaeus's into the psychoanalytic version of the primordial state, we will arrive at our explanation. The static harmony of the organ-less, complete, mother-child dyad is always already disturbed by a structural flaw; the mother's relation to her child remains ever enigmatic, at least partially.[35] The child cannot comprehend the mother's comings and goings; where or why she goes; what she wants from her child to make her want to stay. This is not a phenomenological account; it has to do rather with the materiality of the signifier and thus with the fact that the mother's desire is unconscious, that is, as unknowable to the mother as it is to the child. The enigma of their relation severs the dyad from the start. From the beginning the mother is lost to the child, as is that complete and absolute pleasure which her presence brought (would have brought). What prevents this loss from being catastrophic – from bankrupting life of all pleasure and thus making death preferable to life's desolation – is the riddling remainder the mother leaves behind, the very signifier that causes the separation. This mute, inert signifier, which refuses to yield up its meaning, to enter into any dialectical/diacritical relation to other signifiers – this object-like, 'thing-presentation', as Freud called it, distinguishing it from the conscious 'word-presentations' of ordinary language – derails the drive from its path of total destruction. Rather than pursuing the Nothing of annihilating dissatisfaction, the drive both *breaks up* and *brakes* as it contents itself with these small nothings, the meaningless traces of the now absent mother, which it repeatedly circumscribes. The now *partial* drives have each found an object that *satisfies* them.

The absolute pleasure, or *jouissance*, of the primordial, inanimate past may be forever lost, but this small dose of surplus *jouissance* emerges as a reminder of that past and, of course, of its loss. It is clear from this that, in contrast to the ordinary pleasure that everyday objects bring, *jouissance*, attached as it is to the memory of an originally lost object – *das Ding* – is a painful, immoderate pleasure. Freud's initial observation that the psyche is ruled by pleasure is maintained, but the concept of pleasure is no longer simple; it splits to produce this second, unmasterable sort. The organ-less body that was the original dyad may be irredeemably destroyed, but certain body parts, or organs, develop to mark the various places where the child was once one with its former wholeness. But what does the term *bodily organ* mean here? Obviously, these organs do not coincide with those defined by bio-physiology or bio-politics. While the organs of nineteenth- and twentieth-century bio-physiology belong, in Freud's vocabulary, wholly to the perception-consciousness system – which temporarily registers, but also *shields the psyche against,* external stimuli – the organs defined by psychoanalysis have their origin in a system that *opposes* the perception-consciousness system, namely, the memory system, where *memory* concerns the archaic past, which is incapable of being 'remembered' in the psychological sense, that is: made to appear as an image before the subject. Drive stimuli are nothing but the 'enigmatic signifiers' or opaque demands from that past, husks or pure forms of meaning which the drive circumscribes, tracing out on the body of the child places where it was once connected to the body of the mother, but which now mark her withdrawal. All drives are death drives because they aim, Freud argues, to reproduce an initial state no longer available to the subject.

Two phrases of this description simplify certain complexities and may thereby mislead: *the drive circumscribes* and *tracing out on the body.* In fact, the drive is less a force or thrust that circles a separate thing, the empty form of the demand, than the force of the demand itself, the pressure it exerts.[36] Recall Freud's definition in 'Instincts and their Vicissitudes': a drive is 'a measure of the demand made upon the mind for work in consequence of its connection to the body'.[37] In other words, *drive is the demand,* or pressure, *of the enigmatic, primordial demand.* Also, Lacan's definition in *The Four Fundamental Concepts*: 'the drive represents no doubt, but *merely* represents, and partially at that, the curve of fulfilment of [death] in the living being.'[38] All we have of the death drive are merely these representations, the signifiers of a demand; but they do not represent something – that is, they *merely* represent, without representing anything – because they are opaque, indecipherable. The demand does not name a specific object, then, it does not demand something in particular.

Freud is often thought to be a determinist precisely because he asserts that the subject is driven to reproduce an initial state, to recapture or find again an original lost object, but this is a psychoanalytically naive misreading of what he wrote. The drive (or original, indecipherable demand) does not mandate a specific, parentally-defined duty, it simply *demands work.* Freud is here far from Jung – who concocted the notion of archetypes in order to aver the continuation in the psychic life of every subject of 'some archaiac relation, some primitive mode of access of thoughts, some world that is there like some shade of an ancient world surviving in ours' (*S XII*, p. 153) – and close to Kant. For, like the moral law – and unlike the archetype – the imperative of the drive is to act, not to perform a specific act or think a specific thought. But how does the drive press this demand? By tracing out, impressing, on the subject's body an object that *represents* this demand, a part of the body of the Other to which the subject was once joined but from which it is now detached. On the subject's body, then, this ghostly overlay of the Other's (or, once its own, now lost, and thus Other): phantom organs. Properly speaking, however, *on* is wrong; the subject has no body *before* the activity of the drive brings it into being. It is only through the drive that the subject is corporealized, comes into possession of its bodily organs. This is Freud's profound point: the subject is able to perform its bodily functions – to see, hear, eat, speak, and so on – not because it is endowed from birth with sense organs, in the bio-physiological sense, that is, with eyes, ears, a mouth. Rather, these bio-physiological organs owe their existence to the subject's capacity to use them, which capacity depends on the pressure or demand for work exerted by the objects of the drive. In brief: the gaze is the condition of the possibility of the eye, the voice is the condition of the ear, the breast the condition of the mouth, and so on. It is not only thought, but the very existence and functioning of the body and its organs that require as their condition of possibility certain necessary forms, or objects; certain representations of the drive.

How does this alter the commonplace understanding of these functions: seeing, hearing, speaking, and the rest? What does it mean to say that the objects of the drive – or demands from the past – are their conditions? These are large questions, to which it is possible and appropriate to give here only a few brief responses. First, these functions cannot be considered as purely cognitive, that is, as divorced from the body. Since they are 'ignited' by unconcious pleasure, or *jouissance*, they have, necessarily, a bodily origin. There is for psychoanalysis no such thing as a 'pleasure of the mind', since the body is considered to be pleasure's only support. Second, there is in the psychoanalytic account no simple subject–object relation whereby an individual could encounter, through a process of direct contact or impingement, the outside world. Between subject and object a third term intervenes: the *object a*, or the object of the drive, which is the condition both of the subjectivity of the subject and the objectivity of the object. This object, by representing some part of the subject which is now lost to it, not only splits the subject from itself, but also splits the subject from the external world insofar as this world will no longer be encountered directly, but will be 'filtered through' the *object a*; will always refer itself to it.

Which means this: not only does no signifier refer directly to the world, but neither does it refer directly to another signifier (as Saussure would have it), without first referring to the *object a.* This seems to be what Lacan means by his classic formulation: a signifier represents a *subject* for another signifier. The *object a* as cause of the subjective *division* – hence of the subject, as such – becomes a kind of 'focal point' of all the signifiers. The problem is that it is too easy to overlook the phrase *subjective division* and thence to interpret Lacan's and similar formulations as evidence of *subjectivism,* as a statement about the (psychologically) subjective constitution of the world. Yet, the opposite is true; this restates a *materialist* position along the lines proposed recently by Badiou, who summarized it thus: that view which defines materialism as a theory of the determination of the subjective by objective conditions has been philosophically discredited. Materialism means, rather, that human existence is capable of being 'benumbed' (fixed and fascinated) by what happens to it, by the event.[39]

The difference between being determined by objective conditions and being benumbed by the event is the *object a,* about which it is impossible to say that it belongs exclusively either on the side of the subject or on the side of the external world.[40] According to Lacan, however, fantasy *protects us from* the Other's demand. This definition introduces a significant ambiguity. First it simply means that fantasy substitutes the *object a* for the subject, making the former and not the latter the absolute object of the Other's desire. But the fantasy does not have only this salutary effect, it also has a stultifying dimension. For in fantasy the subject adopts the Other's absolute object as the *sine qua non* of its *own* desiring. In taking the Other's object as its own, the subject is 'protected' against the Other itself. The Other as such is 'domesticated', converted into that 'otherness-to-self' whereby the subject locates the real core of its being in an object outside the series it is possible to possess. The event appears as a rupture of this fantasy structure in this sense: in the event, the opaque demand of the Other – signalled by the *object a* – appears as extrinsic to the subject, as coming from outside. The subject benumbed by the event is like the Wolf Man who stares fascinated and transfixed by the gaze of the wolves appearing in a window in his dream. The hard, opaque gaze of the wolves, in which Lacan locates the real core of the dream, proves that *the world looks back at us, is exterior to us.* The world makes demands on us, commands us to act. This is different from saying that it imprints itself on us, determines how we should act.[41]

With a little reflection one sees that the existence of this demand alters our understanding not only of how the subject relates to its world, but also how the individual subject relates to the species. Listen to what Freud says about this matter:

> No external vicissitude can be experienced or undergone by the id [or: by the drive] except by way of the ego, which is the representative of the external world to the id.

Nevertheless, it's not possible to speak of direct inheritance in the ego. *It is here that a gulf between an actual individual and the concept of a species becomes evident.* (my emphasis)[42]

We have here definitively taken our leave of the *eternal* realm of animal existence where, as Aristotle pointed out, this gulf is closed as a result of the fact that the individual animal obeys the instinctual dictates of its species. We are also far from the merely *mortal* realm described by Feuerbach in which individual researchers inherit knowledge from the past and pass it on to the future, forming a continuous sequence of laboring (and lapsing) bodies in order to abolish the gap between individual merit and recompense, virtuous hard work and happiness, which the modern era opened up: the whole species reaps the profit the individual never collects. For Freud, the gulf between work and reward can never be reabsorbed because *work* (or the active response to the pressures of the drive/archaic demand) *alters* profoundly the world in which the response intervenes – and alters, too, the subject who responds. There is thus no stable place, no fixed sphere, where accounts could conceivably be kept. The game and the stakes keep shifting, precisely because of the demand's ever-renewed insistence on being interpreted. There is no species, in a sense, only individuals.

But if this is so, then how is progress possible? The simple answer, proffered by theoretical cynics is: it's not; there is no progress. Kant, less cynical than these, did not abandon the possibility, and even gave a fumbled answer to the question: 'because the soul is immortal'. What he should have said, we have been suggesting, is: 'because the body is immortal'. This substitution does not transfer to the body the attributes of the soul. For, to say that the body is immortal is not to deny the inevitability of biological death, it is to contest the reduction of the body to biological functions. What forestalls this reduction is the fact that, for us, it is not we, but the *Other* who does not die, who leaves behind a trace that awakens us to our bodies, opening our senses not to a merely empirical reality, but to the reality of the *event*. To bow before the anger or will of others, to be moved to pity by their pains and sorrows, is to behave like the chorus in Greek tragedy, which surrenders itself to external circumstances. To be moved by the event is something quite different. For here it is no longer a question of pathos, of a passive suffering of what comes to us from outside, but of an active engagement with that which is encountered as not being there, as absent. This engagement precipitates an alteration of the subject so radical it requires a separate concept to name it: *resubjectification* is one term, *conversion* another.[43] It is the only form of progress Lacan or Kant, the respective authors of these terms, countenance: ethical progress.

The Obdurate Desire to Endure

Freud had a name for it, too, *Haftbarkeit* – or *perseverance* – with all the ethical connotations the word conjures up. Lacan invokes Freud in a final naming of what Antigone does: she perseveres. Her implacable resolve to honor her brother is attributable not to some 'will to destruction' or 'will to nothing' (as Anouilh's portrayal of her as a 'little fascist', hellbent on annihilating all opposition, suggests), but to *Zwang*, the compulsion of the drive. While the two have in common a turning away from the merely empirical world, the former is constituted solely by the negative movement of dissatisfaction and deflection, while the latter is constituted by an original *satisfaction* and *affirmation* of the object it circles.

Stressing that the trajectory of deflection is deflected or halted and the drive satisfied effectively distinguishes drive from a will to destruction, but it may also stir up a different confusion. We know from Freud that unconscious satisfaction sometimes binds the subject to her symptoms. Someone will repeat, as though stuck in a rut from which she is unwilling to propel herself, a pattern of behavior that inconveniences her, or even brings pain, all for the sake of the exorbitant, *unconscious* satisfaction she derives from it. What is it that distinguished the perseverance of Antigone from these neurotic repetitions? The answer has, in a sense, already been given. Antigone's perseverance does not consist in the repetition of a 'pattern of behavior', but of the performance, in the face of enormous obstacles, of a creative act, and it results not in the preservation of the very core of her being – however wayward or perverse – but of its complete overturning. Antigone's perseverance is not indicated by her remaining rigidly the same, but by her *metamorphosis* at the moment of her encounter with the event of her brother's death and Creon's refusal to allow his burial. She remains faithful throughout not to herself, but to the terrible misfortune – or *ate* – that befalls her. It is only because *Antigone* begins *after* the event has taken place that some are led to mistake its heroine as simply obstinate, as incapable of altering her path. She is, it's true, unyielding before Creon, whose human laws and foibles she cannot abide, but before the inhuman law that manifests itself in the event that, unrepresented, precedes the play, *she metamorphoses herself*, transforms herself so thoroughly that the process has to be described in mythological terms, as inhuman rather than heroic. Metamorphosis has nothing to do with the all-too-human tendency to bend under the weight of adversity, and the wild, bird-like cries Antigone emits upon learning that her brother's body has been exposed once again – after she had carefully covered it with a fine dust – do not humanize her; quite the contrary. The image she presents is *not* one of pathos; it destroys the point of identification rather than encouraging us to identify with her.

This description of the difference between ethical perseverance and neurotic repetition does not obviate the need to analyze their structures. We will need to know how the satisfaction of the symptom differs from the satisfaction of sublimation in order to understand what metamorphosis means. Let us begin with this basic observation: the demand of the Other is not a general one; it is addressed to the subject, uniquely. The singularity of this address is what burdens the subject, who is solely responsible for heeding the demand, for figuring out what the Other wants from her, and from no one else. But if the address is truly unique, then the demand cannot designate it ambiguously – that is, through signifiers – for this would open the possibility that the message was meant for others. It follows that the demand must indicate its addressee deictically, must point to her *in the flesh*. This is in fact what happens; the Other 'hails' the subject by grabbing her by the scruff of the neck, as it were, by seizing her in the flesh. This manner of hailing is what accounts for the inhibition of part of the subject's body or body function. That part which is inhibited or restricted is too strongly eroticized, Freud tells us, offering the example of the obsessional who cannot write because the process of writing has assumed an erotic meaning for him. If the eroticized part indexes the Other's demand, and the inhibition the subject's surrender to that demand, the satisfaction of the symptom seems to be the Other's rather than the subject's own.

The *inhibition of the body* is not the same thing as the *inhibition of the drive*, or sublimation; in fact, sublimation releases the body from inhibition, from symptomatic repetition. Keep in mind the obsessional who cannot write. It is commonly assumed that what releases his writing hand and the flow of his thoughts is the de-eroticization of writing and thinking. The drive to know, in general, is thought to follow from an unlinking of *jouissance* from the process of thinking, of acquiring knowledge. Knowledge would thus begin with the subtraction of sex. This is not so. The drive to know results from an unlinking of *jouissance* not from knowledge, but from the *supposed subject of knowledge*, that is, from the Other who demands one-knows-not-what, but who – or, so the subject supposes – knows a thing or two about *jouissance*.

How does this unlinking come about? Through the substitution of form for flesh. The *object a* – that is, a nondialecticizable- or thing-representation, which cannot signify, or which has no semantic content, but is only the form of language – replaces the flesh of the subject as the index of the Other's demand. It is necessary to be as precise as possible here. This formal element substitutes for the flesh, not for the body of the subject; for, as was argued earlier, this *object a* is, on the contrary, the condition of the possibility of the body. Nor does this form disengage itself from *jouissance*, rather, as the mark of the Other's pressure on the subject, it vehicles *jouissance* (enjoyment being always a matter of the stimulus coming from the Other, which the subject cannot easily separate from itself). The *object a* – which *is* the death drive, or all we ever get of it – both directs the subject toward the inanimate state of reunion with the Other and dams up or inhibits this path. For, like the zero which begins the series of numbers, it begins the series of signifiers, or opens the field of representation in which the subject will now (as a result of this sublimation or substitution of form for flesh) actively engage itself. The subject thus engages symbolic life, but in the name of the lost Other, not to represent the demand of the Other, but to 'point to it', or, as Lacan often says, to encircle it.

The act of Antigone, her sublimation, cuts across the alienating Hegelian division between the universal and the particular. She does not elevate her brother to the status of 'imperishable individuality', does not salvage particularity from contingency, but finds a way of honoring his – and beyond this, her family's – singularity or *ate*: that which belongs to them and no one else. This she does not by pointing him out in the flesh, but by performing a public, symbolic act which is able to 'designate' him in his uniqueness. In virtue of what does Antigone act? She tells us when she mourns, 'If my husband had died, I could have had another, and a child by another man, if I had lost the first, but with my mother and father in Hades below, I could never have another brother.' (ll. 908–912) Is this not the equivalent of our expression, 'They broke the mold'? Her brother is unique and it is this fact that motivates her act.

If to act, in the sense of *Haftbarkeit*, to persevere, means to keep faith with the event (with that which is exterior to ourselves, with the demand coming from the Other), then an act always consists of an intervention in the symbolic that will attest to that demand. Fittingly, Antigone does not expose her brother's body to public view, she *covers* it. Dusting his body, she elevates an object of almost no meaning – dust – to the dignity of *das Ding*, to the dignity of that unrepresentable singularity of her family *ate*. It is as if that which is most precious to her, the absolute condition of her being, her *object a*, had suddenly become figurable as an ordinary object. But what sort of object is this? One that the strong winds accompanying the event easily blow away, leaving a hole in the symbolic world, the hole her brother's absence makes in it. It is often remarked that this scene of burial, this scene of Antigone's pivotal act, is set curiously off-stage and that the wording of the messenger's report further obscures Antigone's agency in it. This is only appropriate. The true act will always resist narrativization, since it explodes the very stuff of narrative: the 'underlying substance' upon which narrative transformation depends. There is no subject who presides over the act, no Promethean figure straddling the interval between its 'before' and its 'after'. The act is that which effects a cut, a break, in narrative time. The important point not to be overlooked is that Antigone herself is *a being of dust*. At the core of her being we find not something that endures throughout time, something whose status is ontological, but that which we might call her ethical status. Her strength lies not in her capacity to remain unchanged despite all contingencies, but in her capacity to metamorphize herself in response to the demand of the Other that these contingencies comport.

It follows from the above that the true act, sublimation, is distinct from idealization, with which it is nevertheless often confused.[44] The object of the drive is always a sublimated object, not an idealized one. It would be silly to argue, for example, that Antigone idealizes her brother's body or the dust she uses to cover it. These objects are, on the contrary, *insignificant* in themselves, and they are not points of identification for Antigone, as are all idealized objects. The confusion between idealization and sublimation is, however, instructive, for it forces us to consider what it is about sublimation that leads to the miscue. We do not have to look far to find the source of confusion, for it resides in the widely acknowledged fact that the sublimated object does not 'fill our stomachs', as it were, it is not directly filling or used. One could say, with Lacan, that the sublimated object 'has the effect ... of suspending, lowering, disarming desire'; it sets up a barrier that prevents us from attempting to devour the object. (*S VII*, p. 238) The sublimated object is one toward which the subject bears a *disinterested* or *detached* relation, that is, one does not approach it as an object that can satiate us, as an object of need can.

The sublimated object and the idealized object are similar, then, in that between them and the subject a barrier is erected that prevents us from treating them as objects of consumption (as is Polynices's body to the birds of prey) or of use. They are *dissimilar* in that only the sublimated object can be said to be *devoid of interest* (I would say, 'in the Kantian sense', but it is this sense that needs to be clarified) or *de-idealized*. The point seems to be this: unlike idealization, sublimation delights not in the object itself, but *in the act of installing it*, that is, in wresting *jouissance* from the Other's hold, insofar as this liberation of *jouissance* initiates what Kant had referred to as 'the free play of the faculties'. Antigone is able to act on behalf of her brother, to honor him and the family *ate*, through this act of *detachment* from him. The sublimated *object a*, which installs the enabling limit or initiates the detachment, has no other value than this; its very nature is to be replaceable. And the *perseverance* of Antigone consists in this replacement, in pursuing the unlinking of *jouissance* from the Other's knowledge and taking responsibility for the value she gives this *ate*. Sublimation is then Freud's indispensable contribution to the 'labor theory of value'.

Our position has been that, while Creon and Antigone may be described as similarly intransigent – it is this very intransigence that testifies to the insistence of the drive in both – there is a world of difference between them. It is now time to say in what this difference consists and so we turn to a section in *Beyond the Pleasure Principle* where Freud, quoting a phrase from Faust's *Mephistopheles*, speaks of a 'driving factor which will permit of no halting at any position attained, but, in the poet's words, "*ungebändigt immer vorwärts dringt* [presses ever forward unsubdued]."' (*SE*, vol. 18 p. 46) The description seems to apply to both Creon and Antigone, though Freud says that this driving factor is such that 'no sublimations will suffice to remove' it. What accounts for this unsubduable pressure? Here is Freud's answer: 'it is the difference in the amount between the pleasure of satisfaction which is *demanded* and that which is actually *achieved* that provides the driving factor which will permit of no halting.'

Why will no act of sublimation remove this factor? As Freud and Lacan both say, every sublimation is only partial, or: the sublimated object is always only a partial object. This does not mean that the object is extracted from a whole of which it is a part, but that it 'deceives' us into believing there is something beyond it; it presents itself as covering over a vastness that it does not allow us to glimpse. It is from this point that the distinction between Antigone's perseverance and Creon's obstinacy can be drawn. Perseverance would seem to be the ethical decision – in light of the partialness of every sublimation – to continue to pursue fresh sublimations. (It is important to catch the difference between this notion of fresh or *new* sublimations and the more common but incorrect notion of an *increase* of sublimation. The first notion acknowledges that sublimation concerns the setting up of an object, not an intensifying of some 'process of purification'.) The act of sublimation thus entails the invention of new ways of keeping faith with the lost or dead Other, even to the point of abandoning every last vestige of one's being, that is, of the very object upon which one's fantasy depends. One must be clear on this point: sublimation leads, not necessarily to a surrendering of one's life, but to a surrendering of one's primary fantasy. Antigone's metamorphosis is such an instance of *giving ground*; it is simultaneously a surrendering of the grounding substance that supports fantasy and a grounding of the world in the act.

Rather than pursuing new sublimations, Creon *idealizes the difference between the satisfaction demanded and that which is achieved*, in other words, he submits to the superego imperative. In the *Ethics* seminar, Lacan translates this imperative this way, 'Carry on working. Work must go on. . . . As far as desires are concerned, come back later. Make them wait.' (*S VIII*: p. 315). One takes from this a precise definition of the superego as nothing but the *idealization* of repressed satisfaction, where *repressed* refers simply to that bit of satisfaction which is structurally unachievable.

The superegoic fixation of Creon and the perseverance that drives Antigone's sublimation thus bear different relations to the primordially lost *jouissance* and to the demands of the Other. Superegoic fixation is the dogged pursuit of *dissatisfaction*, in that the point of this obstinacy is to *preserve the difference* between the pleasure any ordinary object is able to afford and the guarantee of absolute *jouissance* which the object-cause of desire promises. The superego commands us to hold out for this absolute enjoyment of our absolute past and thus to scorn the mundane pleasures that are nothing in comparison to it. The commandment to 'Enjoy!' only an impossible pleasure thus enslaves us to an idealized, dead past. As opposed to perseverance, this pursuit of unachieved satisfaction resists renewed sublimations – precisely because it is only by remaining the same that it stands any chance of measuring its progress. But here *progress* has lost its ethical meaning of *conversion* and comes to refer simply to the *accumulation* of more and more of the same. And the relatively insignificant, de-idealized dust of Antigone becomes something more like the *soil* of modern nation-states or the *blood* of their citizens' mortal bodies. Perseverance locates enjoyment, not in an unachievable past nor in an out-of-reach object, but in the body eroticized by the performance of the act.

Notes

This is for you, Johnny.

1. Jean-Pierre Vernant, 'Greek Tragedy: Problems of Interpretation', in *The Stucturalist Controversy*, ed. Richard Macksey and Eugenio Donato, Baltimore and London: Johns Hopkins University Press, 1972, pp. 278 and 288.
2. Ibid., pp. 278–79.
3. This is the place to note that anachronism formed part of the very substance of Athenian tragedy; as Vernant remarks, 'the surprising fact, often pointed out, is that there are more archaisms in Greek tragedy than, for example, in the epic.' (Ibid., p. 283). While the Chorus, which was made up of Athenian citizens, responded to dramatic situations remarkably similar to their own, they did so in a lyrical, elevated language that appeared antiquated in comparison with normal speech. Contrarily, the dramatic protagonists of the tragedies represented legendary figures from the past, but spoke in the rhythms and idiom of the current day. This curious anachronistic stuff of tragedy is precisely what the films of Pier Paolo Pasolini and Jean-Marie Straub and Danielle Huillet attempt to redeploy.
4. A history of the relation of the German Idealists to Sophocles's *Antigone* can be found in George Steiner, *Antigones*, Oxford: Clarendon, 1984.
5. G.W.F. Hegel, *Aesthetics: Lectures on Fine Art*, trans. T.M. Knox, Oxford: Clarendon, 1975, p. 464.
6. G.W.F. Hegel, *The Phenomenology of Spirit*, referred to in the text as *P* trans. A.V. Miller,

Oxford: Clarendon, 1977, para. 468; all subsequent references to this work will be to this edition and will be indicated in the text by paragraph numbers.

7. Sophocles, *Antigone*, ed. and trans., Hugh Lloyd-Jones, Cambridge MA: Harvard / Loeb Classical Library, 1994, p. 45.

8. Jacques Lacan, *Seminar VII: The Ethics of Psychoanalysis* (referred to in the text as *S VII*), ed. Jacques-Alain Miller, trans. Dennis Porter, London: Routledge, 1992, p. 88; further references to this seminar will made in the text.

9. Sigmund Freud, 'Civilization and Its Discontents', *The Standard Edition of the Complete Psychological Works of Sigmund Freud* (referred to in the text and future footnotes as *SE*), vol. 21, trans., James Strachey, London: Hogarth, 1957, p. 80n. Mary Ann Doane, in her fascinating essay, 'Sublimation and the Psychoanalysis of the Aesthetic', (*Femmes Fatales*, New York and London: Routledge, 1991) also highlights this footnote.

10. Jacques Lacan, *Seminar XII: The Four Fundamental Concepts of Psycho-Analysis* (referred to in the text and future footnotes as *S XI*), ed. Jacques-Alain Miller trans. Alan Sheridan, London: Hogarth Press 1977, pp. 210–215.

11. Sigmund Freud, 'The Ego and the Id', *SE*, vol. 19, p. 58.

12. Claude Lefort, 'The Death of Immortality? (referred to in the text as *L*),' *Democracy and Political Theory*, Minneapolis: Minnesota Press, 1988, p. 256; further references to this essay will be indicated in the text.

13. Hans Blumenberg, *The Legitimacy of the Modern Age* (referred to in the text as *B*), trans. Robert M. Wallace, Cambridge and London: MIT Press, 1983, p. 443; further references to this work will be made in the text.

14. An examination of the Blumenbergian concept of the 'reoccupation of positions' would be a good way to explore the contrast with Lefort further. My own sense is that Blumenberg's notion is a functionalist one, but I could not argue that here.

15. In 'What is an Author?', (*Language, Counter-Memory, Practice*, ed. and trans., Donald Bouchard and Sherry Simon, Ithaca: Cornell, 1977, Michel Foucault reserves for two authors – Marx and Freud – this singular and immortal status. One might answer the essay's question this way: an author is a writer who, for us, does not die, to whose text we continue to return and whose place is not occupied by any intellectual successor.

16. Immanuel Kant, *Critique of Practical Reason*, trans. Mary Gregor, Cambridge: Cambridge University Press, 1997, pp. 102–3.

17. See Lewis White Beck, *A Commentary on Kant's Critique of Practical Reason*, Chicago: University of Chicago Press, 1960, pp. 270–271; and Alenka Zupančič, 'Kant with Don Juan and Sade', in *Radical Evil*, ed. Joan Copjec, London and New York: Verso, 1996, pp. 118–119.

18. Aristotle, *Economics* 1343b24; quoted by Hannah Arendt in *The Human Condition*, Chicago: University of Chicago Press, 1958, p. 19.

19. Walter Benjamin, 'Critique of Violence', *Illuminations*, ed. Peter Demetz, trans. Edmund Jephcott, New York and London: Harcourt Brace Jovanovich, 1978, pp. 298–99; Benjamin then adds, in order to forestall any ahistorical objection: 'The antiquity of all religious commandments against murder is no counterargument, because these are based on other ideas than the modern theorem.'

20. Giorgio Agamben, *Homo Sacer: Sovereign Power and Bare Life*, trans. Daniel Heller-Roazen, Stanford: Stanford University Press, 1998, p. 3; further references to this source will be marked in the text.

21. Ibid., p. 5.

22. Michel Foucault, *The Birth of the Clinic*, trans. A.M. Sheridan Smith, New York: Vintage, 1975, p. 145.

23. Benjamin, 'Critique of Violence', p. 299.

25. Agamben, *Home sacer*, p. 88.

26. Ibid., p. 182.

27. Ibid., p. 187.

28. Ibid., pp. 181–82.

29. Alain Badiou, 'Being by Numbers', Lauren Sedofsky interview with Badiou, *Artforum*,

October 1994, p. 87. Badiou further summarizes his own mathematical, and resolutely atheistic, project by stating, 'The philosophical destiny of atheism, in a radical sense, lies in the interplay between the question of being and the question of infinity . . . Mathematics secularizes infinity in the clearest way, by formalizing it. The thesis that mathematics is ontological has the double-negative virtue of disconnecting philosophy from the question of being and freeing it from the theme of finitude.' The covertly theological theme of the 'finitude of man', epitomized by the Heideggerian phrase 'being-towards-death' and vaunted by deconstruction, is rigorously challenged by Badiou, who remains faithful (in his carefully theorized sense of this term) to Lacan on this issue.

30. Philippe Ariès's *Essais sur l'Histoire de la Mort en Occident, du Moyen Age à nos jOurs*, Paris: Seuil, 1975, is one of the sources on which Lefort draws for his analysis of immortality in the modern era.

31. Sigmund Freud, 'Instincts and Their Vicissitudes', *SE* vol.14: p. 125.

32. The contrast is never stated this starkly. Instead, instinct is described as an innate, biological 'knowledge'/pressure toward sexual reproduction, while the drive is said to be a kind of derailment of this trajectory; drive then becomes a kind of failed instinct. This description is misleading because it (1) allows a normative viewpoint to take hold, even as it attempts to counter it; (2) obscures the true aim of the drive, which is away from rather than toward the empirical world; (3) muddies the conceptualization of human sexuality; and (4) effaces the double paradox of the death drive. My restatement of the contrast is a strategic intervention designed to help rectify these problems.

33. Sigmund Freud, *Beyond the Pleasure Principle, SE*, vol. 18: pp. 121–22; further references to this work are indicated in the text.

34. Plato, *Timaeus*, p. 33 b-d.

35. The term 'enigmatic signifier' is, of course, the invention of Jean Laplanche; see his excellent work on the drive in *Seduction, Translation, Drives*, a dossier compiled by John Fletcher and Martin Stanton, London: Psychoanalytic Forum/Institute of Contemporary Arts, 1992.

36. Compare this important correction by Laplanche, 'When I read this quotation I wondered whether I had written (in *New Formations for Psychoanalysis*) that "the drive is the force behind representatives", since for me the drive is a force of the representatives themselves and not "behind" them,' (Ibid., p. 73). This is an absolutely crucial point; what it says is this: the drive *is* these *sublimated* objects.

37. Freud, 'Instincts and their Vicissitudes', pp. 121–22.

38. Lacan (*S XI*, p. 177) says *sex* rather than *death*, but goes on to explain that *sex* cannot be understood in the vulgar sense, that its relation to death (again, in the psychoanalytic sense) determines its meaning in the human realm. See note 32, above.

39. Alain Badiou, *Saint Paul: La fondation de l'universalisme*, Paris: PUF, 1997, p. 70.

40. In film theory, generally, the gaze is supposed to be on the side of the Other, exclusively; what is ignored is the fact that it is *also* on the side of the subject. This error is parallel to the one that interprets the bobbin in the *fort-da* game as a representation of the mother, rather than as an object detached from the mother which now represents a lost part of the *subject*. In each case the error is the result of not taking the corporeal dimension into account.

41. Is this not the logic of the third *Critique*, where Kant says, in regard to teleological judgement, that the subject faces the natural world not as a chaotic welter of forces, but as though it were endowed with purpose? We must not disregard his repeated denials that this view of nature is based on an analogy with our own.

42. Sigmund Freud, *The Ego and the Id, SE*, vol. 19, p. 56.

43. Lacan describes the event not simply as something that takes place once and for all, but as that which is subject to 'many restructurings . . . *nachträglich*, at a later date.'

('Function and field of speech and language in psychoanalysis', *Ecrits: A Selection*, trans. Alan Sheridan, New York: Norton 1977, p. 51)

44. A recent example of this common error can be found in Kaja Silverman's *The Threshold of the Visible World*, New York and London, Routledge, 1996.

9 ANTIGONE AGONISTES: Urban Guerilla or Guerilla Urbanism?
The Red Army Faction, *Germany in Autumn* and *Death Game*

THOMAS ELSAESSER

Burying the RAF

On April 20, 1998 a letter addressed to the State Prosecutor's Office in Karlsruhe arrived at the Reuters News Agency bureau in Bonn, declaring the voluntary dissolution of the RAF, the Red Army Faction, West Germany's 'urban guerilla' movement from the 1970s. The date was as symbolically overdetermined as many of their often violent actions had been in previous decades. Since the date of the dissolution was Hitler's birthday, commentators wondered if this was a hoax, though whether on the part of the remaining RAF activists or the Federal Office of Criminal Investigation, none could be sure. If this traumatic display of urban disruption and political dissidence had indeed come to an end, it was probably not unconnected with the media blitz that six months earlier – in October and November 1997 – had 'covered' the twentieth anniversary of the turbulent weeks known as the 'hot autumn of 1977' or *Deutsche Herbst.* The televisual *mise-en-scène* of national recollection appeared to achieve what the police and the security services had failed to accomplish: the burial of the RAF along with its mythology, by once more staging it. This essay asks what was at stake in the mythology, and what did its burial help to over-expose?[1]

To much of the world, the RAF is mostly remembered as the Baader-Meinhof group, after Andreas Baader and Ulrike Meinhof, two key protagonists of the so-called 'first generation'.[2] At the time of the 'hot autumn' Ulrike Meinhof was no longer alive; she had hanged herself on May 9, 1976 while awaiting trial. Since Baader, Horst Mahler, Gudrun

Ensslin and Jan Karl Raspe were also in prison, it was the 'second generation' who claimed responsibility for a series of 'political' actions in 1977: foremost among them the kidnapping (on September 5) of Hans Martin Schleyer, Chairman of the German Federation of Industry and a Director of Daimler Benz; the hijacking (on October 13) of a Lufthansa plane filled with German tourists, which was forced to land in Mogadishu, Somalia; and a demand that the RAF prisoners be freed. The 'hot autumn' was the aftermath of these actions: the storming of the plane by a German élite unit, the discovery of Schleyer's body in the trunk of a car in France, and three presumed suicides inside the Stammheim maximum security prison near Stuttgart, where Raspe, Baader and Ensslin took their lives (on October 18), after learning of the failure of the Mogadishu hijack to force their release. Although acts of violence continued to be attributed to RAF members not rounded up or killed in the subsequent dragnet searches, arrests and shoot-outs with the police, by Christmas of 1977 the German government was confident enough to declare the 'terrorist threat' to be over and to call for public life to return to 'normal'.

As we know, however, the tremor of the events lingered on, not only in Germany. Because both the state and its youthful opponents had, for however brief a moment, shown themselves capable of ruthlessness, violence and open confrontation so extreme that it had torn the unexpectedly flimsy fabric of the post-war political consensus, the RAF episode also became a turning point for armed militant action elsewhere.[3] In Germany, the recoil and the soul-searching went deeper than the events of May 1968 had done, as if a different kind of 'knight's move' had been made, backtracking into German history but also forward into an altogether discontinuous political space. Thanks to a number of films identified with the then still relatively 'New' German Cinema, this crisis of West German self-understanding and self-presentation was thematized on an international platform as well: art-cinema audiences saw or read about *The Lost Honour of Katharina Blum, Knife in the Head, Mother Kuster's Trip to Heaven, The German Sisters, The Third Generation, Stammheim.*[4] Above all the omnibus film *Germany in Autumn*, shot partly during the funeral of Schleyer, was a first response among the filmmaking community, meant to bear witness to the impact the kidnap and the suicides were having, across a number of contextualizing narratives.[5]

Neither the films nor a slew of books managed to lay the episode to rest, though.[6] It was as if the events – at once demanding an explanation and, in their emblematically dense textuality, inviting hermeneutic excess – had proven so eminently interpretable because they also inscribed themselves in several other histories, where revolutionary violence, the 1960s student protest movement, and even the phenomenon of international terrorism and governmental reprisals figure only obliquely. This point is raised not in order once more to depoliticize post-1968 radicalism and the German autumn, but rather to recover the events' political dimension, which is to say, their possible significance for the 1990s. One episode from *Germany in Autumn*, as well as the framing story, in retrospect provoke second thoughts, especially when compared to the coverage from 1997, which included, I shall argue, an explicit rewriting of *Germany in Autumn* through repetition: the made-for-television film *Todesspiel (Death Game)*, commissioned by ARD from WDR and NDR, and directed by Heinrich Breloer, at a cost of DM7m – for German television an enormous budget.[7]

Death Game

Breloer is one of the top television makers in Germany, a specialist in political thrillers, and known for vivid, suspenseful storytelling. He established his reputation with a number of docu-dramas, combining archive footage, dramatic re-enactments and interviews, often picking political scandals or high-profile corruption cases, such as a notorious tax subsidy housing scam by Co-op officials (*Kollege Otto*, 1991). Sometimes called 'the Oliver Stone of Germany', his most famous film prior to *Todesspiel* was an investigative TV-portrait of Herbert Wehner, party chairman and *éminence grise* behind the social-democrat (SPD) government of Willy Brandt.[8]

Given Breloer's knowledge of the internal power structure of the SPD and his familiarity with many of the party's leading figures, he was an obvious choice as director for a look back at the crisis of 1977. The hot autumn had occurred during the early days of the social democrat government of Chancellor Helmut Schmidt, whose first political test this was, after he had suddenly been obliged to take over from the popular and internationally much more famous Brandt, who resigned after a spy scandal. *Death Game* was made in two parts, alternating its points of view, focusing first on the kidnap victim Hans Martin Schleyer and his state of mind during what would prove to be the last days of his life; then, the perspective of ex-Chancellor Helmut Schmidt and his crisis team, inter-viewed extensively and re-living the difficult, possibly fatal choices – fatal perhaps to West Germany's democracy, and certainly fatal to quite a number of individuals; and finally, the perspective of one of the hostages, who, after a happy Mallorca holiday, was caught in the nightmare of the Mogadishu airfield, sitting for three days and nights in his own sweat and urine, doused with duty-free liquor so he could be lit as a human torch, shouted at by Palestine guerillas and forced to witness the casual killing of the pilot. We are also given glimpses of Andreas Baader, morosely solitary or manically busy in his overstuffed, untidy prison cell at Stammheim.[9]

The multiple perspectives make for high drama and intense human interest, but they also cunningly disguise a significant absence. *Death Game* shifts attention almost entirely away from the perspective that, twenty years earlier, had been the locus of identification of so many writers and filmmakers: the 'terrorists' and their relatives (*The German Sisters*), 'innocent' bystanders and reluctant protesters (*Katharina Blum, Mother Kuster, Knife in the Head*) the 'political' prisoners (*Stammheim*) and their funeral (*Germany in Autumn*).

Death Game was a hit, a *Strassenfeger*, which is a TV programme that sweeps the streets clean of people on the nights it is broadcast. It appears to have been especially popular among younger audiences, for whom the terrorists were by now political dinosaurs, but who were fascinated by ex-Chancellor Schmidt's narrative. Identifying with the state not as a political entity, but as an institution whose mechanisms of power are rarely laid as bare as during such a crisis, viewers could follow the unfolding events with a technocrat's appreciation of complex institutional and legal processes. This is also the stance adopted by the pragmatist Schmidt during filming and in TV-interviews that allowed him to relive the drama.

This audience interest stands in sharp contrast to that which greeted the events originally, among officials and the young. In 1977, media attention was fixed on the phenomenon of 'sympathizers': students, young unemployed, writers and intellectuals who before condemning the RAF outright, wanted to know more about their motives. Suspecting the available public information to be biased, these sympathizers asked themselves with anguish where they stood in the ensuing debates about violence that split families and estranged life-long friends.[10] To the press, the terrorists seemed to pose a threat less because of their violent acts than because they inspired not just universal revulsion, but sorrow and even sympathy. Like a virus, terrorism appeared contagious, transmissible through verbal contact, requiring discursive efforts to 'isolate' it.[11] A notorious editorial spoke of the 'marshy hinterland of sympathy' that had to be 'dried out', left-liberal demands for prisoners' rights that had to be quarantined, in an effort to suppress the flow of energy and empathy running between a violent minority and the mass of others.[12] Almost all the episodes in *Germany in Autumn*, for instance, convey a climate of paranoia: anyone might be a terrorist, or worse still, anyone might take one for a terrorist. To some (including myself) this paranoia seemed at the time beside the point. I can recall the strange thrill when first hearing about the exploits of the RAF in 1972: the sudden appearance of a Bonnie-and-Clyde gang in the stodgy West of *petit bourgeois* Germany lent the events a surreal improbability. There was the

RAF's own revolutionary discourse: though stridently anti-American and pro-Vietnam, it became 'authentic' only where it referred itself to Germany and its political post-war record. The fact that the RAF spoke of Germany's murky and unmastered past set a novel agenda, and their boldness in targeting members of the judiciary and the business sector – known safe havens for high-ranking ex-Nazis, never held publicly accountable for their actions – hit a raw historical nerve, from which any paranoia on the left and the hysterical witch-hunt for sympathizers by the right seemed intended merely to detract. For others, the RAF's approval was even less overtly political but just as revolutionary: the idea that one could go underground, change one's identity, reinvent a life, and start all over again. The fiction of forging papers, putting on smart clothes, robbing a bank, driving fast cars (BMWs became known as '*Baader-Meinhof-Wagen*') and living dangerously was irresistible, and having the moral right to do so by mouthing Marxist slogans was not as cynical a stance as it might sound.

As can be surmised, little of this ambivalence has made it into Breloer's film. With an apparently wider distribution of attention and interest, *Death Game* works hard to create a special space of empathy around ex-Chancellor Schmidt, his intricate reasoning and calculus of consequences, taking time to dwell also on the personalities of the men Schmidt relied on when reaching for a decision whether to buy Schleyer free and risk letting the prisoners go, whether to abandon the victims of air-piracy to their fate or send a potentially abortive and (in terms of human lives) costly rescue mission. The docu-drama exudes the gravity of the reason of state, ponders the agonizing hours of lonely men at the top, and circles around the problem of how a democratic state manages the mass media. Hence one topical interest and source of appeal: *Death Game* is about spin-doctors and government spokesmen, about how to contain a 'situation', where in the end, it does not seem to matter whether the crisis is a burst oil-tanker, a sex scandal or this particular story of hostage-taking, kidnap, murder and multiple suicide. The fascination is with how men in positions of power deal with emergencies while seemingly keeping cool in public, which is another reason why the film naturally drifts towards Schmidt's advisers, his *Krisenstab*.

These men turn out to be recruited partly from among old war-time comrades of Schmidt, when he was a Wehrmacht officer on the Eastern Front. In one of the most astonishing turns, the film is able to invoke the spirit of Stalingrad and 'the Russian campaign' as naturally as a British politician might invoke the spirit of Dunkirk, or an American President the national resolve after Pearl Harbour. Asked to describe what it was like to wait for the next message from Schleyer's kidnappers or worry if the decoy messenger in Geneva would make contact, State Secretary Hans-Jürgen Wischnewski recalled the dawn mornings on the Eastern Front, waiting for Polish or Russian 'partisans' to attack, while Klaus Bölling, another member of the *Krisenstab*, argues that he kept a cool head only because the soldierly virtues of the Wehrmacht had been drilled into him, in contrast to some other politicians, who foolishly demanded that an RAF prisoner should be publicly executed for each hostage murdered in Mogadishu.

To the extent that *Death Game* is about these former soldiers and their self-representation, it ironically grants the RAF one of its basic points, namely that senior politicians of the Federal Republic were bound together by a military, para-military code of conduct or even an outright Nazi past, and that they formed what were known as *Seilschaften*, old boy networks.[13] Inadvertently perhaps, *Death Game* was replying to the controversy caused by Daniel Gold-hagen's *Hitler's Willing Executioners*, which had dented once more the notion of a clean-cut division between professional soldiers and SS units, between army conscripts and the police battalions. More damaging still to the idea of the 'correct' conduct of the basically 'decent' Wehrmacht – so important to the self-understanding of its successor, the Bundeswehr – was an exhibition that first opened in Hamburg in 1997, which challenged this particular myth head-on, by showing scores of photos taken by soldiers themselves, of the most unimaginable cruelty and atrocities committed by the army in the east.[14] *Death Game* valorizes once more the 'front experience' and its ideals of masculinity (dating as far back as World War I),[15] promoting the impression that if it had not been for the military men at the helm, Germany's ship of state with its fragile cargo of democracy might have sunk in 1977.

With such a re-focusing on ex-Chancellor Schmidt and his wartime comrades, doubling the twenty years after the 'hot autumn' with the fifty-five years after Stalingrad, itself echoing the 'storms of steel' of Verdun in 1917, *Death Game* not only tried to 'redress' the moral balance and level the empathetic score, but actually inverted the dominant mythologies that had already at the time given the events of autumn 1977 their dramatic shape. In *Death Game* it is as if a major player had come back to claim the hero role in a piece of theatre that had cast him as the villain. The 1977 play was called *Antigone*: the 'return' of 1997 traded on this knowledge, suggesting a re-reading of the mythic constel-lation which the re-staging set out to repeal.

Antigone in Germany

Sophocles's *Antigone* has a long and involuted history in Germany, especially since G.W. Hegel's commentaries on the play in his *Phenomenology of Spirit* had made Antigone the epitome of an irreconcilable opposition between the discourse of the state and the demands of the family:

> since the community only gets an existence through its interference with the happiness of the family, and by dissolving self-consciousness into the universal, it creates for itself in what it suppresses and what is at the same time essential to it an internal enemy – womankind . . . the everlasting irony of the community.[16]

Hegel's friend, the poet Friedrich Hölderlin, published a German translation in 1804, and ever since, *Antigone* has stood for those confrontations which, after the French Revolution, oppose not only individual conscience and state power, but two kinds of law, defying any form of government to distribute justice evenly among its citizens, without showing up the limits which tragically flaw the very attempt.[17]

Thus, when halfway through *Germany in Autumn* a sketch directed by Volker Schlöndorff (and written by novelist Heinrich Böll) turns on a cancelled television production of the Sophocles play, Antigone's name trails with it an entire post-romantic politics of interpretation, connoting rebellion and opposition to the state, as well as an order of refusal and resistance of such categorical negation that it challenges the foundations of any form of government. This is a subject of evident relevance in West Germany, since the Bonn government considered itself the sole legal representative of the German Reich, an ambiguous mandate given the Nazi legacy, and precisely the one contested by the RAF's violent protest. The appearance of Antigone in *Germany in Autumn* is thus overdetermined: it raises the question whether the film, by pointing to her presence, already specifies a particular reading of the historical-political dimension of the events with which *Germany in Autumn* is concerned. Is *Antigone* the hermeneutic key, in other words, for more than some merely accidental features of the 'hot autumn'? Does she, thanks to Hegel and Hölderlin, embody or allegorize a recurring constellation in the history of modern Germany? Or, given the belated – and for the viewers of 1997 evidently plausible – reversal of the relationship between state and individual, does *Antigone* become the master-mythology of 1977 only because she served also to mystify what was at stake?

The Hot Autumn: Tragedy and Anagnorisis?

Germany in Autumn premiered in March 1978, only six months after the fatal events.[18] They in turn had brought to a head eight years of often violent and occasionally tragi-comic encounters between the RAF, the press, the German government, its security authorities and police forces. Of these encounters, only the period of the last weeks in October and the beginning of November 1977 appear in *Germany in Autumn*, with the documentary footage mainly centred on two funerals: that of Hans Martin Schleyer and that of Ensslin, Baader and Raspe. Also included are parts of a television interview with Horst Mahler in his prison cell, where he condemns the hostage taking but tries to give the RAF a context and a history: as long as German fascism survives in the guise of Western German capitalism, there will be people desperate enough in their protests to put themselves above the law.

Horst Mahler's argument, with its reference to the Nazi past, instantiates one of the most powerful figurations around the RAF, namely the 'return of the repressed'. At the time, this return was understood by the militant activists as the playing out of a tragically necessary operation: provoking the government with violent and bloody attacks on its officials, its security installations and its top judges, the RAF wanted the political élite to show its true nature. By 'tearing the mask off the face of power' the terrorist expected the public to see what hid behind capitalism and economic prosperity: the old fascist state and its obedient servants. Hence the overdetermined and emblematic figure of one of their chief kidnap victims: Hans Martin Schleyer, figurehead of German indus-try and prominent member of the political class it represented, behind whose *Biedermann* appearance the RAF wanted to expose the fervent SS officer he strenuously denied ever having been. In captivity, Schleyer was apparently several times interrogated by his guards as to his Nazi past, and photos of him in SS uniform circulated in the left-wing press.

Germany in Autumn tries to seize this 'return of the repressed' as one of its major structuring devices, while avoiding the 'theatricalized' logic of the RAF's argument about 'unmasking' the German establishment. The film nonetheless thematizes how the West German state – its legitimacy contested by some of its most intelligent (and some argued, most self-sacrificing)[19] young people – thinking of itself as besieged, resorted to measures that went to the limit, and maybe beyond, of what was legal and constitutional. It shows the government provoking the resistance, if not forfeiting the loyalty of many former social-democrat (SPD) intellectuals, among them Tiresias figures such as Günter Grass and Max Frisch – the latter seen in the film addressing the SPD party conference. There, a murmur of dissenting voices muffling more strident controversies could also be observed among the moderate party members, making up a credible Chorus. If Helmut Schmidt then still seemed an unlikely Creon (and the deposed, 'exiled' Willy Brandt only remotely recalled 'Oedipus at Colonus'), the thoroughness and often ruthlessness of the authorities in dealing with what was judged the terrorist threat did suggest that even the Social Democrats were prepared to use strong-arm tactics to restore order, making some cry 'police state'. To observers outside Germany (such as, famously, Jean-Paul Sartre)[20] the dawn raids on and interrogation of thousands of activists or political opponents were too reminiscent of Nazism to be acceptable. In addition, at the height of the crisis, public opinion was massively manipulated by the tabloid press and Christian Democrat politicians. There was a news blackout during much of the month that the Schleyer kidnap drama unfolded, while the quality papers were either censoring themselves or fearing official censorship.[21]

The self-censorship of television is explicitly connected in the film to the Antigone story. At issue in the Schlöndorff episode of *Germany in Autumn* is the decision of a Broadcast Commission Meeting whether to allow the production (made for a series called 'Youth Meets the Classics') to be aired, or whether, in view of current events, the play is an 'incitement to violence' and ought to be shelved in the interest of public safety. In the exchanges that lead to the decision to ban it, this section evokes some striking contemporary parallels: a state funeral and a contested burial; a woman hanging herself in a prison cell; two sisters; a state in a state of emergency suspending civil rights and curtailing individual freedom; acts of resistance and violence committed out of fiercely held convictions are among the major echoes that provide the episode's central dramatic irony: that a classic tragedy from the canon of Western civilization cannot be shown in a democratic society because it turns out to be 'too political'.

But the irony cuts both ways, and the film exhibits its own sort of *impasse*: it implies the relevance of the parallels, but then denounces the officials who act on the recognition of this relevance. Schlöndorff's intended ideological critique either risks evaporating in self-contradiction or becomes an element that stabilizes the film's mythologization of German history, with its turns and returns, thus creating a sort of *mise en abyme* by which the self-staging of the RAF and the media-management of state institutions are allowed to take on the stature, gravity and allure of an ancient tragedy.

This strategy is most noticeable in the treatment of the two funerals: one an Act of State for a high official, the other the heavily controversial burial for three convicted terrorists, both taking place in one city – not Thebes, but Stuttgart – home town of Daimler Benz *and* of the Ensslin family. In the case of Gudrun Ensslin, it is her sister, Christiane, who fights hardest for the dead activists to be given a proper burial, against public protest and massive threats to her family. Although a generation apart, both Schleyer (as a member of the Hitler youth and the SS) and the terrorists (the RAF being referred to as 'Hitler's children')[22] are seen as heirs to the 'curse' which Nazism had laid upon Germany. By honouring one dead and condemning the others, the state had chosen to cast out part of this legacy, part of this tragic burden or 'pollution' of the body politic.

The confrontation – between state authority and individual conscience, between expediency and resistance, between a law pronounced on behalf of the common good and a law upheld on behalf of an individual's ethical imperative – had produced more doubles: not one but two women who were prepared to commit suicide in prison, Ulrike Meinhof and Gudrun Ensslin, and thus two Antigone figures. The first had flung a categorical 'no' in the face of the German state, initially in print, then in direct action, evidently prepared to take the final consequence of what in her eyes must have appeared an inevitable choice.[23] In the case of Gudrun Ensslin, her suicide coincided with that of her lover, Andreas Baader, who suggested a Haimon figure. There was even an Ismene in the figure of Christiane Ensslin. History and biography had indeed written a tight script.[24]

Once primed by the Sophoclean *Ur*-text and its Hölderlin-Hegel-Brecht hermeneutic, other aspects of the political crisis depicted in *Germany in Autumn* begin to reverberate in the symbolic-theatrical space the film sets up to echo down the years of recent German history. For instance, the trope 'State Funeral and Suicide' returns in *Germany in Autumn* when we learn that the Mayor of Stuttgart, the site of the double funeral, happens to be Manfred Rommel, son of Field-Marshall Erwin Rommel, better known as the Desert Fox. In a World War II newsreel included in the film, the young Manfred can be seen standing beside the coffin of his father, who after the defeat of El-Alamein had been ordered by the Nazis to commit suicide, so that Hitler could give him a State Funeral and celebrate him as a National Hero. Now Rommel Junior in 1977 found himself in the part of the benevolent counter-Creon, for it is he who, as Mayor, orders – 'a quick decision and clean choice', he calls it in the film – that the three terrorists should have a dignified funeral in one of the city's more prestigious cemeteries, rather than be handed to the Stuttgart *vox pop*, who had demanded that the bodies be disposed of 'down the sewers'.

On the other hand, beyond more repetitions and reversals, what sort of cynicism, hypocrisy or expediency is the Rommel reference supposed to imply about the State Funeral of Hans Martin Schleyer? The camera lingers on further parallels between the Rommel State Act and that given to Schleyer. The same forest of flags: the swastika in the newsreel then is replaced by the Mercedes Star now. The same rows of uniformed men: in 1944 in SS uniform, now in sober black suits, but not a few of them with scars on their cheeks, tell-tale signs of having once belonged to the ultra-conservative, duelling student fraternities which, since the Wilhelmine Reich, have supplied Germany with its judiciary, military and industrial élite. Continuities across the rupture, repetitions and returns: that the framing episodes consciously build on these and other dramatic ironies becomes evident when we see shots of the Mercedes Benz assembly line, where the workers down their tools for three minutes of silence, in honour of the dead Schleyer, whose portrait looms over them. As the voice-over commentary informs the viewer, 85 percent of the workers present are foreign 'guest workers', a reference that points forward and backward at the same time: an oblique reminder of the slave labour that firms like Mercedes Benz requisitioned from Nazi armament minister Albert Speer, and forward towards the workers becoming undesirable aliens stealing scarce jobs, the future target of right-wing neo-Nazi resentment in the 1980s. To this can be added another (unstated, but no doubt implied) irony that undercuts both: the workers are now enjoying, albeit for only three minutes, the right to down-tools, which the dead Schleyer, as notorious trade-union basher, had fought hard to eliminate from the statute books.

Fathers and Sons: The Hamlet Figures of Germany

The Rommel reference is, however, an instance of another trope, related to the Antigone story and central to several other interpretive strategies implemented in *Germany in Autumn*. A farewell letter by Schleyer to his son, written immediately prior to his death, opens the film. In it the doomed hostage gives a candid assessment of his predicament, warning the son against harbouring illusions about any possible lack of resolve on the part of the terrorists, and implicitly accusing the government of having sacrificed him as a result of political calculations.[25] This double father-son nexus, linking Rommel and Schleyer, both victims of the Fatherland, the better for it posthumously to honour them, also echoes in the *Antigone* television production that ends with the messenger describing how Haimon killed himself, out of hatred and disgust, when he saw his father Creon cowardly turn and run, after the son had raised his sword against him.

Such an emphasis on father–son relations in *Germany in Autumn* was itself symptomatic of a wider semantic and ideological field, what one might call the attempt to 'oedipalize' Germany's recent political past, using the family romance as a conceptual-psychoanalytic model to figure some of the continuities across the political breaks in West Germany, as well as to explain the more extreme features of the breakdown of the family, illustrated by one of the RAF killings, when the director of the Deutsche Bank, Jürgen Ponto, answered the doorbell of his villa to his own god-child, unaware that she was a decoy, calling on him so that her terrorist accomplices could assassinate him.

The emergence of these explicitly oedipal cultural references first occurred in West German literature: from about 1975 onwards, a wave of autobiographical fiction hit the bookstores, mainly by writers in their thirties. Starting with Bernward Vesper's *Die Reise*, these self narratives took the form of extended suicide notes, often addressed to, and trying to settle old scores with a recently deceased parent.[26] Vesper's novel, for instance, tells the story of the son of a well-to-do Nazi writer, trying to resolve the conflict between loving and fearing his father as a father, and hating what he stood for. Unable to confront his father's ardent Nazism, now turned into an ultra-right, but once more highly respectable conservatism, the hero suffers silently parental disappointment fed by the father's sentimental nostalgia for his own 'heroic' youth. Oedipal rebellion finally takes the form of the son's championing of the Palestinians as his cause, and he is drawn into militant student actions, together with his girlfriend. She, however, falls under the spell of a trigger-happy, working-class activist, and the two of them, wanted by the police, escape to Sicily, where they are to be trained by Libyans as international terrorists. Too sensitive to commit acts of violence, and recognizing in his sexual rival the same ruthlessness shown by his own father, the hero kidnaps his small son and brings him home, where else but to his father's now abandoned house.

Vesper committed suicide before he had completed what is in fact a *roman à clef*, insofar as the girlfriend in the story was Gudrun Ensslin and his rival Andreas Baader. Analyzing *Die Reise*, the critic Michael Schneider observed that the parent generation's conspiracy of silence had 'been bitterly avenged. Since German fathers had failed to indict themselves for their monstrous pasts, they were on trial by proxy by the radicalized sons and daughters in 1968 and thereafter. And since the fathers themselves had taken pains to be sure that they would only be seen as fathers, and not as political beings, their offspring chose to do precisely the opposite in the aftermath of their abrupt political awakening [thanks to the Vietnam War].'[27] As defeated world conquerors, the unpunished but also unreconciled fathers had to re-establish their own sense of identity by wielding an iron authority within the home. But – this is not only Schneider's argument – the family resulting from such flawed authority could only breed murderous distrust between fathers and sons or daughters.[28] Yet the chance discovery by a bereaved son of shoe-boxes full of old photographs or war diaries locked in desk-drawers did not necessarily lead to objective investigations: 'The specific interest which released this literary return to the past was not at all primarily an interest in the fathers and the dark areas of their past, but rather, and to a much greater extent, an interest in [the sons'] own beginnings. The look back [...] is a retrospective look to the roots of their own emotional lives, to the influences at work on them, and to the psychological legacy they thereby have to carry.'[29]

In other words, these sons not only did not identify with the official optimism of the West German economic miracle, they also did not have a genuine stake in any (socialist) alternative. Instead, they identified with the latent emotions, the ones that the forced optimism and strident efficiency tried to hide. Seeing the fathers' cover-up, seeing through it, but being sons by flesh and blood, they also had to deal with their own internalization of the father, whose hidden guilt and shame, according to Schneider, returns in the son as self-destructive melancholy. To quote one of these sons: 'the wound had folded inwards'.[30] For the paradox was that only in the wake of disillusioned and disillusioning political activity – the aftermath of the failure of the extra-parliamentary left – did these ambivalences find words, expression and (dramatic) representation. Significantly enough, the key figure became Hamlet – who in Hegel (and Lacan) is the 'modern' complement of Antigone. To quote once more Schneider: 'It was as if the ghosts of their fathers had suddenly appeared before them in Nazi uniforms, and their living fathers, with whom they had sat down at the supper table for twenty years, had been indicted in the most horrible collective crime committed by any generation this century.'[31]

Schneider sees the RAF's theatrical metaphor as apt. The bombings, hostage takings and terrorist acts were nothing less than 'murderous and suicidal' attempts to 'tear off the mask' of official authority behind which they had reason to suspect the guiltily fretting faces of their own fathers. To take Schneider's analogy further: the Schleyer kidnapping was the RAF's staging of 'The Mousetrap' to catch the conscience of a king by the name of Helmut Schmidt, while Schleyer is himself a Claudius who has the bad luck of being guarded by someone more resolute than Hamlet, for his captors did not spare him the way Hamlet spared Claudius when he overheard him praying. Such an emphasis on the father–son axis in literature, in political activism and in *Germany in Autumn* suggests that the German protest movement was anti-authoritarian rather than egalitarian, that despite a Marxist political discourse, it was caught in the ruses of patriarchy: a feature from which the women's movement had to extricate itself, perhaps by countering this 'Hamletization' of German post-war history with its own 'Antigonizing'?

Fassbinder's *Antigone*

This might indeed be the 'feminist' aspect of *Germany in Autumn*, even if the majority of its directors were men. Against it, one could argue that, paradoxically, the part that most challenges any kind of oedipalization is not the Schlöndorff/Böll segment, but the one directed by Rainer Werner Fassbinder, featuring Fassbinder himself, along with his lover Armin Mayer and his mother Lilo Pempeit. The episode shows Fassbinder, alternately naked and wrapped in an untidy bathrobe, restless and sweating, in his sombre Munich apartment, frantic about the news blackout, cynically incredulous about the Stammheim suicides, in fear of possible police raids and house searches, on the verge of a nervous breakdown, finally collapsing on the floor in a fit of uncontrollable, hysterical weeping.

At the heart of the politics of the segment is a heatedly impromptu but in fact meticulously scripted interrogation to which Fassbinder subjects his mother in the kitchen, where he thematizes the duties of dissent for citizens in a democracy under siege; the human rights of murderers; the special horror provoked in ordinary men and women by terrorists who might have reasons for acts with which one could not disagree. As Fassbinder hectors and lectures his mother, he extracts from her the common-sense caution of the 'normal' German about not wanting to risk one's neck, and finally, the admission that she would much prefer in such a situation to be ruled by an authoritarian Führer, 'but a gentle benevolent one', rather than face the responsibilities of free speech. Challenging his mother, berating his homosexual lover, phoning his former wife for comfort – after denouncing marriage in a television interview as an artificial coupling – Fassbinder stages a series of encounters meant to cast doubt on the fictional-narrative closure on which a founding myth of West German democracy was built, namely that (masculine) ideals of self-discipline, responsibility, and citizenship – the Helmut Schmidt values which *Death Game* was to revive nostalgically twenty years later – had done away with the authoritarian personality.

Considered as such, Fassbinder's self-display is an act of resistance, and a double Antigone gesture, directed partly at the film into which Alexander Kluge has bound him. For ultimately, three perspectives intersect also in *Germany in Autumn*, though they do not segue into or even complement each other, as they do in Breloer's film. Firstly, Kluge's generational line from 'fathers to sons cross-wise' most explicitly evokes the Hamlet–Claudius intertext. In Schlöndorff-Böll's 'Antigone', sister confronts sister in the encounter of Antigone with Ismene, a theme Margarethe von Trotta (then married to Schlöndorff, and his collaborator on *Katharina Blum*) was to take up in *The German Sisters*, while in Fassbinder's episode there is an exchange between mother and son, as if to make so over-explicit their primary bond, that it de-oedipalizes the lineage from (guilty) father to (guilty) son analyzed by Schneider.

While Kluge's segments explore, as we saw, the echoing parallels of a double funeral symmetrically inverted, and create, across the axis of two fathers and two sons, a story intended to hold together the disparate moments of this film of many voices, they also effectively 'contain' German history, by setting up a more or less orderly series of mirrors to balance the two periods; Germany in the 1940s and in the 1970s. But as Fassbinder's episode makes clear, neither such doubling for the sake of structure, nor the proliferation of situations alluding to the classical Antigone can 'domesticate' the fantasmatic power emanating from the events. Fassbinder in a sense tries to write a different kind of asymmetrical exchange into the representations, offset in turn by Kluge's own anti-Antigone in a minor (tragi-comic) key, his heroine Gabi Teichert, a teacher who, at a loss where to find German history, goes out – instead of burying a body – to dig for it with a shovel in the frozen ground. Fassbinder's episode puts before us not an absence or an unburied body, but 'a body too much': violent, obese, naked, grossly material; he confronts the viewer, indeed assaults the viewer – demanding an Antigone to mark the site where mourning has not taken place, to remind us of the irreducible singularity involved in her predicament.

In a sense, Fassbinder's staging is in the spirit of Sophocles's Antigone more than is the Antigone sketch of Schlöndorff/Böll. By thematizing both of Antigone's impossible choices – that of the unburied body and that of her angry confrontation with Creon, Fassbinder enacts an almost classical reciprocity, as expressed in the play's stychomythia – the exchange of sentences – when he argues with his mother. Re-creating and, at the same time, inverting the encounter between Creon (power, state, future father-in-law) and Antigone (individual, female, daughter), formal equivalences that underline different orders of non-equivalence of inequality, in-justice – while all the time keeping before our eyes the fact that the power, the potential for resistance, comes from this non-equivalence between son and mother, between male and female subjectivity. Fassbinder's own (terrorising) self-righteous intransigence and his mother's moral candour of the sensible, if cowardly, pliable 'pragmatist' confront each other, while – emphasized by the abrupt cuts and montage effects – a retching, weeping, shaking Fassbinder remains 'uncovered' by the symbolization or representations offered to him by his lover Armin. Unless one takes this excess, which takes the place of representation, as an act of exposure that undoes the uncovering, Fassbinder's sexualized self-exposure enforces, by its frontality towards the spectator, an impossible convergence of 'look' and 'gaze'. What seems an unselfconscious display of shameless vulnerability is in fact a form of exhibitionism that tries to turn the machinery of surveillance – in *Germany in Autumn* the state is present through patrol-car sirens wailing at night and mounted policemen wielding camcorders filming the mourners at the Ensslin funeral – into 'showing itself' and thus allowing Fassbinder to manifest a kind of defiant compliance in which the spectator is necessarily implicated as much as s/he is excluded.

When (re)turning to the Antigone episode of Schlöndorff/Böll after Fassbinder's, one cannot help wondering if the former does not subtly 'hand over' its own heroine. By placing the discussion of the television production at the centre of *Germany in Autumn*, and making the metaphoric links between Sophocles's play and a version of political events ('rebellious women', 'a suicide', 'a government that stands firm') the ironic hinge between the classical play and the contemporary events, Schlöndorff/Böll's Antigone is drawn into Alexander Kluge's mirror mazes of uncanny repetitions and doubling symmetries – a mirroring also evidenced by the 'doubles' inside the episode, for instance, letting Ismene and Antigone speak a number of 'distancing prologues' as if with one voice. Where the play – as well as Hölderlin, Hegel, Brecht or Straub/Huillet's renderings – speaks of the radical incommensurability of the subject and the state, Kluge and Schlöndorff are seduced by symmetry, balance and repetition. They allow their narrative to achieve almost 'classical' closure, which contaminates their version of German history, not only because such a spirit of heavily underscored dramatic ironies and structural parallels seems remote from the singularity of Antigone's act, and contrary to the direction in which her ethical narrative propels her: twice having to make a choice, where she has to take sides against herself, but also because it attempts to 'master' the German past by letting it slide into the master-narrative of fathers and sons.

That *Germany in Autumn* is thus more conciliatory than its makers might have intended also highlights an historical problem – one that the reversal of perspective so deftly effected by *Death Game* makes explicit. Rewriting the very tropes of tragedy, it lets Creon take control of the play and, with it, of the 'hot autumn'. Here, too, an act of handing over was on offer, the tacit reconciliation with the previous generation, where former soldiers 'father' future captains of industry, as the television-nation unites in sympathy with the necessarily sacrificial victim Schleyer and the patriarchal-patrician Schmidt, attentively listening to the latter's case on behalf of his conscience, his plea for letting pragmatism prevail over dissent, and his categorical 'no' to the terrorists also in retrospect, which is to say, for now and in the future. After this *coup d'état par l'état*, where might the ground be located from which the RAF could have continued – even within the law? But then, what jagged terrain has been abandoned in such a suture, such a progress towards closure?

Reversals and Rehearsals: *'unheimlich'* or *'klammheimlich'*?

The historical problem just alluded to concerns Germany's Social Democrats. After leaving the centre of politics and the ground of national identity to the Christian Democrats for more than fifty years, they feel the need to restake their claim and to prove themselves patriots, making their contribution to the nation's generational lineage, so to speak, by producing 'good fathers'. *Death Game* does this ideological work of national consolidation with great rhetorical force and narrative skill, 'replying' to *Germany in Autumn* while promoting its own political agenda, now with an eye to the imminent post-Kohl era where another pragmatic, social democratic government is waiting in the wings. For the sake of coming to power, they are ready even to bury their differences with the 'Greens', themselves parliamentary descendants of the militants of 1968.[32] It took *Death Game* to make explicit the hint that Kluge and Schlöndorff might already have inscribed in their film the possibility of a revisionist remake, for Breloer assigns to his film, too, the task of mourning-work and memory-management for a nation still – and after unification, once more – negotiating historical breaks. For the sake of this binding and healing, a double betrayal then, of the tragic female heroine and of the tragi-comic avenger-terrorists? A repetition that buries a body and banishes a ghost by definitely separating post-war history and politics from Sophocles and Shakespeare?

Death Game has another contemporary agenda insofar as it resolutely refuses to repeat the dominant representational gesture of the 1970s, which was to see West Germany invariably as possessing no present except as 'post-'. For instance, for *Germany in Autumn* to cast the events of 1977 in the shape of classical tragedy – even if it was a tragedy with a revolutionary heroine – was to make the present of 1977 first and foremost a function of the past, encasing it, as indicated, in the paradigm of the 'return of the repressed'. The repetitions of *Death Game*, by contrast, wrest from the events of 1977 a pastness that refers itself to a present situated in 1997. It does so, not by denying the link to Nazism and the war, but by thematizing it explicitly as proof of a continuity and a tradition (that of soldierly virtues), rather than a 'return of the repressed' or of a past unmastered. On the basis of this central reversal – the shift in identification from hunted terrorists to beleaguered soldiers called upon to serve the democratic state – the film constructs a continuity, that of Social Democrats remaining patriots by serving their country in war just as honourably as they stand by the nation in conditions of near civil war.

Yet what applies to the Social Democrats now was also true of the RAF then: their messages, too, were doubly coded. The RAF's pamphlets may have spoken of the Nazi past, and their intuitive recourse to Hamlet's play-within-the play strategy may have been nothing if not an archetypal case of provoking the 'return of the repressed'. Yet the means they deployed, at once expressively metaphoric and excessively literal, also connoted something else, and supported another voice, another discourse. If we go back to what was said about the fascination with the RAF at the time – the troubled question of 'sympathizers' – then it seems that these supporters were themselves split. The older generation of liberals, such as Heinrich Böll or Günter Grass, subscribing to the 'return of the repressed', saw the motives for these apparently senseless acts of violence rooted in the past. They argued for a dialogue with West Germany's disaffected youth, recognizing in the RAF's bloody acts the force of a familiar history, in which the worst excesses of left-wing, but also fascist, street terror from the Weimar years staged an *unheimlich* return. But for the younger generation the sympathy was not generated by a sense of the *unheimlich*. Rather, theirs was a sympathy that became known as *klammheimlich*, after a notorious student manifesto had expressed 'vicarious satisfaction' (*klammheimliche Freude*) at the death of one of the RAF's most prominent victims, the Prosecutor General Siegfried Buback.[33] The outrage that followed this seemingly callous expression of collusion in murder, however, somehow missed its target. Today it is clear that a significant element in the RAF's popular appeal lay in the many kinds of vicariousness their emergence onto the scene permitted their own generation to engage in. Even if neither the acts of violence nor the RAF's political goals were perceived as viable, their modes of interaction, their moral high ground and tactics of intervention were sensed as absolutely contemporary and, often enough, as the vital social vanguard. That was because their politics effected an aesthetic break and their practice embedded itself in a culture of direct action taking shape on several (not always explicitly politicised) fronts. Even more than to the romantic Hollywood cliché of the outlaw gang on the run, Baader, Meinhof, Ensslin and Raspe belonged to the culture of the happening, to graffiti art and fluxus events, to street theatre and the Living Theatre: their energy was turned outward, and seemed like the ratchet-action of ferocious escalation on situationist urban *dérives*. True, some of the RAF's stunts were uncannily reminiscent of scenes from movies – not necessarily Hollywood movies: the baby pram pushed in front of Schleyer's car to make his driver break seemed borrowed from Eisenstein – other spectacular actions involving bank raids or car chases re-enacted scenes from Godard's *Bande à Part* or *Weekend*, and if one is to believe Stefan Aust, the antics later at Stammheim prison read as if the Marx Brothers had strayed into a Mack Sennett prison caper.[34] The double-coding involved in this role playing and its references to the cinema had its strategic place in the perpetual exchange of misinformation and disinformation between the RAF, the police, and the press. The pram story is a good example: was it for real or was it a fiction? Was it something the police invented, in order to show just how inhuman the terrorists were (the RAF 'women' perverting the most basic maternal instincts?) or was it the terrorists, 'citing' the Odessa steps scene from *Battleship Potemkin* or the 1918 Spartakist uprisings in Berlin and Munich, in order to inscribe themselves into the historical iconography of Revolution? These post-situationist dress-rehearsals for the great 'all-change' contained too much and too little 'reality', allowing a perpetual ambiguity of reference and intent to hover over the proceedings. Yet it was also proof of an intense involvement on both sides, which even created, in the figure of Horst Herold, the information-gathering computer expert and Head of the Federal Office of Criminal Investigation – a sort of 'Juve' who with passion and dedication pitted his wits against the RAF's various 'Fantomas'.[35]

Inhospitable Cities

Listening to the RAF 'live' must have been embarrassing to some of their sympathizers, even in 1977: arrogant, jargon-ridden, self-obsessed, their pronouncements seemed to lack all playfulness or the marks of the political prankster. Instead of leaving room for possible irony, the phrase that baptised the foam-padded closet in which Schleyer was kept – 'the people's prison' – appeared irritatingly pompous, while the truly appalling words used to announce Schleyer's assassination were rightly judged 'contemptuous' not only of *his* life but of 'human life'. When journalists recalled these moments in 1997, they easily managed to sustain moral distance by quoting the RAF's more outrageous statements, talking of hubris, bathos, or sniggering at the convoluted rhetoric.[36] But with the sound turned off, as it were, the TV-footage of mass demonstrations, the newspaper pictures of barred faces, or the grainy photos of bombed cars in leafy side-streets spoke a different language. True, they spoke of violence, of crowds, of confrontation, but they also brought into view something that makes keeping distance a more difficult task, because the distance in time makes the proximity in another register all the more striking. What becomes evident is that the RAF's preferred theatres of action – the street, public buildings, department stores, nondescript underpasses – designate a topography of visual signs now omnipresent: the city, the urban scene on the move. One suddenly becomes aware to what extent these 'urban guerillas' – and the police that controlled the crowds – were not only part of the more general transformation of the civic realm and the public sphere, but actually played a leading role in making the changes visible. This public sphere in the making has, as we know, radically re-coded the cities of the developed world, producing new kinds of mobility, reflecting changed working conditions and leisure habits, imposing new ways of inhabiting and using the domestic environment; in short, making space itself a political category.[37]

Viewed in this light, the RAF can be seen as a possible answer, not to Alexander Mitscherlich's famous *The Inability to Mourn*, where the eminent Freudian social-psychologist tried to present his own reading of *Antigone* and explain West Germany's amnesia regarding the Nazi period, but to another – then almost equally controversial – Mitscherlich book, *Die Unwirtlichkeit der Städte* ('The Inhospitability of Cities'), in which he lambasts contemporary town planning and modernist high-rises for breeding family violence, destroying communities and laying waste the historically grown city centres more terminally than allied bombing raids had done in 1944–45.[38] If one subtext to the RAF's urban guerilla tactics is furnished by Mitscherlich's jeremiad, then it does so with a twist: many of the phenomena Mitscherlich eyed with growing despair as symptoms of social entropy, the RAF used productively, even creatively. The blight of suburban anomie, the anonymity of apartment blocks, where no one talks to his or her neighbours, and where shopping, service industries and the cash-nexus define the quality of life: these became subject to situationist *divagation* or Brechtian acts of *Umfunktionieren*. The rent for the three-room apartment in a dormitory town near Cologne, into which Schleyer was bundled and where he was held for six weeks, was paid for in cash, as was the three months' deposit. Less than two minutes from the off-ramp of a major interstate Autobahn, it was located on the third floor of a fifteen-storey high-rise, with convenient underground parking and a service lift: a building where not even the janitor could later remember who exactly had lived there.[39]

To search out the sites where the RAF kidnapped their victims, found their safe houses or clashed with the police is thus to inspect a strangely familiar and yet dislocated topography. The RAF attacked the industrialists and bankers in their quiet villa side streets, but they found refuge in the new urban high-rises. That the RAF justified their actions with the sins of omissions in German postwar history or the anti-imperialist, pro-Vietnam struggle seemed to pale in comparison to their brutal, actual presence but also phantom-like elusiveness in the new traffic-free pedestrian shopping areas, where the sins of commission were architectural, or in the newspapers' daily headlines and on the ubiquitous 'wanted' posters in every post office, where the brutality was typographical. But their ubiquity, proximity and simultaneous 'underground' existence also owed much to the way they occupied and made use of those sites which Marc Augé has called *les non-lieux*, typically contemporary 'non-spaces': motorway off-ramps, suburban tramway crossings, industrial estate wastelands, the sprawl of housing conglomerations.[40] Breloer, in *Death Game*, develops a keen eye for such sites, in the way he deploys the newspaper and TV material, effectively contrasting it in his re-enactments with some of the more symbolically overdetermined or falsely idyllic locations, as in the final scene, where he constructs a veritable tableau out of the setting and circumstances of Schleyer's killing: in the middle distance, a body slumping forward on a grassy mount, against the evening sun, with impressively 'Germanic' trees spreading their branches in the background.

The irony is poignant also for my argument. Are we, with these sites, still in the world of the tragic stage? I do not mean that *Death Game* belongs to the genre of the television docu-drama while *Germany in Autumn* still follows a distinct film aesthetic. Rather, an additional doubt arises about the latter's Antigone parallel, but also about my claiming to detect the return of Creon in the former: the parallels and contrasts rely too confidently on the pertinence and validity of the theatrical metaphor. True, its cultural currency gives the 'drama' of the hot autumn a powerful pathos, but it also hides a number of historical blind spots emerging from these representations of urban mutations. For instance, by ignoring the blurry iconicity of identikit photos, the gaudy language of the slogans, posters and graffiti, or the terrorists' irruptive presence in the urban fabric, the theatrical analogy can be accused of dignifying 'common criminals' with the gravity of a high tragedy. But perhaps more to the point, it also risks mis-identifying the medium in which the events not so much unfolded but were subsequently to take on a good deal of their historical significance.

The street not as metaphor for the stage, but as synecdoche for urban space: this does not mean that the 'Antigone' and 'Hamlet' effects discussed above did not exist – they clearly did, since they were so readily seized upon. But could such interpretive moves themselves have become mere vestiges of a political culture that in its cognitive mapping had made the theatrical stage central, rather than the city, the media, and the urban scene? Put more pointedly, was the RAF in 1977 harbinger also of a shift from the (élite) politics of stage/parliament/agora to the (street) politics of an event-and-entertainment culture, across the switch from literature and drama to the photographic, print and electronic media?

Whether the terrorists were aware of such changing space semantics is another question. Their rhetoric might suggest not, but other evidence makes it plausible that they were. For the RAF's deployment of the signs of the streets and the sites of urban space, their command of the sloganed caption, the video tape and the photomontage curiously aligns them with a West Germany reconstructing itself in the 1960s, not only as a Western-style pluralist liberal democracy, but also one that self-consciously constructs for itself a set of brand-name logos. The chain of associations that the RAF iconography – encompassing the means as well as the targets of their actions – evokes is nicely summed up in the pun already quoted, namely the re-naming of the revamped BMW as the *Baader-Meinhof-Wagen*. Around this other mythology (derived from Barthes rather than the Bard), and encapsulated in the colourful figure of Andreas Baader, one can begin to trace another sort of transformation.[41] It locates the RAF in the slipstream of a shift which, while not unconnected with urbanism is nonetheless distinct from it, namely that of an also elusively ubiquitous youth culture, where fast cars, leather jackets, macho attitudes and violence came to play a very ambiguous role, since they could also stand for radical depoliticisation. But one evident irony of the appearance of a figure like Baader lies in the fact that a blindingly shrill anti-American rhetoric existed side by side with behaviour, dress codes and forms of expression that were nothing if not American. Perhaps one should not forget that growing up geographically and culturally adjacent to the massive presence of US Armed Forces, first as the occupying power, then as the visible reminder of NATO and the Cold War, also left a legacy among German adolescents, dreaming of (what must have seemed) these American GIs' glamorous lives, lived on the edge and in material plenitude. As young Germans stared through barbed wire into the compounds where their 'others' played basketball or drove open-top cars, envy mingled with admiration. Some of the envy resurfaced later as anti-Americanism, without quite quenching the admiration, now became desire for mimesis and impersonation.

What interferes with this reverse identification and builds up a different texture of associations, feelings and values is the equally ambiguous – because at once valorized and vilified – prominence of specifically German icons of the economic miracle, reflecting the arrogant establishment (but also *petit bourgeois*) complacency of '*wir sind wieder wer*' ('once again, we amount to something'). Apart from the automotive prowess behind the logos of VW, BMW, Porsche and the Mercedes star, one thinks of the Lufthansa icon on the Mogadishu plane, or the smart uniforms of the GSG 9 rescue mission: a forest of symbols of (post-war) Germany, which seemed to want to compete with US American symbols such as the golden arches of McDonald's, the Coke bottle or Levis jeans. The RAF participated in these 'design features' of the West German soul at the same time as it vociferously rejected them. Amidst such oscillating semiosis, in which the mimetic impulse of 'acting out' and 'putting on' were central, the drama of the RAF and the hot autumn would seem to be at odds with notions of 'working through' or the purging of fear and pity, implicit in the 'tragic' genre of Antigone that gave the events their metaphoric space, but it was equally at odds with the 'classical narrative' by which *Germany in Autumn* tried to mould modern German history into a unity across the break of 1945.

If one can speak of a public sphere poised between theatricalization and mediatization, then the RAF marked a significant rupture: their enunciated was 'theatrical', their acts of enunciation were often cunningly 'medial'. Put differently, the RAF's ideology may already at the time have seemed stilted, expendable, second-hand,[42] yet it was their mode of address that made them credible and, with it, authenticated the bond between the terrorists and their contemporaries. The RAF 'got it right' as far as the mediality of their message was concerned, even if what they said may have been stagey and self-conscious, and their actions politically obtuse as well as obscene. This 'enunciative apparatus' was, I am suggesting, linked to what one now understands by 'popular culture' or mainstream youth culture, but which at the time was clearly more ambiguous, poised between the urban guerilla tactics of violent and bloody actions, and what would be the RAF's 'guerilla urbanism', the media-literate, but also harsh and brittle interventionism, which held people in thrall. Not only that: it gave the '68 student generation its sense that they were challenged into having a response, that they were called upon to be counted either 'in' or 'out'. This may have been the true drama of 'sympathizers': to feel interpellated, but not sure in the name of what.

Street Violence as the Street Credibility of a Super Band

The dilemma is illustrated by an autobiographical essay published in *Die Beute*, a neo-left 1990s magazine, in which articles on Raymond Williams, 'Manhattan after Warhol and Nan Goldin', and Courtney Love stand alongside pieces dissecting German museum culture or the demise of radical German filmmaking. In 'Fractures from the Field Hospital of an Undeclared History', Michael Dreyer describes how he first reacted to the RAF as a schoolboy, or rather, how in the cotton-wool world of a protected family life, he tried to make sense of the radio bulletins and the television news as he sat in his room or walked the streets in the evenings.[43] For Dreyer, the RAF's street violence was not only street theatre, it was a kind of 'music' ('no more/mere words'). He felt their political violence as a percussion cutting into the monotone of his everyday, a form of bodily 'sensation' which, rather like rock music, delivered non-verbal expression and opened up a new subjective space. He also compares their actions to Walt Disney's definition of animation: 'plausible impossibility'. Such recollections are doubly surprising, for their endorsement of aestheticized violence, but also for remembering the RAF as nonverbal, when in fact, with their pamphlets, statements and messages to the press, they were hyperverbal. This slip of memory would, however, confirm that the verbal was not perceived as words, but as material signs, and the signs not as messages, but as shapes, sounds and colours.

Dreyer's recollections are thus useful as the record of a disavowed but also over-cathecting form of identification. He speaks of the RAF as Germany's only 'super band' ('the Crosby, Stills & Nash principle of armed struggle'), and concludes that the RAF was engaged in what he calls a 'style war'.[44] disguised as 'international Marxism': the terrorists literally shot past the 'form' and 'issue' debates of political activism to fame, and, for their sympathizers, unconsciously embodied a German version of pop, yet to be defined as to idiom, medium or mode of participation. For others, the RAF even carried on the interventionist work of a particular literary *avant garde*, and the pop-polemicist and cultural analyst Dietrich Diedrichsen wonders:

> where are we to locate the symbolic rupture between the early enthusiasm of Ensslin or Vesper for modern poetry, and the full-blown RAF-diction, present in the lower-case typewritten messages, influenced by sub-culture colloquialisms, shaped by decisionist rhetoric, and celebrating orgies of one-line sententiousness?[45]

Diedrichsen goes on to trace the fault lines of a poetics of revolt, perhaps indebted to Brecht, but choosing a terseness closer to advertising and market-ing, driven by a self-conscious promotion of casualness, anti-establishment life-styles and street credibility. The demands were all about 'the political struggle' and 'international solidarity': what made an impression (and often the head-lines of the tabloids) were the fast cars, the girls and the guns. One comes back to Andreas Baader, profiling himself as the incarnation of the narcissistic, self-styled working class hero, good at break-outs, shoot-outs and bombings.[46] But such a stance also disguises the culture clash within the RAF (which included a writer, Ulrike Meinhof, and a lawyer, Horst Mahler), as well as between the RAF and university-educated literature students, making the first-generation more like the rear view mirror – belated, heavily moralized and fiercely protestant – of 'sex, drugs and rock'n'roll' rather than its extension by other means. The culture clash, however, does highlight the absence of a (home-grown) pop culture in Germany well into the 1970s, including the cinema, where Wim Wenders's obsession with US rock bands and R.W. Fassbinder's pastiches of B-feature gangster films, at first, and then Sirkean melodramas, put this lack into sharp relief. Unlike Britain, Germany did not answer the US 'invasion' with the wit, irony or creative mimicry of the Beatles or Rolling Stones. And unlike France, with its situationist May '68 slogans of *l'imagination au pouvoir*, Germany's political youth culture was almost solely university-based, theory-driven, and (this being post-war Germany) more earnest, more system-atic, more bloody-minded (and in the end, more traumatized and traumatizing) than even the Italian or Japanese violent protest movements.[47]

The presence in the streets, the organization into 'cells', the lightning raids on banks or bankers' homes could thus count as part of a thoroughly ambiva-lent modernism represented by the RAF, helping a youth culture to take off, but which then veered off in quite a different direction. On the other hand, one wonders if the techno-fetishism of a Jan Carl Raspe or Andreas Baader did not anticipate the yuppie side of this youth culture, inventing electric gadgets, rewiring loudspeakers to serve as radio receivers and mail-dropping video tapes to TV broadcasters, even before the computer and the portable telephone made communication 'electronic', 'mobile' and 'multi-media.'

Emblematically, the RAF deployed novel forms of communication also in the wider sense, in that they soldered together a great many different circuits of energy, bringing together, hot-wiring so to speak, different areas of politics, institutional life, the press. They clearly had an ambivalent relation to the new means of communication, half 'inventing' a modern communication infrastruc-ture out of the bric-a-brac of minimal prison furniture, retooling that which, under a democracy, they were entitled to use against the state, thus persuading their lawyers to make statements to the media about imperialism, Zionism, police brutality. The 'secret' mode of the *Kassiber* that passed among the prisoners in solitary confinement, or made their way mysteriously between the high security tract and the RAF's underground 'cells' outside, strangely com-bined with the 'public' mode of media bulletins, press interviews and spectacu-lar actions. Modes of contact in prison, among themselves and between blocks are described in detail in Stefan Aust's book (and in the film *Stammheim*), including the guards putting mattresses on the doors during the day but removing them at night and the use of radio wires as two-way circuits for speech and messages. Baader hid his hand gun in a record player, and used the water pipes in his cell as a communication system, after the guards had finally found out how he had 'adapted' the prison intercom. Having trained as bomb- and booby-trap experts, Baader and especially Raspe were do-it-yourself geniuses, experts with wire, electricity, radio sets, transistors and transmitters. At the height of the crisis, even the maximum security prisons proved impossible to keep 'closed' or the prisoners 'isolated', just as the press was no longer 'independent' or the government 'leak-proof'. In the move to mediality, two public spheres, the press and the prison, may temporarily have changed places, taking over from two traditional political 'stages': the (bourgeois) parliament and the (proletarian, but also fascist) street.

In such a transfer, the much-noted self-obsession of the group, with its clandestine networks and bulletins to the press, might not have been so self-absorbed after all, since it provided a permanent commentary on the importance it attached to the 'material' side of communication. The RAF's peculiar form of mediality being perhaps their more lasting legacy, this new urbanist communication (typified by the city as non-space, and the prison cell or private study as command-and-control centre) would signal also a dramatic overlay of inside and outside, of architectural, carceral and electronic space. At the time, if it was seen at all, this space was discussed in 'panoptic' terms or as the curse of 'reversibility',[48] but now it might be more appropriately analyzed in the manner suggested by Virilio, for whom paradigmatic of contemporary urban space are the security arrangements at a modern airport.[49] Hence another ambivalence of the RAF's 'street-credibility': it was difficult to tell whether the new surveillance city was the RAF's 'natural' element, or whether they were critiquing it by forcing it to show itself. A fine dividing line runs between the kidnapper and the media star, between the bank robber and the super group. As the politically soft-edged focus of Michael Dreyer's essay shows, the 'style wars' argument leads to either cynicism or aporia, either it ignores the violence or is willing to read it as 'music' to postmodern, postpunk ears.

But how else to confront the fact of the RAF's violence? Can it be regarded as a 'language'? Did its particularly spectacular form merely indicate the violence of electronic communication, now disguised and normalized – having left behind the 'modern' violence of administered discourse to mutate into Paul Virilio's zonal violence of electronic passes, x-ray screens, security areas? What if the RAF's spectacular violence was a theatrical way of representing and staging the wrenching dislocation of the postwar world economic order which in the 1970s followed upon the Six Day War, the war in Vietnam, the oil crisis? Can one argue that the violence of the RAF was, despite its very real victims, essentially symbolic?

Symbolic violence in this sense would connote the use of spectacle in order to interrupt the circulation of goods and people, to render visible the security zones and spaces of exclusion, to let flare up the last ambiguous moment of a politics of the street, before the street becomes 'safe' for shopping, for the multiplex cinema and the mall, for market research and opinion polls? The question repeats itself: was the RAF the last (violent) snapshot of a political culture of the street – ambiguously coded in both right- and left-wing terms – that was trying to uphold essentially 'democratic' principles of the forum and the agora, or was it already operating in the space of the spectacle it seemed to attack, but could not but help to usher in, finally?[50]

If symbolic violence, then a further question might be: did the RAF at some level understand themselves as 'artists', engaged after all in making West

Germany the stage for a 'learning play' in the Brechtian tradition, taking such liberties with the lives of officials because they considered them to be 'actors' like themselves? And is this what their 'sympathizers' in the style wars obliquely picked up: the spectacle of a new 'media politics' bursting upon the scene? Perhaps the RAF was trying to produce a different kind of 'art' altogether: not spectacular, but 'conceptual', by making visible deeper, irreconcilable contradictions, articulating a series of deadlocks in the body politic, in the fabric of democracy itself? If so, the deadlocks fell back on themselves. They were denied success not only with their enemies, but also with their friends, since even for their sympathizers, they succeeded in outlining at most a moment of 'culture', an 'aesthetization of politics' in the form of a (dangerous) life-style, complementing and facilitating a shift in (imaginary) self-representation. It would mean that their success at having created sympathizers actually connoted the failure of their intervention, both as street 'artists' and as 'political' protagonists.

A Symbolic Mandate?

A double failure, then, as artists and as political activists. In fact, this double failure could be seen to spell another kind of success for the opponent: the possibility that the RAF's actions and tactics 'played straight into the hands' of the government, their own sworn enemy. Such, at any rate, was the tenor not only of the retrospective assessments on the right. The view on the left of the result of the 'hot autumn' has always been that the state cynically played up the terrorist threat in order to usher in a 'law-and-order' society, using the RAF as intimidation against reformist social movements, a stick to beat the moderate left with, but also as justification to invest in security equipment, surveillance technology, the introduction of electronics into the bureaucracies at federal, regional and local levels. It was as if capitalism, shifting gears towards the information society, had to invent terrorism in order to legitimate a (temporary?) curtailment of civil liberties and even human rights, as a politically expedient, broadly acceptable argument to allow the new military-industrial, electronic-surveillance complex to ease itself into place. It is a version of events endorsed, for instance, by the writer F.C. Delius as recently as June 1997:

> Whereas for the terrorists their on-air 'live' cop-show replaced political analysis, the RAF was a welcome gift to the police, to the security services, parts of the press and the conservative political parties. The gigantic process of paramilitary upgrading of the federal bureau of criminal investigation, the secret services and border police was surely not resisted by those thus served. The RAF was useful [also in other respects]:

never had it been easier to paint anyone who was young or left-wing, who was engaged on behalf of liberal, progressive or social causes into the same corner with terrorists.[51]

Fassbinder, in his 1978 film *The Third Generation*, had already appeared to put forward a similar view, when he showed his terrorists masterminded and plied with drugs by an industrialist keen to secure government contracts for his electronic hardware and business computers.[52] That the film can also be read differently was not noted at the time, yet in the face of the fact that even on the left the RAF came to be regarded as a tool of the state, it may be necessary to break open this apparently devastating but perhaps too facile irony. What this 'mirroring' of the state by the RAF flattens is the underlying dynamic of identification: not the kind of imaginary identification noted above, on the part of the RAF's political or pop sympathizers, but the act of symbolic identification, where the RAF saw itself interpellated, from an instance that challenged the members to become 'more themselves' than they were, but also challenged the state to speak from a position, to own up to the place, from which it made its subjects political citizens: a necessarily and fundamentally contradictory place.

Such an observation is prompted by two thoughts. Firstly, it implies that one consider the RAF from the point of view of subjectification and regard them as 'desiring subjects'. Secondly, it means 'taking seriously' their politics, not in the sense of endorsing their political goals or methods, but recognizing their founding gesture, as it were, namely their demand to assume a political role, to assume a political mandate. One might say that if at first glance it looks as though the RAF ultimately mirrored the state, then it is equally appropriate to say that the RAF took the state at its word, mirrored the demand made upon the individual by the state, accepted the symbolic mandate that is implied in being a citizen. The RAF demanded that the state not only take its citizens seriously, but that the state take itself seriously as the space of the *polis* (where everyone is answerable at once to himself and the community) rather than the space of the *police* (where everyone is answerable only to himself and to statistics).

This symbolic mandate can be seen as an historical one. It may enjoin one to offer resistance in a situation when the state exceeds its legitimacy, when the state commits a wrong, in this case the perceived collusion of Germany with the US waging an imperialist war in Vietnam. Here, a fatal displacement operated: the RAF was the resistance that German citizens had never managed to organize when it mattered, for instance, resisting the Nazis or opposing the persecution of the Jews. The RAF was in this precise sense not the 'return of the repressed', but involved in a situation of *Nachträglichkeit*, engaged in making up for something that had been omitted in the past, desirous to assume a role, across a historical gap, that was marked by shame, guilt, self-hatred. Under these circumstances, speaking of 'mutual symbiosis', as does Delius, may not quite strike the right note, although it recognizes that something other than pure antagonism played across the confrontation between the state and the terrorists. The RAF was not only attacking the state: it was also 'addressing' it, their mode of address being that of 'symbolic identification'. That such an awareness was even shared by some of those thus addressed is attested by security chief Horst Herold's remark 'I loved Andreas Baader'.[53]

What was at stake in the wider context touches the crisis of historical subjectivity and political agency for which the events of May 68 still stand as the muted beacon. It could be called a double crisis of the subject: the political ramifications of the post-68 period showed that in Western Europe, with the absence of a militant working class, there no longer existed even the possibility of a collective revolutionary subject. At the same time, the bourgeois order could no longer claim, in the face of such massive disaffection as manifested itself in the anti-war protests, to embody in its leaders the representative subject, mandated to act on behalf of and in place of society and its members.[54] The RAF might be said to have highlighted one of the political double-binds in which liberal democracies necessarily find themselves: they exist to guarantee equality before the law, yet because this very principle contradicts the expression of uniqueness and particularity, difference reappears elsewhere in the system, whether in the form of youth protests or identity politics. The question raised by such phenomena as urban guerillas or 'revolutionary cells' was thus, 'How is the singular connected to the collective?' – to which one answer was the figure of the terrorist, at once the existential subject (by his mimicry of 'armed struggle'), the embodiment of the singular (the saint or cult figure), and the self-conscious martyr (the ascetic, prepared to sacrifice him/ herself). The terrorist is a representative, but – so one might argue – with a false mandate, trying to inscribe him/herself 'positively' into history (or its religious equivalent, immortality). In the absence of a 'representative' who can credibly figure both the singular and the collective (which is the false promise of the fascist leader), the terrorist necessarily buys into 'representation' in the form of spectacular action and the highest visibility.[55] Yet to the extent that the terrorist 'responds' to this double-bind within the dominant political system of representation, s/he is a figure that shadows, mirrors or even mimics the official state, nowhere more so than in the challenge to the state's 'monopoly on violence.'

Outside the Law

One of the crucial points about the RAF is that its existence was the result of
an act of separation: they started by putting themselves outside the law. It
almost seems as if they undertook certain actions, committed certain offences,
went 'underground', first and foremost in order to draw a line, to instantiate a
break.[56] Historians are tempted to see the origins of RAF within a continuum,
namely that of the post-68 movements to create alternative communities. For
instance, it is often argued that the RAF emerged from the Berlin communes
movement, whose social protest potential and revolutionary energies came from
partly historical, partly anarchist-inspired hopes to break up the patriarchal
structures of the German bourgeois family (the so-called anti-authoritarian
movement), and that it was informed by the broader currents of sexual
liberation and feminism. In one sense this is true, although it is worth recalling
that the communes were also, more prosaically, a reflection of the specific
housing situation in West Berlin, with its large student population, as well as its
large 'bourgeois' apartments which, economically, were only viable through
multiple occupancy (the so-called *Wohngemeinschaften*). The student communes
– and in their wake, the 'revolutionary cells' – initially represented an opening
up of the nuclear family to other forms of or new experiments in group
solidarity and bonding. They also promoted a new kind of body-politics, acting
ideally as the vanguard of a new interpersonal proximity, pursuing ideals not
only of how to share and redistribute goods and services more equitably, but
also how to redefine privacy and communality, as well as the material and
immaterial spaces of everyday existence.

Clearly, some of the aims of the RAF can be identified with these currents,
but in other respects, it only became the RAF after it had made a break with
them, semantically secured by their initials (connoting the double nemesis of
the Third Reich: the Red Army and the Royal Air Force) and politically
manifested by their use of arms. This resort to violence is usually treated as a
'cause', that is, as the moment when legitimate political opposition turned into
criminal behaviour, marking the beginning of the escalating spiral that finally
ended in murder and suicide. Yet the resort to violence can also, from another
vantage point, be seen as an effect, the consequence brought about by the fact
that certain citizens no longer felt themselves to be represented by the state,
which corresponded to the crisis on the left that followed the formation of
alternative communities, namely the withdrawal from the polis, or the public
sphere, into the personal. Clearly, finding ways of occupying large apartments
economically, or reorganizing the domestic sphere – however important these

goals were in the context of slogans such as 'the personal is the political' – ceased to be conceived as adequate political acts. It must have seemed to the RAF that it was only by putting themselves outside the law that they could constitute a 'political group', and again, not in the practical sense of organizing a non-authoritarian *Wohngemeinschaft*, or in the formal sense of registering as an extra-parliamentary opposition, a sort of NGO for internal affairs, but in the sense of being political subjects and constituting a 'we'. In this respect, the RAF was both a 'family' (in Hegel's sense of 'enmity to the state') and the very opposite of a family (in the sense of the hippie communes, student communities or post-nuclear families). The RAF's was the negative, utopian, suicidal attempt to constitute a political ground, under the unique conditions in which they found themselves. For to be able to say 'we' in post-war Germany meant above all to contest a history: primarily the disastrous history of saying 'we' under Nazism, when one part of the nation redefined the criteria of inclusion and not only excluded from this community legitimate citizens, but segregated and exterminated them on the basis of this redefinition. The specificity of the conditions pointed backward to the fascist abuses of the notion of national identity embodied in the Aryan *Volksgemeinschaft*, but also sideways to the Stalinist abuses of the notion of a proletarian collectivity in the GDR.

In practice, it may seem as if the RAF were only able to refer to a 'we' by an act of equally radical exclusion or appropriation. But if one returns to the question of what constitutes a political subject, then the RAF must be considered not only historically, but also hermeneutically, since their role as 'political activists' was complicated by their status as 'political subjects'. Not surprisingly, perhaps, it is at this point that the figure of Antigone returns. The RAF, by putting itself outside the law, or rather by making the act of becoming 'criminals' the founding gesture of its group identity, might be said to have made an 'Antigone gesture': the 'Antigone move,' as it were. Just as Antigone became in Western political thought the 'ethical' subject *par excellence* as a consequence of the fact that her place outside the law is for any mortal a non-place, so the RAF's so-called self-obsession could be regarded as the consequence of their knowledge of the non-place from which they were speaking as well as of the urban 'non-space' they were inhabiting. It gives them, if only in retrospect, the freedom to speak to us about the very difficulties of saying 'we', especially in the 1990s, when the various ethnic, tribal, postnational and postcolonial groups are staging such apparently compelling comebacks. Perhaps the real tragedy of the RAF was that their particular ways of stepping outside the law in order to constitute an identity – precisely because they did not allow for traditional symbolizations such as 'class', 'nation' or 'the people' – was merely able to engender 'imaginary' identifications around either bank robberies, prison break-outs and killing sprees, or designer labels, rock music and fast cars. All this raises a crucial question: what sort of 'we', what group identity, is symbolizable in a civic, political sense?[57] To this question various answers are currently offered: from the identity politics of political correctness (according to Jacques Rancière, this answer is always at risk of conflating a non-symbolized singularity with a non-symbolizable universal such as race or religion)[58] to the new forms of nationalism, in which the ethnic-geographic 'thing' once more sanctions violence 'within the law', in the form of civil wars and ethnic cleansing.

The Self-Dissolution of the RAF

Perhaps the most familiar contemporary site of group formation – at once parasitic on the civic and its absolute negation – is television, where the audience watches real events as they happen or as they are restaged and replayed. In light of this new 'we' – the global/local virtual community manufactured the virtual 'we' manufactured by the televisual media event and its mode of address – the subjectivation instanced by *Death Game* indeed spelled the death of the RAF, not only historically, but also in the very terms of the symbolic mandate to which they thought they were responding.[59] This form of 'community' no longer needs to be able to symbolize a political entity such as 'the people' or the revolutionary subject, any more than it needs an urban environment, whether inhospitable, theatrical or communal: a media event, as the German phrase indicates, is a *Strassenfeger* – it sweeps the streets clean, historically and politically.

The letter of April 20, then: whether it was sent on Hitler's birthday as a reminder of his legacy or because it was also the eve of a possible amnesty hearing for some ex-members of the RAF still held in prison must remain a matter of speculation. But in a curious sense, the RAF may never have been more true to its historical and political meaning than when it dissolved itself in the wake of the massive act of 'sympathy' or imaginary identification that the German television audience manifested toward *Death Game*'s rewriting of *Germany in Autumn*: a piece of national history was thereby recuperated. Between the apparent alternatives of either the return of an atavistic ethnic 'we', or the emergence of the virtual, transitory 'we' of the television audience, no political ground remained. More crucially, the very possibility of a non-ground appeared to be foreclosed by the sheer proliferations of these (dis-) embodiments of a 'we', the decorporealization of that on which politics alone can be found and which it constantly confounds.

Notes

1. I want to thank Michael Wedel (Berlin), Ulrich Kriest (Stuttgart) and Peter Kramer (Norwich), as well as Eric Ames (Berkeley) for their assistance with source material and additional research.
2. The best-known English-language account is Jillian Becker, *Hitler's Children? The Story of the Baader-Meinhof Terrorist Gang*, New York/Philadelphia: Lippincott, 1977.
3. Among the studies of terrorism in an international, historical perspective, see Anthony M. Burton, *Urban Terrorism: Theory, Practice, Response*, New York: The Free Press, 1975; Martha Crenshaw, ed., *Terrorism, Legitimacy, and Power*, Middletown, Conn.: Wesleyan University Press, 1983; Noam Chomsky, *The Culture of Terrorism*, Boston: South End Press, 1988; Edward S. Herman and Gerry O'Sullivan, *The 'Terrorism' Industry*, New York: Pantheon, 1990.
4. A complete filmography can be found in P. Kraus, N. Lettenewitsch, U. Saekel et al., eds., *Deutschland im Herbst: Terrorismus und Film*, Munich: Münchner Filmzentrum, 1997, pp. 118–133.
5. Among the many essays on *Germany in Autumn* mention should be made of Miriam Hansen, 'Alexander Kluge's Contribution to *Germany in Autumn*', *New German Critique* nos. 24–25, Fall/Winter 1981–82, pp. 36–56; Felix Guattari, 'Like the Echo of a Collective Melancholy' in *Semiotexte*, vol. 4, no. 2, 1982, pp. 102–110; Marc Silverman, '*Germany in Autumn*' in *Discourse* no. 6, Fall 1983; pp. 48–52; Anton Kaes, *From Hitler to Heimat*, Cambridge MA: Harvard University Press, 1989, pp. 22–28; Joachim Paech, 'Zweimal "Deutschland im Herbst": 1977 und 1992', *Kinoschriften*, Vienna, no 4, 1996, pp. 87–105.
6. The literary reflection came in the 1980s: novels like F.C. Delius's trilogy *Deutscher Herbst* (1981–1992), Christian Geissler's *Kamalatta* (1988), Reinald Goetz's *Kontrolliert* (1988); investigative journalism like Stefan Aust's *Der Baader-Meinhof Komplex* (1985) and Michael Sontheimer, Otto Kallscheuer, eds., *Einschüsse. Besichtigung eines Frontverlaufs* (1987).
7. WDR and NDR are two of the larger and more prestigious German regional television channels that supply the central network ARD with programming. For a production history and the book of the film, see Heinrich Breloer, *Todesspiel – Eine dokumentarische Erzählung*, Cologne: Kiepenheuer und Witsch, 1997.
8. In Breloer's *Wehner – die unerzählte Geschichte* (1993) Herbert Wehner, a king-maker and wily tactician, comes across as a sort of Iago to Willy Brandt's Othello, masterminding Germany's role in the Cold War as well as shuttle-cocking for the so-called *Ostpolitik*, thanks to the contacts he had kept with his former Communist comrades from the days in political exile in Moscow and Stockholm.
9. For a critical assessment of Breloer's film, from the political left, see Ulrich Kriest, Rember Hüser, 'Rechtzeitig', in *Deutschland im Herbst*, pp. 48–60.
10. The best general account is still Stefan Aust, *The Baader-Meinhof Complex*, New York: Harcourt Brace, 1989. Aust, a left-wing journalist and friend of Alexander Kluge, later became editor of the news magazine *Der Spiegel*. He had himself been a pro-Meinhof sympathizer, but later became embroiled in public rows with Horst Mahler and other ex-RAF members. See *Die Zeit*, 6 June 1997, p. 44.
11. 'Ausgrenzung' (isolating the 'terrorist' element) became the key word. See Heinrich Böll, 'Diese Art der Stimmungsmache', in H. Boencke, D. Richter, eds., *Nicht heimlich und nicht kühl, Ästhetik und Kommunikation*, Berlin, 1977, pp. 75–82.
12. Some of the documents are to be found in Henner Hess, ed., *Angriff auf das Herz des Staates*, Frankfurt: Suhrkamp, 1988.
13. For a stunning account of one such *Seilschaft*, extending all the way into the foundation of *Der Spiegel*, see Lutz Hachmeister, *Der Gegnerforscher*, Munich: C.H. Beck, 1998.

14. Hannes Heer and Klaus Naumann, eds., *Vernichtungskrieg; Verbrechen der Wehrmacht 1941–1944*, Hamburg: Hamburger Editions 1995 and J.P. Reemtsma, 'Die Mörder waren unter uns', *Sueddeutsche Zeitung*, August 24, 1996.

15. For different evaluations of this masculinity and its (gender) politics, see amongst others, Karlheinz Bohrer, *Aesthetik des Schreckens*, Frankfurt: Suhrkamp, 1986, Klaus Theweleit, *Male Fantasies*, Minneapolis: University of Minnesota Press, 1990 and Helmut Lethen, *Cool Conduct*, University of California Press, forthcoming.

16. G.W. Hegel, *Phenomenology of Spirit*, p. 288, para. 475, here quoted from Patricia Mills, *Woman, Nature and Psyche*, Princeton: University of Princeton Press, 1987, pp. 25–26.

17. See the essays by Hans-Joachim Ruckhaeberle on the history of *Antigone* in German post-war theatre from Bertold Brecht to Julian Beck's Living Theatre, Peter Handke, Heiner Müller and Straub-Huillet, in *poetics politics: documenta X – the book*, Ostfildern: Cantz, 1997, pp. 48–53, 250–251, 488–489, 648–653.

18. The idea came from a distributor, the Filmverlag der Autoren, which had just changed hands. After having been owned by a number of filmmakers, among them also Wim Wenders and R.W. Fassbinder, the Filmverlag was bought out and baled out by Rudolf Augstein, the editor of Germany's powerful news magazine *Der Spiegel.*

19. Heinrich Böll, 'Will Ulrike Gnade oder freies Geleit?', *Der Spiegel* no. 3, 1977.

20. Hans Egon Holthusen, *Sartre in Stammheim: Literatur und Terrorismus*, Stuttgart: Klett-Cotta, 1982.

21. T. Botzat, E. Kiderlen, F. Wolff, eds., *Ein deutscher Herbst. Dokumente. Berichte. Kommentare*, Frankfurt: Verlag Neue Kritik, 1978.

22. As indicated in Jillian Becker's title *Hitler's Children? The Story of the Baader-Meinhof Terrorist Gang*, cited above.

23. Among Meinhof's journalism, only her pamphlet advocating the rehabilitation of youth offenders appears to be in print. Ulrike Meinhof, *Bambule. Fürsorge für wen?* Berlin: Klaus Wagenbach, 1995. A brief extract from a pamphlet 'Revolt' can be found in *Semiotexte: The German Issue*, vol. 4, no. 2, 1982, pp. 152–158. Meinhof is also the heroine of a Danish novel, published in 1996.

24. These two daughters of a Swabian protestant clergyman, who passed on to them a passionate idealism and a fierce sense of justice, became the subject of another famous film of the New German Cinema, Margarethe von Trotta's *The German Sisters*.

25. The sense of official hypocrisy – strongly felt by the members of the Schleyer family at the funeral itself – was also alluded to by the Federal President Walter Scheel, who in his funeral oration said: 'the face of terrorism makes us blanch. But we ourselves may have to look more often into the mirror.'

26. Bernward Vesper, *Die Reise*, Reinbek: Rowohlt, repr. 1995.

27. Michael Schneider, 'Fathers and Sons Retrospectively', *New German Critique*, no. 31, Winter 1984, pp. 11–12.

28. That this distrust did much to shape the forms the protest movement took in West Germany is made clear in another autobiographical essay, Christoph Meckel's *Suchbild*, Frankfurt: Fischer, 1983. There, among the most traumatic memories are instances where the father projected his own insufficiency onto his children, abusing parental power to confirm himself and strengthen his own battered ego, setting a pattern which in the son provoked violence against both himself and seemingly 'innocent' targets.

29. Schneider, 'Fathers and Sons Retrospectively', p. 23.

30. Paul Kersten, *Der alltägliche Tod meines Vaters*, quoted in Schneider, p. 41.

31. Schneider, 'Fathers and Sons Retrospectively', p. 9.

32. Gerhard Schroeder, at the time of writing the SPD Chancellor-candidate, is of the generation of Baader and Meinhof, and he models himself consciously in the image of Schmidt. Furthermore, he has taken into his shadow-cabinet the 'green' deputy Otto Schily, who in 1977 came to prominence as one of the lawyers who defended the Stammheim prisoners.

33. 'Nachruf' (signed: 'a Mescalero from Göttingen'), *ASTA: Göttinger Nachrichten*, May 1977.

34. Stefan Aust, *The Baader-Meinhof Complex*. But see also the report of the prison guard's account in *WDR Info*, November 1996.

35. Herold, who once claimed that one had to be able to sympathize with a terrorist in order to fight a terrorist, is himself one of the tragi-comic victims, having been confined for the past twenty years to a life inside an army compound, for fear of reprisals. Dirk Kurbjuweit, 'Gefangen für alle Zeiten', *Die Zeit*, 8 August 1997, p. 8.

36. Hellmuth Karasek, 'Deutschland im Herbst', *Der Tagesspiegel* 25 June 1997, p. 21; Heinrich Breloer, quoted in *WDR Info*, November 1996; Mariam Lau, 'Der Deutsche Herbst als Exorzismus', *Merkur* no. 585, December 1997, p. 1092.

37. The literature charting these changes is now too vast to more than signal in a footnote. Besides classics such as Jane Jacobs, *The Death and Life of Great American Cities*, New York: Random House, 1961, Manuel Castells, *The Informational City*, Oxford: Blackwell, 1989, and Richard Sennett, *The Conscience of the Eye*, London: Faber & Faber, 1990, one could mention recent collections such as Michael Sorkin, ed., *Variations on a Theme Park*, New York: Hill & Wang, 1992, R.T. Le Gates and F. Stout, eds., *The City Reader*, London: Routledge, 1996 and N.R. Fyfe, ed., *Images of the Street* London: Routledge, 1998.

38. Alexander Mitscherlich, *The Inability to Mourn*, London: Tavistock, 1975 and Alexander Mitscherlich, *Die Unwirtlichkeit der Städte* Frankfurt: Suhrkamp, 1965.

39. See 'Der Herbst der Terroristen', *Der Spiegel* no. 38, 15 Sept 1997, p. 43.

40. Marc Augé, *Non-places: Introduction to an Anthropology of Supermodernity*, London: Verso, 1995.

41. Baader's portrait featured prominently in 'Deutsche Photographie 1890–1990', an exhibition at the Bonn Museum of the Federal Republic, January to June 1997.

42. See Mariam Lau, 'Der Deutsche Herbst als Exorzismus,' *Merkur* no. 585, December 1997, pp. 1080–1092.

43. Michael Dreyer, 'Das muss genäht werden: Frakturen aus dem Lazarett einer ungeschriebenen Geschichte', *Die Beute. Neue Folge*, 1998, pp. 171–185.

44. Ibid, p. 174.

45. Dietrich Diedrichsen, 'Der Boden der Freundlichkeit', *Die Beute. Neue Folge*, 1998, pp. 44–45.

46. 'We were a bit like media stars', admits Astrid Proll, one of the first generation RAF members, for most of the 1970s in hiding in London, who has called Baader a 'James Dean lookalike' in *The Guardian Weekend*, August 28, 1998, p. 25. Baader also recalls the Martin Sheen character in Terrence Malick's *Badlands*, 1973, himself a reworking of the media-consciousness of Clyde in Arthur Penn's *Bonnie and Clyde*, 1967.

47. When a German popular culture finally did emerge towards the end of the 1980s, it was both middle-class and middle-aged: sex comedy, sit-coms, football and talk-shows, that is quite different from British 'pop' in the 1960s (when music, fashion, movies and art briefly fed from the same social-subversive energies), and instead directly reflecting the suburban TV culture imported from the US.

48. 'Everything in terrorism is ambivalent and reversible: death, the media, violence, victory. Who plays into the other's hands? . . . Fascination allows no distinction to be made, and rightly so, for power finally does not make any either, but settles its accounts with everyone, and buries Baader and Schleyer together at Stuttgart in its incapacity to unravel the deaths and rediscover the fine dividing line.' Jean Baudrillard, 'Our Theatre of Cruelty', *Semiotexte* vol. 4, no. 2, 1982, p. 109.

49. 'As the state's last gateway, the airport became, like the fort, the harbor or the train station of the past, the place of the necessary regulation of exchange and communication. For this reason, it also became the perfect field for intense control and high surveillance experimentation. An "air border patrol" was developed, and their antiterrorist exploits made headlines, as, for example, in the case of the GSG.9 German guards' intervention in the Mogadishu hijacking several thousand kilometers

from their jurisdiction.' Paul Virilio 'The Overexposed City', in Jonathan Crary and Michel Feher, eds., *Zone* nos.1/2 (n.d.), p. 16.

50. Henri LeFebvre, *The Production of Space*, Oxford: Basil Blackwell, 1991; Michel de Certeau, *Heterologies*, Minneapolis: Minnesota University Press, 1956; Guy Debord, *The Society of the Spectacle*, New York: Zone Books, 1994.

51. F.C. Delius, 'Die Dialektik des Deutschen Herbstes', *Die Zeit*, 25 July 1977, p. 3.

52. The title is explained by Fassbinder: 'The first generation was that of '68. Idealists, who thought they could change the world with words and demonstrations in the street. The second generation, the Baader-Meinhof group, moved from legality to the armed struggle and total illegality. The third generation is today's, who just indulges in action without thinking, without either ideology or politics, and who, probably without knowing it, are like puppets whose wires are pulled by others.' R.W. Fassbinder, *Die Anarchie der Phantasie*, Frankfurt: Verlag der Autoren, 1986 p. 106.

53. Dorothea Hause, *Baader und Herold – Beschreibung eines Kampfes*, Berlin: Fest, 1997.

54. Fassbinder spoke of West Germans as living in a 'democracy handed to them as a present' (a common phrase at the time: 'Modell Deutschland: die geschenkte Demokratie', *Die Anarchie der Phantasie*, p. 138). This implies a question about the 'agency' the political subject can assume or put on (if only through mimicry) in reply to repression: 'we're not in control, and therefore not responsible', thus hinting at one kernel of (inverted) truth in the emergent 'victim' cultures of the 1980s and 1990s.

55. A similar dilemma of how to respond to the symbolic mandate coming from a cult following has faced pop stars. The black rapper of the 1990s, for instance, 'represents' a constituency which demands that his street-credibility of violence is not merely verbal and in the music. Tupac Shakur, the 'gangsta rapper' whose mother was a Black Panther militant, exposed himself to 'getting real', with fatal results. But as he is supposed to have said, 'all good niggers, all niggers who change the world, die in violence'. *The Economist*, October 1996.

56. As Astrid Proll put it: 'Everyone carried a gun. That was a membership card', *The Guardian Weekend*, 28 August, 1998, p. 25.

57. This is the gist of the conversation that Fassbinder has with his mother in *Germany in Autumn* about whether terrorists are criminals protected by the law or a species of perpetrator to which the law does not apply and where thus a more atavistic demand for retribution is called for.

58. See Jacques Ranciere, 'The Political Form of Democracy' in *documenta X – the book*, Cantz, 1997, p. 801.

59. Another sign of the televisual 'we' was the attempt made in the media in 1997 to bring together the victims, such as the son of Hans Martin Schleyer, and ex-members of the RAF, in the hope of finding some common ground, however vain and absurd this attempt in practice proved to be. Television shows presume that there is always the space of 'talk'. No wonder it proved impossible to recover across the televisual face-to-face the displaced dialogues of German history, the generations, of responsibility and accountability.

NOTES ON CONTRIBUTORS

ARIELLA AZOULAY is Director of Curatorial and Critical Studies at the Camera Obscura School of Art in Tel Aviv. Her book, *Toward a Critique of Museual Economy in and around Israeli Art*, is forthcoming (in Hebrew). She is currently writing about Walter Benjamin, art, and the modern display of death.

ETIENNE BALIBAR, Professor of Philosophy at Paris X, is the author of numerous books in English and French, including *Masses, Classes, Ideas; Race, Nation, Class* (with Immanuel Wallerstein) and *Reading Capital* (with Louis Althusser).

LAUREN BERLANT teaches English at the University of Chicago. She is now working on the final volume in her national sentimentality trilogy, *The Female Complaint: The Unfinished Business of Sentimentality in American Culture*. The first two volumes, *The Anatomy of National Fantasy: Hawthorne, Utopia, and Everyday Life* and *The Queen of America Goes to Washington City: Essays on Sex and Citizenship*, have already appeared.

JOAN COPJEC teaches in the Departments of English, Comparative Literature, and Media Study at the University at Buffalo where she is also Director of the Center for the Study of Psychoanalysis and Culture. Her book, *Read My Desire: Lacan against the Historicists*, will soon be followed by *The Ethics of the Absolute All: Sex, Sublimation and the Body*.

SAMUEL DELANY is a writer of science fiction and fantasy, including the *Neveryon* tetralogy. He is also an essayist and theorist; among his works of non-fiction, his memoir, *The Motion of Light and Water: East Village Sex and Science Fiction Writing, 1960–1965*, is probably best-known. He teaches in the Department of English at the University at Buffalo.

ROSALYN DEUTSCHE is an art historian and critic who lives in New York City. She is the author of *Evictions: Art and Spatial Politics*.

THOMAS ELSAESSER is Professor of Art and Culture at the University of Amsterdam and is Chair of Film and Television. He has written and edited numerous books, including *Early Cinema: Space, Frame, Narrative; Fassbinder's Germany: History, Identity, Subject*; and *Cinema Futures: Cain, Able, or Cable?*

DEAN MACCANNELL is Chair of Landscape Architecture at the University of California, Davis. His books include *The Tourist: A New Theory of the Leisure Class* and *Empty Meeting Grounds*.

SASKIA SASSEN teaches in the Department of Sociology at the University of Chicago. She is the author of several books on global cities, including *Cities in a World Economy*; *Losing Control?: Sovereignty in an Age of Globalization*; and *Globalization and Its Discontents*.

MICHAEL SORKIN is principal of Michael Sorkin Studio in New York City and Director of the Institute of Urbanism at the Academy of Fine Arts, Vienna. He is the author of *Exquisite Corpse: Writings on Buildings*; *Local Code: The Constitution of a City at 42 Latitude*; and *Wiggle* (a collection of studio projects); he is also the editor of *Variations on a Theme Park*.

INDEX